rrac

Women and Religion

**Recent Titles in
Women and Society around the World**

Women and Violence: Global Lives in Focus
Kathleen Nadeau and Sangita Rayamajhi, Editors

Women and Health: Global Lives in Focus
AnnJanette Alejano-Steele, Editor

Women and the Military: Global Lives in Focus
Ruth Margolies Beitler and Sarah M. Gerstein

Women and Religion

Global Lives in Focus

Susan M. Shaw, Editor

Women and Society around the World

An Imprint of ABC-CLIO, LLC
Santa Barbara, California • Denver, Colorado

Library of Congress Cataloging-in-Publication Data

Names: Shaw, Susan M. (Susan Maxine), 1960- editor.
Title: Women and religion : global lives in focus / Susan M. Shaw, editor.
Description: Santa Barbara, California : ABC-CLIO, [2021] | Series: Women and society around the world | Includes bibliographical references and index.
Identifiers: LCCN 2021008704 (print) | LCCN 2021008705 (ebook) | ISBN 9781440871962 (hardcover) | ISBN 9781440871979 (ebook)
Subjects: LCSH: Women and religion.
Classification: LCC BL458 .W56374 2021 (print) | LCC BL458 (ebook) | DDC 200.82—dc23
LC record available at https://lccn.loc.gov/2021008704
LC ebook record available at https://lccn.loc.gov/2021008705

ISBN: 978-1-4408-7196-2 (print)
    978-1-4408-7197-9 (ebook)

25 24 23 22 21   1 2 3 4 5

This book is also available as an eBook.

ABC-CLIO
An Imprint of ABC-CLIO, LLC

ABC-CLIO, LLC
147 Castilian Drive
Santa Barbara, California 93117
www.abc-clio.com

This book is printed on acid-free paper ∞

Manufactured in the United States of America

Contents

Series Foreword

Women's roles in society and the issues they face differ greatly from those of their male counterparts. In some corners of the world, women may manage households but are deemed unworthy of an education; in other areas, women scientists are pioneers in their fields, juggling family life and their careers. Gender inequality looms in all aspects of life, from employment to education to opportunities in sports and the military. What are the challenges, issues, and achievements women around the world face?

The *Women and Society around the World* series looks at women's lives as they pertain to various issues. The volumes cover topics such as

- Health;
- Violence;
- Religion;
- Sexuality;
- The military;
- Sports;
- Education; and
- Technology, among others.

Each volume begins with an introductory background essay on the volume's topic and is followed by a general chronology of significant world events pertaining to the topic. Eight chapters follow, focusing on the world's regions: United States and Canada, Latin America and the Caribbean, Europe, North Africa and the Middle East, Sub-Saharan Africa, Central and East Asia, South and Southeast Asia, and Oceania. All chapters include a list of further reading resources, and a selected bibliography at the end of each volume provides students with additional print and electronic resources for further research needs.

The chapters examine women in each region with broad brushstrokes, highlighting specific examples of key customs and policies in specific countries that help to illuminate cultural nuances among countries within each region. They can be read alone or be reviewed cumulatively to make cross-cultural comparisons. The volumes are ideal for high school students doing projects, undergraduate students writing research papers, and even general readers interested in learning about women's lives.

The goal of the *Women and Society around the World* series is to depict the roles of women worldwide by exploring the major issues they face and the accomplishments they have made, especially in terms of bridging the gap in gender inequality and fighting for basic human rights. While readers will learn about the challenges that half of the world's population face, they will also discover the empowering ways women succeed and overcome social and cultural barriers in their daily lives.

Introduction

Susan M. Shaw and Shannon Garvin

Religion is a powerful force all around the world. For women, religion can be an institution of limitation, oppression, and even violence. It can also be a space of welcome, empowerment, and resistance—sometimes at the same time. Of course, women's experiences of religion vary greatly, not only across religious traditions but also across race and ethnicity, nationality, sexuality, social class, ability, and age. The lens that helps us identify how these various social differences intertwine and affect one another in our lives is called *intersectionality.*

Intersectionality reminds us that women are not a uniform group; rather, they experience *sexism* (the systemic mistreatment of people based on gender) in different ways based on the interactions of all of these social differences within institutions such as religion, family, education, and the state. So, for example, many conservative Christian groups in the United States believe in a God-ordained manhood and womanhood, but conservative Christian expectations of womanhood are based on stereotypes of *white* womanhood—dainty, hyperfeminine, and submissive. Yet, dominant cultural and stereotypical notions of Black women in the United States as strong, dominant, and unfeminine prevent them from ever meeting these expectations (McCluney 2018).

This volume takes a decidedly feminist approach in exploring women in the world's religions. *Feminism* is a tool that helps us examine how gender is at work so that women can resist being dominated and pushed to the margins and then identify ways to transform social institutions to be inclusive, equitable, and just. Feminism recognizes that the mistreatment of women is not simply a matter of individual men behaving badly: sexism is *systemic*—built into the structures of society through beliefs, language, and institutions that shape relationships between men and women as well as *transgender* and *gender-nonconforming* people (people whose sense of gender does not fit neatly into either category of women or men). We call this assumption of only two genders the *gender binary*.

The gender binary reinforces sexism by forcing people into one category or the other and then arranging those categories in a hierarchy with men over women; this is called *patriarchy*. Sexism is a driving force behind discrimination against women. It is pervasive and present in all the major systems that affect women—including religion. As such, there are many similarities across religions in the specific aspects of women's experiences that we will examine: sexism limits women's freedom to access high leadership positions; dictates gender-related religious practices and roles; portrays women in limited ways in sacred texts; restricts their control of their own sexuality and fertility; excludes or condemns them if they are lesbian, bisexual, or transgender; and makes them subject to violence by people of other faiths as well as their own.

As a feminist work, then, this volume pays attention to *gender arrangements*, the ways in which beliefs, relationships, and institutions force people into patterns of behavior. In religion, that means we examine what various faiths teach about women and men, how faith practices include or exclude based on gender, what religions teach about LGBTQ people and how they treat them, and what religions suggest about the roles of women and men in the family and in religious leadership. Feminism is concerned with social justice, and so we also ask what should be done to move toward *gender justice* to ensure people of all genders are treated with dignity, are provided equitable resources and opportunities, and are not limited or mistreated because of gender.

Each chapter in this volume follows a similar outline so that readers can easily compare and contrast different regions of the world. The first section of each chapter provides an overview of women in religion in the region with an emphasis on women in each of the major world religions as well as in more localized and indigenous religions. The second section of each chapter explores key issues faced by women in religion in the region.

MAJOR WORLD RELIGIONS

Major world religions have a particularly powerful impact on women's lives. Because of colonization and the power of the Western world, Christianity, in particular, has shaped women's lives not only in the United

States and Europe but in every country colonized by Western forces or targeted by Christian missionaries, sometimes working hand in hand with colonial governments.

Christianity, Judaism, and Islam are the three *monotheistic* (belief in one God) *Abrahamic religions* (descended from Abraham, whom the Bible tells us was called by God to be the father of many nations). I prefer to think of them all as the "Abraham, Sarah, and Hagar" religions because the women also played an important role in the origin stories.

Christianity centers on Jesus as God's child who came to show the way of redemption. Broadly, Christian denominations are Catholic, Orthodox, and Protestant and encompass a wide range of beliefs and religious practices. The Catholic Church and Orthodox churches exclude women from the priesthood. Among Protestants, some denominations, such as Southern Baptists, oppose women's ordination, while others, such as United Methodists and Episcopalians, support women's ordination. Christians also disagree on a number of issues of gender and sexuality, ranging from women's roles in the home to marriage equality to reproductive rights.

Judaism focuses on the right relationship with God expressed in the right behavior based on God's law. Judaism has four distinct branches: Orthodox, Conservative, Reform, and Reconstructionist. These branches differ in their interpretations of Jewish law as well as their religious observances. Broadly speaking, Jews believe in one God with whom each person can have a relationship. They believe God still works in the world and expects them to live ethical lives as God's people. Jewish views on women vary, from Orthodox Judaism's belief in separate spheres for women and men to the acceptance of women rabbis in the other branches of the faith.

More than two billion people in the world are Muslim. The countries with the largest Muslim populations are Indonesia, Pakistan, Bangladesh, India, and Turkey. That list probably surprises you because we often associate Islam with the Arab world, and it is true that most Arabs are Muslim; however, most Muslims are not Arabs. Muslims share the core beliefs that there is only one God and Muhammad is God's messenger. Muslims also practice daily prayers and fast, pay an annual tax to benefit the poor and other beneficiaries, and take a pilgrimage to Mecca once in a lifetime, if possible. Around 90 percent of Muslims are Sunni Muslims, who believe the Prophet did not appoint a successor. Shi'a Muslims believe Muhammad appointed his son-in-law Ali ibn Abi Talib as his successor. Most Muslims do not believe women should lead gender-mixed prayers in the mosque, and many hold to traditions, such as women entering the mosque through a separate door and praying behind the men or behind curtains. Feminist Muslims push back on these restrictions, calling for greater equality in mosques.

As we approach Asian religions, we must be aware of how deep historical and cultural differences require us to imagine ways of thinking and being beyond traditional Western ways of observing religion. An Asian understanding of life itself, as it developed from 2500 to 1500 BCE in China, does not include a distinction between beings who hold a physical form and those who do not. Existence is merely that, existence. Existence can take a physical or nonphysical form. It can also change, moving back and forth and in and out of a physical form, in one whole reality within the larger cosmos. The process of coming into and being in a relationship with another, rather than "personhood," allows the form of a being to emerge (Sprenger 2016).

Built on the idea that within the cosmos existence life can take on a physical or spiritual form along a spectrum and that existence can dwell apart from the cosmic origin or in harmony with it, the Asian religions of Buddhism and Hinduism came to understand life in a circular rather than a linear sense. One does not simply live a life and then it is over. One continues to live a life over and over until there is a reunion with the cosmos (Buddhism) or the cosmic creator(s) (Hinduism). An Asian worldview is based on familial and cosmic relationships where one exists within a larger whole, not merely as one's own independent self. The goal of life is to be reunited with the divine creator or the cosmos, and it does not support an exclusive and individualized self/person existing apart from others. A distinctly Asian understanding of religion also does not make a Western or Greek assumption that conversion from one religion (belief system) to another requires a wholesale change of beliefs and lifestyle (Jenkins 2008); it allows a blending together of traditions.

The lives of both women and men are greatly influenced by their basic beliefs about the nature of reality. In women, the power of life and death is easily seen in the birth of a child or the loss of that child and its mother in the act of birth. Likewise, the power of life and death is seen in the earth as crops are planted for food; they either grow well with rain and sun or they die of drought and the people starve. The observations of these great powers seen in women and the earth caused early Asian philosophers to view women as the holders of a great creative power with the potential for both life and destruction. Women in Hinduism and Daoism are tied to the creative power of the cosmos, while men are reflective of the corollary physical power (Kohn 2008). A cosmic gynophobia (fear of uncontrolled feminine creation) pervades

Asia, where "woman is the living microcosmic image of the macrocosm, the manifest body of the Great Goddess" (Arvind 2004). This ancient indigenous hope and fear in relation to women and their sexuality informs the basic practices of each South and Southeast Asian religion and culture.

While women in South and Southeast Asia have held an exalted position in the scheme of life, they have also been seen as the primary threat to the men who have sought to organize and control the civil and religious power of local and national civil governments, from the ancient Chinese emperors to the modern democratic and autocratic governments. A handful of traditional matrilineal tribes exist in Southeast Asia, but the creative power of women and their sexuality primarily came to be revered under a mantle of fear rather than respect.

Hinduism is the oldest religion in the world, dating back around four thousand years. With nearly a billion followers, Hinduism is the third-largest religion, following Christianity and Islam. Most of the world's Hindus live in India. Hindus worship Brahman and recognize other gods and goddesses and multiple paths to God. They believe life is a continuous cycle of life, death, and reincarnation. The goal of life is to achieve *moksha* and end the cycle of reincarnation by becoming part of the absolute soul. Hindu religious texts both extol women as leaders, including the highest goddess, and limit women's roles to wives and mothers.

Buddhism is the world's fourth-largest religion with nearly six million practitioners. Buddhists also believe in a cycle of reincarnation, which ends when someone is able to release his or her attachments and achieve Nirvana, a state of freedom from suffering. The three primary practices in Buddhism are virtue, meditation, and enlightenment. Like other major religions, Buddhists divide themselves into a number of sects with different beliefs and texts. Although Buddha insisted that women and men are of the same value, Buddhist practices through time have not always reflected equality. Buddha himself eventually allowed women to join monasteries, but Buddhist nuns are subject to much stricter rules than monks.

Confucianism, as a civil religion, with its desire to support organized society in service to the Chinese emperors did not diminish women so much as merely define their place as lower than men. Hinduism, while elevating the creative power of women to reverence, lost sight of women having any other purpose or value outside of their sexuality. Daoism originally elevated women as the slightly stronger power in the yin over the yang but lost influence to Confucianism. Buddhism taught that all people could become enlightened, but it struggled with separating women's intent in seeking their own enlightenment with the basic assumption that all women are dangerous sexual forces who distract men in their seeking. In each religion, a system developed in fearful response to the Asian under- standing of women as holding the creative and destructive powers of the cosmos in its physical form (Langenberg 2018). This primary belief in creative power and the fear associated with it combined over the centuries with the reinforced civil organizational systems of Confucianism to keep women in a guarded and confined space where life could safely exist and men could use their physical power to keep the creative power of the uni- verse in check and under control (Andaya 2006).

Many people in the world practice other religions that perhaps are not as widespread but still shape the lives of women who participate in them. For example, in her chapter on South and Southeast Asia, Shannon Garvin notes the plight of nuns in Jainism who are strictly subordinated to monks. Indigenous religions also play an important role in women's lives, particu- larly in those precolonial traditions that valued women and their power. As Kali Furman, Jennifer A. Venable, Leida Karibu (L.K.) Mae, Luhui Whitebear, and Rebecca J. Lambert note in chapter 1, Indigenous women in North America have always been involved with ceremonial practices. As Karen J. Shaw and Anuncia Escala point out in chapter 2, in Mexico, indigenous beliefs and Catholic beliefs merged in the Virgen de Guada- lupe and folk saints. In chapter 3, Janet Lockhart also notes the develop- ment of Wicca in England, which combines elements of ancient goddess worship, magic, and ethical precepts focused on peace and respect.

New religious movements (NRMs) are especially interesting because they often resist traditional norms, though they may just as likely position women as secondary; many are male dominated and promote anti-LGBTQ positions. Some NRMs do not seem that "new," such as the Church of Jesus Christ of Latter-day Saints, the Church of Scientology, Jehovah's Witnesses, and the Nation of Islam, but compared with the ancient major religions, these groups are indeed newcomers.

ISSUES WOMEN FACE IN RELIGIONS

Key issues discussed in the second section of each chapter include colo- nization, women's leadership, gendered practices, sacred texts, LGBTQ issues, the intersection of religion and politics, and religious violence against women.

Colonization

One of the key factors to understand in exploring women's experiences in religion worldwide is the impact of the Christian missionary enterprise as a part of the colonial project (the taking of other people's lands and resources and exerting political power over them). Throughout the world, the missionary effort has upended cultures and contributed to the devaluing of women. As Mary-Antoinette Smith explains in chapter 5, on sub-Saharan Africa, Christian missionaries were complicit with European imperialists in the name of "God, Gold, and Glory" to spread Christianity and to extract the resources of African peoples. Botswanan feminist theologian Musa Dube has added "gender" as the fourth *G*, noting the ways in which missionary and colonial enterprises were gendered. In chapter 1, Kali Furman, Jennifer A. Venable, Leida Karibu (L.K.) Mae, Luhui Whitebear, and Rebecca J. Lambert point out the harm done to Indigenous people, particularly women, in North America because of Christian missionaries' belief in the inherent sinfulness of Indigenous women's bodies, which provided a religious foundation for rape, trafficking, and servitude. The ongoing effects of colonialism are seen in the persistent rates of poverty; lack of access to employment, health care, housing, food, and clean water; and violence against women in Indigenous communities.

Women's Leadership

The issue of women's leadership in the religions of the world is key to women's placement and power in these faiths. There are few religions in which women experience full parity with men, and so, in many ways, religion continues to function as a social institution that helps to maintain the system of patriarchy. That often leads us to wonder why women participate in religion at all, when it so rarely treats them equally. Radical feminist philosopher Mary Daly made this point about Christianity. She had been a Catholic but came to the conclusion that Christianity was inherently patriarchal and unredeemable for women. She instead became a practitioner of women- and earth-centered religion. As Shannon Garvin notes in chapter 7, on South and Southeast Asia, Buddhist nuns continue to fight for recognition of their ordination. For one thousand years in Sri Lanka, no Theravada nuns were ordained; the practice was revived in the 1990s, but the Sri Lankan government still does not recognize these nuns' ordination. In 2005, Amina Wadud, an African American convert to

Islam, became the first woman to lead mixed-gender prayers, setting off both waves of support and a backlash that included death threats.

Gendered Practices

Women's bodies are a central site of religious conflict. In many religions, women's bodies are seen as powerful and fearful, and religious beliefs, practices, and leaders work to control and regulate them. For example, in chapter 1, Kali Furman, Jennifer A. Venable, Leida Karibu (L.K.) Mae, Luhui Whitebear, and Rebecca J. Lambert point out that among evangelicals in the United States, the idea of *purity* has taken hold in ways that both define and limit young women's sexuality. In chapter 4, Hanan Hammad and Amina Zarrugh discuss veiling as a gendered practice within Islam in the Middle East and North Africa. While female genital cutting has been most frequently practiced in North Africa, Karen G. Massey notes in chapter 8, on Oceania, that the practice is on the rise in Papua New Guinea. Still other religious groups see women's bodily autonomy as core to their beliefs and practices. As Karen J. Shaw and Anuncia Escala point out chapter 2, on Latin America and the Caribbean, Catholics for Choice is working in eleven Latin American countries to advocate for reproductive choice.

Sacred Texts

Much of the sexism women face in religions comes from interpretations of sacred texts. For example, Suzanne E. Schier-Happell points out in chapter 6, on Central and East Asia, the problematic sexualizing (reducing people to sex objects) of women in a number of Buddhist texts. Within Christianity, the Bible has been used by conservatives to place wives in submission to husbands and exclude women from ordained ministry. On the other hand, feminist interpreters of the Bible have used the text to argue for women's full equality in the church. Likewise, feminist interpreters of the Qur'an are rereading the text to affirm women's equality in family, society, and the mosque.

LGBTQ Issues

The place of LGBTQ people in religious traditions has been especially controversial in recent times. Although South and Southeast Asian religions often make room for third gender people, in practice, these societies still often discriminate against LGBTQ people. As Mary-Antoinette Smith observes in chapter 5, in sub-Saharan Africa, people have often believed that homosexuality arrived along with colonization and may hold deep prejudice toward LGBTQ people. Evangelical Christianity has infused African culture with antigay rhetoric and belief. Queer African activists point out the irony of condemning homosexuality as a Western import while using Western religion to argue against LGBTQ human rights. In the United States, many Christian denominations have strenuously grappled with the issue, and Orthodox Jews in the United States reject LGBTQ marriage and ordination, though many Reform and Conservative Jewish congregations accept and ordain LGBTQ people.

Intersection of Religion and Politics

While deeply personal, religion is also a social institution that overlaps and interacts with politics, and so it plays an important role in shaping public policy around women's issues. The influence of the Catholic Church and evangelical churches on governments around the world has had a tremendous impact on access to abortion and contraception. In chapter 4, Hanan Hammad and Amina Zarrugh note how religious beliefs affect family law in the Middle East and North Africa. These laws govern marriage, divorce, child custody, and inheritance.

Religious Violence against Women

Violence against women is a pervasive global problem, and religion can intensify gendered violence. In chapter 8, Karen G. Massey suggests the very high rates of violence against women in Oceania are related to evangelical beliefs that women are to be submissive to men. Similarly, in chapter 3, Janet Lockhart points out the problem of domestic violence fueled by religion in Europe. Suzanne E. Schier-Happell explains in chapter 6 that, in Afghanistan, burqa laws were enforced by the Taliban before the U.S.-led war there, and now, even though these laws no longer apply, many women feel the need to wear the burqa to protect themselves from male harassment and family or social pressure.

CONCLUSION

Of course, a single volume on women and religion around the world can only offer the briefest of overviews. We do hope we have raised important issues, highlighted diverse women and their participation in and resistance to religion, and pointed you toward resources where you can learn more in depth. Because religion is such an important facet of both individual lives and public policy, understanding religion's impact on women's lives is a necessary part of feminist work toward transforming the world in regard to inclusion, equity, and justice.

Collaboration is also an important feminist practice, and this volume is the result of a wonderful collaboration of authors and editors. We are grateful for the authors who embraced this task with enthusiasm and took on the daunting assignment of covering topics of women and religion in entire regions of the world in around ten thousand to twelve thousand words: Anuncia Escala, Kali Furman, Shannon Garvin, Hanan Hammad, Rebecca J. Lambert, Janet Lockhart, Leida Karibu (L.K.) Mae, Karen G. Massey, Suzanne E. Schier-Happell, Karen J. Shaw, Mary-Antoinette Smith, Jennifer A. Venable, Luhui Whitebear, and Amina Zarrugh. I also greatly appreciate Kaitlin Ciarmiello, my capable editor at ABC-CLIO, who asked me to do this second project for the press and who provided guidance, clarity, and immeasurable support. I also thank Jane Nichols, our Women, Gender, & Sexuality Studies librarian at Oregon State University, who created an online resource guide for the authors.

FURTHER READING

Andaya, Barbara Watson. 2006. *The Flaming Womb: Repositioning Women in Early Modern Southeast Asia*. Honolulu: University of Hawai'i Press.

Arvind, Sharma. 2004. *Goddesses and Women in the Indic Religious Tradition*. Leiden, Netherlands: Brill.

Jenkins, Philip. 2008. *The Lost History of Christianity: The Thousand-Year Golden Age of the Church in the Middle East, Africa, and Asia—and How It Died*. New York: HarperOne.

Kohn, Livia. 2008. "Sexual Control and the Daoist Cultivation." In *Celibacy and Religious Traditions*, edited by Carl Olson, 241–264. New York: Oxford University Press.

Langenberg, Amy Paris. 2018. "An Imperfect Alliance: Feminism and Contemporary Female Buddhist Monasticisms." *Religions* 9(6): 190.

McCluney, Courtney. 2018. "For the Bible Tells Me So: Justifying Gender Discrimination Based on Biblical Text." Spark, August 10, 2018.

https://medium.com/national-center-for-institutional-diversity/for
-the-bible-tells-me-so-justifying-gender-discrimination-based-on
-biblical-text-83c61dd4e639.

Sprenger, Guido. 2016. "Dimensions of Animism in Southeast Asia." In
Animism in Southeast Asia, edited by Kaj Århem and Guido
Sprenger, 31–54. London; New York: Routledge.

Chronology

ca. 24,000 BCE
The Venus of Willendorf, one of the earliest-known figures of the human body, is carved in what is now Austria by an anonymous Paleolithic artist.

3100 BCE
The first phase of Stonehenge is completed.

2285–2250 BCE
Enheduanna becomes the first-known holder of the title of priestess in the Akkadian Empire.

2050–1470 BCE
Minoan Crete flourishes. Archaeological evidence later shows a high level of gender equality and worship of the goddess.

1700–1100 BCE
The first of the Hindu Vedas is composed.

1250–600 BCE
The Upanishads are composed.

Sixth Century BCE
The first woman receives Buddhist ordination, Mahapajapati Gotami, the aunt and foster mother of Buddha.

Sixth–Fifth Century BCE
Gautama Buddha is born.

551 BCE
Confucius is born.

300 BCE
Buddhism arrives in Southeast Asia.

ca. 4 CE
Jesus of Nazareth is born.

313
Emperor Constantine makes Christianity the state religion of the Roman Empire.

570
The Prophet Muhammad is born.

1067
Arwa al-Sulayhi becomes the sole ruler of Yemen after reigning with her first two husbands. She was the longest-reigning ruler of Yemen. She was also a *da'i*, a Muslim who uses dialogue to invite people to convert to Islam. She became the first woman to achieve the rank of *hujjat*, the highest rank a *dai'i* can achieve.

Thirteenth Century
Japanese abbess Mugai Nyodai becomes the first female Zen master in Japan.

1373
Julian of Norwich receives visions, or "shewings," while she is seriously ill. These visions became the basis for her *Revelations of Divine Love*.

1484
The European witch hunts begin with Pope Innocent VIII's papal bull *Summis desiderantes*.

1517
Martin Luther posts his Ninety-Five Theses on the door of All Saints' Church in Wittenberg.

1531
La Virgen de Guadalupe emerges in Mexico as a symbol of faith. Despite her association with Catholicism, she represents Indigenous women's voice and power. She is revered by people of many religious and spiritual backgrounds.

1534

Henry VIII declares himself supreme head of the Church of England and breaks the English Church from Rome.

1637

Anne Hutchinson is tried in Massachusetts for espousing "free grace" theology and challenging colonial authorities.

1651

Sor Juana Inés de la Cruz, a Mexican Catholic nun who wrote, taught, and argued for the education of women, is born. She dies in 1695.

1660

Quaker Margaret Fell publishes "Women's Speaking Justified, Proved and Allowed of by the Scriptures, All Such as Speak by the Spirit and Power of the Lord Jesus and How Women Were the First That Preached the Tidings of the Resurrection of Jesus, and Were Sent by Christ's Own Command before He Ascended to the Father (John 20:17)."

1775

Pope Benedict XIV explicitly condemns women serving the priest at the celebration of Mass in his encyclical *Allatae Sunt*, of July 26, 1755.

1790

Four Discalced Carmelite nuns form the first Catholic convent in the United States.

1791

The United States enshrines freedom of religion in the Bill of Rights as an amendment to the U.S. Constitution.

1853

A Congregational Church ordains Antoinette Brown Blackwell, the first woman ordained as a minister in the United States.

1879

Mary Baker Eddy founds the Church of Christ, Scientist (Christian Science).

1925

Pioneering anthropologist Margaret Mead begins studying male and female identity in several cultures in Oceania, paving the way for more research to be conducted with a female perspective.

1935
Regina Jonas (Germany) is the first woman ordained as a rabbi.

1940s
Wicca is developed in England by Gerald Gardner.

1956
The United Methodist Church votes in favor of "full clergy rights" for women, although the church remains divided on abortion, LBGTQ+ rights, and women's leadership.

1960
An internal armed conflict begins in Guatemala and lasts for thirty-six years. During that time, around two hundred thousand people, mostly Indigenous Mayans, are killed or disappeared. The army and paramilitary use rape as a tool of war during the genocidal conflict.

1964
Addie Davis is the first woman to be ordained by a Southern Baptist church.

1968
Radical lesbian feminist Mary Daly publishes her groundbreaking *The Church and the Second Sex.*

1970
The Unitarian Universalist Association is the first mainstream religious group in the United States to recognize LGB clergy and call for an end to anti-LGB discrimination.

A Catholic bishop secretly ordains several women priests under communist repression in then Czechoslovakia. After the communist era ends, their ordinations are not recognized by the church.

1972
The first LGBT synagogue in the world, Beth Chayim Chadashim, is founded in Los Angeles.

The first openly gay minister is ordained in the United Church of Christ, Rev. William R. Johnson.

1974
WomanSpirit magazine starts publishing women's writings on spirituality as part of a larger movement of feminist critique of patriarchal systems of

religion. This energy also develops into a collaborative homestead, the Oregon Women's Land Trust.

1978
The American Indian Religious Freedom Act is passed in the United States, making ceremonial practices and the possession of sacred objects legal for members of federally recognized tribes.

1979
Starhawk writes *The Spiral Dance* to challenge heteropatriarchal spirituality and iconography.

Mother Teresa is awarded the Nobel Peace Prize for her work among the poorest people in India.

1981
The Mātā Amṛtānandamayī Math (MAM) is founded to carry out the spiritual and charitable work of Mata Amritanandamayi, or Amma, the hugging saint, an Indian guru from Kerala, India.

1984
The Southern Baptist Convention, the largest Protestant denomination in the United States, adopts a resolution opposing women's ordination.

1986
Randall Terry founds Operation Rescue, an aggressive antiabortion organization that blocks the entrances to abortion clinics.

1987
Haiti recognizes Vodou as a national religion.

1989
The academic organization Weavers is formed as the first women's advocacy arm of the South Pacific Association of Theological Schools. The organization paves the way for women's voices and leadership in theological education in the region.

1990
The first female Anglican bishop is installed in New Zealand.

1996
Women's Ordination Worldwide is founded with the mission of gaining admission of Roman Catholic women to all ordained ministries.

2000

The Catholic Bishops of Australia approve the formation of the Council for Australian Catholic Women, whose purpose is to promote the participation of women in leadership, decision-making, and other ecclesial ministries in the church and to study theology in light of women's experiences and perspectives.

2003

The 24th General Synod of the United Church of Christ passes the resolution "Affirming the Participation and Ministry of Transgender People within the United Church of Christ and Supporting Their Civil and Human Rights."

2004

Wearing men's clothing and a false beard and mustache, a woman tries to deliver a *Jumah khutbah* (Friday Prayer) in Bahrain, but she is found out by the congregation before she has the chance.

The Marriage Law is established in Chile to allow women access to divorce and the morning-after pill and to produce an anti-AIDS campaign.

2005

In India, an amendment to the Hindu Succession Act gives married women the right to inherit their father's property. Previously only men in the family had this right.

Amina Wadud becomes the first woman to lead mixed-gender prayers in a mosque. At the service in Manhattan, about one hundred women and men are seated together with no gender segregation.

2006

South Africa becomes the first African nation to legalize same-sex marriage.

Katharine Jefferts Schori is the first woman elected as a primate in the Anglican Communion. She serves as the presiding bishop of the Episcopal Church of the United State until 2015.

2007

The Catholic Church recognizes sins as social structures built on institutional violence and earmarks resources of the church for the poor. It also establishes a moral vocabulary for activists and sprouts movements such as the Mothers of the Plaza del Mayo.

2008

The first female Anglican Bishop is installed in Australia.

2010

Argentina becomes the first Latin American nation to legalize same-sex marriage.

2011

The first woman is elected as prime minister of Australia.

The annual Slut Walk begins in Buenos Aires in response to the Catholic Church's declaration that the only purpose for sex is fertilization, not enjoyment for women.

The Council of Europe Convention on preventing and combating violence against women and domestic violence (also known as Treaty 210 or the Istanbul Convention) is opened for signatures. In 2020, many nations still have not ratified it.

2013

The first Muslim woman is elected to Parliament in Australia.

2014

Findings in the *Family Health and Safety Studies* conducted by the United Nations Population Fund indicate that the region of Oceania is one of the most dangerous places in the world for women to live. Violence against women in the region is twice the global average.

Antje Jackelén becomes the first woman in the Church of Sweden to hold the post of archbishop.

2016

Sherin Khankan becomes the first woman imam in Scandinavia when she opens a woman-led mosque in Denmark.

Karne Oliveto becomes the first openly lesbian bishop in the United Methodist Church.

Joanna Penberthy becomes the first woman bishop of the Church in Wales.

The government of Myanmar begins a genocidal attack on the Rohingya Muslim population that includes systemic rape and other forms of sexual violence against women.

2017

The Tibetan Buddhist spiritual leader suggests that a woman could be the next Dalai Lama but adds that she would have to be pretty. Soon after, he apologizes for that comment.

"Mama Kiota" of Niger receives the Tisch College Global Humanitarian Citizen Award in recognition of her lifetime of work for Muslim women's rights, education, and peace.

Russian president Vladimir Putin signs a law decriminalizing family violence. The Russian Orthodox Church supports the law, citing male authority and female submission as the basis of the traditional family.

2018

The Catholic bishops in New Zealand acknowledge the church's shortcomings in providing love and care to groups who have felt a very real sense of rejection by the church, such as the LGBTQ community. The bishops further say that concrete actions will be enacted to prove church leaders' commitment to becoming an inclusive church.

A woman from Kerala is the first woman imam in India to lead the *Jum'ah khutbah* for a mixed-gender congregation.

The Catholic Church of Latin America Synod on Women declares that the church must appreciate the role of women and end the practice of using women solely as submissive laborers in the parish.

2019

Archbishop of Canterbury Justin Welby consecrates Rose Hudson-Wilkin, the first Black woman to become a bishop in the Church of England.

Majority-Catholic Austria legalizes same-sex marriage.

Pope Francis acknowledges that clergy abuse of children and women, including nuns, is "a problem."

ONE

North America

Kali Furman, Jennifer A. Venable, Leida Karibu (L.K.) Mae, Luhui Whitebear, and Rebecca J. Lambert

WOMEN IN THE RELIGIONS OF NORTH AMERICA

In North America, which includes Canada, the United States, and Mexico, religion plays an important role in many women's lives, from their faith practices and identity formation to the impacts of religious doctrine on their positions in society and politics. Christianity is the dominant religion in North America, with Christians making up nearly 78 percent of the region's population (Pew Research Center 2015b). There are many Christian faith traditions, including Catholics; Protestant evangelical denominations, such as Southern Baptists and the Lutheran Church–Missouri Synod; mainline Protestant denominations, such as the Episcopal Church, the Presbyterian Church, and the United Church of Christ; and other independent and community churches.

The second-largest religious group in North America, accounting for just over 17 percent of the population, is unaffiliated with any particular religion (Pew Research Center 2015b). These "Nones" are mostly individuals who hold religious beliefs similar to those who identify with a religious tradition; the minority of the "Nones" are agnostic or atheist (Killen and Silk 2004). In the United States, the "Nones" account for 22.8 percent of the country's population, with the largest concentration found in the Pacific Northwest (Pew Research Center n.d.; Killen and Silk 2004). In Canada, religiously unaffiliated people make up 29 percent of the population, and in Mexico, they are almost 5 percent (Central Intelligence Agency n.d.-b; Lipka 2019).

The next largest religious group in North America is the Jewish community, with 1.8 percent of the population. They are followed by Buddhists at 1.1 percent, Muslims at 1.0 percent, and Hindus at 0.7 percent.

The religious life of women in North America is diverse and has a long and at times complicated history. Indigenous peoples have faced centuries of colonialism and forced assimilation into settlers' religious practices. Nonetheless, Indigenous peoples have resisted and, as discussed throughout this chapter, have maintained Native religious practices in different forms. Women's resistance to oppression can also be seen in the rise of feminist theology within their religious communities.

It is important to consider the experiences of women in religions in conjunction with other social forces, such as racism, classism, homophobia, ableism, and transphobia. As Black feminist poet Audre Lorde (2007) said, "There is no such thing as a single-issue struggle because we do not live single-issue lives." This chapter highlights the ways religion can be a source of opportunity, strength, and faith as well as how it can be used to enact oppression.

Christianity

Christianity remains the majority religion in North America, although it has recently decreased notably. Christians make up 55 percent of the population in Canada, 65 percent in the United States, and over 90 percent in Mexico (Lesley 2016; Lipka 2019; Pew Research Center 2019b). Women's roles within Christianity have varied over time and across denominations. Examples of women's issues in a few of the diverse branches of Christianity are discussed in the following sections.

Roman Catholicism

Catholicism is the largest branch of Christianity in North America; it comprises 39 percent of the population in Canada, 25 percent in the United States, and 81 percent in Mexico (Pew Research Center 2013; McGill 2015; Lipka 2016b). Although Christian and secular writers contend that women have always been integral to the church in a multitude of ways, they also agree that women's work does not receive the acknowledgment it deserves (Kroeger 1988). Women's roles continue to reflect the historical marginalization of Catholic women, who still cannot be ordained as deacons or priests and, in some instances, are prohibited from completing other ministry duties because of gender (Ecklund 2005, 136).

Catholic women continue to face oppressive and traditional pressures that negatively and disproportionately affect them. In particular, the Catholic Church has openly made stances against contraception, abortion, divorce, and gay marriage (O'Loughlin 2016). In the United States, an estimated 50 percent of Catholics agreed with the church's stances against abortion and gay marriage, but the majority disagreed with the church about contraception and divorce being inherently sinful (O'Loughlin 2016).

Protestantism

Protestants make up the largest group of Christians in the United States (although they represent a wide divergence in beliefs and practices), with an estimated 25.4 percent of the population identifying as evangelical and 14.7 percent as mainline Protestant (Masci and Smith 2018). Protestantism includes many drastically different denominations and independent churches, such as Adventists, Baptists, Methodists, Presbyterians, Pentecostals, and Lutherans. Because Protestantism encompasses such a vast range of denominations, churches, and believers, its traditions, values, practices, organization, and members range from very conservative to very progressive. They differ in political affiliation as well as beliefs about social issues such as abortion and marriage equality. While Protestant women are more religious than Protestant men, both groups have seen a decline in church participation in recent years. More Protestant women are pastors than even a decade ago, but they still represent only a fraction of pastors.

Evangelicalism

In general, evangelicalism stresses personal salvation through Jesus Christ and understands the Bible as the final authority on faith-related issues (Smidt 2007, 32). Evangelical Christianity bases its understandings of women and men on biblical interpretations of separate gendered spheres of behavior that are rooted in biological determinism (the idea that the genitals one is born with determine one's gender and therefore one's social role, whom one is attracted to, and one's general behavior). The ideal family structure, then, is a heterosexual marriage with the man as the head of the household and the woman as the domestic worker and child rearer. Gallagher and Smith (1999) describe a "pragmatic egalitarianism" in many evangelical marriages, where women (and men) reconcile their ideals of masculine headship and feminine submission with the necessary realities of mutual respect and the need for compromise. Although a small percentage speak about "mutual submission" and respect, most evangelicals, while believing in equality before God, desire to "stand apart from" mainstream society and egalitarianism, even as they are influenced by feminism in the practical execution of household duties (Gallagher and Smith 1999).

Christian Fundamentalism

Most evangelicals are fundamentalists. Christian fundamentalism, based on biblical literalism, is politically conservative, and it rejects a clear separation of church and state (New 2014). Fundamentalism is defined by clear subcultural boundaries, authoritarian leaders, a sense of engagement in an ultimate battle between good and evil, and ill preparation to deal with people who are different from themselves (Shaw 2020). Fundamentalism is also characterized by male dominance: "religious fundamentalism is understood as a patriarchal politics of identity in which a male religious elite attempts to maintain its power over women and other males in both the religious and social spheres" (Madigan 2011, 2). A common theme remains the subservience of women and the control of men over women.

Fundamentalist Christians believe that the Bible is the inerrant and infallible word of God, which means that it is theologically, historically, and scientifically accurate and unchanging across time and place. They read the biblical text to teach women's responsibility for the Fall in the Garden of Eden and women's submission to husbands and pastors. Because believers are uncompromising, women have few opportunities to challenge the patriarchal paradigm. For fundamentalists, progressive movements toward the equality of women and other marginalized populations are a threat to "traditional moral values" because these movements undermine hierarchies of gender and the requirements for submission.

Ethnic Minority Churches

A number of uniquely African American/Black/diasporic African religious traditions exist in Canada, the United States, the Caribbean, and Latin America, such as the African Methodist Episcopal Church (AME), the African Methodist Episcopal Zion Church (AMEZ), and the Church of God in Christ. These diverse churches combine the influences of European, African, and local Indigenous religions with an emphasis on the Black experience (Keller, Ruether, and Cantlon 2006).

One reason for the historical practice of Christianity in Black communities is the way in which baptism and other Christian rites conveyed legal rights and freedom under slavery (Beasley 2009). During the slave era in the United States, Black religious gatherings and churches became the center of African American communities, and this tradition continues; Black churches serve as a stronghold in African American communities' political and social lives (McMickle 2002). Unlike predominantly white

Although often excluded from leadership, Black women are the core of active participants in the Black church in the United States. Many Black churches serve as centers for organizing and addressing issues of social justice. (iStockPhoto.com)

churches, Black churches have regularly been expected to address social issues that impact their members, such as civil rights (McMickle 2002). During the civil rights era, some Black churches also became the heart of coalition building and were active in organizing protests and marches in tandem with their Christian teachings. Others rejected becoming involved in anything political.

In Black churches, most active participants are women, although most leaders are men (Lowen 2019). Despite this disparity, Black women persist as congregants (Lowen 2019). Although most Black women cannot ascend to the role of spiritual leaders, their work contributes to the organization and growth of church communities. Black women tend to work behind the scenes in roles as ushers, trustees, or financial supporters (Williams 2018).

For many immigrant Christians, churches function as social hubs and community centers in the face of cultural and racial bias (Hong 2015). The creation of country-specific churches gives new immigrant Christians social and communal gathering spaces with familiar cultural context (Sanchez and Gilbert 2016). For example, Korean American churches share some racial and class characteristics that are embedded in the immigration process. Scholars have discussed the "dual functions" of racial and ethnic churches. They function for the assimilation (in this case, the Americanization) of church members as well as the preservation of their traditional cultures (Kim 1997, 123). Similar to women in Black churches, Korean American women are the majority of attendees in their community churches (1997, 124). However, they continue to exist mostly in the background of the congregation and not in formal leadership roles.

Buddhism

An estimated 1.2 percent of people in the United States and 0.9 percent in Mexico identify as Buddhist. Buddhism remains one of the smallest religious groups in Canada, making up 1.1 percent of the population (Statistics Canada 2013; Boorstein 2020). A number of factors affect the ways Buddhism is shaped and practiced in North America.

Buddhism gained popularity in the United States in the 1960s (Seager 2012). As interest in the religion grew, two forms of Buddhism emerged: immigrant and convert (Seager 2012). The convert stream of Buddhism is an Americanized or Western version of the religion that has selected the traditions of the religion it wants to follow, such as meditation (Bender and

Cadge 2006). The immigrant stream of Buddhism connects more with Asian traditions, including a focus on "memory, solace, and spiritual practice grounded in ethnic, linguistic, and ancestral identity" (Seager 2012, 5).

In the 1990s, Buddhism in the United States embraced social activism while supporting women in their desire to be leaders (Seager 2012). Gender equity became a priority in the convert community, elevating women into practitioner positions they had not previously held (Seager 2012).

The influence of Buddhist nuns in North America can be seen in the "interfaith dialogue" trend. One key component has been the "hybridization" of religions, which occurs when religions move between geographical spaces and adapt and transform as a result of historical, cultural, and environmental influences. According to Bender and Cadge, "Our analyses suggest not only that Catholic engagement with Buddhism is constructing and shaping Americans' views of 'Buddhism,' but that these constructions develop together, as Buddhist and Catholic nuns come to understand their unique historical positions through imagining and engaging the other" (2006, 231).

One example of this is the utilization of Buddhist "forms," such as meditation and mindfulness, within Catholicism. Some Catholic nuns have incorporated Buddhist practices as a way to deepen their Catholic reflection, referring to their silent meditations as embodied and labeling such practices as "Christian Zen" (Bender and Cadge 2006, 234). However, not all Buddhist nuns appreciate the inclusion of their practices within the Catholic faith and hold that utilizing only certain aspects that feel useful, without understanding the beliefs that should accompany such practices, falls short of the goal of Buddhism as organically whole. Bender and Cadge state that "by understanding meditation forms as tools, these Buddhist nuns see the Catholic nuns participating in the very same American picking and choosing they often encounter among their students and are trying to overcome in their teachings about Buddhism as a holistic religious/philosophical tradition" (2006, 234).

While many Buddhist nuns reject this kind of hybridization, others embrace and foster it as part of their own practices. In the 1980s, Reverend Sik Kuan Yen, a nun from Hong Kong, created the Thousand Buddha Temple in Massachusetts (Dugan 2007, 34). She believes that interfaith collaboration and partnership is important because all religions "work for the good of society" (Dugan 2007, 34). Many Buddhist women involved in interfaith dialogue have translated their religious practices into social activist work, such as prison ministry, community education, and university education (Dugan 2007, 39, 40, 41).

Hinduism

The majority of Hindus in North America are immigrants from India, Sri Lanka, Malaysia, and the Caribbean; a minority are converts (Narayanan 2006, 659). Hindus in North America mostly embrace the Vedanta school of Hinduism, which focuses on the ancient Sanskrit Upanishads and their teachings about spiritual liberation (Narayanan 2006, 659).

Similar to women in other religions in North America, Hindu women have a range of experiences. The oppression of Hindu women stems from a patriarchal social structure undergirded by gendered ideologies justifying their lower status and subordination (Derné 1994, 203). Hinduism declares women as having "different natures than men," implying women's inferiority is based on their biological or "female" bodies (Lindley 2006, 29). Such gendered constructions hold implications about the "purity" and immorality of women and serve to rationalize the control of women's movements inside and outside their homes (Derné 1994, 203). A fundamental component to the gender division is a norm requiring women's "modest" behavior, where they are expected to remain pure, self-sacrificial, and nurturing as mothers and wives (Derné 1994, 205).

Most literature regarding the evolution of Hindu women in the United States falls into one of two categories. Some scholars argue that the migration and settlement of Indian women in the United States led to their empowerment and equality; others hold that Hindu immigrants have actually created and upheld a more oppressive model that censures any feminist analysis about gendered abuse or violence (Kurien 1999, 948).

Sociologist Prema Kurien argues that the Hindu immigrant woman is "constructed as a virtuous and self-sacrificing homemaker, enabling the professional success of her husband and the academic achievements of her children through her unselfish actions on their behalf" (1999, 650). Restrictions placed on Hindu women are gender and caste specific. Because, for some, "inappropriate" behavior from women can easily damage a family's integrity, social restrictions are important in regulating and monitoring women's movements. Honor among families is maintained by a daughter's marriage within a "respectable" and appropriate family. Because such a huge weight is placed on this notion of honor, a number of Hindu men take extra precautions to ensure their daughters' moral behavior outside of the home before marriage (Derné 1994, 207). Similarly, married Hindu women are often not independent, unless they have gained permission from their husband (Derné 1994, 208).

On the other hand, Kurien explains that because many women have received a higher education and do have professional positions, some argue that Hindu women do have equality with Hindu men in the United States (1999, 650).

Islam

The Muslim community in North America is steadily growing across Mexico, Canada, and the United States, with the smallest population in Mexico, estimated in 2010 to be 110,000 people (approximately 0.1 percent of the population) (Rogers 2011). Mexico City in particular is experiencing a growth of the Muslim population, as are some rural communities (Strochlic 2017).

In the United States, the Muslim population is wide ranging and diverse, with Muslim people coming from many ethnic and cultural backgrounds, including immigrants and people born in the United States. A 2017 Pew Research Center study estimates there are approximately 3.45 million Muslims in the United States (Mohamed 2018). Muslim women comprise many racial and ethnic identities, including Sunni, who are the majority; Shia, who account for up to 20 percent of U.S. Muslim women; and a small minority of women who are Sufi and cut across racial and ethnic lines (Haddad 2006). Because of the diversity of Muslim women, there is no universal set of experiences and faith practices. However, the roles of women in Muslim culture tend to be tied to their family relationships and responsibilities, their age, and their role and status in their community, which many Muslim women actively explore and try to expand.

The ways in which Muslim women navigate their faith in relation to family, tradition, heritage, and the dominant U.S. culture overlap with Islamophobia at the individual and societal levels, especially since the events of September 11, 2001. Following the attacks, there was a dramatic rise in hate crimes against Muslim communities and individuals who were perceived to be Muslim. From 2000 to 2006, the American Civil Liberties Union (ACLU) reported a 674 percent increase in hate crimes against Muslims in the United States (Al Wazni 2015). Muslim women in the United States and around the world often became targets because of the visibility of their Islamic dress, particularly the hijab (the traditional hair and neck covering).

The status of Muslim women and the hijab became a focal point of Islamophobia for states, individuals, and Western feminists. The U.S.

About 3.5 million Muslims live in the United States. Muslim women negotiate differences across Muslim sects and cultural differences that define
women's roles as well as the dramatic rise in Islamophobia in the past
twenty years. (Lei Xu/Dreamstime.com)

government (and often white feminists) constructed the hijab and especially the burqa as symbols of oppression and used Muslim women's attire
to justify the U.S. invasions of Afghanistan and Iraq (Abu-Lughod 2002;
Al Wazni 2015). Many Western feminists also took up the trope of veiled
Muslim women as victims of oppression and did not consider what the
choice to wear a hijab means for Muslim women or account for their
agency in their own lives and communities.

Research demonstrates that for Muslim women in the United States,
wearing the hijab is an active choice (Al Wazni 2015). Muslim women's
decisions regarding Islamic dress, contrary to the stereotypes and miscon-
ceptions discussed above, are "not about coercion, but about making
choices, about 'choosing' an identity and expressing a religiosity through
their mode of dress" (Haddad 2006, 10).

Muslims in Canada account for 3.2 percent of the general population,
slightly more than one million people (Central Intelligence Agency n.d.-a).

In Canada, roughly three-quarters of Muslim women are immigrants (Marcotte 2010). Similar to Muslim women in the United States, Muslim women in Canada come from diverse ethnic, cultural, and national backgrounds, resulting in a wide range of experiences, beliefs, and practices. The Canadian Council of Muslim Women is an important organization whose mission is to "affirm our identity as Canadian Muslim women and promote an understanding of our lived experiences through community engagement, research, influence on public policy and our strive for positive change" (Canadian Council on Muslim Women 2020). The organization provides programming and tool kits to address the practical needs of Muslim communities across Canada.

Judaism

North America holds three of the fifteen countries with the highest populations of Jewish people: the United States is second, Canada is fourth, and Mexico is fourteenth (Sawe 2018). Starting in the 1680s, New York became the first main settlement area for Jews coming to the United States; additional population growth occurred in Rhode Island, Pennsylvania, Virginia, and Massachusetts (Levenson 2012). Currently, New York State has the largest population of Jewish people, with 7 percent of the population identifying as Jewish (Sandstrom 2016).

There are three branches of Judaism: Orthodox, Reform, and Conservative. The Orthodox branch includes the ultra-Orthodox and Modern Orthodox groups (Lugo, Cooperman, and Smith 2013). Orthodox Jews observe more traditional practices, including following the Sabbath and dietary limitations (Robinson 2013). This branch of Judaism believes in the strict interpretation of the Torah, which outlines daily worship practices, dietary restrictions, the study of the written laws, and the separation of women and men in the synagogue. Reform Judaism recognizes an evolving approach to the practice of the religion, allows women and men to sit together in the synagogue, and holds a confirmation ceremony for girls, a bat mitzvah, similar to the bar mitzvah ceremony for boys. Reform Judaism does not adhere to the strict worship or dietary practices of Orthodox Judaism. The Conservative branch maintains certain traditional practices while making allowances for modern changes, such as not separating women and men in the synagogue (Israel-Cohen 2012). Conservative Judaism aligns with Reform Judaism in terms of scholarship but adheres to Jewish law on issues such as dietary restrictions.

During the second wave of U.S. feminist activism, Jewish feminists challenged the limited roles and rights they had within their religion, which resulted in an expansion of rights and access to positions of leadership. Both Reform and Conservative Judaism allow women to be rabbis (Hyman 2009). Even within Orthodox Judaism, women have made some advances. In 2006, the *New York Times* featured a story about Dina Najman, who became a spiritual leader within the Jewish Orthodox community. She was not, however, referred to as a rabbi; she was given the title of "head of congregation" (Lugo, Cooperman, and Smith 2013) and was not allowed to lead services, read from the Torah, start prayer, or preside over ceremonies (Lugo, Cooperman, and Smith 2013).

The Church of Jesus Christ of Latter-Day Saints

The Church of Jesus Christ of Latter-day Saints (LDS), also known as the Mormon Church, was formed in 1830 in upstate New York. Today, the church's 6.7 million members comprise 1.6 percent of the population in the United States. There are also nearly 198,000 members in Canada and almost 1.5 million members in Mexico (Church of Jesus Christ of Latter-day Saints 2020a, 2020b, 2020c).

Women have always had an important role in the LDS Church and are central figures in LDS families, particularly in their roles as wives and mothers. Much of the early scholarship on Mormon women focused on their roles in the settlement of Utah, the growth and expansion of the church, and the development of the Relief Society, a church-based organization that focused on social and civic involvement as well as spiritual growth (Holbrook and Bowman 2016). The Relief Society is still an important component of Mormon women's lives, with a focus on "increasing personal faith and righteousness, strengthening homes and families and seeking out and helping those in need" (Church of Jesus Christ of Latter-day Saints 2012). The Relief Society provides opportunities for women's leadership, service work, teaching, and training for sermon delivery.

As in other religious groups, LDS women have a variety of gender-related experiences, although agency is a central theme in the lives of many. In discussing an extensive Mormon women's oral history project, Claudia Bushman emphasizes the role of agency: "As we try to record what contemporary LDS women of all stripes have to say, we see them interpreting teachings and creating personal doctrine for themselves, making and justifying their choices based on their own preferences and circumstances" (Holbrook and Bowman 2016).

Missionary work ties all of these components together and is one of the most significant and visible aspects of the LDS Church. Many women consider missionary work "a personal responsibility" and fulfill this faith-based obligation by participating in missions as well as by "raising children, particularly sons, who willingly serve the LDS Church as full-time missionaries" (Bushman and Kline 2013, 169). In 2014, the church lowered the missionary age for women from twenty-one to nineteen, resulting in an increase in their numbers (Human Rights Campaign n.d.-c).

Since the 1970s, Mormon feminists have bridged their faith and the feminist movement for women's equality and gender justice (Brooks, Steenblik, and Wheelwright 2016). They have participated in social activism and worked to build community with each other to explore the relationship between gender and faith. For example, on December 16, 2012, Mormon feminists all over the world staged an action to raise awareness of feminist issues by wearing pants to their Sunday church services. This pushed back on the unofficial, but socially enforced, traditional gendered dress customs (Brooks, Steenblik, and Wheelwright 2016).

Neo-Paganism/Wicca

Women's traditional knowledges of plant-based healing, medicine making, and embodied understandings have roots in the Indigenous knowledge of the inhabitants of what came to be known as the United States and in Indigenous and traditional knowledge brought by settlers, slaves, and immigrants from around the world. Neo-paganism and Wicca, particularly their feminist iterations, are reclaimed/revived religions that reject colonial Christianity in favor of (Mother) Goddess-centered theologies. In *The Spiral Dance*, first written in 1979, feminist Wiccan Starhawk describes Wicca as a "challenge to the spiritual supremacy of patriarchal males and male images" (1999, 7).

American New Age, Wiccan, and neo-pagan movements gained their impetus from the social movements of the 1960s, drawing ritual practices from British, German, African, Indian, and Native American traditions. Neo-pagan religions and Wicca draw guidance for the present and the future from the past, whereas New Age beliefs function from an imagined future and seek to create a present from that future.

Wiccans and neo-pagans are often associated with witchcraft and have been affected by the colonial histories of the Inquisition, the witch hunts of Puritan New England, and a blend of Native American, African, and European ideas about witches. "Witches, everyone agreed, were people who performed harmful acts and threatened community order" (Games 2010, 3). A large part of the work of early American feminist Wiccan philosophers such as Starhawk and Zsuzsanna Budapest is reclaiming women's threat to patriarchy and rejecting the ways women are taught to deny themselves for others.

Feminist Dianic Wicca and lesbian separatist collectives grew out of the environmental activism of the 1960s and the women's movement. Zsuzsanna Budapest started the Susan B. Anthony Coven No. 1 in 1971, whose manifesto is included in her classic book *The Holy Book of Women's Mysteries* (1986, 12–13). The first Feminist Dianic Wicca organization, it is for women only and sees all goddesses as manifestations of the one Goddess.

In the 1970s, *WomanSpirit* magazine was printed in Oregon as a place for women's writing on spirituality as part of a larger political movement of feminist critique of patriarchal systems of religion. In Oregon during the same era, the OWL (Oregon Women's Land) Farm became the Oregon Women's Land Trust; it was intended to create a space for women to live in spiritual harmony with the land. Starhawk's writing on ecofeminism and awareness of connections to the natural world led to her discussions of new ways of leadership and the need to transition from masculinist systems of "power over" as integral to (lesbian) feminist spiritual and political movements.

Diasporic African Religions

For African women in North America, religious beliefs and practices may be influenced by Indigenous African religions, colonially imposed Christianity, slavery, collaborations with North American Indigenous religions, other diasporic religions, and neo-pagan practices (Keller, Ruether, and Cantlon 2006). Ifa/Yoruba followers created the Oyotunji African Village in 1971 in Sheldon, South Carolina; it is a communal living space and polygamous community, complete with its own theology and scripture (Ashcraft-Eason, Martin, and Olademo 2009). Afro-Cuban traditions of *orisha* (spirit) possession or Santeria in the tradition of *Regla de Ocha* and Palo Mayombe exist primarily in Cuba and the United States. *We*, in which women are active participants, is also distinct to Cuba but is not built on African origins (Ashcraft-Eason, Martin, and Olademo 2009). Founded by Cynthea Jones and Patricia Storm in the 1990s, Diana's Grove is a multimodal spiritual community retreat center in the foothills of the Missouri Ozarks. Diana's Grove provides a safe space for the expression of Earth-based spiritual beliefs and women's leadership practice (Ashcraft-Eason, Martin, and Olademo 2009).

Indigenous Religions

In North America, Indigenous women have always been involved with ceremonial practices. Western religion has a complicated history in Indigenous communities because it has often harmed those communities, but it has also helped preserve Indigenous languages and practices when Indigenous ceremonies were outlawed.

There are not many organized Indigenous religions in North America. Among the most prominent is the Native American Church, which can be described as a "pan-Indian" religious movement (a practice of Indigenous origin adopted as a common cultural practice across multiple Indigenous communities). The Native American Church's roots come from the Indigenous peyote (an hallucinogenic drug made from a cactus) cultural and ceremonial practices in Mexico that spread north. The use of Christian-based sacramental practices became a means to continue practicing Native America customs. The Native American Church has allowed Indigenous communities to exert self-determination, religious sovereignty, and cultural revitalization. Women's roles in the Native American Church are focused on meal preparation, which is part of the ceremonial practices, and participation in the ceremony itself.

Organized religion has influenced Indigenous ceremonies in North America in other ways. One of the most prominent is *Dia de los Muertos* (Day of the Dead), which has origins in Indigenous cultures from Mexico. During Spanish colonial rule, Indigenous practices were outlawed. Blending various practices allowed Indigenous people to continue some of their traditions while embracing the colonizers' Catholic religion. *Dia de los Muertos* takes different forms in different regions. The observance centers on celebrating ancestors, loved ones who have passed on, and one's own mortality. It coincides with the Catholic All Saints' Day, which also honors those who have passed on, making the intermingling of traditions possible.

New Religious Movements

The term *new religious movement* (NRM) can be misleading, as many of the religions associated with this title are actually centuries old. NRMs are often negatively referred to as *cults* or *sects*, but they challenge these conceptions. In general, NRMs are not part of mainstream religions (such as Christianity and Judaism). Examples of NRMs include Indigenous religious movements, Baha'i, Scientology, the Nation of Islam, Shaker, and Jehovah's Witnesses.

Indigenous Religious Movements

NRMs have emerged from Indigenous communities as a way to reclaim cultural identities, practices, and connections to land and to counter the ways in which religion has been used as a tool of colonial oppression.

Among the numerous current Indigenous-based religious movements is Idle No More, a Canadian First Nations–based effort, which was established in response to environmental justice and treaty rights efforts. Women rose to the forefront of these efforts based on ancestral responsibilities to their communities and lands. Idle No More was a call to action to bring Indigenous ceremonies into the streets and buildings that occupy Indigenous lands. These ceremonies were not to serve as a performance but as a way to begin healing relationships with each other and with the lands. Idle No More quickly spread through the use of social media and was adopted by Indigenous communities in the United States.

Scientology

Scientology is a spiritual movement based on the ideas of L. Ronald Hubbard, who is also known for his popular fiction books. Scientologists believe that all people have suppressed power that can be regained through "audits" that help them clear themselves of the things that block access to that power, allowing them to self-actualize. The Church of Scientology is

---

UNITARIAN UNIVERSALISTS: A "RADICAL" RELIGION

Unitarian Universalism (UU) was born when two Christian groups joined their voices in the United States in 1961. It has historical roots but is a "new" religion.

The doctrines of *Unitarians* (the oneness of God) and *Universalists* (salvation for all) were accepted in the early Christian church but were later declared heresy. Both groups supported free will and choice in religion and believed in the dignity and worth of all people.

Today, Unitarian Universalists support diversity, inclusion, and social justice. Their teachings are drawn from monotheistic religions such as Christianity, humanism, Earth-centered religions, science, writings of thoughtful and compassionate people (past and present), and each individual's experience.

Janet Lockhart

---

structured hierarchically; local churches are independent, though they operate from a basic set of principles (Encyclopedia.com 2020). Ministry is available to women and men. The movement claims that there are no limitations based on gender, race, or ethnicity, and anyone who is dedicated to the work can be a minister (Scientology n.d.).

The Nation of Islam

The Nation of Islam was founded in 1930 at a time when African Americans were looking for an alternative to Christianity (Fleischer 2005). The movement's goals are to address the needs of African Americans, but it has been criticized for promoting anti-Semitism and anti-LGBTQ positions because of the belief that these groups are inferior. The Southern Poverty Law Center has labeled it a hate group. Although leadership in the Nation of Islam is male dominated, some women do hold leadership positions. Ava Muhammad, who in 2005 held the highest position as national spokesperson, said that "the role of women in the Nation of Islam is really no different than it is in any other religion. Christianity, Judaism and Islam—all of which are necessary for the enlightenment of humanity—all suffer from a similar affliction of being overly male-dominant, even in the interpretation of scripture" (Fleischer 2005). Although women are making progress in leadership roles, they are still held to traditional gender roles, such as caretakers for the household (Fleischer 2005).

BAHÁ'Í: SPIRITUAL UNITY

The core principles of the Bahá'í faith include the Unity of God, the Unity of Religion, and the Unity of Humanity. Bahá'í is widespread across the world, but the United States has the second-largest population.

Bahá'í promotes equality regardless of gender or race. Religious texts state there is no difference between women and men, and they specify that women may serve in leadership positions.

However, Bahá'í women still encounter some challenges. Sacred texts are framed from a male perspective and refer to men, suggesting to readers that men are central and at the top of a hierarchy. Many Bahá'í followers challenge these readings and claim unequivocal equality among men and women.

**Kali Furman, Jennifer A. Venable, Leida Karibu (L.K.) Mae,
Luhui Whitebear, Rebecca J. Lambert**

ISSUES OF RELIGION IN NORTH AMERICA

The Impact of Christian Missionaries on the Colonial Project

Christian missionaries in North America played a significant role in the colonial project. Colonizers held that Indigenous people did not have souls, so they took on the mission of saving them through the adoption of Christianity. However, even as colonizers evangelized Indigenous people, they also enslaved and murdered them. Women in particular were subjected to the racist and misogynistic violence of rape, sex trafficking, and forced servitude. Because colonizers viewed Indigenous women's bodies as sinful, they insisted that Indigenous women deserved mistreatment and assault. The lasting effects of colonization can be seen in the staggering contemporary rates of violence against Indigenous women, including the epidemic of murdered and missing Indigenous women across the United States, Canada, and Mexico (Deer 2015, x; Whitebear 2019, 86).

After, and sometimes during, the waves of genocide and disease that Indigenous people faced, the introduction of boarding schools and missions began. The purpose of these colonial projects was to assimilate Indigenous children and strip them of their cultural identities. Religion was a primary factor in these projects. Women served central roles as teachers and nuns in the residential schools and missions, shaping the experiences of the children both in the schools or missions and when they returned home. The impacts today can be seen through the high suicide, drug addiction, alcohol addiction, and domestic violence rates in Indige-nous communities (Centers for Disease Control and Prevention 2013).

Understanding the critical roles Christian missionaries played in the colonial projects that dispossessed Indigenous people of their lands and African people of their freedom helps all people understand the complex-ity of the current struggles faced by all communities of color. These strug-gles have deep roots fueled by settler colonialism. The good done now in the forms of housing development, school infrastructures, and other ways of helping struggling communities are new in comparison to these lega-cies. If they come at the cost of adopting the religion they are sponsored by, it is worth examining whether this is another iteration of these legacies.

Women in Religious Leadership

Although some would argue that women have made strides in religious leadership in North America, there is still much to be done to reach par-ity with men. Of the one hundred largest churches in the United States, only one has a female senior pastor, and she is a co-pastor with her hus-band (*Outreach Magazine* n.d.; Mekhail and Ngu 2018). While the num-ber of women serving in religious organizations continues to rise, their roles in leadership are sometimes limited, which is justified through patriarchal ideals and religious texts (Fiedler 2010). A major divide among many Christian denominations continues to focus on the leader-ship roles of women.

Mainstream Protestant denominations such as the United Church of Christ, the Presbyterian Church (U.S.A.), American Baptist Churches USA, the Episcopal Church, the Evangelical Lutheran Church in America, and the United Methodist Church ordain women and accept women in all leadership positions. Despite this, only about 11 percent of congregations in the United States are led by women (Masci 2014). Many of the largest denominations in the United States, including Southern Baptists, still do not support women's ordination (Masci 2014).

In May 1956, the United Methodist Church voted in favor of "full clergy rights" for women, believing "in the full equality of women and the impor-tance of women in decision-making and leadership positions at all levels of the church" (United Methodist Church n.d.-b). According to the United Methodists, women can be leaders because women and men are equal in all ways in the eyes of God; thus, the role of religious leader should be extended to those who are called to the ministry (United Methodist Church n.d.-a). The Episcopal Church consecrated its first woman presiding bishop, Katharine Jefferts Schori, in 2006 at the Washington National Cathedral.

Southern Baptists, the nation's largest Protestant denomination, fought a more than decade-long battle over women's ordination in the 1980s, as local Southern Baptist churches began to call and ordain women as pastors. By the mid-1990s, fundamentalists had taken over the Southern Baptist Convention, and churches supporting the ordination of women or LGBTQ rights were forced out. The organizations that formed as a result—the Cooperative Baptist Fellowship and the Baptist Alliance—support women's ordination, but only the Baptist Alliance affirms LGBTQ rights.

In the United States, the Leadership Conference of Women Religious (LCWR) is an association of Catholic women leaders who center their work on social justice activism in collaboration with the Catholic Church (Leadership Conference of Women Religious n.d.). LCWR reflects the leadership work of Catholic women and also the conflicts that they have and continue to face. In 2009, the Vatican began a seven-year investigation of the LCWR and all women religious in the United States, claiming they were too "radical" in their practices and conflicted with Catholic doctrine and tradition (Gibson 2012). The organization was censured by the church for being in alliance with "radical feminist themes" because the LCWR did not speak out enough against same-sex marriage, reproductive choices—such as birth control and abortion—and women's ordination (Gibson 2012). Regardless of the scrutiny this group faced, they continued to address the most pressing social justice issues, and they spoke out against the sexual abuse of nuns by members of the clergy (Leadership Conference of Women Religious 2019).

Other religious traditions in North America have seen a growing shift in the roles of women as religious leaders. For example, the female guru (religious teacher) is an increasingly relevant role within Hindu religious life. Scholar Karen Pechilis contends that female gurus "maintain dialogue with their tradition and recognize kinship with it, but they are also innovative within that context, by their distinctive contributions to tradition and by distinguishing themselves from each other" (2004, 5).

Women's participation in leadership positions in Judaism varies across branches of the religion. More progressive forms began to accept women as rabbis in the 1970s (Sandstrom 2016). A pioneering moment for women in Orthodox Judaism occurred in 2017 when three women were formally ordained (Smokler 2013). This group of women completed all the training and demonstrated a deep knowledge of Jewish texts and were given the title of Maharat, a term for leader. Although they were not given the title of rabbi, all three women practice at the same level as rabbis (Smokler 2017).

Although women in Islam often participate as teachers and preachers, they are not typically given religious leadership roles (Bano and Kalmbach 2012); however, women have begun to challenge this exclusion. For example, Amina Wadud, a professor of Islamic studies and an African American convert to Islam, led a mixed-gender group of worshippers in a Friday prayer in 2005, making her the first woman to lead prayers in a mosque (Bano and Kalmbach 2012).

Women make up about 65 percent of the membership of Jehovah's Witnesses in the United States (Lipka 2016a). Jehovah's Witnesses hold that men should have authority over women and that women's role is to support the household (Chryssides 2008). Women are allowed to engage in door-to-door outreach but are not given leadership authority.

Women in the Church of Jesus Christ of Latter-day Saints (LDS) are assigned mothering and caregiving roles, such as tending to the sick and keeping the home in order (Brooks, Steenblik, and Wheelwright 2016). Many members of the LDS Church, including women, do not support women in leadership positions (Lipka 2016a), and they are excluded from decision-making in the institutional church (Brooks, Steenblik, and Wheelwright 2016). Although there are distinctive barriers for Mormon women in church leadership, women do play an important role in LDS communities. Mormon feminists have actively organized and fought for the place of Mormon women in church structures.

In Mexico, 2019 marked the ten-year celebration of the ordination of women in the Mexican Lutheran Church (ILM) (LWF LAC Communications Network, México 2019). In 2009, Rev. Maria Elena Ortega and Rev. Ángela Trejo Haager were ordained. Rev. Karina García Carmona, ordained in 2015, shared how she believed such changes gave rise to a surge of female leadership and empowerment as well as a more nuanced gender perspective within the church (LWF LAC Communications Network, México 2019).

Canadians have a unique commitment to building coalitions across churches, which has been a positive initiative for the involvement of women. A number of "interfaith Canadian women's coalitions" have been created to address social justice issues (Trothen 2006, 1285). For instance, the National Council of Jewish Women of Canada mainly advocates for families, disabled people, and poor people in the Jewish community, and while the Ecumenical Network of Women of African Heritage focuses on building connections between women of African heritage and stands against racism (Trothen 2006, 1285). Such groups give hope for women's positions within religious institutions and provide the foundation for addressing the intersection of social justice issues.

Gendered Religious Practices

Gender roles within religious practices are often based on socially constructed expectations for women and men, reinforcing the gender binary (classification of gender into only two options—male and female).

According to religious scholar Susan Hill Lindley, Hindu women commonly practice traditional vows (or *vratas*). While men and women utilize this practice, women do so more frequently. Such vows reflect a particularly humble and ethical sacrifice in exchange for a temporal prayer, such as a speedy recovery of a loved one or protection from harm for their families, especially their husbands, brothers, or male children (Lindley 2006, 29).

Although the notion of chastity is common within Christianity for men and women, the weight of "purity" and thus "saving" oneself for marriage is clearly directed more firmly toward girls and women, who ultimately bear the consequences and the stigmas that accompany sex before marriage. In the 1990s, Christian abstinence groups encouraged a culture of chastity, where "purity balls" and the gifting of purity rings to daughters from Christian fathers became widespread (Fahs 2010, 116). These formal events imitated weddings, including extravagantly decorated reception halls, wedding cakes, and dancing, with the daughter wearing a wedding dress and the father a tuxedo. At the end of the event, the daughter made a covenant with her father to stay "pure" until she is married and can give her "gift of virginity" to her husband (Deneson 2017). While the father promised his daughter's chastity to God, the daughter promised to remain "pure" to both her father and her future husband.

Through such rituals, girls are taught that their value and worth are inseparable from and dependent upon their bodies, and their morality is tied to their sexuality (Valenti 2009). Fahs argues that this "obsession with restraining sexual expression has led to a sex-obsessed culture of chastity. . . . This particular construction of sexuality in a highly gendered social space that reinforces women's oppressed sociosexual status as the property of men, inadequately prepares them for negotiating the terms of their sexual health, and encourages them to seek out chastity clubs and social spaces that construct an identity based on enforced repression of sexual desire and expression" (Fahs 2010, 117). Purity vows and the accompanying rituals echo other religious sentiments that regard women as property, as sexually deviant, and as the mere constitution of their physical bodies. These practices also reinforce heterosexual relationships as the only possible romantic and intimate narratives.

Women in Sacred Texts

One of the most important woman figures in sacred texts across multiple religions is Mary of Nazareth. Mary is the mother of Jesus in Christianity, Islam, Baha'i, and the Church of Jesus Christ of Latter-day Saints, although each of these religions (and their subdenominations) have their own perspectives on her role and level of importance. For example, in Catholicism, Mary as the Virgin Mother is venerated as a model of ideal womanhood (Hamington 1995). Christian feminist scholars and theologians have made critical analyses of the impact of patriarchy on these interpretations of Mary and argue for more critical and nuanced readings of her as a historical, religious, and cultural figure (Hamington 1995).

Mary is a revered figure in Islam and is the only woman referred to by name in the Qur'an (Wadud 1999). Despite this, women-focused readings of the Qur'an reveal the multiple ways women are included. As Wadud explains in *Qur'an and Woman: Rereading the Sacred Text from a Woman's Perspective* (1999), there are two primary distinctions in how women can be interpreted in the sacred text—as individuals and as members of society. While much of the Qur'an is focused on the role of women on earth as members of a social system, the consideration of women as individuals is important because "the Qur'an treats the individual, whether male or female, in exactly the same manner: that is, whatever the Qur'an says about the relationship between Allah and the individual is not in gender terms" (Wadud 1999, 34). Therefore, spiritually, the rights of women are not separate from the rights of men in the sacred text.

Wadud's work not only addresses the presence of women in the Qur'an but also provides an example of one of the important aspects of feminist theological work: bringing a feminist lens to the reading of sacred texts. Feminist interpretations of sacred texts gained prominence in the 1970s and the 1980s. The works of Jewish feminist scholar Judith Plaskow and Catholic feminist theologian Elisabeth Schüssler Fiorenza provided groundbreaking feminist interpretations of Jewish and Christian scriptures that helped launch the field and have had a profound and lasting impact on feminist religious studies. Plaskow and Schüssler Fiorenza cofounded the *Journal of Feminist Studies in Religion*, now the oldest interdisciplinary and interreligious feminist academic journal in the field of religious studies.

LGBTQ People and Issues in Religions

In 1968, a group of twelve people gathered in the Rev. Troy D. Perry's living room in San Francisco, California, to begin what would become the Metropolitan Community Church, the first sexuality- and gender-affirming church in the region (Metropolitan Community Churches 2016). Unfortunately, in recent years, there has been a steady decline in attendance and support for the early front-runners of the gay church movement, such as the Metropolitan Community Church, Dignity (Roman Catholic), the Alliance of Christian Churches, and the Evangelical Network (Cartier 2014), because of an increase and diversity of accepting congregations, aging founding members, and younger churchgoers seeking less identity-focused religious spaces (Elaine n.d.).

Many conservative Christian traditions do not affirm LGBTQ people and feel targeted by society's increasing acceptance of them. This fear of change and a desire to maintain rigid heteronormative gender and social roles have led to anti-LGBTQ court challenges under the aegis of "bathroom bills" (which would force transgender people to use the bathroom matching the sex they were assigned at birth) and "religious freedoms" that would, for example, allow health-care workers to refuse to treat LGBTQ people.

In 2018, the U.S. Supreme Court decided *Masterpiece Cakeshop v. Colorado Civil Rights Commission*, in which a Christian cake shop owner refused to make a wedding cake for a gay couple. In a narrow decision, the court decided in favor of the baker, but it did not address the larger question of whether businesses can deny service to LGBTQ people based on religion.

CONVERSION THERAPY: PUNISHMENT OR CURE?

Conversion therapy (or reparative therapy) is a controversial psychological treatment meant to change a gay or lesbian person's sexual orientation to heterosexual (straight). However, therapists and former patients say that the treatment is not only ineffective but also harmful.

In the last decade or so, a number of U.S. states have banned conversion therapy. Even some religious authorities now say the treatments involved, being punitive, are not in line with biblical principles.

However, religious and medical authorities still disagree about whether homosexuality itself is problematic. Conservative Christians deem it a sin and believe homosexual desires can be overcome by faith. On the other hand, the American Psychological Association describes homosexuality as a "normal and positive variation of human sexual orientation" (American Psychological Association n.d.).

Janet Lockhart

American Psychological Association. n.d. "Resolution on Appropriate Affirmative Responses to Sexual Orientation Distress and Change Efforts." Accessed December 31, 2019. https://www.apa.org/about/policy/sexual-orientation.

Same-sex (gender) marriage and legal protections have been primary rallying points for LGBTQ equality. Same-sex marriage has been recognized since 2005 in Canada and 2015 in the United States. Same-sex marriages are available in over forty-four Native American Tribal Nations, and almost forty more recognize marriages performed in other jurisdictions (Pew Research Center 2019a). In the Church of Jesus Christ of Latter-day Saints, same-sex marriages are not allowed, and engaging in same-sex sexual activity is grounds for denial of temple access and ordination (Human Rights Campaign n.d.-c). The Episcopal Church, a part of the worldwide Anglican Communion, has been well ahead of other Anglican churches in recognizing LGBTQ ordination and marriages. At this writing, the United Methodist Church is in the process of splitting over LGBTQ issues.

Orthodox Jews, on the whole, continue to reject LGBTQ marriage and ordination, even as there are moves toward individual acceptance. To a degree, Reform and Conservative Judaism accept LGBTQ members and permit the ordination of openly LGBTQ people. The Jewish Institute of Religion seeks to create change by empowering students to know more about LGBT issues and to be able to create and sustain welcoming congregations, while also working against heterosexism and homophobia (Jewish Institute of Religion n.d.).

Many LGBTQ Muslims engage in community building as a form of activism and as a way of mitigating the impact of being both sexual/gender and religious/ethnic minorities (Kugle 2013). Organizations such as Muslims for Progressive Values and the Muslim Alliance for Sexual and Gender Diversity both seek to support Muslims in their faith and to advance understandings of Islamic theology that allow for acceptance of LGBTQ people ("MASGD Core Values" n.d.; Muslims for Progressive Values 2019).

Hindus are generally supportive of marriage equality, and there are references to third gender people, gender-fluid (moving among genders) deities, and the identification of same-sex experiences as enjoyable in Hindu scriptures. The Hindu American Foundation notes that there is no reason to ostracize or reject LGBTQ people (Human Rights Campaign n.d.-b). Buddhism holds no specific tenets of faith regarding LGBTQ people or their service as monks or nuns, except for celibacy, although this can vary between temple and monastery (Human Rights Campaign n.d.-a).

Women at the Intersection of Religion and Politics

Reproductive rights provide an example of struggle for women at the intersection of religion, politics, and gender. Religious-based ideas about women's bodies as bearers of life have impacted women's right to determine whether they want children. These rights include not only access to abortion and birth control but also the choice to have children and whether or whom to marry.

In Mexico, abortion laws are determined by the state governments, so access to the medical procedure varies throughout the country. Since 2007, abortion has been legal in Mexico City, but the majority of Mexican states only allow women to have an abortion if their life is in danger. In Canada, following a 1988 Supreme Court ruling, abortion began to be treated like any medical procedure and has no national law regulating it (Abedi 2019). Because of this, the provinces in Canada each have their own approach to managing the procedure, meaning that each province's politics, funding, and the number of and distance to medical facilities determine the level of regulation and access to the procedure. While abortion has been legally viewed as a constitutional right in the United States

By far, Jews in the United States support abortion rights. These Jewish women are participating in a pro-choice rally at the State Capitol in Missouri. Jewish law allows for abortion, and Jews in the United States tend to be strong supporters of separation of church and state. (Joe Sohm/ Dreamstime.com)

since the 1973 *Roe v. Wade* U.S. Supreme Court decision, every state except Oregon has passed laws significantly restricting access to abortion since then. Recently, in the case *Burwell v. Hobby Lobby*, the court ruled that some corporations can block women employees' insurance coverage for birth control if it is in contradiction with the owners' religious beliefs.

Religious women, including queer and trans women, have been at the forefront of efforts to overturn oppressive laws and pass laws protecting reproductive rights. The interfaith Religious Coalition for Reproductive Choice, which began in 1967, helps women gain access to safe abortions. What started as an underground collective has grown to a more organized entity that focuses on reproductive rights, health, and justice while centering the intersections of race, class, and religion (Religious Coalition for Reproductive Choice 2020).

Sexuality and gender identity also provide examples of the intertwining of religion and politics. Religious opposition to queer sexuality and gender diversity have shaped laws across the United States. For example, South Dakota passed legislation in 2020 that allows for health-care providers to deny services to trans and gender-diverse patients based on providers' ethical, moral, philosophical, or religious beliefs. Particularly troubling is that South Dakota Senate Bill 109 (SB 109) claims it is "an Act to provide protections for health care decisions governed by conscience," which means that the provider has the right to deny potentially life-saving treatment for someone based on their gender identity or sexuality (South Dakota Legislature 2020), placing a care provider's beliefs and principles above the lives of people needing treatment.

Religious Violence against Women

Rhetorical and theological violence form the basis for all other religious violence against women (and other marginalized people). Once theologies condone subordination of any group, their mistreatment can be justified. Views of women as innately subordinate, beliefs about wives' submission to their husbands, ideas of honor and shame, and beliefs about women's bodies as inherently sinful are to some degree shared by Christianity, Judaism, and Islam because they developed in proximity to each other in the Middle East (Jeffreys 2011).

Religions have both the potential to be a source of solace for the women who practice them and to be a source of harm, particularly if abuse is justified through doctrine, sacred text, or religious practice (Fortune and Enger 2005). For example, battery and rape in the context of marriage can be normalized as a wife's Christian duty of submission, and sexual assault can be ignored if the perpetrator repents (Shaw 2018).

Large-scale abuses of women and children take place in a variety of contexts: the Catholic sex-abuse scandals, abuse in Native American boarding schools of all denominations (Shaw 2019a), and sexual assault scandals in the Southern Baptist Convention (Shaw 2019b). Abuses occur where power imbalances are normalized, whether between genders or between priests and congregants. In evangelical denominations, where repentance is all that is required, survivors can be left dealing with trauma while also being expected to forgive so that the abuser, having repented, can move on with his or her life (Shaw 2018).

Theologies of the fixed nature of gender and control of women overlap with racism and colonialism. When women are multiply marginalized, personal and institutional violence become even more glaring and difficult to overcome. For example, Hong writes about the ways in which Korean Shamanic folktales and Christian practices combined to create complex moral webs for her growing up and the ways that this helped her to navigate the heteropatriarchy inherent in white society and in Korean societies struggling to deal with downward mobility due to racism and anti-Asian sentiment. Facing opposite behavioral expectations at home and at school is a point of internal conflict for many second-generation immigrants, as Hong found in her study (Hong 2015).

Religious groups often use the idea of an "ethics of compassion" to frame harm as a benefit to society. Historically, we see this in missionary efforts in the region to convert Indigenous people, which furthered cultural assimilation and Indigenous erasure. Religiously framed programs to "improve" humanity through controlled reproduction targeted poor, Indigenous, Black, and Latina women. Contemporary compassion framing includes deeply caring language in both ex-gay and postabortion ministry while campaigning strongly against legal protections for LGBTQ people or a woman's right to choose (Burack 2014). Combined with Islamophobia, compassion framing results in unwillingness to listen to women's decisions about veiling and perpetuates harassment and violence against women in hijab (Hoodfar 2001).

Women's Resistance to Religious Oppression

While religion has been used as a tool of oppression, particularly to reinforce Eurocentric male-dominated control, women across time and differences have resisted. An early example of how white women have countered religious oppression through allyship can be seen through the humanization of Indigenous people. During the early contact periods in the Americas, Europeans used religion to diminish the humanness of Indigenous people as a way to exploit labor and to murder, rape, and torture them. Once the colonial period began and women came to the Americas to start families, the inhumane practices did not end, but women, based on their religious views, did take a stand against some of the atrocities and advocated for the humane treatment of Indigenous people.

Women also resisted religious oppression through the sexual liberation movements and struggles for reproductive rights during the 1960s and 1970s. Regulation of women's bodies by men under the interpretation of religious texts gave women little say over what happened to them. Whether it was the normalization of spousal abuse, the value placed on women's bodies based on their ability to bear children, the sexualization of women's bodies, or other forms of oppression, religion has been used as a means to justify these oppressions. For example, the National Right to Life Committee relies on right-wing Christian ideologies to prevent women's right to abortion. The rhetoric of these antichoice groups has led to bombings of abortion clinics, harassment of doctors and nurses who work at them, and the humiliation of women who leave them. These acts of violence are justified and sanctioned by antichoice groups by using terminology that suggests they are acting to protect life.

Religious beliefs have also given rise to resistance to oppression. In Canada, the Pro-Choice Action Network helped establish a clinic that provided abortion services despite their being illegal in Canada until 1988 (Pro Choice Action Network n.d.). Their efforts have grown to include safer sex education and legal lobbying against antichoice laws. Catholics for Choice is another faith-based organization that focuses on "a woman's moral and legal right to follow her conscience in matters of sexuality and reproductive health" (Catholics for Choice 2020). Based in Washington, DC, this organization works with sister organizations in Latin America and Mexico, such as Catholics for the Right to Decide. This work is especially important given the high rates of femicide in Mexico, particularly along the U.S.-Mexico border.

Another form of women's resistance to religious oppression has been the development of feminist theology. Feminist theology is a diverse movement and field of study that encompasses many religious and cultural perspectives and is closely related to liberation theology. Broadly speaking, feminist theologies reconsider religious traditions, texts, practices, and imagery through a feminist lens. In the context of North America, feminist theologies are present in womanist theologies, Christian feminist theologies, Asian American women's theologies, Latina feminist theology, and in specific religious traditions in relationship to women and feminism, such as Judaism, Islam, and Buddhism (Ruether 2007).

FURTHER READING

Abedi, Maham. 2019. "How Abortion Rights Work in Canada—and Whether They Could Be Put at Risk." *Global News*, May 24, 2019.

Abu-Lughod, Lila. 2002. "Do Muslim Women Really Need Saving? Anthropological Reflections on Cultural Relativism and Its Others." *American Anthropologist* 104 (3): 783–790.

Al Wazni, Anderson Beckmann. 2015. "Muslim Women in America and Hijab: A Study of Empowerment, Feminist Identity, and Body Image." *Social Work* 60 (4): 325–333.

Anti-Defamation League. n.d. "Anti-Semitism in the US." Accessed April 2, 2020. https://www.adl.org/what-we-do/anti-semitism/anti-semitism-in-the-us.

Ashcraft-Eason, Lillian, Darnise Martin, and Oyeronke Olademo. 2009. *Women and New and Africana Religions.* 1st ed. Women and Religion in the World. Santa Barbara, CA: ABC-CLIO.

Bano, Masooda, and Hilary Kalmbach, eds. 2012. *Women, Leadership and Mosques: Changes in Contemporary Islamic Authority.* Women and Gender: The Middle East and the Islamic World, vol. 11. Leiden, Netherlands; Boston: Brill.

Barnes, Robert. 2019. "Supreme Court Passes on Case Involving Baker Who Refused to Make Wedding Cake for Same-Sex Couple." *Washington Post*, June 17, 2019.

Beasley, Nicholas M. 2009. *Christian Ritual and the Creation of British Slave Societies, 1650–1780.* Race in the Atlantic World, 1700–1900. Athens: University of Georgia Press.

Bender, Courtney, and Wendy Cadge. 2006. "Constructing Buddhism(s): Interreligious Dialogue and Religious Hybridity." *Sociology of Religion* 67 (3): 229–247.

Berger, Helen A. 2003. *Voices from the Pagan Census: A National Survey of Witches and Neo-Pagans in the United States.* Studies in Comparative Religion. Columbia: University of South Carolina Press.

Boorstein, Michelle. 2020. "Famed Buddhist Nun Pema Chodron Retires, Cites Handling of Sexual Misconduct Allegations against Her Group's Leader." *Washington Post*, January 17, 2020.

Brooks, Joanna, Rachel Hunt Steenblik, and Hannah Wheelwright. 2016. *Mormon Feminism: Essential Writings.* Oxford, UK; New York: Oxford University Press.

Brooten, Bernadette J., and Jacqueline L. Hazelton, eds. 2010. *Beyond Slavery: Overcoming Its Religious and Sexual Legacies.* 1st ed. Black Religion, Womanist Thought, Social Justice. New York: Palgrave Macmillan.

Budapest, Zsuzsanna Emese, and Jan Huston. 1986. *The Holy Book of Women's Mysteries*. Oakland, CA: Z. E. Budapest.

Burack, Cynthia. 2014. *Tough Love: Sexuality, Compassion, and the Christian Right*. SUNY Series in Queer Politics and Cultures. Albany: State University of New York Press.

Bushman, Claudia L., and Caroline Esther Kline. 2013. *Mormon Women Have Their Say: Essays from the Claremont Oral History Collection*. Salt Lake City, UT: Greg Kofford Books.

Canadian Council on Muslim Women. 2020. "Our Mission." https://www.ccmw.com/our-mission.

Cartier, Marie. 2014. *Baby, You Are My Religion: Women, Gay Bars, and Theology before Stonewall*. 1st ed. Gender, Theology and Spirituality. New York: Routledge.

Catholics for Choice. 2020. "About Us." https://www.catholicsforchoice.org/about-us/.

Centers for Disease Control and Prevention. 2013. "CDC Health Disparities & Inequalities Report." https://www.cdc.gov/minorityhealth/CHDIReport.html.

Central Intelligence Agency. n.d.-a "Canada—The World Factbook." Accessed January 11, 2021. https://www.cia.gov/the-world-factbook/countries/canada/.

Central Intelligence Agency. n.d.-b "Mexico—The World Factbook." Accessed January 11, 2021. https://www.cia.gov/the-world-factbook/countries/mexico/.

Central Intelligence Agency. n.d.-c "United States—The World Factbook." Accessed January 11, 2021. https://www.cia.gov/the-world-factbook/countries/united-states/.

Chryssides, George D. 2008. *The A to Z of Jehovah's Witnesses*. 104th ed. A to Z Guides 104. Lanham, MD; Plymouth, England: Scarecrow Press, Inc.

Church of Jesus Christ of Latter-day Saints. 2012. "Relief Society History." September 29, 2012. http://newsroom.churchofjesuschrist.org/article/relief-society-history.

Church of Jesus Christ of Latter-day Saints. 2020a. "Facts and Statistics: Canada." http://newsroom.churchofjesuschrist.org/facts-and-statistics/country/canada.

Church of Jesus Christ of Latter-day Saints. 2020b. "Facts and Statistics: Mexico." https://newsroom.churchofjesuschrist.org/facts-and-statistics/country/mexico.

Church of Jesus Christ of Latter-day Saints. 2020c. "Facts and Statistics: United States." https://newsroom.churchofjesuschrist.org/facts-and -statistics/country/united-states.

de Beauvoir, Simone. 1972. *The Second Sex*. Harmondsworth, UK: Penguin.

Deer, Sarah. 2015. *The Beginning and End of Rape: Confronting Sexual Violence in Native America*. Minneapolis: University of Minnesota Press.

Deneson, Amy. 2017. "True Love Waits? The Story of My Purity Ring and Feeling Like I Didn't Have a Choice." *The Guardian*, February 18, 2017.

Derné, Steve. 1994. "Hindu Men Talk about Controlling Women: Cultural Ideas As a Tool of the Powerful." Sociological Perspectives 37 (2): 203–227. https://doi.org/10.2307/1389320.

Drogus, Carol Ann. 1994. "Religious Change and Women's Status in Latin America: A Comparison of Catholic Base Communities and Pentecostal Churches." Helen Kellog Institute for International Studies Working Paper #205.

Dugan, Kate. 2007. "Buddhist Women and Interfaith Work in the United States." *Buddhist-Christian Studies* 27: 31–50.

Ecklund, Elaine Howard. 2005. "Different Identity Accounts for Catholic Women." *Review of Religious Research* 47 (2): 135–149.

Eisler, Riane Tennenhaus. 1988. *The Chalice and the Blade: Our History, Our Future*. 1st Harper & Row paperback ed. San Francisco: Perennial Library.

Elaine. n.d. "Find an Affirming Church." Gaychurch.org (blog). Accessed January 23, 2020. https://www.gaychurch.org/find_a_church/.

Eller, Cynthia. 2000. *The Myth of Matriarchal Prehistory: Why an Invented Past Won't Give Women a Future*. Boston: Beacon Press.

Encyclopedia.com. 2020. "Church of Scientology." https://www .encyclopedia.com/philosophy-and-religion/other-religious-beliefs -and-general-terms/miscellaneous-religion/church-scientology.

Fahs, Breanne. 2010. "Daddy's Little Girls: On the Perils of Chastity Clubs, Purity Balls, and Ritualized Abstinence." *Frontiers: A Journal of Women's Studies* 31 (3): 116–142.

Falk, Mallory. 2019. "Religious Leaders Stand Up for Immigrants at Border." High Plains Public Radio, August 1, 2019. https://www.hppr .org/post/religious-leaders-stand-immigrants-border.

Fiedler, Maureen. 2010. "Women as Religious Leaders: Breaking Through the Stained Glass Ceiling." HuffPost, October 18, 2010. https:// www.huffpost.com/entry/women-religious-leaders_b_766006.

Fleischer, Jeff. 2005. "Nation of Islam Women Look Up and Out." Women's eNews, August 2, 2005. https://womensenews.org/2005/08/nation-islam-women-look-and-out/.

Fortune, Mary, and Cindy Enger. 2005. "Violence against Women and the Role of Religion." VAWnet, March 2005. https://vawnet.org/material/violence-against-women-and-role-religion.

Gallagher, Sally K., and Christian Smith. 1999. "Symbolic Traditionalism and Pragmatic Egalitarianism: Contemporary Evangelicals, Families, and Gender." *Gender and Society* 13 (2): 211–233.

Games, Alison. 2010. *Witchcraft in Early North America*. American Controversies. Lanham, MD: Rowman & Littlefield Publishers.

Gibson, David. 2012. "Vatican Orders Crackdown on American Nuns." Religion News Service, April 18, 2012. https://religionnews.com/2012/04/18/vatican-orders-crackdown-on-american-nuns/.

Gorham, Candace R. M. 2013. *The Ebony Exodus Project: Why Some Black Women Are Walking Out on Religion—and Others Should Too*. Durham, NC: Pitchstone Publishing.

Green, John. 2004. "Evangelicals v. Mainline Protestants." Frontline. https://www.pbs.org/wgbh/pages/frontline/shows/jesus/evangelicals/evmain.html.

Griffith, R. Marie, and Barbara Dianne Savage. 2006. *Women and Religion in the African Diaspora: Knowledge, Power, and Performance*. 1st ed. Lived Religions. Baltimore, MD: Johns Hopkins University Press.

Gross, Rita M. 1993. *Buddhism after Patriarchy: A Feminist History, Analysis, and Reconstruction of Buddhism*. Albany: State University of New York Press.

Haddad, Yvonne Yazbeck. 2006. *Muslim Women in America: The Challenge of Islamic Identity Today*. New York: Oxford University Press.

Hamington, Maurice. 1995. *Hail Mary? The Struggle for Ultimate Womanhood in Catholicism*. New York: Routledge.

Holbrook, Kate, and Matthew Burton Bowman. 2016. *Women and Mormonism: Historical and Contemporary Perspectives*. Salt Lake City: University of Utah Press.

Hong, Christine J. 2015. *Identity, Youth, and Gender in the Korean American Church*. 1st ed. New York: Palgrave Pivot.

Hoodfar, Homa. 2001. "The Veil in Their Minds and on Our Heads: Veiling Practices and Muslim Women (1997)." In *Women, Gender,*

Religion: A Reader, edited by Elizabeth A. Catelli, 1st ed., 420–446. New York: Palgrave.

Human Rights Campaign. n.d.-a. "Stances of Faiths on LGBTQ Issues: Buddhism." Accessed January 24, 2020. https://www.hrc.org /resources/stances-of-faiths-on-lgbt-issues-buddhism/.

Human Rights Campaign. n.d.-b. "Stances of Faiths on LGBTQ Issues: Hinduism." Accessed January 24, 2020. https://www.hrc.org /resources/stances-of-faiths-on-lgbt-issues-hinduism/.

Human Rights Campaign. n.d.-c "Stances of Faiths on LGBTQ Issues: The Church of Jesus Christ of Latter-Day Saints." Accessed January 24, 2020. https://www.hrc.org/resources/stances-of-faiths-on -lgbt-issues-church-of-jesus-christ-of-latter-day-saint/.

Hyman, Paula E. 2009. "Jewish Feminism in the United States." Jewish Women's Archive, Encyclopedia of Jewish Women. https://jwa.org /encyclopedia/article/jewish-feminism-in-united-states.

India Today. 2015. "Hindu Population up in US, Becomes Fourth-Largest Faith." May 13, 2015. https://www.indiatoday.in/world/story/hindu -population-up-in-united-states-becomes-fourth-largest-faith -252755-2015-05-13.

Israel-Cohen, Yael. 2012. *Between Feminism and Orthodox Judaism: Resistance, Identity, and Religious Change in Israel*. Jewish Identities in a Changing World, vol. 20. Leiden, Netherlands; Boston: Brill.

Jacobsen, Jeanna, and Rachel Wright. 2014. "Mental Health Implications in Mormon Women's Experiences with Same-Sex Attraction: A Qualitative Study." *Counseling Psychologist* 42 (5): 664–696.

Jeffreys, Sheila. 2011. *Man's Dominion: The Rise of Religion and the Eclipse of Women's Rights*. New York: Routledge.

Jewish Institute of Religion. n.d. "Institute for Judaism, Sexual Orientation & Gender Identity." Hebrew Union College-Jewish Institute of Religion. Accessed January 20, 2020. http://ijso.huc.edu/.

Kaplan, Dana. 2009. *Contemporary American Judaism: Transformation and Renewal*. 1st ed. New York: Columbia University Press.

Keller, Rosemary Skinner, Rosemary Radford Ruether, and Marie Cantlon. 2006. *Encyclopedia of Women and Religion in North America*. Bloomington: Indiana University Press.

Killen, Patricia O'Connell, and Mark Silk. 2004. *Religion and Public Life in the Pacific Northwest: The None Zone*. Religion by Region. Walnut Creek, CA: Rowman AltaMira Press.

Kim, Jung Ha. 1997. *Bridge-Makers and Cross-Bearers: Korean-American Women and the Church*. American Academy of Religion Academy Series, vol. 92. Atlanta, GA: Scholars Press.

Kroeger, Catherine. 1988. "The Neglected History of Women in the Early Church." *Christian History Magazine*. https://christianhistoryinstitute.org/magazine/article/women-in-the-early-church.

Kugle, Scott Siraj al-Haqq. 2013. *Living Out Islam: Voices of Gay, Lesbian, and Transgender Muslims*. New York: NYU Press.

Kurien, Prema. 1999. "Gendered Ethnicity: Creating a Hindu Indian Identity in the United States." *American Behavioral Scientist* 42 (4): 648–670.

Leadership Conference of Women Religious. 2019. "LCWR Statement on the Sexual Abuse of Sisters by Clergy." February 7, 2019. https://lcwr.org/media/news/lcwr-statement-sexual-abuse-sisters-clergy.

Leadership Conference of Women Religious. n.d. "About LCWR." Accessed April 2, 2020. https://lcwr.org/about.

Lesley, Alison. 2016. "81% of Mexican Adults Are Catholic & More Facts on Religion in Mexico." World Religion News, February 16, 2016. https://www.worldreligionnews.com/religion-news/81-of-mexican-adults-are-catholic-more-facts-on-religion-in-mexico.

Levenson, Alan T. 2012. *The Wiley-Blackwell History of Jews and Judaism*. Chichester, UK: John Wiley & Sons.

Lindley, Susan Hill. 2006. "Women in Protestant Church Societies and Bureaucracies." In *Encyclopedia of Women and Religion in North America*, edited by Rosemary Skinner Keller and Rosemary Radford Ruether, 1:23–33. Bloomington; Indianapolis: Indiana University Press.

Lipka, Michael. 2016a. "A Closer Look at Jehovah's Witnesses Living in the U.S." Pew Research Center, Fact Tank: News in the Numbers, April 26, 2016. https://www.pewresearch.org/fact-tank/2016/04/26/a-closer-look-at-jehovahs-witnesses-living-in-the-u-s/.

Lipka, Michael. 2016b. "A Snapshot of Catholics in Mexico, Pope Francis' Next Stop." Pew Research Center, Fact Tank: News in the Numbers, February 10, 2016. https://www.pewresearch.org/fact-tank/2016/02/10/a-snapshot-of-catholics-in-mexico-pope-francis-next-stop/.

Lipka, Michael. 2019. "5 Facts about Religion in Canada." Pew Research Center, Fact Tank: News in the Numbers, July 1, 2019. https://www.pewresearch.org/fact-tank/2019/07/01/5-facts-about-religion-in-canada/.

Lorde, Audre. 2007. "Learning from the 60s." In *Sister Outsider: Essays & Speeches by Audre Lorde*, 134–144. Berkeley, CA: Crossing Press.

Lowen, Linda. 2019. "African American Women in the Black Church." ThoughtCo, February 12, 2019. https://www.thoughtco.com /african-american-women-black-church-3533748.

Lugo, Luis, Alan Cooperman, and Gregory A. Smith. 2013. *A Portrait of Jewish Americans*. Washington, DC: Pew Research Center's Religion & Public Life Project. https://www.pewforum.org/2013/10/01 /jewish-american-beliefs-attitudes-culture-survey/.

LWF LAC Communications Network, México. 2019. "Mexican Church Marks 10 Years of Women's Ordination." Lutheran World Federation, December 4, 2019. https://www.lutheranworld.org/news /mexican-church-marks-10-years-womens-ordination.

Madigan, Patricia. 2011. *Women and Fundamentalism in Islam and Catholicism Negotiating Modernity in a Globalized World*. Religions and Discourse, vol. 53. New York: Peter Lang.

Marcotte, Roxanne D. 2010. "Muslim Women in Canada: Autonomy and Empowerment." *Journal of Muslim Minority Affairs* 30 (3): 357–373. https://doi.org/10.1080/13602004.2010.515816.

Masci, David. 2014. "The Divide over Ordaining Women." Pew Research Center, Fact Tank: News in the Numbers, September 9, 2014. https://www.pewresearch.org/fact-tank/2014/09/09/the-divide -over-ordaining-women/.

Masci, David, and Gregory A. Smith. 2018. "5 Facts about U.S. Evangelical Protestants." Pew Research Center, Fact Tank: News in the Numbers, March 1, 2018. https://www.pewresearch.org/fact-tank /2018/03/01/5-facts-about-u-s-evangelical-protestants/.

"MASGD Core Values." n.d. Accessed January 24, 2020. http://www .lgbtmuslimretreat.com/muslim-alliance.php.

McGill, Brian. 2015. "Catholicism in the United States." *Wall Street Journal*, September 28, 2015. http://graphics.wsj.com/catholics-us/.

McMickle, Marvin Andrew. 2002. "'The Black Church,' a Brief History." African American Registry. https://aaregistry.org/story/the-black -church-a-brief-history/.

Mekhail, George, and Sarah Ngu. 2018. "Scoring America's 100 Largest Churches for Clarity (2018)." Church Clarity. https://www .churchclarity.org/resources/scoring-americas-100-largest -churches-for-clarity-2018.

Mekhail, George, and Sarah Ngu. 2019. "Score Definitions." Church Clarity. https://www.churchclarity.org/score-definitions.

Metropolitan Community Churches. 2016. "MCC Statement of Faith: As Adopted at General Conference XXVI, Victoria, British Columbia, Canada." https://www.mccchurch.org/mcc-statement-of-faith/.

MJL. 2020. "Judaism and LGBTQ Issues: An Overview." My Jewish Learning, January 24, 2020. https://www.myjewishlearning.com/article/judaism-and-the-lgbtq-community-an-overview/.

Mohamed, Besheer. 2018. "A New Estimate of U.S. Muslim Population." Pew Research Center, Fact Tank: News in the Numbers, January 3, 2018. https://www.pewresearch.org/fact-tank/2018/01/03/new-estimates-show-u-s-muslim-population-continues-to-grow/.

Movsesion, Mark L. 2019. "Masterpiece Cakeshop and the Future of Religious Freedom." *Harvard Journal of Law and Public Policy* 42 (3): 711–751.

Muslims for Progressive Values. 2019. "LGBTQI Resources." https://www.mpvusa.org/lgbtqi-resources.

Narayanan, Vasudha. 2006. "Hinduism in North America Including Emerging Issues." In *Encyclopedia of Women and Religion in North America*, edited by Rosemary Skinner Keller and Rosemary Radford Ruether, 2:659–693. Bloomington; Indianapolis: Indiana University Press.

New, David S. 2014. *Christian Fundamentalism in America: A Cultural History*. Jefferson, NC: McFarland.

O'Loughlin, Michael J. 2016. "Poll Finds Many U.S. Catholics Breaking with Church over Contraception, Abortion and L.G.B.T. Rights." America: The Jesuit Review, September 28, 2016. https://www.americamagazine.org/faith/2016/09/28/poll-finds-many-us-catholics-breaking-church-over-contraception-abortion-and-lgbt.

Oregon Women's Land Trust. n.d. "Herstory." Accessed April 1, 2020. http://www.oregonwomenslandtrust.org/herstory.

Outreach 100. n.d. "Largest Churches in America." Accessed January 23, 2020. https://outreach100.com/largest-churches-in-america.

Parent, Mike C., and Kevin Silva. 2018. "Critical Consciousness Moderates the Relationship between Transphobia and 'Bathroom Bill' Voting." *Journal of Counseling Psychology* 65 (4): 403–412.

Pearson, Jo. 2010. "Resisting Rhetorics of Violence: Women, Witches, and Wicca." *Feminist Theology* 18 (2): 141–159.

Pearson, Joanne. 2007. *Wicca and the Christian Heritage: Ritual, Sex and Magic*. London; New York: Routledge.

Pechilis, Karen. 2004. "Introduction." In *The Graceful Guru: Hindu Female Gurus in India and the United States*, edited by Karen Pechilis, 3–50. Oxford, UK: Oxford University Press.

Pew Research Center. 2013. "Canada's Changing Religious Landscape." Pew Research Center's Religion & Public Life Project (blog), June 27, 2013. https://www.pewforum.org/2013/06/27/canadas-changing -religious-landscape/.

Pew Research Center. 2015a. "Buddhists." Pew Research Center's Religion & Public Life Project (blog), April 2, 2015. https://www .pewforum.org/2015/04/02/buddhists/.

Pew Research Center. 2015b. "North America." Pew Research Center's Religion & Public Life Project (blog), April 2, 2015. https://www .pewforum.org/2015/04/02/north-america/.

Pew Research Center. 2019a. "In a Politically Polarized Era, Sharp Divides in Both Partisan Coalitions." https://www.people-press.org/wp -content/uploads/sites/4/2019/12/PP_2019.12.17_Political-Values _FINAL.pdf.

Pew Research Center. 2019b. "In U.S., Decline of Christianity Continues at Rapid Pace." Pew Research Center's Religion & Public Life Project (blog), October 17, 2019. https://www.pewforum.org/2019 /10/17/in-u-s-decline-of-christianity-continues-at-rapid-pace/.

Pew Research Center. n.d.-a. "Mainline Protestants—Religion in America: U.S. Religious Data, Demographics and Statistics." Accessed April 2, 2020. https://www.pewforum.org/religious-landscape-study /religious-tradition/mainline-protestant/.

Pew Research Center. n.d.-b. "Religious Landscape Study." Pew Research Center's Religion & Public Life Project (blog). Accessed January 24, 2020. https://www.pewforum.org/religious-landscape-study/.

Pike, Sarah M. 2004. *New Age and Neopagan Religions in America. Columbia Contemporary American Religion Series*. New York: Columbia University Press.

Pro Choice Action Network. n.d. "About Us." Accessed March 31, 2020. https://prochoiceactionnetwork-canada.org/aboutus/aboutus.shtml.

Religious Coalition for Reproductive Choice. 2020. "History." https://rcrc .org/history/.

Reuters. 2020. "Methodist Church Announces Plan to Split into Pro- and Anti-Gay Branches." *The Guardian*, January 3.

Robinson, Ira, ed. 2013. *Canada's Jews: In Time, Space and Spirit.* 1st ed. Jews in Space and Time. Brighton, MA: Academic Studies Press.

Rogers, Simon. 2011. "Muslim Populations by Country: How Big Will Each Muslim Population Be by 2030?" *The Guardian, Datablog* (blog), January 28, 2011.

Ruether, Rosemary Radford. 1967. *The Church against Itself; an Inquiry into the Conditions of Historical Existence for the Eschatological Community.* New York: Herder and Herder.

Ruether, Rosemary Radford, ed. 2007. *Feminist Theologies: Legacy and Prospect.* Minneapolis, MN: Fortress Press.

Sanchez, Delida, and Dorie J. Gilbert. 2016. "Exploring the Relations between Religious Orientation and Racial Identity Attitudes in African College Students: A Preliminary Analysis." *Journal of Black Studies* 47 (4): 313–333.

Sandstrom, Aleksandra. 2016. "Women Relatively Rare in Top Positions of Religious Leadership." Pew Research Center, Fact Tank: News in the Numbers, March 2, 2016. https://www.pewresearch.org/fact-tank/2016/03/02/women-relatively-rare-in-top-positions-of-religious-leadership/.

Sawe, Benjamin Elisha. 2018. "Countries with the Largest Jewish Populations." WorldAtlas, May 23. https://www.worldatlas.com/articles/countries-with-the-largest-jewish-populations.html.

Scientology. n.d. "Official Church of Scientology: What Is Scientology?" Accessed April 1, 2020. https://www.scientology.org/what-is-scientology/.

Seager, Richard Hughes. 2012. *Buddhism in America.* Rev. and expanded ed. Columbia Contemporary American Religion Series. New York: Columbia University Press.

Shaw, Susan. 2018. "How Evangelical Theology Supports a Culture of Sexual Abuse." *Ms.*, September 27, 2018. https://msmagazine.com/2018/09/27/evangelical-theology-supports-culture-sexual-abuse/.

Shaw, Susan. 2019a. "From Sexism to Sex Abuse in Southern Baptist Churches." *Ms.*, February 12, 2019. https://msmagazine.com/2019/02/12/sexism-sex-abuse-southern-baptist-church/.

Shaw, Susan. 2019b. "In the Wake of #NunsToo, It's Time for Repentance and Conversion." *Ms.*, February 7, 2019. https://msmagazine.com/2019/02/07/wake-nunstoo-time-repentance-conversion/.

Shaw, Susan. 2020. "On Christianity and Donald Trump." *Ms.*, January 14, 2020. https://msmagazine.com/2020/01/14/on-christianity-and -donald-trump/.

Składanowski, Marcin. 2016. "Women's Dignity or Church Tradition? Christian Anthropology in the Debate about the Ordination of Women." *Roczniki Teologiczne* 63 (7): 275–288.

Smidt, Corwin E. 2007. "Evangelical and Mainline Protestant at the Turn of the Millennium Taking Stock and Looking Forward." In *From Pews to Polling Places: Faith and Politics in the American Religious Mosaic*. Religion and Politics, edited by J. Matthew Wilson, 29–51. Washington, DC: Georgetown University Press.

Smokler, Erin Leib. 2013. "A Historic Graduation Ceremony for Orthodox Women." *Daily Beast*, June 17, 2013. https://www.thedailybeast .com/articles/2013/06/17/a-historic-graduation-ceremony-for -orthodox-women.

South Dakota Legislature. 2020. "Senate Bill 109: An Act to Provide Protections for Health Care Decisions Governed by Conscience." 95th Legislative, 456th sess., 2020, S. Doc. 20.662.10. https:// sdlegislature.gov/Legislative_Session/Bills/Bill.aspx?File=SB109P .html&Session=2020&Version=Introduced&Bill=109.

Starhawk. 1999. *The Spiral Dance: A Rebirth of the Ancient Religion of the Great Goddess*. 20th anniv. ed.. New York: HarperOne.

Statistics Canada. 2013. "2011 National Household Survey: Immigration, Place of Birth, Citizenship, Ethnic Origin, Visible Minorities, Language and Religion." https://www150.statcan.gc.ca/n1/daily -quotidien/130508/dq130508b-eng.htm.

Strochlic, Nina. 2017. "See the Small Mexican Town Embracing Islam." *National Geographic*, November 7, 2017.

Trothen, Tracy J. 2006. "Canadian Women's Religious Issues." In *Encyclopedia of Women and Religion in North America*, edited by Rosemary Skinner Keller and Rosemary Radford Ruether, 3:1283–1290. Bloomington; Indianapolis: Indiana University Press.

Udis-Kessler, Amanda. 2008. *Queer Inclusion in the United Methodist Church*. New Approaches in Sociology. New York: Routledge.

United Methodist Church. n.d.-a. "Why Do We Have Social Principles?" Accessed April 2, 2020. https://www.umc.org/en/content/ask-the -umc-why-do-we-have-social-principles-where-did-they-come -from.

United Methodist Church. n.d.-b. "Why Does the UMC Ordain Women?" Accessed April 2, 2020. https://www.umc.org/en/content/ask-the-umc-why-does-the-united-methodist-church-ordain-women.

Valenti, Jessica. 2009. *The Purity Myth: How America's Obsession with Virginity Is Hurting Young Women.* Berkeley, CA: Seal Press.

Wadud, Amina. 1999. *Qur'an and Woman: Rereading the Sacred Text from a Woman's Perspective.* New York: Oxford University Press.

Whitebear, Luhui. 2019. "VAWA Reauthorization of 2013 and the Continued Legacy of Violence against Indigenous Women: A Critical Outsider Jurisprudence Perspective." *University of Miami Race & Social Justice Law Review* 9 (1): 75–89.

Williams, Corey. 2018. "For Black Women at Church It's More Than the Aretha Eulogy." *Denver Post*, September 10.

TWO

Latin America and the Caribbean

Karen J. Shaw and Anuncia Escala

WOMEN IN THE RELIGIONS OF LATIN AMERICA AND THE CARIBBEAN

In Latin America and the Caribbean, religion plays a dominant role in the lives of women. While participation in religions has steadily declined in the late twentieth and early twenty-first centuries, the majority of people in Latin America and the Caribbean still identify with some form of religion, though there has been a significant shift in both the strength of historical religions and their practices (WorldAtlas 2019a).

The two prominent Christian groups in this region are Roman Catholics and Protestants, with Protestants being represented by historically traditional religious groups—Anglican, Methodist, Baptist, Seventh-day Adventist, Lutheran, Presbyterian, Church of the Nazarene, Mennonite, and Moravian—and a fast-growing movement of the Pentecostal faith through the Assemblies of God, the Foursquare Church, and the United Pentecostal Church/United Latin American Pentecostal Church (Jesus Solo Igelesia Pentecostal Unida or IPU) (Bartel 2018).

Ninety percent of people within this region identified as Roman Catholic in the 1970s, but a 2014 Pew Research study found that only 69 percent now identify as Roman Catholic, even though 84 percent reported being raised in that faith tradition (Lipka 2014). The study also found that "people in the Central American nations of Honduras, Nicaragua, Guatemala and El Salvador are among the most religiously committed and socially conservative. By contrast, people in the 'Southern Cone' countries of Argentina, Chile and especially Uruguay are among the most secular, with relatively low levels of religious commitment" (Lipka 2014).

Alongside, and sometimes combined with, these core religions are many syncretistic religions and new religious movements (NRMs). Among these communities, some practice liberation theology, and others incorporate native Mayan polytheistic practices, primarily in Guatemala and Honduras, and pre-Christian traditions in the Andean regions. Indigenous beliefs in the region center on the respect and worship of nature. Practiced among descendants of the African diaspora are Santeria (primarily in Cuba and the Caribbean); Spiritism, Candomblé, and Macumba (in Brazil); Obeah (primarily in Guyana); Vodou (primarily in Haiti); and Rastafarianism (primarily in Jamaica). Most of the religious practices mentioned are results of syncretism—a creative process that blends elements of Indigenous religions with elements of the colonizers' religions—which was initiated by the oppressed to preserve some of their original beliefs.

Candomblé is a syncretistic religion practiced primarily in Brazil. It combines elements of Yoruba, Fon, Bantu African religions, and Catholicism. Candomblé means "dance in honor of the gods." Practitioners perform special dances that allow them to be possessed by orixas, lesser deities that control their destinies. (Marina Endermar/Dreamstime.com)

EARLY FEMINIST: SOR JUANA INÉS DE LA CRUZ

Juana Ramirez was an unusual fifteenth-century woman in New Spain (Mexico). Hungry for theological knowledge and disinclined to marry, she became a Catholic nun. This allowed her to read, write, teach, and cook. To her, the secular process of food preparation was as valid a way for women to contemplate and understand the world as theological study.

Sor (Sister) Juana Inés de la Cruz became famous for her brilliant writing, pro-woman stance, and theology of God as wisdom *and* love. Although religious authorities forced her to recant her arguments, her belief remained unshaken. She wrote, "She studies, and disputes, and teaches, and thus she serves her Faith; for how could God, who gave her reason, want her ignorant?" (Nieves 2017).

Janet Lockhart and Karen J. Shaw

Nieves, Juliany González. 2017. "23 Latin American Women and USA Latinas in Theology and Religion You Should Know About." Global Church Project, July 31, 2017. https://theglobalchurchproject.com/18-latin-american-female-theologians-know/.

The Catholic image of the Virgen de Guadalupe in Mexico is a crucial icon transformed from the Aztec goddess Tonantzin. Indigenous followers of Catholicism held to the hope of the Virgin of Guadalupe, a brown-skinned virgin who, traditions says, appeared to Juan Diego on a hill outside of Mexico City in 1531 and who gave direct access to the divine for Indigenous and mestizo/a populations. In Argentina, people seek help and solace through folk saints such as La Difunta Correa, Gauchito Gil, and Miguel Angel Gaitan.

Other faiths within the region include Islam (primarily in Guyana and Haiti but small pockets across the region), Hinduism (the third-largest population of Hindus in the Western Hemisphere is in Suriname), Judaism (primarily in Argentina but small pockets across the region), Buddhism (primarily in the Caribbean), Santeria (Cuba), Jehovah's Witnesses, and the Church of Jesus Christ of Latter-day Saints (Mormon Church; growing quickly in Guatemala). Other new religious movements represented in the region include Bahá'í, Hare Krishna, Scientology, Wicca, Pachamama, and African Shamanism.

One significant growing group is those who identify as atheist or non-religious. Bolivia and Cuba have increasing numbers of people who do not associate with any religion, and in Costa Rica, those identifying as nonreligious are the second-largest population. Believing that the church relegates women to a position of inferiority, many in Argentina are leaving religion rather than substituting one conservative religion for another (Edgerton and Sotirova 2011/2012). Uruguay has the highest percentage of agnostics and atheists in the Western Hemisphere, ranking sixth in least religious countries in the world (WorldAtlas 2019b). This trend, which mirrors the international trend toward a shrinking interest in religious engagement, is most often found in the urban centers of the region.

Roman Catholicism

The Roman Catholic Church still figures strongly in the lives of Latin American and Caribbean people, not only in their faith practices but also in the historical entanglement of the Catholic Church and governments. Across Latin America, the Catholic Church often developed the governmental infrastructure and, as a result, also built and influenced schools, hospitals, health care, and acceptable standards of living.

In the days leading up to the late twentieth century, when nine out of ten people in the region identified as Roman Catholic, presidents and generals were required to be Roman Catholic. The church built most public and private schools, and they were either run by or influenced by the church's values, religious teachings, and moral code. As recently as 2004, when the health minister of Peru proposed a plan to provide sex education and distribute contraceptives in the schools, Bishop Antonio Baseotto suggested he "be thrown into the sea with a rock around his neck" (Hagopian 2008). Even though the relationship between the Roman Catholic Church and government has weakened, the church still controls many of the political views and laws regarding sex (Edgerton and Sotirova 2011/2012).

In Paraguay, where almost 90 percent of the population identifies as Roman Catholic, most of its government leaders also align with Catholicism. Peru exhibits the strongest Roman Catholic influence in government. Its clergy is subsidized by the government, and religion is a required subject in both private and public schools (WorldAtlas 2019c).

A Catholic-based theology known as liberation theology is rooted in Latin America's struggles against oppression. It argues that true salvation cannot occur without liberation from social, political, and economic oppression. It does not, however, take into account the oppression that occurs within the church, particularly for women and LGBTQ people.

With its primary focus on race and class, liberation theology does not consider gender and the plight of women (Pena 1995). Ultimately, Catholic feminists developed feminist theologies that gave women within the church a voice against patriarchy and scriptural interpretations that maintain gender oppression. The mantra of women at the Confederation of Latin American Religions became the following: "Liberation requires the total transformation of society and its liberation of women from social structures that marginalize women and poor indigenous people."

Catholic feminist theology led to the Catholics for Choice movement through which "women in Latin America, as always, have reinterpreted, reimagined, and reclaimed spaces and places in the making of the contemporary church, both Catholic and Protestant. They have forced open dialogues to consider feminist readings of the Bible, the role of women in leadership, and the very colonial inheritance that they are responding to" (Bartel 2018).

As Catholicism began to falter under its break from governmental relationships and the people's tiring of conservative values that controlled all aspects of their lives, the church began to break with tradition and seek new alternatives to its long-standing priorities and to take on characteristics of religions growing in popularity. The Catholic Charismatic Renewal movement combined the popular aspects of the growing Pentecostal religion with tried and true Catholic belief. With the addition of the concept of being filled with the Holy Spirit, followers gained a more personal relationship with the divine and were able to exhibit that relationship through speaking in tongues, prophesying, exorcism, divine healing, and interpreting dreams, all of which were considered to be more easily attained by women (Chestnut 2003). By including these practices in the Catholic Church, followers were given the benefit of the Virgin Mary combined with the woman-centric attributes of Pentecostalism, elevating women's place in the church.

In some parts of the region, Afro-Brazilian and Afro-Caribbean religions combined with Catholic traditions to create Macumba, Umbanda, Candumblé, and Santeria. In Brazil, the Universal Church of the Reign of God, founded by Edir Macedo, uses the model of priesthood leadership from Catholicism but elevates the priest to the role of a "superhero" who speaks as the direct voice of God. The church uses mass media and dramaturgy to play out this superhero image (Levine 2009).

In Haiti, Catholic-Vodou Syncretism has led to a safe environment for traditional Vodou followers, who make up a majority of people on the

---

IEMANJÁ: MANY-FACETED GODDESS

Iemanjá (also Yemanjá, Yemaya, or Yemoja) is a Yoruba *orisha* (deity) of the waters, who was carried from West Africa with the human beings who were brought as slaves to South America and the Caribbean.

Under the oppression of slavery, Iemanjá was worshipped in secret, or she was syncretized (merged) with other figures, such as the Virgin Mary. This influence can be seen, for example, in the fact that some of her images are now light-skinned rather than her original dark skin.

Iemanjá is many things: mother of all goddesses, queen of the seas, protector of fishermen and of children, female creatrix, and spirit of the moon. At her annual festival in Brazil, participants throw gifts into the ocean and ask for her blessings. Like the waters, Iemanjá can be nurturing and protective as well as fierce and destructive.

Janet Lockhart

---

island, to worship publicly. As with other Afro-Caribbean religions, this partnering of faiths allows for a broader reach for the Catholic Church while at the same time recognizing and giving space for Indigenous religions and religions brought by oppressed peoples, such as enslaved Africans. Protestant Christians (primarily Baptists, Pentecostals, and Adventists) decry Vodou in any form.

Beyond internal shifts, the Catholic Church also changed how it worked within the world. As the church began to separate from government, it moved toward a human rights and social justice agenda. Spurred on by activism in other religions and by the growing outcry from liberation and feminist theologians, the church took on a pivotal role in the search for justice and in placing justice and human rights in the forefront of political discourse. Having once been the primary participant in the injustice and violence carried out against the people of the region, the church began to play an intimate role in reparations, although the church still collaborates with oppressive regimes in some places.

Brazil, Chile, El Salvador, Peru, and Guatemala saw the Catholic Church become the defender "of classic human rights (to be free from arbitrary arrest, abuse, and torture and to reject the impunity of political leaders, military, and police)" and the advocate for "general rights to collective organization (by the landless, by slum dwellers, by Indigenous communities) and to health and education" (Levine 2010). This action led to the concept of "social sin" as part of liberation theology and the idea that human rights and justice violations are, in essence, a sin against humanity and a sin in the eyes of the divine.

This humanitarian agenda, however, not only reengaged the wavering followers of the Catholic faith but also enraged the oppressors and the now fractured governments that had long depended on the church to back up their oppressive and patriarchal agenda. The church became a target of violence from corrupt militaries, gangs angered by the church's interference in their drug trade and illegal activities, and individuals whose oppressive actions were publicly decried. At the height of the church's social sin agenda, the National Council of Evangelicals of Peru created the first human rights organizations, taking focus away from the human rights agenda in churches as that responsibility passed on to those emerging organizations. As a result, many of the churches reverted back to their government relationships and brought back Christian nationalism.

But the Roman Catholic Church never regained the political ties that it once had. In Venezuela, under the leadership of Hugo Chávez, the government took control of Catholic schools and removed religion from public schools. In Argentina, liberationists attempting to sever ties between the government and the church were marginalized, tortured, exiled, and killed. Nestor Kirchner's leadership in government became the democratic shift that separated the church and government and made room for religious pluralism because Catholicism no longer held the power it had historically enjoyed as a government-sanctioned religion. It was the chink in the armor that other religions needed to establish foundations in the region (Levine 2009).

One final adaptation of the Roman Catholic Church in this region is "Catholic My Way." As the population of the church has become less conservative, traditional beliefs have been challenged (e.g., gay marriage, LGBT rights, abortion) as have traditional expectations (e.g., attendance, confession). Priorities for Catholic followers have shifted from moral issues to concerns around employment, poverty, economic crisis, personal security, and access to health care and education. In countries such as Chile and Argentina, this can be seen in their shifting support for key issues. In Chile, more Catholics identify with the left-leaning Christian Democratic Party than with conservatives, and in Argentina, 90 percent of Catholics believe sex education should be taught in schools (Hagopian 2008).

Despite this seemingly "open" version of Catholicism, Catholic clergy in the region still predominantly hold to traditional values. They believe that human life is defined as conception to natural death. They oppose embryonic stem cell research and cloning, the morning-after pill, assisted suicide, and abortion; they support Indigenous rights, migrant needs, and land struggles; and they condemn poverty, inequality, and Indigenous land abuses. In response to pluralism, many of the Catholic churches are also returning to secular partnerships in government and politics to enforce their moral agenda on abortion, marriage, and LGBTQ and women's rights (Hagopian 2008). In Ecuador, women have the fewest rights of all women in the region. A woman gives up her rights to property and money to her husband under the Catholic-based law, and upon his death, all property goes to male children or male relatives, who then have the choice to take on the support of the woman or not (Wilson 2014).

Protestantism

The Protestant movement in the region has been the most significant force in unseating the Roman Catholic Church from its place in the homes and governments of the people. Colonial missionaries brought in virtually every Protestant belief, leaving behind small numbers of each Protestant religious group across the region. These colonial religions often became syncretized with Indigenous religious practices, creating a blended religion that resonated with the population. However, the colonization of religions has been seen more as a "takeover" of Indigenous religions than a mode of giving voice to marginalized people (Hallum 2003). Others argue that it was and is the creativity of Indigenous-mestizo and Afro-Latino communities that creates the path for surviving beliefs and practices, despite violent conquest and imposition. Darien J. Davis, in his article "La Santería: Una Religion Sincretica," sees syncretism as a form of protest against the dominant culture (Davis 2015).

In Guyana, the colonial missionary movement, combined with the migration of Hindu followers from India, minimized the influence of the Roman Catholic Church. With the further migration of African slave populations to Guyana, Protestant Christian practices became syncretized with African beliefs, leading to today's blended Western and African religion.

Syncretic religions often developed because it was the only way for Indigenous practices to survive when European colonizers arrived with both their Protestant (usually Anglican) religions and a large population of enslaved Africans. People in St. Vincent and the Grenadines held to polytheistic beliefs and the worship of nature as a representation of the divine. Today, a form of Protestant religion remains that includes Indigenous belief in the power of dreams and their interpretation as spiritual events. Services often include rituals meant to keep evil spirits at bay.

Honduran Protestants have developed a syncretic religion that combines Mayan rituals, including animal sacrifice, with Christian thought. In Jamaica, Protestant missionaries brought Christianity to enslaved people and ideas about abolition. Owners were threatened by the conversion of enslaved people because of Christianity's potential to disrupt the dominant social order. Evangelical Christianity fostered rebellion and joined forces with Black nationalism to improve the lives of Black Jamaicans. For the people of St. Kitts and Nevis, British rule led to a predominantly Protestant Anglican population, with only small pockets remaining of the Indigenous practice of Obeah, a belief in witchcraft and curses (WorldAtlas 2019d).

Within Protestant faiths, women are predominantly subordinated to men in the decisions of the home and the religion. A 2014 Pew Research study found that the Protestant religions were more likely to oppose same-sex marriage and to expect women to "obey" their husbands (Lipka 2014).

Pentecostalism—A Protestant Movement

Despite the number of Protestant religions in the region, none has had a transformative impact like Pentecostalism. Brazil led the Pentecostal movement in the region in the 1970s, with followers believing that this newly emerging religion created a "community of spiritual medics" that could provide both emotional comfort and support along with prayer and ritual acts of healing. Growing at a rate of over twenty million new followers each year at the height of its establishment, women make up two-thirds of the Pentecostal membership in the region. But accurate statistics have remained challenging because (1) in the early days of the movement, the Roman Catholic Church still controlled much of the information flow with its power in government and education, so the movement was downplayed; (2) Pentecostal churches are not required to document membership or file significant reports of finances or activities; and (3) with women at the core of the movement, they have been historically ignored in religious research (Hallum 2003).

In Guatemala, where followers of Pentecostalism are quickly equaling those of Catholicism, people have resonated with the end-time theology and suffering for sins, as they have been forced from their homelands because of the violence of civil war. They have exchanged the associated poverty and corporate marginalization in their Indigenous communities for the violence of the urban centers—gang war, drugs, alcoholism, crime, and domestic abuse. End-time theology gives them hope for healing and restoration in Christ's new world (Levine 2010).

Why have women in the region been so drawn to Pentecostalism? Most researchers agree that the strongest pull is the belief that it improves their lives both inside and outside of the home. Many of the women transitioning to Pentecostalism have experienced or are still experiencing domestic violence, absentee fathers, extreme poverty, partner substance abuse, and isolation. Women, particularly in Latin America, are seeking faith communities that answer their daily problems of health (healing), isolation (small and large group worship and activities), hunger (shared resources), and access (networking) (Chestnut 2003). Pentecostal churches give these women limited power within their belief system, access to information for overcoming their circumstances, a community, and a voice. Within the emerging Pentecostal movement, women are seeing an opportunity to play a more significant role through their leadership in worship services, hosting home groups (small group worship services held in their homes), and leading service programs for the hungry and marginalized.

Pentecostalism focuses on the priesthood of all believers. In other words, anyone can directly access the Holy Spirit and can be filled with the Spirit, allowing them to prophesy, heal, and channel the Spirit to others. Women are considered to be most receptive to the Holy Spirit, elevating their status within the religion. Through the *cultos a domicillo*, or "services in the home," women can also read, interpret, and share the scriptures and their inspirations from the divine.

Further, when a man is still in the home, this newly found belief system that is shared within the home often leads to his conversion to Pentecostalism. By this passive conversion activity, women are able to directly impact the machismo that has led to abusive and neglectful behaviors without an obvious targeted effort. As a result, the women are now able to let the church direct the men's behavior, leading to a change in the home environment. The additional benefits are that the man becomes a contributor to the home's finances and upkeep again, and the woman is in a safer and healthier situation (Brusco 2010).

Because the tenets of Pentecostalism include fidelity, avoidance of alcohol and drugs, and care for the family, women who lead the men in their households to conversion have fewer instances of sexually transmitted diseases and domestic violence, and they have the backing of the church in expecting men to contribute to the household finances. With so many services and activities, members are not only provided with a safe space, social support, and shared meals but are also given opportunities that support their tenets and pull men away from harmful or tempting activities.

For the growing number of women-led households, Pentecostal churches also provide a community of support that keeps them out of deep poverty. Members of the church pool resources such as childcare, finances, and food, and the expected tithes to the church provide funds for emergency relief. Pentecostalism "provides its members with a safe place to suspend availing roles and statuses and temporarily inhabit new and rewarding ones" (Brodwin 2003).

In Bolivia, four out of five households are led by women, many of whom were abandoned by their husbands. As peasant culture has deteriorated, the migration to urban centers has forced women into roles as domestic servants and street vendors, where they experience classism, racism, and gender discrimination. In their involvement with Pentecostal churches, these women have found a sense of equality, an escape from social isolation, and a religious calling. However, the challenge lies in the organization of the church that still ultimately subordinates women and puts the burden of faithful living on them rather than on men (Gill 1990).

The rebirth theology of Pentecostalism resonates with women who have endured deeper rights violations and abuses because it provides hope of total rebirth, not just from their "sinful nature" but from their circumstances of hopelessness. In a small village in Guatemala, almost every man was killed during the Guatemalan Civil War, leaving women heads of household who were ill prepared for their role. Pentecostal churches rallied around these women, providing emotional support, food, financial resources, and education for meaningful skills to become self-sufficient. For these women, it was a rebirth into a new life (Hallum 2003).

Beyond their improved sense of power and purpose through leadership in the church and access to support for their varying home environments, women find community in Pentecostalism. All roles, except the leading pastor role, are available to women, and social class barriers are equalized. Women are given status that is unavailable to them in mainstream society (Brusco 2010). Because Pentecostalism attracts

**MAYAN WOMEN IN GUATEMALA
FIGHTING FOR JUSTICE**

Since the Spanish conquest, Mayan women have struggled for gender and racial justice, inspired by their beliefs in the sacredness of the world and their ceremonies for healing, gratitude, and guidance. Today's Mayan women rely on their spirituality to strengthen them for the fight for justice. Many of these women are human rights defenders, standing up for dignity and resources for Guatemala's Indigenous people and protecting the earth from environmental degradation.

For example, Lolita Chávez, who is Maya Quiché, works in defense of the land and women's rights. She is a member of the Council of K'iche Peoples for the Defense of Life, Mother Nature, Land and Territory (CPK). Lolita has faced off with the government and mining, hydroelectric, logging, and agricultural corporations that exploit Mayan resources without the consent of the communities. In return, she has been targeted for harassment and death threats and had to leave the country in 2017 for her own safety. That same year, she was a finalist for the European Parliament's Sakharov Human Rights Prize.

Susan M. Shaw

people from the lowest socioeconomic classes in many parts of the region, members often tend to be less educated and poorer. In Argentina, only 20 percent of Pentecostals have secondary degrees, and 22 percent live in poverty, compared to 60 percent of non-Pentecostals holding higher degrees and 10 percent living in poverty (Koehrsen 2016). Pentecostalism has provided a forum for weakening the impact of economic crises and disparagements between classes by providing an environment where deep relationships are formed across classes and life situations (Gill 1990).

Finally, women find their voice in Pentecostalism because—despite the paid staff being men—women plan and lead the majority of the services and small group activities within the religion. In a typical Pentecostal service, women are likely to begin the service with a parade of song, dance, and, at times, speaking in tongues. Women will prophesy from the floor, speaking out the words they believe the Holy Spirit has given them. In home groups, women plan and lead the conversations in their homes, again prophesying and interpreting scriptures, and in evangelizing, women, often the wives of the pastors, organize and carry out evangelistic activities and participation in humanitarian efforts.

The Assemblies of God is the most dominant of the Pentecostal churches. While women run the service, the men remain on the stage in positions of authority. Although given a broad range of leadership opportunities within the church, women still follow clear gender-identified roles and support a subordinate relationship with men (Brusco 2010).

The Evangelical Movement

Almost 20 percent of the population in Latin America identifies as evangelical. "Evangelical pastors embrace varied ideologies, but when it comes to gender and sexuality, their values are typically conservative, patriarchal and homophobic. They expect women to be completely submissive to their evangelical husbands. And in every country in the region, they have taken the strongest stands against gay rights" (Corrales 2018). The evangelical movement is quickly becoming one of the most political in the region, with relationships between evangelicals and political leaders gaining strength, particularly in Brazil, Costa Rica, and Peru (Puglie 2018). In Guatemala, former president Rios Montt, who was responsible for genocide within that country, also identified as evangelical. This "marriage" between religion and politics has so blurred the dividing lines that many campaign promises are built around commitments to incorporating conservative evangelical beliefs into law. The evangelical mayor of Rio de Janeiro, Marcelo Crivella, said, "I told God I wouldn't . . . move a son from the altar to politics, but I confess I was wrong. One day, this nation will elect an evangelical president, and then . . . we'll take the Gospel to all nations of the Earth" (Puglie 2018).

Other Major Religions

Other major religions arrived in the region through emigration from countries where followers were fleeing oppression and being relocated by force through the slave trade. Judaism grew as the Jewish community fled Germany and other European countries during the reign of Hitler and the Nazi regime, with largest population now in Argentina. Overall, Judaism accounts for less than 2 percent of the population.

Both the Muslim and Hindu faiths grew through the emigration of people from India and Africa. In the smallest country of the region, Suriname, the most multicultural, multireligious community exists, with Islam

and Hinduism trailing only Pentecostalism. These faiths are often combined with Indigenous practices of polytheism and nature and ancestor
worship. Guyana and Trinidad and Tobago also have larger populations of
Hindus. While accounting for larger percentages on these islands, the
overall population of Muslims and Hindus in the region, like Jews, is small
(WorldAtlas 2019e).

Mostly Tamil-speaking Hindus in Guyana, Trinidad, and Suriname
worship Mother Kali. In Trinidad, a syncretistic worship of Mother Kali
sees her as the Catholic Virgin Mary. This Catholic La Divina Pastora,
meaning "the Divine Shepherdess," was adapted as a dark-skinned Virgin
Mary and is worshipped on Good Friday. She is credited for traveling with
the Indian people across the ocean to their new home (Naidu 2007).

Making up one-third of the Suriname population, Hinduism offers a bit
of a mixed message to women. While the religion reveres women through
its goddess worship and its belief that women have the ability to channel
goddess energy, women are still subordinated to men and are held to a
strict code of dress and behavior. As Hinduism embraces equality (as in
the movement for women to have access within temples in India), this
could have a positive effect on the position of Hindu women within this
region.

Living as Muslim in the region brings significant challenges. One
example is in Haiti, where "the government does not recognize Islam as an
official religion because Islamic practices such as polygamy, belief in the
death penalty, and the practice of adopting Islamic names after conversion
are incompatible with the law" (U.S. Department of State, Bureau of
Democracy, Human Rights, and Labor 2018). Muslims must obtain civil
marriage licenses because marriages within the mosques are not recognized. Further, many Muslim women experience violence for wearing the
hijab and struggle to obtain government identification because it requires
them to remove their hijab for the photo (U.S. Department of State, Bureau
of Democracy, Human Rights, and Labor 2018).

Buddhism arrived in the Caribbean through the emigration of Chinese
people fleeing persecution and seeking a more peaceful life. Buddhism
remains most popular in the Caribbean, though it is practiced by less than
2 percent of the population. Jnanadakini became the first Mexican woman
to be ordained into the Triratna Buddhist Order. Her goal is to utilize the
"strength of practical faith in the face of great political and economic dif-
ficulties," and she has been carrying this movement throughout the continent with specific focus in Venezuela (Jnanadakini 2017).

Indigenous and Syncretistic Religions and New Religious Movements

Across the region, many Indigenous religions and new religious movements (NRMs) have representation, and parts of these religious practices are quite often combined with traditional religions to create a worship experience unique to the region. As previously mentioned, Santeria, commonly practiced in Cuba, combines Catholicism with African rituals brought by enslaved Africans. Ancient polytheistic Mayan religions in Guatemala and Honduras are often woven into the practices of Catholicism and Pentecostalism. Obeah, a folk religion of Africa, is combined with Hindu and Protestant religions in Guyana. Also in Guyana, Roman Catholic beliefs are interwoven with Hindu beliefs that manifest the goddess Mother Kali as a brown-skinned Virgin Mary (Naidu 2007). This process of syncretism has ensured that Indigenous religions are able to live alongside and within modern religions, protecting the history and value of

Indigenous Mayans have retained many of their religious practices that they now use as a form of empowerment and resistance as they engage in activism against racism, poverty, violence against women, and environmental degradation in Guatemala. (Lucy Brown/Dreamstime.com)

their practices, although some scholars see this as another form of colonizing Indigenous religions.

In Jamaica, a unique and slowly growing new religious movement is Rastafarianism. Founded in the 1930s as a way for the Black community to reclaim power that had been stripped from them by white people (or Babylonians, as they call them), Rastafarianism was built as a patriarchal religion that placed men in complete control of the religion and of women. Followers worship Haile Selassie I, the emperor of Ethiopia, as the incarnation of Jesus. There are strict Bible-based (Hebrew/Christian Bible) rules around the allowed behavior, dress, and involvement of women, including the following:

- Females are not called to Rastafarl except through a male. Only a man can make a woman "sight" Rastafarl. She therefore cannot be a leader in any Rastafarl ritual.

- Males are the physical and spiritual head of the female as well as the family. The female must seek the man's guidance in all things spiritual. He also accepts the responsibility for "balancing" her thoughts.

- A female cannot experience the "highest heights" of Rastafarl if she is without a king-man or head.

Females are unclean whenever they have an issue of blood. From these premises came certain behavioral restrictions or taboos:

- The female cannot share the chalice of the males. This excludes her from experiencing the communal nature of the culture in a direct way.

- The female should always have her head covered when praying (1 Corinthians 11:5–6), since she is always expected to be receptive to spiritual instruction.

- An unclean female cannot approach a ritual gathering of males, nor should she prepare meals for any males during that time.

- A woman is expected to be obedient and receptive to guidance as well as have a willingness to learn (Rowe 1980).

Modern-day Rastafarianism is in a tug-of-war with traditional Rastafarianism as young women speak out for their rights to their bodies and to being engaged in all levels of worship. Rastafarian men have begun marrying Babylonian (white) women, bringing them into the rituals of the religion. Like other religions in the region, developing factions are creating space for more inclusion (O'Gilvie 2018).

On the opposite end of the spectrum from Rastafarianism is Spiritism, a predominantly white middle-class movement, mainly practiced in Brazil, based on the writings of Hippolyte Leon Denizard Rivai under the pseudonym Allan Kardec (whom he claimed was one of his incarnations). Kardec borrowed elements from Christianity, Eastern religions, and parapsychology to create Spiritism. From Christianity, Kardec took ethical values while rejecting doctrines such as the Trinity, the divinity of Christ, and the existence of miracles, angels, demons, heaven, and hell. He focused on the idea of religion within the limits of reason alone that dominated liberal theological circles at the time (Vasquez 2001).

Spiritism moved to Brazil as a part of a combination scientific and religious experience that could attract the middle-class elite to the community through either knowledge or faith. The basic belief is that humans are immortal spirits who temporarily live in physical bodies to attain intellectual and moral improvement for themselves. The science of the Spiritism movement attracts medical professionals and academics, while the focus on contact with the spirit world through mediums attracts those looking for religion and a higher power (Hess 1987). Umbanda, a popular religion in Brazil, brings together varying combinations of Spiritism, Catholicism, and African-based religions. It is practiced across class and racial lines. Women within Spiritism, especially Umbanda, are highly regarded as mediums. In this role, they are able to access a sense of power that takes them out of their daily lives of oppression and aligns them with other religious leaders (Lerch 1982).

One of the most misunderstood and misrepresented religious practices in the region is Vodou. With most of the practicing population in Haiti, Vodou has comfortably blended with Catholicism in recent times, but this was not the case when enslaved Africans first brought the practice to Haiti. During this time, enslaved people were prohibited from practicing Vodou, and their temples and shrines were destroyed, forcing followers to develop underground societies called "Maroons" where they could gather and worship. The followers of Vodou have reclaimed their religion through the renaming and rebranding of it as Vodou.

One point worth noting is the negative impact of Voodoo on the Vodou religion. The name *Vodou* means "God" or "Spirit." The sensationalism of secular Voodoo in movies, books, and other Western entertainment is the antithesis of actual Vodou. The belief that Vodou is an "evil" practice involving sacrifices, curses, and dark magic has led to many priestesses, or manbo, holding their services in hidden spaces and covering up their association with the religion to avoid persecution and physical harm (Michel 2001).

In 1987, the new Constitution of Haiti recognized Vodou as a national religion alongside Catholicism, but by this time, many of the Vodou temples were practicing a unique form of worship that combined Catholic rites and ceremonies with Vodou to "normalize" the religion and allow for its public practice (Michel 2001).

As with other religions, those who follow Vodou seek protection and guidance during hardships and also expect to be punished when they are willingly wrong, but Vodou has no equivalent of heaven or an afterlife. It, instead, provides a philosophy and a code of ethics that are built into spiritual concepts and regulate social behavior. Followers are offered the opportunity for revitalization through ancestral African traditions and a place to air complaints, to organize, to resist, and to act (Michel 2001).

The manbo, or Vodou priestess, is held in highest regard in Vodou, elevating women to a leadership status. Because Vodou is considered a belief of the lower classes, though, the elite of Haiti who practice Vodou do so underground while snubbing it in public. As a result, Vodou priestesses, while held in high regard within the religion, are more often aligned with lower socioeconomic classes in public life.

Another new religious movement is Santeria ("Way of the Saints"). Santeria is an Afro-Caribbean syncretic religion based on Yoruba beliefs and traditions combined with Roman Catholic elements. It grew out of slave trade in Cuba, where the largest population of followers in the region is located. Followers of Santeria believe that Orishas (mortal spirits) are manifestations of Olodumare (God) that will help them to reach their destiny if the followers perform the appropriate rituals. But the Orishas can only exist if they are worshipped by human beings.

Women are an integral part of Santeria. Priests may be a *babalorisha* (Father in the Spirit) or *iyalorisha* (Mother or Wife in the Spirit). Santeria deities are often linked with Catholic saints, such as Saint Barbara (justice and strength) and Our Lady of Charity (the Yoruba goddess of the river) (BBC 2014).

ISSUES OF RELIGION FOR WOMEN IN LATIN AMERICA AND THE CARIBBEAN

The Impact of Christian Missionaries on the Colonial Project

Clear examples of the legacy of missionary colonialism can be found in this region. Christian missionaries, visiting the region under the guise of bringing their religious "opportunities" to the people, instead brought in white colonial thinking, practices, and culture that began to be woven into the fabric of Indigenous people, sometimes virtually eradicating traditional practices. These colonial religions were often "forcibly and violently imposed by the European 'conquerors' in the 15th and 16th centuries through the complete annihilation or partial assimilation of pre-Columbian religious beliefs and practices" (Cevallos 2005). Despite these influences, many contemporary descendants of the Mayan and Aztec cultures have managed to retain core elements of their traditions, many times by forming syncretic religions that incorporate the colonial religious rituals and beliefs with Indigenous traditions.

To understand the impact that colonialism had on women specifically, it is important to look back to the lives of Aztec women prior to the arrival of the colonists. Women had equal legal and financial rights with men and were revered as healers and priestesses. While women's work of weaving, spinning, sweeping, cooking, and caring for children was focused within the home, it was highly valued and had sacred significance with the home as a place of power. In fact, childbirth was equated with the work of a warrior.

With the arrival of the colonizers, conservative Western religious values were forced on the people of the region, replacing women's power with women's subordination. Families were destroyed by foreign diseases brought in by the colonizers and by the forced labor of both women and men that led to exhaustion and death. People were murdered by colonizers who saw their traditional practices as "savage" rather than trying to understand the value and importance of those practices. Even the very names of people were stolen as new Western names were given to them (Gale 2005). "Many religions have destroyed what we are, and it is sad to see the contempt that the new generations have for what we once were. They think that the traditional beliefs of the Mayans (the main indigenous ethnic group in Central America) are witchcraft, or satanic" (Cevallos 2005).

Colonialism and religion also went hand in hand in other ways. In some places, such as Guatemala, evangelical religions were said to have been planted by governments, including the United States, as a way of protecting their political and economic interests in the region (Cevallos 2005).

Colonialism was not only responsible for the desecration of Indigenous religions and families, but it was also the source of poverty in this region, as colonizers stole land, resources, and livelihoods from the native people for their own gain. This practice continues today as Western cultures destroy lands once owned by Indigenous people to access hydroelectric power, fertile soils for agribusiness, and natural resources through mining, timber, and other precious materials. This desecration is often done in the name of the church, as in Ecuador, where sects "pacify, divide and tame the people, subordinating them to the interests of the dominant powers or big corporations, like the oil companies" (Cevallos 2005).

In the Caribbean, Indigenous populations were largely destroyed by colonial contact and exploitation. The economies that existed prior to the British invasion were virtually eliminated or marginalized by colonial corporate interests, primarily sugar plantations, and social order was reconstructed according to the colonizers' views of the natural order, which included white superiority and Black slavery (Clarke 1983).

Women in Religious Leadership

Despite great strides through women's movements and the expansion of humanitarian efforts around social justice and human rights, women in the largest and most populated religions of Latin America and the Caribbean are subordinated to men. As the Roman Catholic Church has struggled with its historical patriarchal hierarchy, women have begun to find their voice through versions of Catholicism that allow for practices derived from evangelical, Pentecostal, and humanitarian influences. Through the addition of both evangelical and Pentecostal practices within the worship services, women have been given the opportunity to lead portions of the service, to be seen as conduits of the faith through their channeling of the Holy Spirit (prophesying and speaking in tongues), and to go out into their communities to share their beliefs and recruit members to the church. Through the addition of humanitarian efforts in the church, women have had the opportunity to develop and lead human rights campaigns, health and wellness efforts in impoverished communities, and cooperatives that share food and resources.

While some have argued for a "Francis Effect" (the influence of Pope Francis) that more significantly encompasses the aims of liberation theology (Levine 2014), the church has not moved in any transformational way to recognize women through ordained leadership. At the April 2018 Synod on Women, the Pontifical Commission declared that "the Catholic Church in Latin America must recognize and appreciate the role of women and end the practice of using them solely as submissive laborers in the parish" (Esteves 2018). However, they fell short when in the process of this declaration, they went on to say, "In order for priests to benefit from 'feminine genius,' it is important for married women and consecrated women to participate in the formation process."

Women in the Catholic Church have begun to raise their voices in other ways. An annual "slut walk" was begun in Buenos Aires and spread to Nicaragua, Guatemala, and Costa Rica after Catholic clergy said the only purpose of sex is fertilization, insinuating that women should not have sex for enjoyment. With chants of "Get your rosaries off our ovaries" and "Jesus loves sluts," women stood up to the majority religion and gave voice to the marginalized (Edgerton and Sotirova 2011/2012).

In some traditional Protestant churches, women have access to leadership roles within the church, serving as pastors, lay leaders, and deacons. The Lutheran, Mennonite, Presbyterian, Episcopalian, and Methodist Churches allow for and encourage the professional leadership of women within the church structure. More conservative groups, such as Baptists, maintain the subordination of women through belief in the divine authorship of the Bible and its literal interpretation as a guide for life and church organization.

Pentecostalism, while elevating women as leaders in worship services and home-based group gatherings, maintains women's subordination by allowing only men on the stage in the worship services and by only hiring men as paid staff. In recent years, there has been a small shift, as women have been invited to co-pastor with their husbands, but the husband is still the only paid staff member. Women, however, are regarded as the most receptive to the Holy Spirit, enjoying direct communion that cuts men out of the relationship and elevates women as equals in access to the divine (Zibechi 2008). Bernice Martin, in her article "The Pentecostal Gender Paradox," questions why women still embrace a religion whose tenets only call for baptism of the Holy Spirit and a call to ministry as the basis for leadership, and yet men are still the only ones allowed to lead (Brusco 2010).

One irony in this relationship between women and the Pentecostal churches is in the expectations placed upon them. Women are set up to take the burden of men's behaviors. If a woman is in relationship with a man who is not in the church, she is called to "lead" him to the church, where he is then given an opportunity to be called to lead. This reinforces a belief in women's natural inferiority and places the responsibility for men's behavior on them (Gill 1990).

An example of internalized oppression and patriarchy can be seen in the Pentecostal churches of Haiti, one of the most conservative institutions of this religion. Men exercise authority and control over women's sexuality by dictating how women dress, claiming that it is the responsibility of women through their dress and demeanor to "safeguard morality through natural containment." Women must dress conservatively, covering their heads and legs, and if a woman is sexually assaulted, the blame is placed on either her clothes or her behavior. Women within this religion denigrate those of other religions for their failure to follow the same beliefs and blame them for the moral downfall of their society and for any violence that occurs against those "outside" women (Brodwin 2003). As a result, the "leadership" of women becomes an enabler of the patriarchy by using that leadership to maintain the oppression of women within and outside of the church.

Indigenous religions in the region allow the most opportunity for women as leaders, and many of them rely on what is perceived as women's unique capacity for channeling spirits and nurturing relationships between followers and the divine. Women fill the role of priestess, medium, spiritual guide, and interpreter of dreams, and in polytheistic beliefs, images of the divine are often in female form. For example, in Guatemala, Indigenous women take on important obligations called cargos, sometimes brought on by a visitation from a saint in a dream or vision. Cargos take the form of prayers, work such as preparing food or weaving cloth, or work in collaboration with their husbands to honor a particular saint. These works ensure the well-being of their communities and "underscore the complementarity and interdependence between males and females" (Gale 2005).

Women in Sacred Texts

Much of Indigenous religion is passed down through the spoken word in stories of divine interventions, visitations by spirits and ancient leaders, prophetical dreams, and the personalization of traditional religious stories. The appearance of the Virgin of Guadalupe as a brown-skinned virgin gave the peasant masses relatability to a majority religion that was often celebrated in a language they could not even understand.

The Catholic and Protestant faiths rely on the Bible and their various interpretations of it as a guide for living. As such, women are subordinated through the male-authored texts and are given strict guidelines for their clothing, sexuality, bodies, and behavior. Even as Pentecostals give women a support system and a way out of abusive relationships and extreme poverty, they subordinate women to the men in the church and to God (Levine 2009).

Feminist theological readings of the Bible, however, utilize gender theories as tools for analyzing the texts in a way that reveals the structure of the text (e.g., male authors, differing versions from multiple authors, hints of women being present and engaged but no clear recognition of women in the text). This analysis then opens up a new relationship with the text that is liberating for women and, in the eyes of feminist theologians, is the wish of God for women who, like men, are created in God's likeness (Cardoso Pereira 1997).

LGBTQ People and Issues in Religions

For LGBTQ community members in the region, religion is much like anywhere else. While the overarching theology speaks out against the LGBTQ community, individual churches and groups embrace the community and ignore the long-standing traditions of their religion. Evangelical churches have built the strongest stance against LGBTQ rights, particularly the right to marry, and have politicized this stance to draw the conservative population in the region into voting for evangelical candidates (Puglie 2018). In Brazil, the evangelical members of Congress undercut LGBTQ legislation and participated in the impeachment of leftist president Dilma Rousseff. When an evangelical pastor was elected mayor of Rio de Janeiro, one of the world's most LGBTQ-friendly cities, evangelical leaders in the regional called for their countries to imitate the "Brazilian model" to shift the capacity for government to make decisions in favor of LGBTQ rights (Corrales 2018). This strong anti-LGBTQ belief contributes to a high level of violence against the LGBTQ population. A 2015 study by the Inter-American Commission on Human Rights found that nearly 600 LGBTQ murders occurred across Latin America from January 2013 to March 2014 (Brigida 2018). In 2017 alone, there were 387 murders and 58 suicides among the LGBTQ population (Trithart 2018).

Another challenge facing the LGBTQ community is the return of the conservative idea of *gender ideology*. Growing out of the 1990 Catholic opposition to the expansion of sexual and reproductive rights for women, this thinking has been reawakened by opponents of LGBTQ rights to categorize movements around sexual orientation and gender identity as efforts to impose an "ideology" that will subvert traditional gender roles and destroy the family. This viewpoint has been politicized to influence conservative votes against LGBTQ rights (Shaw and Albarracin 2019).

However, Latin America has also led the way for LGBTQ rights in the face of the growth of the conservative evangelical movement. Argentina was the first Latin American nation to legalize marriage equality (followed by Colombia, Brazil, and Uruguay) and has enacted some of the most progressive transgender rights laws in the world. A 2012 ruling ensures that transgender people have access to change their gender on government documents without first having to receive psychiatric counseling or transition surgery. Argentina also requires that public and private medical facilities provide free hormone therapy and gender reassignment surgery (Brigida 2018).

One place of religious refuge for the LGTBQ community in Latin America is in the practice of Santeria. A Yoruba-originated religion once considered primitive, Santeria is the most popular Afro-Cuban religion and is, in fact, the most practiced religion in Cuba. Male homosexuality

Santeria is a syncretistic religion combining elements of Yoruba religions and Catholicism. Practiced in Cuba and other Caribbean countries, as well as by immigrants in the United States, it affords women powerful roles as santeras, priests who can be overtaken by the Orishas, spirits that are manifestations of Olodumare (God). (Sandra Foyt/Dreamstime.com)

and cross-gender identity are an essential part of Santeria's mythology, philosophy, and practice (Morad 2008).

In the Caribbean, LGBTQ Haitians have found refuge in the unlikely religion of Vodou. With very few legal rights in Haiti, the LGBTQ community operates mostly underground, unable to cohabit, to spend the night in a hotel with a same-sex partner, or to access much-needed health care services. Within the Vodou *peristil* (place of worship), Haitian LGBTQ people are not only safe but welcomed, both as participants and as leaders. Some Vodou spirits are even considered to be LGBTQ themselves. In a time when being part of the LGBTQ community could result in beatings, punishment, or death, the Vodou peristil is a welcome refuge (Ahmed 2016).

Women at the Intersection of Religion and Politics

For many women in the region, their religions have given them the leadership skills and training to enter political life. Women began to emerge in politics in the region in the mid-1990s, finding leadership roles in Colombia, Honduras, Venezuela, and Bolivia. Ecuador elected Rosalia Arteaga as president, and Nicaragua followed with the election of Violeta Barrios de Chamorro. In the twenty-first century, Michelle Bachelet was elected as president of Chile twice, and Cristina Fernandez de Kirchner in Argentina, Dilma Rousseff in Brazil, and Laura Chinchilla in Costa Rica all served as presidents of their countries. Argentina passed a quota law that requires 25 percent of Congress be women, and Guatemala places Mayan women in Congress through the mobilization of women's labor groups.

Despite these major advances for women in the region, they still tend to reject feminism because their religion calls for women to serve in the traditional roles of mother, caregiver, and community builder (Hallum 2003). Pentecostal women are discouraged from participating in events or activities outside of the church, particularly those aligned with the Roman Catholic Church or Pachamama (Indigenous Earth Mother religion). This separation from society keeps them further subordinated to the church and further separated from engaging in societal change (Gill 1990).

In a region where the Roman Catholic Church has historically held the most significant role in politics and government, a distinct move away from this partnership has occurred. The majority of governments are now fully separated from the church, and two-thirds of the population believe the church should have no influence on the government or the people's vote

(Hagopian 2008). This notion is deepened now that the values of the Catholic Church often cut across political parties, making it more difficult to align with a particular group and influence elections and policy decisions.

A growing religious influence on politics in the region is the evangelical movement. As has been shown in the section on Protestantism, Latin American countries, in particular, have increasingly embraced the conservative values of the evangelical movement, electing into office evangelical pastors, performers, and church leaders. The impact of these elected officials and their constituents is felt most deeply by marginalized communities, especially women and LGBTQ community members, as votes concerning abortion, women's and LGBTQ rights, marriage equality, and health care are centered around conservative values and beliefs.

Religious Violence against Women

Religious discrimination and violence against women in the region are varied across the Caribbean and Latin America. Despite a small Jewish population in the region, anti-Semitism is common across Latin America, along with anti-Muslim rhetoric. Within the Caribbean, Muslim women face discrimination for wearing the hijab and are currently required to remove it for identification photos. Rastafarians have suffered instances of having their hair cut in public because of their trademark dreadlocks. And Protestants have been kidnapped and harmed in parts of the region with heavy gang activity.

Those identifying as Christian are the particularly vulnerable in the region if they advocate a social justice agenda. In Colombia, Alba Mery Chilito Peñafiel and Alicia Castilla are examples of the risk that Christian women take in living out their religious values through activism. In 2013, Chilito was murdered for speaking out against the drug cartel that had killed her husband, daughter, and son-in-law and was later recognized as a martyr by the Catholic Church. Castilla, the wife of a pastor, was murdered by a left-wing guerilla group after she began a support group for the families of victims when that same group murdered her husband. Sister Yolanda Ceron Delgado was martyred in 2001 outside of the church by a right-wing paramilitary man angered over her 1993 reform that returned 1.3 million acres of land to peasants (Allen 2015).

Although the Catholic Church has experienced a small resurgence in its relationship with governments across the region, for the most part, all religions find themselves at risk as they speak out against the corrupt powers within governments and their communities. In 2014, Maria Francisca Sevilla, a co-pastor with her husband of the Church of God for Life Ministry, was murdered by two gang members to whom she refused to pay a "war tax" to ensure the church's safety during gang wars.

These violent activities by gangs and corrupt government are assisted in Argentina and Guatemala by a ban on public mourning. This action not only removes religious freedom by stifling the traditional religious grieving processes but also assists the perpetrators in covering up atrocities and destroying historical memory by extricating the death and funeral process from the church, where most records are kept. This makes it almost impossible to reconstruct the atrocity and bring about any liberatory justice (Levine 2010).

Violence is not just carried out by those outside of the church. More and more violence within the church is being revealed. The Catholic Church in the late twentieth and twenty-first centuries has seen an unprecedented revelation of violence against children by its religious leaders. In Argentina alone, sixty-six priests, nuns, and brothers have been accused since 2001 of abusing dozens of people, most of them children (Pisarenko 2017).

In Chile, special prosecutors are examining cases involving 104 potential victims, half of whom were underage when the reported offenses took place, by nearly 70 clergy and laypeople. At mass, followers arrive with banners and signs demanding that "all bishops resign," as they have learned that bishops have both ignored sexual violence and have also committed acts of violence themselves (Bonnefoy 2018). For Brazil, estimates show that at least 10 percent of all clergy within the Catholic Church are sexual offenders (Phillips and Hooper 2005).

It is not only members of the Catholic Church who have been subject to sexual abuse; nuns working within the church have also begun to come forward with allegations of abuse—"thanks to the universal tradition of sisters' second-class status in the Catholic Church and their ingrained subservience to the men who run it" (Winfield and Muhumza 2018). After years of subordination to the male leadership of the Catholic Church, the women have found their voices and are speaking out.

Violence associated with religion is not limited to physical violence. The lack of control over their own bodies is an ongoing challenge for women in Catholicism and some institutions of Protestantism. One of the longest and most contentious conversations is around abortion. Conservative Roman Catholics in the region believe there is no valid reason for abortion, and they still define life as conception to death, particularly in the poorest communities. For young women in impoverished areas with little or no access to contraception or sex education, the lack of legal abortion access leads to higher mortality rates due to pregnancy and delivery complications when the mother is too young for the pregnancy or abortions are being performed by unskilled practitioners. September 28 is now the annual Day for the Decriminalization of Abortion in Latin America in honor of the lives lost to illegal abortions and complicated pregnancies and childbirth.

Nicaraguan president Daniel Ortega formed an agreement with the Catholic cardinal to prohibit emergency abortions in exchange for the cardinal's support of Ortega's radical government ideals. This has maintained a conservative view of reproduction-based sexuality and has enforced an abstinence-based model of sex education that is not working. Twenty-two percent of adolescent girls report having sex before the age of fifteen, and Latin America has the second-highest teen pregnancy rate in the world (Edgerton and Sotirova 2011/2012).

Further complicating the situation is the expectation that women's bodies are controlled by men's desires and that women are expected to "control" men's behaviors by their dress and behavior. In 2004, when the Marriage Law in Chile allowed for divorce, the morning-after pill, and an anti-AIDS campaign that distributed condoms, churches spoke out about moral and cultural degradation rather than about social justice issues that led to the need for the Marriage Law. In 2000, in Argentina, in a public outcry resulting from the collapse of the economy and the rise of the anti-neoliberal government, oppositionists spoke against the availability of abortion in cases of rape and assisted reproduction for LGBTQ couples. They went on to blame the downfall of the economy on "a moral crisis rooted in a secularist culture that demoralized the concepts of marriage and family and certain perceptions of gender that have opened up new models of relationships between the sexes" (Hagopian 2008).

Women's Resistance to Religious Oppression

Women in the region have not simply accepted their fate. In parts of the region, women have begun to follow the new religious movement of Santa Muerte, a sort of female grim reaper who punishes those who would oppress, marginalize, and harm women. Catholics for Choice (CDD) in Nicaragua has joined ten Latin American countries and the United States in an effort to give women ownership over their reproductive rights and to recognize the needs of the LGBTQ community. Their motto is "Sex education to decide.

Contraception to avoid abortion. Legal abortions to prevent death." In Argentina, women have been behind the successful National Program of Sexual Health and Procreation, passed in 2002, that guarantees sex education in the schools. Further, they have gained legal abortion in emergencies, legal divorce, and same-sex marriage (Edgerton and Sotirova 2011/2012).

In what is identified as "zones of crisis," boundaries between religious tradition and reality are blurred. But in reality, religion in zones of crisis must be relevant and capable of meeting the people's needs of safety, security, food, health, and social justice (Rubin, Smilde, and Junge 2014). Women in churches in these regions are using creative opportunities to speak out through church-based radio and theater. In these safe spaces, women are able to discuss sensitive social and political topics, such as sexual abuse, social inequality, and authoritarian government.

In response to housing and food insecurity for young women who are also heads of households, the Pentecostal women's movement created a Homeless Workers Movement to provide support by sharing what they have received through the church. Under the leadership of the Pastoral Land Commission, in 2005, women in Brazil partnered with the Campaign to Overcome Misery and Hunger in an effort to give back lands stolen from Indigenous peoples and to denounce discriminatory labor laws based on gender and race (Hagopian 2008).

In 2007, following landmark declarations by the Catholic Church that sin is more than individual failings but social structures built on institutional violence and that preference should be given to the poor when considering the resources of the church, the Latin American Catholic Church established a moral vocabulary for activists (Levine 2009). Women's movements grew out of these types of declarations, such as the Mothers of the Plaza del Mayo, a movement of Argentine mothers that campaign for their children who have been "disappeared" during the military dictatorship, pursuing the government for answers and working for justice and peace in the region.

FURTHER READING

Ahmed, Beenish. 2016. "Queer Haitians Find a Refuge in Vodou." Advocate, October 31, 2016. https://www.advocate.com/current-issue/2016/10/31/why-queer-haitians-are-turning-vodou.

Allen, John L., Jr. 2015. "Christians in Latin America Are Numerous, but Still Vulnerable." Crux. December 30, 2015. https://cruxnow.com

/faith/2015/12/christians-in-latin-america-are-numerous-but-still
-vulnerable/.

Bartel, Rebecca C. 2018. "Women & Christianity in Latin America." In
*Encyclopedia of Women in World Religions: Faith and Culture
across History*, edited by Susan de Gaia, 180–185. Santa Barbara,
CA: ABC-CLIO.

BBC. 2014. "Religions: Santeria." https://www.bbc.co.uk/religion/religions
/santeria/.

Bonnefoy, Pascale. 2018. "Catholic Church Faces Reckoning in Chile as
Sex Abuse Scandal Widens." *New York Times*, July 31, 2018.
https://www.nytimes.com/2018/07/31/world/americas
/chile-pope-francis-catholic-church-sexual-abuse.html.

Brigida, Anna-Catherine. 2018. "Latin America Has Become an Unlikely
Leader in LGBT Rights." Quartz, June 6, 2018. https://qz.com
/1288320/despite-its-catholic-roots-latin-america-has-become-an
-unlikely-lgbt-rights/.

Brodwin, Paul. 2003. "Pentecostalism in Translation: Religion and the
Production of Community in the Haitian Diaspora." *American
Ethnologist* 30: 85–101.

Brusco, Elizabeth. 2010. "Gender and Power." In *Studying Global Pentecostalism: Theories and Methods*, edited by Allan Anderson,
Michael Bergunder, André Droogers, and Cornelis van der Laan,
74–92. Berkeley: University of California Press.

Cardoso Pereira, Nancy. 1997. "The Body as Hermeneutical Category." *Journal of Latin American Biblical Interpretation* 54(3): 235–239. https://
onlinelibrary.wiley.com/doi/10.1111/j.1758-6623.2002.tb00149.x.

Cevallos, Diego. 2005. "Religion—Latin America: Indigenous Peoples
Divided by Faith." Inter Press Service News Agency, May 6, 2005.
http://www.ipsnews.net/2005/05/religion-latin-america-indigenous
-peoples-divided-by-faith/.

Chestnut, R. Andrew. 2003. "Pragmatic Consumers and Practical Prod-
ucts: The Success of Pneumacentric Religion among Women in
Latin America's New Religious Economy." *Review of Religious
Research* 45 (1): 20–31.

Clarke, Colin. 1983. "Review: Colonialism and Its Social and Cultural
Consequences in the Caribbean." *Journal of Latin American Studies* 15 (2): 491–503.

Corrales, Javier. 2018. "A Perfect Marriage: Evangelicals and Conservatives in Latin America." *New York Times*, January 17, 2018. https://

www.nytimes.com/2018/01/17/opinion/evangelicals-politics-latin -america.html.

Davis, Darien J. 2015. "La Santeria: Una Religion Sincretica." Prezi, October 21, 2015. https://prezi.com/ti0u308eeh3l/la-santeria-una -religion-sincretica/.

Edgerton, Anna, and Ina Sotirova. 2011/2012. "Sex and the Barrio: A Clash of Faith in Latin America." *World Policy Journal* 28 (4): 34–41.

Esteves, Junno Arocho. 2018. "Pontifical Commission for Latin America Proposes Synod on Women." National Catholic Reporter, April 11, 2018. https://www.ncronline.org/news/people/pontifical-commission -latin-america-proposes-synod-women.

Gale, Thomas. 2005. "Gender and Religion: Gender and Mesoamerican Religions." Encyclopedia.com. https://www.encyclopedia.com /environment/encyclopedias-almanacs-transcripts-and-maps /gender-and-religion-gender-and-mesoamerican-religions.

Gebara, Ivone. 2008. "Feminist Theology in Latin America: A Theology without Recognition." *Feminist Theology* 16 (3): 324–331.

Gill, Lesley. 1990. "'Like a Veil to Cover Them': Women and the Pentecostal Movement in La Paz." *American Ethnologist* 17 (4): 708–721.

Hagopian, Frances. 2008. "Latin American Catholicism in an Age of Political Pluralism: A Framework for Analysis." *Comparative Politics* 40 (2): 149–168.

Hallum, Anne Motley. 2003. "Taking Stock and Building Bridges: Women's Movements and Pentecostalism in Latin America." *Latin American Research Review* 38 (1): 169–186.

Hess, David. 1987. "The Many Rooms of Spiritism in Brazil." *Luso-Brazilian Review* 24 (2): 15–34.

Isasi-Diaz, Ada Maria. 1996. *Mujerista Theology: A Theology for the Twenty-First Century.* Maryknoll, NY: Orbis Books.

Jnanadakini. 2017. "Jnanadakini—Bringing the Dharma to Latin America." Interview by Candradasa. May 2, 2017. https://www.radio .com/podcasts/buddhist-voices-35577/27-jnanadakini-bringing-the -dharma-to-latin-america-215041643.

Koehrsen, Jen. 2016. "Pentecostalism in Tension." In *Middle Class Pentecostalism in Argentina: Inappropriate Spirits*, edited by Jen Koehrsen, 94–118. Leiden, Netherlands; Boston Brill.

Lerch, Patricia B. 1982. "An Explanation for the Predominance of Women in the Umbanda Cults of Pôrto Alegre, Brazil." *Urban Anthropology* 15: 237–261.

Levine, Daniel H. 2009. "The Future of Christianity in Latin America." *Journal of Latin American Studies* 41 (1): 121–145.

Levine, Daniel H. 2010. "Reflections on the Mutual Impact of Violence and Religious Change in Latin America." *Latin American Politics and Society* 52 (3): 131–150.

Levine, Daniel H. 2014. "The Francis Effect." *Americas Quarterly* (Fall), November 5, 2014. https://www.americasquarterly.org/content/pope-francis-effect.

Lipka, Michael. 2014. "7 Key Takeaways about Religion in Latin America." Pew Research Center, Fact Tank: News in the Numbers, November 13, 2014. https://www.pewresearch.org/fact-tank/2014/11/13/7-key-takeaways-about-religion-in-latin-america/.

Michel, Claudine. 2001. "Women's Moral and Spiritual Leadership in Haitian Vodou: The Voice of Mama Lola and Karen McCarthy Brown." *Journal of Feminist Studies in Religion* 17 (2): 61–87.

Morad, Moshe. 2008. "'Invertidos' in Afro-Cuban Religion." Gay & Lesbian Review, March 1, 2008. https://glreview.org/article/article-679/.

Naidu, Janet. 2007. "Retention and Transculturation of Hinduism in the Caribbean." *Guyana Journal.* https://www.worldhindunews.com/retention-and-transculturation-of-hinduism-in-the-caribbean/.

Nieves, Juliany González. 2017. "23 Latin American Women and USA Latinas in Theology and Religion You Should Know About." Global Church Project, July 31, 2017. https://theglobalchurchproject.com/18-latin-american-female-theologians-know/.

O'Gilvie, Diana. 2018. "Tug of War: Traditional Rastafarian Women in Modern Jamaican Society." Griots Republic, February 2018. http://www.griotsrepublic.com/tug-war-traditional-rastafarian-women-modern-jamaican-society/.

Pena, Milagros. 1995. "Feminist Christian Women in Latin America: Other Voices, Other Visions." *Journal of Feminist Studies in Religion* 11 (1): 81–94.

Phillips, Tom, and John Hooper. 2005. "Scandal of Sexual Abuse by Priests Shocks Brazil's 125 Million Catholics." *The Guardian*, November 26, 2005. https://www.theguardian.com/world/2005/nov/26/brazil.religion.

Pisarenko, Natasha. 2017. "Clerical Sex Abuse Disclosures Skyrocket in Pope's Argentina." NBC News, October 27, 2017. https://www

.nbcnews.com/news/latino/clerical-sex-abuse-disclosures
-skyrocket-pope-s-argentina-n815146.

Puglie, Frederic. 2018. "Evangelicals' Newfound Political Clout in Latin America Unnerves Politicians, Catholic Church." *Washington Times*, February 19, 2018. https://www.washingtontimes.com/news /2018/feb/19/latin-american-voters-turn-evangelicals-social-con/.

Rowe, Maureen. 1980. "The Woman in Rastafari." *Caribbean Quarterly* 26 (4): 13–21.

Rubin, Jeffrey W., David Smilde, and Benjamin Junge. 2014. "Lived Religion and Lived Citizenship in Latin America's Zones of Crisis: Introduction." *Latin American Research Review* 29: 7–26.

Shaw, Ari, and Mauricio Albarracin. 2019. "Fragile Rights? New Challenges for LGBTQ People in the Americas." Open Global Rights, March 6, 2019. https://www.openglobalrights.org/fragile-rights -new-challenges-for-LGBTQ-people-in-the-americas/.

Trithart, Albert. 2018. "Costa Rica's 'Religious Shock': The Political Price of Same-Sex Marriage in Latin America?" IPI Global Observatory, February 8, 2018. https://theglobalobservatory.org/2018/02 /costa-rica-election-shock/.

U.S. Department of State, Bureau of Democracy, Human Rights, and Labor. 2018. "Haiti 2018 International Religious Freedom Report." https://www.state.gov/wp-content/uploads/2019/05/HAITI-2018 -INTERNATIONAL-RELIGIOUS-FREEDOM-REPORT.pdf.

Vasquez, Manuel A. 2001. "Battling Spiritism and the Need for Catholic Orthodoxy." In *Religions of the United States in Practice*, vol. 2, edited by Colleen McDannell, 449–461. Princeton, NJ: Princeton University Press.

Wilson, Tamar Diana. 2014. "Violence against Women in Latin America." *Latin American Perspectives* 41 (1): 3–18.

Winfield, Nicole, and Rodney Muhumza. 2018. "After Decades of Silence, Nuns Talk about Abuse by Priests." AP News, July 27, 2018. https:// apnews.com/f7ec3cec9a4b46868aa584fe1c94fb28.

World Atlas. 2019a. https://www.worldatlas.com/articles/which-is-the -largest-religious-group-in-south-america.html.

World Atlas. 2019b. https://www.worldatlas.com/articles/major-religions -practiced-in-uruguay.html.

World Atlas. 2019c. https://www.worldatlas.com/articles/religious-beliefs -in-peru.html.

World Atlas. 2091d. https://www.worldatlas.com/articles/religious-beliefs
    -in-saint-kitts-and-nevis.html.
World Atlast. 2019e. https://www.worldatlas.com/articles/religious-beliefs
    -in-trinidad-and-tobago.html.
Zibechi, Raul. 2008. "Pentecostalism and South America's Social Move-
    ments." Upside Down World, October 15, 2008. http://upsidedownworld
    .org/archives/international/pentecostalism-and-south-americas-social
    -movements/.

THREE

Europe

Janet Lockhart

WOMEN IN THE RELIGIONS OF EUROPE

Europe is an enormous region that comprises nearly fifty countries. Geographically, it stretches from Russia in the east to Portugal in the west and Norway in the north to Malta in the south. Culturally, Europe also includes Greenland and Iceland as well as parts of Cyprus, Georgia, Armenia, and Turkey. It is home to over seven hundred million people and includes a huge variety of ethnic groups, languages, cultural traditions, and religious practices.

Historically, Europe has collectively been referred to as "Christendom." This is appropriate in the sense that today Europe as a whole is widely Christian, although not the same Christianity as in its early centuries. Modern Christianity in Europe is divided into three branches: Orthodox, Catholic, and Protestant. About 35 percent of the Christians in Europe are Orthodox (Pew Research Center 2011). Catholics make up about 45 percent of European Christians and Protestants about 18 percent.

Christianity was divided into the Orthodox (generally, Eastern) and Catholic (Western) traditions during the Great Schism of 1054 CE. Protestantism arose in Germany as a break with Catholicism in the early 1500s.

These branches of Christianity are further divided (sometimes greatly). Orthodox Christianity includes Eastern Orthodox (practiced mostly in Europe) and Oriental Orthodox (practiced in Armenia and Africa). Catholicism includes the Roman Catholic Church as well as the Eastern or Oriental Catholic Church (primarily in Eastern Europe). Some consider the

Church of England, also called Anglican (Episcopalian in Scotland), to be Protestant, and others view it as partway between Protestant and Catholic. Protestants in Europe include Lutherans, Calvinists, Adventists, Anabaptists, Baptists, Methodists, Pentecostals, Mennonites, Presbyterians, Quakers, Unitarians, and Reform. Some consider Unitarian Universalists to be Protestants; others believe they are not strictly Christians, as they draw on a variety of religious and secular sources.

The other monotheistic religions (those that recognize a single god) are present in smaller numbers in Europe. Several European countries are predominantly Muslim, and others have growing Muslim minorities. There are also Jews (Reform, Conservative, and Orthodox) in many countries, although to a much smaller degree (less than half of 1 percent in most countries) than before World War II and the Holocaust.

Other religions, such as Buddhism, Hinduism, and Jainism, are practiced by less than half of 1 percent of the population in any given country. Ethnic/Indigenous religions and new religions, such as the neo-pagan and Goddess movements, are also observed by a small but, in many areas, growing number of people. A number of countries also report large percentages of "nones"—people who are atheist, agnostic, or not affiliated with any religion (Pew Research Center 2018).

Orthodox Christianity

Orthodox Christianity is the majority religion in many Eastern, Southern, and Central European countries, including Belarus, Bulgaria, Cyprus, Greece, Macedonia, Moldova, Montenegro, Romania, Russia, Serbia, and Ukraine. Orthodox Christians are also a plurality (a large minority but less than 50 percent) in Bosnia and Herzegovina (Sawe 2017). Although some smaller countries, such as Serbia and Cyprus, have higher percentages, Russia has the largest total number of Orthodox Christians at about one hundred million (Pariona 2017a). Most of the Orthodox Christians in the world live in Europe (Pew Research Center 2017a).

In addition to the issues of sexism faced by women in many religions, Orthodox Christian women may also experience particular pressure to bear children and stay home to raise them, struggle to obtain a divorce, face a lack of support from the church hierarchy in cases of domestic violence, and need to move especially slowly and carefully in advocating for change from within the church.

Roman Catholicism

Roman Catholicism is the majority religion in many Western, Northern, and Central European countries, including Andorra, Austria, Belgium, Croatia, France, Hungary, Ireland, Italy, Liechtenstein, Lithuania, Luxembourg, Malta, Monaco, Poland, Portugal, San Marino, Slovakia, Slovenia, and Spain. Catholics are also a plurality in Germany, Hungary, Latvia, the Netherlands, and Switzerland (Pew Research Center 2018). The Roman Catholic Church has also spread greatly outside of Europe.

The Eastern Catholic Church (or Greek Catholic), a branch of Catholicism that holds the same essential principles as the Roman Catholic Church, is present in Belarus, Bulgaria, Croatia, Greece, Hungary, Italy, Macedonia, Romania, Russia, Serbia, and Slovakia. One difference is that Eastern Catholic Churches generally allow married men to be priests (Arnold n.d.).

In addition to the issues of sexism faced by women in many religions, Catholic women are excluded from the priesthood and diaconate, controlled

Each year, thousands of pilgrims journey to Fátima, Portugal, on May 13 for the Feast of Fatima. The feast commemorates the May 13, 1917, appearance of the Virgin Mary to three shepherd children there. (G0r3cki/ Dreamstime.com)

in their sexuality and fertility, and faced with a lack of support from the church hierarchy in cases of abuse.

Protestantism

Protestantism is the majority religion in many Northern and Western European countries, including Denmark, Finland, Greenland, Iceland, Norway, and Sweden. It is a plurality in Germany, Latvia, Switzerland, and the United Kingdom (England, Wales, Scotland, and Northern Ireland). Protestantism in general has spread widely beyond Europe.

In Denmark, Estonia, Finland, Greenland, Iceland, Norway, and Sweden, the majority of Protestants belong to branches of the Evangelical Lutheran Church (Christensen n.d.; Sutherland 2019). In the United Kingdom, the largest Protestant denomination is Anglican/Episcopalian, with about 20 percent of the population (however, a larger percentage in the United Kingdom is nonreligious) (Pariona 2017b).

In addition to the issues of sexism faced by women in many religions, Protestant women may be blocked from rising to the highest levels of church leadership, be unwelcome if transgender, and be expected to remain celibate if they are unmarried, lesbian, or bisexual.

Islam

Today, Islam is the majority in a handful of Eastern European countries, including Albania, Bosnia and Herzegovina, Kosovo, and Turkey. It is a plurality in Macedonia, where about 30 percent of the population is Muslim (and expected to exceed 50 percent by 2050), and in Cyprus and Montenegro (Pew Research Center 2015). In general, Islam was established in these countries, and in some parts of Russia, centuries ago.

A small but growing number of Muslims also live in Western European countries, such as Austria, Belgium, Denmark, France, Germany, Italy, the Netherlands, Spain, Switzerland, and the United Kingdom (Sawe 2018). In general, Muslims have immigrated to these countries more recently (during the last century or so). The Muslim population in Europe is expected to increase from about 6 percent to about 10 percent overall, mostly due to immigration and to a relatively higher birth rate for Muslims (Hackett 2017).

In addition to the issues of sexism faced by women in many religions, Muslim women may also encounter Islamophobia (intolerance of Muslims) and be caught between secular and religious laws in non-Muslim-majority countries.

Judaism

The significance of Jews in Europe is greater than their small numbers indicate. Jewish history includes centuries of migration, settlement, integration, forced relocations, and persecution. In the last century, their numbers were decimated by the Holocaust (the genocide of Jews and other groups) and by immigration to Israel after its establishment in 1948 (Lipka 2015).

The only countries where Jewish populations increased between 1933 and 2015 were Denmark, France, Spain, Sweden, and Switzerland (mostly due to immigration from North Africa). Today, the largest populations of Jews in Europe are in France, Germany, the Russian Federation, and the United Kingdom (Brilliant Maps 2017).

In addition to the issues of sexism faced by women in many religions, Jewish women in general may face anti-Semitism (intolerance of Jews). Orthodox Jewish women may also experience greater limits on their participation in religious roles and especially strict interpretations of their roles as wives, mothers, and homemakers.

Ethnic/Indigenous Religions and New Religions

In many countries, small communities observe ancient ethnic/Indigenous religions that have been handed down from generation to generation; these are generically called "pagan." (*Pagan* means "pre-Christian" or "non-Christian," but it has negative connotations, such as "uncivilized" or "primitive." Some find the term offensive, and others are working to reclaim it with positive connotations.)

Other groups try to reconstruct ancient traditions that have died out or to create similar new traditions; they are often called neo-pagans. Because ancient religions were transmitted orally and were often repressed or destroyed by other traditions, and because modern life is profoundly different from life in ancient times, it can be hard to distinguish between pagan and neo-pagan, so the terms are sometimes used synonymously.

Although ethnic/Indigenous religions varied greatly depending on the climate, the resources people depended on for survival, and the values of the particular peoples in each place, there were some similarities. Ethnic/ Indigenous religions tended to be polytheistic (recognizing a number of deities, both female and male), centered around nature, animist (perceiving a spirit or a soul in all things, including people, animals, plants, and places), and pantheistic (perceiving the sacred in all things). They also often included veneration for ancestors and sometimes a belief in reincarnation (the return of the soul in a new body). Many of the new and reconstructed religions also embody these traits.

Sami Animism/Shamanism

Animism/shamanism is the religion of the hunting and herding Sami people of northern Norway, Sweden, Finland, and parts of Russia. Sami beliefs included polytheism (including Mother, Father, Son, and Daughter deities), animism, pantheism, belief in animal spirits, and an ongoing connection between the living and the dead facilitated by shamans (*noaidi*). The Sami people experienced discrimination, including the loss of their lands, language, and religion. Today, most belong to Evangelical Lutheran or Orthodox Churches. However, they continue to advocate for cultural equality, including preservation of their language and access to their livelihood, reindeer herding (Holloway n.d.).

Romuva

Romuva is a revitalization of the ancient pagan practices of Lithuania. Some say these beliefs have been handed down in an unbroken line; others consider them reconstructed. Romuva includes a belief in the sanctity of nature, a male god of thunder (Perkūnas) and a female mother sun goddess (Saule), and ancestor worship. Romuva was repressed during the communist era, but it was recognized as a "nontraditional" religion in Lithuania in 1995. About 0.2 percent of the Lithuanian population identifies as Romuva (Žemaitis 2018).

Ásatrú

Ásatrú is a revival in Iceland of the ancient Nordic religion as described in the epic *Eddas* (heroic stories and poems written down in the 1200s CE) (Religion Facts 2016a). It is described as a religion of peace, including a reverence for nature and "equality and respect for human rights, especially LGBT rights" (Helgason 2015). Ásatrú includes deities that may be familiar, such as Thor, Odin, and Freyja, but it distinguishes itself from neo-Nazi groups who use some of its imagery and from portrayals of the religion in popular media. Ásatrúarfélagið, the Pagan Association of Iceland, has over four thousand members (1.2 percent of the population) (Iceland Magazine 2018).

Wicca

Wicca is a new religion that was developed in England by Gerald Gardner in the 1940s. It is based on a combination of occult, esoteric, and magical practices. Wicca is polytheistic, with a special emphasis on the Goddess. Wiccans mark the phases of the moon, solstices, and equinoxes with rituals. They distinguish their magic from Satanism. As with Ásatrú,

The summer solstice is the longest day of the year. At Stonehenge, in England, stones align with the rising sun on the solstice, and neo-pagans gather on that day to celebrate life and growth as well as to acknowledge movement toward winter. (Production351/Dreamstime.com)

THE VENUS OF WILLENDORF: ENIGMA

The Venus of Willendorf (Austria) is one of the earliest-known figures of the human body, dating from around 25,000 BCE. The handheld limestone figure is famous for her enormously abundant body, with curvaceous breasts, belly, buttocks, and thighs.

What does she mean? Since she is "prehistoric," we have no written accounts. Early archeologists named her Venus (after the Roman fertility goddess). Others have speculated she was a mother goddess, the ideal survivor in a frigid climate (due to her body fat), a pornographic icon, or a self-portrait.

Little is known about who carved her or why. We can only be sure that someone devoted time, energy, and skill to creating this figure that could be carried along in a harsh environment by a people with few possessions.

Janet Lockhart

Wicca emphasizes peace and respect. Their ethical code of "if it harm none, do as ye will" is based on internal authority rather than a religious text.

In addition to the issues of sexism faced by women in many religions, women in ethnic/Indigenous and new religions may also face discrimination based on their ethnicity or social class as well as their gender and the lack of societal acceptance or legal status of their practices as a "real" religion.

Nonreligious (Secular)

Religious commitment is generally lower in Western Europe than in Eastern Europe. A plurality identify themselves as nonreligious in Belgium, Denmark, Finland, France, Germany, Iceland, Ireland, Luxembourg, the Netherlands, Norway, Spain, Sweden, Switzerland, and the United Kingdom (Pew Research Center 2018). A few Eastern European countries have a plurality of nonreligious people, including Estonia, Hungary, Latvia, and Russia. One country, the Czech Republic, has a majority (72 percent) nonreligious population (Pew Research Center 2017b).

In most of Europe, "nones" are the second-largest religious group (Bullard 2016). Nonreligious people are diverse, but most are young (ages sixteen to twenty-nine). A majority of young people identify as "no religion" in Belgium, the Czech Republic, Denmark, Estonia, Finland, France, Hungary, the Netherlands, Norway, Spain, Sweden, and the United Kingdom and nearly half in Russia and Switzerland (Sherwood 2018). More of the openly atheist are male (although this could be related to a greater freedom to talk about their nonbelief) (Bullard 2016). Women, especially poor women, tend to be more religious (Pew Research Center 2016), whereas women who work paid jobs may be less so (Bullard 2016). In addition to the issues of sexism faced by women in many religions, nonreligious women may face discrimination from the dominant religious traditions in their countries.

There are some differences between secular countries and religious ones. With some exceptions (e.g., some of the Catholic European countries), secular countries are richer than religious ones. Lower levels of religious adherence are also associated with higher levels of personal income or higher levels of education (Noack 2015). Research shows that secularism comes *before* economic growth, not the other way around (Ruck 2018b).

General indicators of well-being also rate secular countries well. Save the Children Federation's (2015) "Mother's Index" showed Norway, Finland, Iceland, Denmark, and Sweden (all with secular pluralities) as the five best countries in the world to be a mother based on maternal and child health and the educational, economic, and political status of women. U.S. News & World Report's "Best Countries for Women" (2019) gave six of the top seven slots to Sweden, Denmark, Norway, the Netherlands, Finland, and Switzerland based on human rights, gender equality, income equality, progress, and safety.

Does this mean that all secular countries are good for women and all religious countries bad? Not necessarily. Research has shown that something besides religion makes a bigger difference in the well-being of women (and men): tolerance for differences and respect for individual rights, including acceptance of divorce, homosexuality, abortion, and jobs for women (Ruck 2018a). When these factors are in place, economic and other measures of well-being rise, regardless of the country or religion. Some researchers suggest that religious countries do not have to fall behind economically or in other measures of well-being. If religious institutions use their resources to advocate for tolerance and individual rights, they can be at the forefront of positive change for women and for all.

ISSUES OF RELIGION FOR WOMEN IN EUROPE

The Impact of Christian Missionaries on the Colonial Project

As part of the Old World, Europe has been inhabited since prehistoric times. It has seen waves of immigration (groups moving into an area), emigration (groups moving out), and colonization, ancient and modern. Europe has been Christianized for hundreds of years, so colonialism is older in Europe than in other parts of the world (e.g., Oceania).

Ancient Europeans followed a variety of religions, now generally called pagan, as previously discussed. Jews also entered Europe during the early days of Roman rule (several hundred years BCE), first in the Mediterranean islands, Greece, and Italy and then migrating to Southern and Central Europe.

By around 100 CE, the ethnic pagan peoples of Southern, Central, and Western Europe had been colonized by the Roman Empire's cultural and religious ways (perhaps confusingly, the Romans are also called "pagan" because they were "pre-Christian" and "non-Christian"). Depending on their circumstances, they were pushed into remote areas, destroyed, forced to assimilate (integrate) the Roman pantheon of gods and goddesses into their own beliefs, or converted to the Roman religion.

In the early 300s, the Roman emperor Constantine made Christianity the state religion of the empire. After the empire fell (between 400 and 500), Christianity remained, and over hundreds of years, it spread throughout Europe (the ruler of Lithuania, the last country to be Christianized, was converted in 1387). Again, the inhabitants, including Jews and pagans, withdrew to remote areas, were expelled, practiced their beliefs in secret, were destroyed, were assimilated, or converted to Christianity.

Christianity also interacted with Islam, which from the seventh to the twentieth century ebbed and flowed in parts of Southern and Western Europe, the countries on the Balkan Peninsula, and Russia. Some of these countries are still majority Muslim, as previously discussed, and some are now majority Christian, particularly Orthodox Christian.

During the communist era in Eastern Europe, religion in general was greatly repressed. After the Soviet Bloc dissolved in 1989, religion returned to some (but not all) of the former communist countries, including Russia, Poland, and Lithuania.

Today, Europe as a whole is widely Christian. As such, Christianity's influence on the continent, and on women, has been profound. Even countries with secularism as a solid "second religion" feel the effects of Christian influence. We will explore some of these effects as we look at women in religious leadership, gendered religious practices, women's portrayals in sacred texts, the experiences and issues of LGBTQ people, women's experiences as religion intersects with politics, religious violence against women, and women's resistance to religious oppression.

Christianity is not limited to Europe. As you will see in other chapters, the influence of Christianity has flowed via settlers, conquerors, missionaries, and explorers to much of the rest of the world, deeply influencing women's (and men's) lives.

Women in Religious Leadership

Women are often excluded from serving in the highest church offices. For example, women cannot be ordained as priests in Orthodox Christianity or Roman Catholicism. Many Catholics and Orthodox Christians (especially in Russia) agree with this exclusion (Pew Research Center 2017b). However, some scholars say women served as deaconesses, priests, and even bishops during the first centuries of Christianity, so the refusal to ordain women is due to patriarchal traditions, not Scripture (McClain 2018; Patheos n.d.-h.).

WOMEN'S ORDINATION WORLDWIDE

Although the Roman Catholic Church stands firm against women's ordination, there *are* about 150 ordained women Catholic priests worldwide.

Collaborating with other associations, Women's Ordination Worldwide (WOW) works to ordain women who are called to serve by God, their consciences, and their communities. Although the ordinations are validly performed by bishops in the line of apostolic succession, the church does not recognize them. It has excommunicated some of the women and forced others to keep their ordinations secret.

WOW affirms there are no scriptural grounds for refusing to ordain women. Its goals are to "free the Church from the sin of sexism and heal divisions that exist because of it" (Women's Ordination Worldwide n.d.).

Janet Lockhart

Women's Ordination Worldwide. n.d. "Membership in Women's Ordination Worldwide." Accessed September 10, 2019. http://womensordinationcampaign.org.

However, there *have* been Catholic women priests. Under communist religious repression in the former Czechoslovakia, a shortage of priests to minister to women (e.g., in prisons) led bishops to secretly ordain seven women. After Soviet repression ended, however, the church did not recognize their ordinations. The women tried to keep their identities secret, and none of them continued as priests (Tarjanyi 2001).

There are also women Catholic priests today, but they are not officially recognized by the church. In fact, most of them have been excommunicated. Nevertheless, since they have been ordained via bishops, within apostolic succession, they practice as priests within their churches (Women's Ordination Worldwide 2019).

In general, Protestant denominations, such as the various Evangelical Lutheran Churches, are inclusive of women in high leadership. In Eastern Europe, the Evangelical Lutheran Church of Estonia has ordained women since 1967. The Church in Finland has had one female bishop, and the Churches of Denmark and Iceland have had a number of female bishops (World Council of Churches 2019; Evangelical Lutheran Church of Finland n.d.-b). The Church of Sweden has a woman archbishop (Sutherland 2019).

The United Free Church of Scotland, the United Reformed Church, the Presbyterian Church in Ireland, the Free Church of England, and the Methodist Church in Great Britain ordain women (Religious Tolerance n.d.; Methodist Church 2014). In Switzerland, the Unitarian Universalists ordain female ministers (European Unitarian Universalists n.d.). In Germany, the Pentecostal Church allows ordination of women, and the

---

"POPE JOAN"?

Some Catholics tell stories of Joan, a woman pope. Different versions say she reigned in the ninth century under the name Pope John VIII; that she brought her Benedictine monk lover with her to Rome, where she became pope; or that she became pope in the twelfth century but, being pregnant at the time, was discovered and murdered when she went into labor.

In the Middle Ages, Joan's existence was taken as history. Today, scholarly sources place Pope Joan in the category of legend, but her story lives on in contemporary Catholicism, illustrating that many people crave the presence of the feminine in their conception of the holy.

Janet Lockhart

Evangelical Church ordains women and has female bishops. The Evangelical Methodist Church in Germany elected its first female bishop in 2005 (People of the United Methodist Church 2019).

The Anglican Church has been divided over the ordination of women as priests and bishops. Many churches began ordaining women as priests in 1993 (Patheos n.d.-a); there are now women bishops in the Church of England, the Church of Ireland, the Scottish Episcopal Church, and the Church in Wales. However, the decision is left to each individual diocese, and not all ordain women. The Evangelical Lutheran Church in Latvia ordained women at one time, but in 2016, it revoked this permission (*Baltic Times* 2016).

In Islam, there is no central governing body or formal ordination process; imams have usually "completed extensive theological studies and have proven themselves strong leaders" (Human Rights Campaign 2018c). There is disagreement among scholars as to whether women should be allowed to lead prayers or serve as imams. There are female imams in Belgium, Denmark (some of them use the playful term "imamas"), France, Germany, Turkey, and the United Kingdom (Iqbal 2018; Miller Llana 2017; Taylor 2018; Yahmid 2008). They work to create more inclusive spaces, fight Islamophobia in Western European countries, follow their religious calling, and help women reclaim their space in mosques. Sherin Khankan, the imam of the first women's mosque in Denmark, says letting women lead prayers is not challenging the Qur'an; it is "going back to the essence of Islam" (Taylor 2018).

Reform and Conservative Judaism allow women to be ordained as rabbis and cantors (chanters/prayer leaders). Orthodox Judaism does not allow women as rabbis, but it recently created an alternate position for women, "albeit with a distinct title, Maharat," an acronym of the first letters of the Hebrew words for a female leader of Jewish law, spirituality, and Torah (Nadell 2016). The first European woman Maharat was ordained in Poland in 2015.

Many of the new and ethnic/Indigenous religions of Europe, such as Wicca and Romuva, promote women to lead rituals and serve in high leadership positions, such as the high priestess (*krivè*) of Romuva (Parliament of the World's Religions 2016).

In general, women have greater access to church leadership roles at lower levels. Orthodox Christian women may perform important work as the wives of priests, and some female scholars teach male seminarians (International Orthodox Theological Association 2019). Orthodox Christian and Catholic women can serve as nuns (working as educators or caring for the sick, displaced, or homeless).

In Bulgaria, the Orthodox Church does ordain women as deacons (O'Connell 2019). The Roman Catholic Church does not do so, and there is debate as to whether women will ever gain this right. The Anglican Church began ordaining women deacons in the 1800s.

The Evangelical Lutheran Churches of Finland and Iceland have a large number of women as pastors and vicars (World Council of Churches 2019). In 2018, the Evangelical Lutheran Church of Saxony (in Germany) passed a religious law aiming for "gender equality in participation" in church governing bodies (Lutheran World Federation 2018).

In many denominations, women are choir directors, lectors (readers), parish educators, lay ministers, or members of local church councils. They also frequently perform other important but unacknowledged work in the upkeep and cleaning of churches, preparing and serving food, leading committees, doing charity work, providing hospitality, and making sure things run smoothly. This work is so vital that in May 2019, German Catholic women staged a weeklong boycott of voluntary church work—"disobedient nonservice"—to call attention to the church's failure to respond to clergy sex-abuse scandals and the refusal to ordain women. One bishop encouraged empathy for women's "very deep wound—that they in the church do not feel accepted in relation to their efforts" (DW 2019).

Gendered Religious Practices

Women and men are often treated differently in religious services and in life outside of church. Orthodox Christian, Mennonite, Unitarian, and Orthodox Jewish women and men sit separately during services. Orthodox Jewish women do not generally act as religious leaders. Muslim women also worship separately from men and may be expected to stay out of a mosque during menstruation or after childbirth (Taylor 2018; Miller Llana 2017). In contrast, Reform and Conservative Jewish services are "completely gender-egalitarian." Unitarian Universalist and Reform Jewish services include "family seating" (rather than separation by gender) (Patheos n.d.-g).

Similarly, religions often treat women and men differently in their family life. Marriage is generally considered a sacrament or a gift from God and intended to be lifelong. The Orthodox Christian Church allows divorce under certain circumstances, but it must be granted by the church, not civil authorities. Divorced people are allowed to remarry (Pew Research Center 2017a). Catholics are forbidden to divorce, although it does happen in practice; divorced Catholics may not remarry in the church as long as the former spouse is alive.

Protestant denominations that allow divorce, at least in some circumstances, include the Anglican Church, the Evangelical Lutheran Church in Sweden, the Evangelical Lutheran Church in Finland, and the Presbyterian Church of Scotland (Religion Facts 2016b).

Islam allows divorce, but there are fewer conditions for when women can initiate divorce than men, who can do so without giving a cause. Divorce can also be initiated by mutual agreement.

In the past, Orthodox Judaism has invoked strict scriptural terms, with wives subject to divorce at their husbands' whim. However, rabbis have often intervened by specifying appropriate grounds for divorce and introducing marriage contracts that protect women (Patheos n.d.-f).

Polygamy (having more than one wife or husband at a time) is forbidden in Christianity and Judaism. Islam allows *polygyny* (marriage of one man to more than one woman) in limited circumstances (Religion Library, n.d.-d). Polygyny is legal only in Sweden, Switzerland, and the Netherlands and only if an already polygynous family emigrates from another country. *Polyandry*, the marriage of one woman to more than one man, is forbidden in Islam and is also illegal in all European countries.

Religions vary greatly in regard to the appropriate expression of sexuality. In Orthodox Christianity and Catholicism, sexual expression is limited to heterosexual marriage. Premarital sex, extramarital sex, homosexual relationships, and, in Catholicism, certain specific sexual acts are forbidden. Adventists, Anglicans, and the Methodist Conference in Great Britain also emphasize heterosexual monogamy, urging unmarried people (gay or straight) to be celibate. In Sweden, the Evangelical Lutheran Church accepts unmarried couples living together and having children (Sutherland 2019). In Finland, the Evangelical Lutheran Church forbids extramarital sex but is somewhat more accepting of premarital sex.

In Islam, sexual expression within marriage is encouraged, for men and women. Similarly, in Jewish traditions, sex within marriage is generally considered natural and good (Patheos n.d.-b, n.d.-d, n.d.-g).

Most religions support the raising of children within marriage; however, there are differences in details. Most Orthodox Christians say that women do have an obligation to society to bear children; however, they differ over whether women should stay home and take care of children and whether a wife should always obey her husband. In general, Orthodox women are more supportive of women's rights than Orthodox men (Pew Research Center 2017a).

Orthodox Jewish women's roles are traditional and include homemaking, child-rearing, and carrying out religious observations in the family's home. Similarly, marriage and childbearing are highly encouraged in Islam. Being a homemaker is valued; however, Islamic teachings do not forbid women from working and receiving wages.

Family planning practices also vary widely. In Orthodox Christianity, contraception was originally banned, but in modern times, it has been approved for use within marriage. Abortion is not sanctioned by the church under any circumstances (Patheos n.d.-c). However, individual Orthodox Christians' opinions of abortion vary widely, from "it should be legal in almost all circumstances" to "it should be illegal in almost all circumstances" (Pew Research Center 2017a).

In the Catholic Church, the only contraception permitted is abstinence, which can include the use of natural family planning (also called the rhythm method), when a couple abstains from sex during the time in the woman's menstrual cycle when she is most likely to conceive. Nevertheless, many Catholics do use contraception (Davies 2014). Abortion is forbidden, and women who have one may be excommunicated (Clowes 2020).

Protestant denominations vary. Contraceptive use was once forbidden in Anglicanism, but now both liberals and conservatives generally accept it (Patheos n.d.-a). The Evangelical Lutheran Church in Sweden allows abortion (Sutherland 2019), but the Church in Latvia forbids it.

The Qur'an is silent on contraception; however, Islamic laws do allow some methods if they are mutually agreed upon by the couple, are not permanent (such as vasectomies or tubal ligations), and do not interfere with the development of the fetus after conception. Early-term abortions may be allowed; late-term abortions are forbidden unless the mother's life is at risk (Huda 2019).

Women in Sacred Texts

Religious texts can serve as roadblocks as well as resources for women (Fortune and Enger 2005). Individual passages are often pulled out of context and used to justify both misogyny and liberation for women.

Feminist scholars stress the importance of examining religious texts in historical context. "Much in the literature of religions is descriptive of the way things *were*, not prescriptive of the way things *ought to be*" (Maguire and Shaikh 2007; emphasis added). In other words, understanding the attitudes and values of the time and the people who wrote down and translated their words can help clarify the intention of the figures who first spoke them.

In 2018, a group of eighteen female Protestant and Catholic theologians developed "A Women's Bible" that examines passages traditionally portraying women as weak or subordinate and reinterprets them in emancipatory terms. Inspired by Elizabeth Cady Stanton's "The Woman's Bible," the editors emphasized placing the passages in historical context, not reading them literally. Rather than "throwing out" the Bible, they say its themes are relevant to women today, including the body, seduction, motherhood, and subordination. According to editor Lauriane Savoy, "Feminist values and reading the Bible are not incompatible" (Tschannen 2019).

Belgian social scientist Ghaliya Djelloul encourages Muslim women to reexamine the holy texts of Islam while keeping gender equality and the effects of colonial history in mind (Djelloul 2018). At the Ibn Rushd-Goethe Mosque in Berlin, "the Koran is read and interpreted from a modern perspective" (Heynders 2018). In Turkey, a country that has long been open to "modernizing," Ankara University's School of Theology has provided training of several hundred women as *vaizes* (senior imams) to explain the "equality, justice, and human rights guaranteed by an accurate interpretation of the Koran" (Piggot 2008).

Scottish Jewish scholar Avivah Gottlieb Zornberg famously interprets the "repressed unconscious of the Torah," emphasizing the often overlooked aspects of desire and the erotic, which also come from the divine, expressed in the texts (Grubin 2004).

Many neo-pagan groups, such as Wiccans, have produced works of scholarship as well as guidebooks and compilations of rituals, songs, stories, and the like. Many of these emphasize the roles of women as empowered, powerful, and spiritually equal to men.

LGBTQ People and Issues in Religions

People who differ from the social and sexual roles assigned to women and men may be considered disruptive or dangerous. The experiences of LGBTQ people are affected by the doctrines of their faith, practices of their local churches and clergy, and factors such as race, social class, ability, and the laws and cultures of the countries they live in. Generally, Western Europeans are more liberal on LGBTQ issues, such as same-sex marriage, while Eastern Europeans are more conservative (Pew Research Center 2018).

Most Orthodox Christian countries are quite rejecting of homosexuality, with majorities in Belarus, Bosnia & Herzegovina, Bulgaria, Moldova, Romania, Russia, Serbia, and Ukraine saying that society should not accept it. Greece is an exception, with slightly over half saying society should be accepting of homosexuality (Pew Research Center 2017a). However, even in Greece, the Greek Orthodox Church considers homosexual acts sinful (Human Rights Campaign 2018b).

Although not officially sanctioned, individual Catholic churches and members may welcome LGBTQ individuals, accept gay clergy, and support same-sex unions. The Catechism says that homosexual orientation is not a sin and that homosexual people should be treated with respect. However, it also describes homosexuality as "intrinsically immoral" and "objectively disordered," and it requires homosexual people to remain chaste (celibate) (Human Rights Campaign 2018f). The Vatican has excluded at least one transgender man from serving as a godfather, saying that he "did not possess the requisite of leading a life according to the faith and to the position of godfather" (San Martín 2015).

Protestant denominations vary. The Methodist Church of Great Britain welcomes LGBTQ people, whereas Seventh-day Adventist Churches believe that sex other than heterosexual monogamy is "contrary to God's plan." In 2017, the Anglican Church voted to welcome the participation of transgender people (Church of England 2018). In general, the Evangelical Lutheran churches in Northern and Western European countries are open and affirming to the membership of LGBTQ people, the recognition of same-sex marriages, and the ordination of women and LGBTQ people (Patheos n.d.-e).

"Islamic individuals and institutions fall along a wide spectrum," with some welcoming LGBTQ people and others rejecting them to the point of violence (Human Rights Campaign 2018c). The Qur'an is often interpreted as including only male and female gender identities and heterosexual relationships. However, "no verse of the Qur'an gives a legal punishment for either homoerotic inclinations or behaviors" (Ahmed and Mendoza 2017). There may be more cultural support for men's sexual expression than women's, however.

"Transgender men and women are recognized and accepted in many Islamic cultures around the world." Although they may still face discrimination, they are more likely to be accepted than homosexual men or lesbians (Human Rights Campaign 2018c). There are inclusive mosques in the United Kingdom and Germany (Iqbal 2018; Heynders 2018).

Judaism also includes a wide variety of attitudes toward LGBTQ people. In the United Kingdom, Reform Judaism and Liberal Judaism welcome the participation of LGBT individuals. Conservative Judaism, which includes politically conservative and liberal members, is divided over LGBT issues (Got Questions 2019). Orthodox Judaism believes gender identity is based on a person's biology at birth; therefore, transgender people are not accepted.

Ásatrú is accepting of people of all races, cultural backgrounds, genders, and sexual orientations (Iceland Magazine 2019). The original Wicca of Gerald Gardner was focused on heterosexual relationships, and some feel that heterosexuality is still the norm. The Dianic tradition of Wicca is exclusively for lesbians, and there has been controversy in various circles about acceptance of transgender people. With no central sacred text and the "do as ye will" ethic, individual covens (Wiccan groups) make their own decisions. In general, the religion today is open and accepting to people of diverse sexual identities (Wiginton 2019).

Same-sex marriages are opposed by the majority of people in almost all the Central and Eastern European countries. The Orthodox Christian Church forbids them, and they are illegal in all of these countries, except Greece, Estonia, and Cyprus, which allow domestic partnerships or civil unions (Pew Research Center 2017a, 53; Lipka and Masci 2019, 1).

Catholic-majority countries with legal same-sex marriages include Austria (the most recent to legalize it, in 2019), Belgium, France, Ireland, Luxembourg, Malta, Portugal, and Spain (Lipka and Masci 2019). Germany and the Netherlands (the first country to legalize it, in 2001), where Catholics are a plurality, also allow same-sex marriages (Felter and Renwick 2019). Andorra, Croatia, Italy, Liechtenstein, Northern Ireland, and Slovenia allow same-sex civil unions or domestic partnerships (Lipka and Masci 2019).

Protestant-majority countries with legal same-sex marriages include Denmark, Finland, Greenland, Iceland, Norway, and Sweden (Lipka and Masci 2019). The Evangelical Lutheran Churches of Denmark, Iceland, Norway, and Sweden perform same-sex marriages (Sutherland 2019; Zaimov 2016). After years of debate, the Evangelical Lutheran Church of Finland allows same-sex marriages, but individual church leaders decide whether or not to perform them (Evangelical Lutheran Church of Finland n.d.-a). Most Evangelical Lutheran Churches in Germany allow same-sex marriages; the Church in Estonia does not.

Same-sex marriages are legal in the United Kingdom. However, the Anglican Church is divided. In some places they are allowed, as long as the partners are monogamous; in other places, they are condemned as heretical (Patheos n.d.-a). The Methodist Conference in Great Britain allows the blessing of same-sex unions, and Quakers in Great Britain approved same-sex marriage in 2009 (Butt 2009). The Mennonite Church in the Netherlands has allowed same-sex marriages since 2001, but the church is divided over the issue elsewhere.

Many Muslims interpret the Qur'an to mean that marriage is only for heterosexual people, but individual mosques and imams are free to decide. National and cultural differences (e.g., between Denmark, where same-sex marriages are legal, and Bosnia and Herzegovina, where they are illegal) may affect individual imams' ability to perform them (LGBTI Equal Rights Association for Western Balkans and Turkey 2016).

Reform and Liberal Judaism conduct same-sex marriages using the *Brit Ahava* ("Covenant of Love") ceremony (Simons and Simons 2016; Human Rights Campaign 2018e), and some Conservative Jewish synagogues perform them (Human Rights Campaign 2018a). Orthodox Judaism forbids homosexual relationships and same-sex marriages (Human Rights Campaign 2018d).

Ásatrúarfélagið priests in Iceland perform same-sex marriages (Iceland Magazine 2019). Many Wiccan covens perform handfastings (marriages) for same-sex couples.

Openly LGBTQ people are not ordained in the Eastern Orthodox and Catholic Churches; however, some gay men may be accepted as Catholic priests (Human Rights Campaign 2018f).

The Evangelical Lutheran Churches in the Netherlands, Norway, and Sweden ordain gay and lesbian clergy (New Europe 2007). The Church in Finland has had at least one pastor who was transgender (Yle 2012). In Estonia, gay pastors can be ordained, but they must remain celibate. In Latvia, LGBTQ people may not be ordained. The Methodist Church of Great Britain allows LGBTQ clergy, as do many Lutheran Churches in Germany and the Reformed Churches of Germany and Switzerland (United Church of Christ 2002).

As there is no formal ordination process in Islam, LGBTQ people with the requisite knowledge and skills may be able to become imams. An openly gay imam founded the first inclusive mosque in Paris (Evening Standard 2016).

Reform and Liberal Judaism ordain LGBT people as rabbis and cantors. Conservative Judaism is divided over whether to accept LGBTQ people as clergy, and Orthodox Judaism forbids the ordination or employment of openly LGBT clergy (Got Questions 2019).

Women at the Intersection of Religion and Politics

Where religion and politics intersect (overlap), women may have to choose between obeying their religious convictions or the laws of their country. They may need the protection of laws against harmful religious practices or against harm from individuals acting under the shield of religion. They may work for greater acceptance of their religion in a country to which they have immigrated. Or they may lobby to influence public policy in an area where they disagree with the leadership of their religion.

Covering/Veiling

In public, Muslim women are often expected to wear a hijab (a head scarf), a niqab (a covering of the hair and lower face), or a burqa (a covering of the whole body) as an expression of modesty (BBC Newsround 2018). After the events of September 11, 2001, these coverings took on negative connotations. In many places, people identified as Muslim were labeled "terrorists." Countries that included Austria, Belgium, Bulgaria, Denmark, France, Germany, Great Britain, Italy, the Netherlands, Russia, Spain, Switzerland, and Turkey considered or passed laws banning clothing that hides the wearer's identity—which included burqas and niqabs (BBC News 2018).

The laws were intended to increase public safety by helping to identify people who carried out terrorist acts, but many also saw them as expressions of Islamophobia. They also forced Muslim women to choose whether to cover themselves in public (as their religion/culture might require), to bare their faces in public (as the law required), or not to appear in public. According to imam Sherin Khankan, "It's important to fight for any women's right to wear the hijab or not, to wear the niqab or not—if it's her own choice and her own free will" (Miller Llana 2017).

Abuses by Clergy

Several decades ago, the Catholic Church was caught in a scandal over priests and bishops abusing children in their dioceses. More recently, it emerged that abusers were also targeting vulnerable women, including nuns. Incidents were reported in Austria, Belgium, Britain, France, Germany, Ireland, Italy, the Netherlands, Poland, and Switzerland. In 2019, Pope Francis acknowledged that abuse had occurred and that it might be ongoing (Bell, Vandoorne, and Smith-Spark 2019).

The abuse included sexual, physical, psychological, and spiritual harm, causing serious, long-term effects for the survivors. One former nun described it as "a murder inside your heart and of your soul" (Bell 2019). The effects can be compounded when survivors are not believed, are blamed or punished for reporting the abuse, or are silenced. Offenders are frequently moved to new districts, with no apparent consequences for their offenses.

As they try to come to terms with their experiences, some survivors report the abuse to police and try to press criminal charges. Others bring civil suits, which may run up against statutes of limitations (abuse survivors often take many years to come to terms, report, and try to get justice against their abusers). Inspired by the #MeToo movement, women are talking about experiences they may have kept secret for years (DeGeorge 2019; Bell, Vandoorne, and Smith-Spark 2019).

Within the church, some national conferences and local congregations have created programs to help sisters in training recognize abusive behaviors, avoid vulnerable situations, and report instances of abuse (DeGeorge 2019). In March 2019, the entire newsroom staff of "Women Church World" (a monthly insert included in *L'Osservatore Romano*, the Vatican's newspaper), resigned over pushback they received from their reports about abuses (Harlan and Pitrelli 2019).

In general, the Vatican has not acknowledged the root of the abuse issue. In February 2019, Pope Francis publicly acknowledged that it was a "problem" (Bell, Vandoorne, and Smith-Spark 2019). In May 2019, he decreed mandatory reporting in cases of known or suspected abuse. However, each diocese is responsible for developing its own reporting system (by 2020); reports will be made to church superiors rather than civil authorities (police), and admissions of abuse made during confession will not be reported. Although these changes will help victims/survivors, support groups are still saying abusers should be fired, reports should be made to police, and files on abusers should be accessible to the public (France 24 2019).

The Vatican has not yet addressed *prevention* of clergy abuse. Insiders say this will require a fundamental shift. Feminist theologian Mary Hunt says the church hierarchy, male domination, and treatment of women as second-class citizens must change: as it is, it constitutes a deep and widespread "spiritual abuse" (DeGeorge 2019).

Religious Violence against Women

Violence against women in Europe, as in the world, is widespread. Violence happens in private and in public. It can be verbal, psychological, emotional, physical, sexual, economic, or a combination of these.

Religious violence has been done against women by members of their own faiths and by members of other faiths and secular institutions. Verbal and psychological violence take the form of negative messages about women, gendered language, and male imagery in sacred texts. Sermons and everyday language also contain negative messages about women's worth, abilities, and reasons for being.

Religious violence can be done against groups, such as terrorist actions, or against individuals, such as verbal or physical aggression in public places or on public transportation. However, the most prevalent form of violence against women is domestic violence. The Istanbul Convention defines *domestic violence* as "all acts of physical, sexual, psychological or economic violence that occur within the family or domestic unit or between former or current spouses or partners, whether or not the perpetrator shares or has shared the same residence with the victim" (Council of Europe 2011). In fact, many more women are injured or killed by domestic violence than by terrorist attacks (Lidia 2018). In many cases, violence against women is sanctioned by the very institutions that should be their sources of protection and comfort: sacred texts, clergy, churches, and religious communities.

Violence against women is not limited to one particular religion. Rates of domestic violence may be quite different between countries with the same majority religion. For example, in 2016, Greece, a majority Orthodox Christian country, had a 19 percent lifetime rate of physical or sexual intimate partner violence against women, whereas in Moldova, another majority Orthodox country, the rate was 46 percent. The rate in Iceland, a majority Evangelical Lutheran country, was 22 percent, but it was 32 percent in Denmark (for comparison, the level for women worldwide is 35 percent) (UN Women 2016). Clearly, violence against women is a pervasive and persistent problem across religions.

On top of pervasive sexism, violence against women can become more likely based on intersecting factors such as "racism, xenophobia [hatred of people from other countries], homophobia as well as discrimination based on age, disability, ethnicity or religion. Women and girls with migrant backgrounds, undocumented migrant women, refugee women and asylum seekers, women and girls with disabilities, lesbian, transgender or intersex women, Roma women and girls, young women and elderly women, homeless women, black women, Muslim women" may all be more vulnerable to gender-based violence (European Disability Forum 2017).

Religion can be a force either to protect women from violence or to make them more vulnerable to it. In Russia, at least one Orthodox Christian Church has provided a shelter for women fleeing domestic violence (Monaghan 2015). However, when Russian president Vladimir Putin signed a 2017 law decriminalizing family violence, the Russian Orthodox Church supported it, saying opposition to domestic violence is an attempt to impose liberal Western values—a "gender ideology"—on Russia (Cauterucci 2017; Zezulin 2017). The church even opposed programs to prevent domestic violence, saying that traditional family relationships are based on male authority and female subservience (Cauterucci 2017; Zezulin 2017).

In Latvia, the heads of the Roman Catholic, Evangelical Lutheran, Latvian Orthodox, and Union of Baptist Churches all opposed ratifying the Council of Europe's Istanbul Convention to prevent and eliminate violence against women. Although Latvia has a high rate of domestic violence (32 percent), it opposed the convention on several grounds, saying that Article 14, related to education, would require children to "deny their sex" in school and that (as in the Russian example) it would change society based on "gender ideology" (Mustillo 2018).

Supporters of the convention suggest that religious opposition is mostly related to the convention's Article 12, which requires countries to work toward eliminating "prejudices, customs, traditions and all other practices which are based on the idea of the inferiority of women or on stereotyped roles for women and men" (Council of Europe 2011). This would require religious leaders to openly look at doctrines that present women as subordinate and gender roles as biologically/spiritually determined and unalterable; therefore, they want to keep the issue silent (Mustillo 2018).

As of July 2019, Latvia had not ratified the Istanbul Convention. Other countries that have not yet ratified the convention include Armenia, Bulgaria, the Czech Republic, Hungary, Liechtenstein, Lithuania, the Republic of Moldova, the Russian Federation, the Slovak Republic, Ukraine, and the United Kingdom (Council of Europe 2019).

Women's Resistance to Religious Oppression

Just as religious oppression affects women differently in different areas, women also resist differently, depending on their challenges and the available resources. Some work within established institutions, such as their local faith communities, to advocate for needed resources or to make worship spaces more inclusive. Others collaborate within their regional faith communities or across denominations to change policies and examine doctrine. Still others work outside established institutions by creating new religious organizations, or they work within nonprofit/nongovernmental organizations.

Women in the Orthodox Church Group

As Orthodox Christianity considers holy tradition extremely important (Patheos n.d.-c), efforts to make changes must proceed slowly and with careful attention to the way questions of doctrine are handled. Women in the Orthodox Church Group, part of the International Orthodox Theological Association, encourages theological scholarship about women's roles in the Orthodox Church, past and present, and supports women's participation in the church's mission. It acknowledges the church's "imperfect record when it comes to its conduct towards women throughout its history" and tries to distinguish between "the liberating message of the Gospel" and "stereotypes of gender inherited from patriarchal societies" (International Orthodox Theological Association 2019). The committee has members in the United Kingdom, Serbia, and Greece.

Catholics for Choice

Internationally, the Catholic Church has a great deal of influence in the education, health care, and political arenas (Vatican City is an independent nation and has Non-Member State Permanent Observer status at the United

Nations). The church uses its influence on public policy-making bodies, such as governments, to support its stance on many issues, including reproductive and sexual behavior and health.

As described elsewhere, church doctrine forbids all sexual acts except those performed within monogamous, heterosexual marriage, and all contraception, except timed abstinence. People who break these restrictions may face obstacles, including lack of information, unavailability of needed services, and shaming or punishment from the church.

Catholics for Choice, a nonprofit organization, challenges some of the historical Catholic teachings about sex and sexuality and emphasizes the also authentically Catholic view that each individual woman's and man's conscience is the "keystone of moral decision making" (Catholics for Choice n.d.). The group advocates family planning, including abortion; safe sex and HIV/AIDS prevention through use of condoms; and religious liberty in making public policy at national and international levels, such as the European Parliament.

Inclusive Mosque Initiative

It may be a common perception that there is no such thing as "Muslim feminism," but some Muslim women design worship spaces that are more inclusive. In 2012, a group of Muslim women in London began the Inclusive Mosque Initiative, a space designed to include Muslims excluded in more traditional mosques: single parents, LGBT individuals, and people with disabilities. "IMI emphasises that it welcomes people 'regardless of religious belief, race, gender, impairments, sexuality or immigration status'" and strives to create peaceful, nonjudgmental places of worship (Iqbal 2018).

Bet Debora

Jewish feminism has a long history in Europe, both before and after World War II. Bet Debora, a group that began in Berlin in 1998, tries to "illuminate the ongoing process of emancipation of Jewish women in Europe" (Bet Debora: Jewish Women's Perspectives n.d.). The group has published journals and produced conferences on themes of gender equality for Jewish women, including participants from Eastern and Western Europe. Its 2019 conference was held in Belgrade, Serbia.

The World Congress: *Keshet Ga'avah* ("Rainbow of Pride")

The World Congress is an international organization based in London that helps smaller groups network, advocates globally, and translates resources. It has held international conferences in Italy, France, and other countries. Its mission is "to be the worldwide voice of Jews of diverse sexual orientations and gender identities (LGBTQIA+)" (World Congress: Keshet Ga'avah 2017).

Kvenna Kirkjan

Kvenna Kirkjan, or "the Women's Church," is an independent group, grounded in feminist theology, within the Icelandic National Evangelical Lutheran Church. The group "preaches what the Bible tells us women about the freedom that we were created to enjoy, talks about God in the feminine gender, encourages the distribution of power, considers new possibilities in service ritual, and uses inclusive language in all its work." Members of the group translate hymns and write new ones with feminist theological elements. They also offer courses on feminist theology (Kvennakirkjan n.d.).

FURTHER READING

Ahmed, Tanvir, and Carolina Mendoza. 2017. "Islamic Sexuality Is More Complicated Than You Might Think." HuffPost, June 24, 2017. https://www.huffpost.com/entry/islamic-sexuality-is-more-complicated-than-you-might-think_b_10616800.

Arnold, Michelle. n.d. "Why Are Eastern Rite Married Men Allowed to Be Ordained Priests?" Catholic Answers. Accessed August 8, 2019. https://www.catholic.com/qa/why-are-eastern-rite-married-men-allowed-to-be-ordained-priests.

Baltic Times. 2016. "Latvian Lutheran Church Officially Bans Women's Ordination." June 4, 2016. https://www.baltictimes.com/latvian_lutheran_church_officially_bans_women_s_ordination/.

BBC News. 2018. "The Islamic Veil across Europe." May 31, 2018. https://www.bbc.com/news/world-europe-13038095.

BBC Newsround. 2018. "What's the Difference between a Hijab, Niqab and Burka?" August 7, 2018. https://www.bbc.co.uk/newsround/24118241.

Bell, Melissa. 2019. "Woman Alleging Abuse by Priest: It's a Murder inside Your Heart." CNN, February 19, 2019. https://www.cnn.com /videos/world/2019/02/19/french-church-abuse-stories-melissa -bell-dnt-cnni-vpx.cnn.

Bell, Melissa, Saskya Vandoorne, and Laura Smith-Spark. 2019. "They Say They Were Sexually Abused by Priests, Then Silenced. Now These Women Are Speaking Out." CNN, February 20, 2019. https://www.cnn.com/2019/02/20/europe/catholic-france-order -women-abuse-intl/index.html.

Bet Debora: Jewish Women's Perspectives. n.d. "History." Accessed July 24, 2019. https://www.bet-debora.net/.

Brilliant Maps. 2017. "Jewish Population of Europe in 1933 and 2015." March 8, 2017. https://brilliantmaps.com/jewish-population-europe/.

Bullard, Gabe. 2016. "The World's Newest Major Religion: No Religion." National Geographic, April 22, 2016. https://news.nationalgeographic .com/2016/04/160422-atheism-agnostic-secular-nones-rising -religion/.

Butt, Riazat. 2009. "Quakers Agree to Same-Sex Marriages (U.K.)." *The Guardian*, July 31, 2009. https://www.theguardian.com/world/2009 /jul/31/quakers-gay-marriage.

Catholics for Choice. n.d. "About Us." Accessed July 24, 2019. http://www .catholicsforchoice.org/about-us/.

Cauterucci, Christina. 2017. "Russia Decriminalized Domestic Violence with Support from the Russian Orthodox Church." Slate, February 8, 2017. https://slate.com/human-interest/2017/02/russia-decriminalized -domestic-violence-with-support-from-the-russian-orthodox -church.html.

Christensen, Christian. n.d. "Religion in Scandinavia: Norse, Christianity, Islam." Accessed January 13, 2021. https://scandinaviafacts.com /religion-in-scandinavia.

Church of England. 2018. "Guidance for Welcoming Transgender People Published." November 12, 2018. https://www.churchofengland.org /more/media-centre/news/guidance-welcoming-transgender -people-published.

Clowes, Brian. 2020. "Does Abortion Really Incur Excommunication?" https://www.hli.org/resources/abortion-and-excommunication/.

Council of Europe. 2011. "Council of Europe Convention on Preventing and Combating Violence against Women and Domestic Violence." April 12, 2011. https://rm.coe.int/168046031c.

Council of Europe. 2019. "Chart of Signatures and Ratifications of Treaty 210." July 18, 2019. https://www.coe.int/en/web/conventions/full-list/-/conventions/treaty/210/signatures.

Davies, Lizzy. 2014. "Catholics and Church at Odds on Contraception, Divorce and Abortion." *The Guardian*, February 9, 2014. https://www.theguardian.com/world/2014/feb/09/catholics-church-contraception-abortion-survey.

DeGeorge, Gail. 2019. "Women Religious Shatter the Silence about Clergy Sexual Abuse of Sisters." Global Sisters Report: A Project of National Catholic Reporter, January 21, 2019. https://www.globalsistersreport.org/news/trends/women-religious-shatter-silence-about-clergy-sexual-abuse-sisters-55800.

Djelloul, Ghaliya. 2018. "Islamic Feminism: A Contradiction in Terms?" Eurozine, March 8, 2018. Translated by Mike Routledge. https://www.eurozine.com/islamic-feminism-contradiction-terms/.

DW. 2019. "German Catholic Women Begin Boycott over Lack of Reforms." May 11, 2019. https://www.dw.com/en/german-catholic-women-begin-boycott-over-lack-of-reforms/a-48699567.

European Disability Forum. 2017. "Violence against Women and Girls: Will Europe Rise Up in 2017?" March 7, 2017. http://www.edf-feph.org/newsroom/news/violence-against-women-and-girls-will-europe-rise-2017.

European Unitarian Universalists. n.d. "The Birth of UU Basel." Accessed August 8, 2019. http://www.europeanuu.org/about-us/euu-fellowships/unitarian-universalists-of-basel-uu-basel/the-birth-of-uu-basel/.

Evangelical Lutheran Church of Finland. n.d.-a. "The Marriage Law." Accessed July 20, 2019. https://evl.fi/current-issues/the-marriage-law.

Evangelical Lutheran Church of Finland. n.d.-b. "Women Ordained for Thirty Years." Accessed July 20, 2019. https://evl.fi/current-issues/women-ordained-for-thirty-years.

Evening Standard. 2016. "What Is It Like to Be Gay and Muslim? Gay Imam Ludovic-Mohamed Zahed Explains." YouTube, February 29, 2016. https://www.youtube.com/watch?v=WFHx5kS0dxA.

Felter, Claire, and Danielle Renwick. 2019. "Same-Sex Marriage: Global Comparisons." Council on Foreign Relations, May 24, 2019. https://www.cfr.org/backgrounder/same-sex-marriage-global-comparisons.

Fortune, M., and C. Enger. 2005. "Violence against Women and the Role of Religion." VAWnet, March 2005. https://vawnet.org/material /violence-against-women-and-role-religion.

France 24. 2019. "Pope Passes Legal Decree Requiring Priests, Nuns to Report Sex Abuse." May 9, 2019. https://www.france24.com/en /20190509-vatican-pope-francis-orders-catholic-church-priests -nuns-report-sex-abuse.

Got Questions. 2019. "What Is Conservative Judaism?" February 14, 2019. https://www.gotquestions.org/Conservative-Judaism.html.

Grubin, Eve. 2004. "A Torah Scholar with a Rock-Star Following." Forward, September 3, 2004. https://forward.com/culture/5264 /a-torah-scholar-with-a-rock-star-following/.

Hackett, Conrad. 2017. "5 Facts about the Muslim Population in Europe." Pew Research Center, Fact Tank: News in the Numbers, November 29, 2017. https://www.pewresearch.org/fact-tank/2017/11/29 /5-facts-about-the-muslim-population-in-europe/.

Harlan, Chico, and Stefano Pitrelli. 2019. "Founder and Staff of Vatican Women's Magazine Step Down, Citing Pressure over Nun Abuse Stories." *Washington Post*, March 26, 2019. https://www .washingtonpost.com/world/europe/founder-and-staff-of-vatican -womens-magazine-step-down-citing-pressure-over-nun-abuse -stories/2019/03/26/c32c591c-4fb0-11e9-88a1-ed346f0ec94f_story .html.

Helgason, Magnus Sveinn. 2015. "Heathens against Hate: Exclusive Interview with the High Priest of the Icelandic Pagan Association." Iceland Magazine, July 25, 2015. https://icelandmag.is/article /heathens-against-hate-exclusive-interview-high-priest-icelandic -pagan-association.

Heynders, Odile. 2018. "Seyran Ates: Female Muslim Leader and Intellectual." Diggit Magazine, February 19, 2018. https://www .diggitmagazine.com/column/seyran-ates-female-muslim -leader-and-intellectual.

Holloway, Alan "Ivvár." n.d. "The Decline of the Sami People's Indigenous Religion." University of Texas at Austin. Accessed July 26, 2019. http://www.laits.utexas.edu/sami/diehtu/siida/christian/decline .htm.

Huda. 2019. "The View of Contraception and Abortion in Islam." Learn Religions, April 27, 2019. https://www.learnreligions.com /contraception-in-islam-2004440.

Human Rights Campaign. 2018a. "Stances of Faiths on LGBTQ Issues: Conservative Judaism." August 1, 2018. https://hrc.org/resources/stances-of-faiths-on-lgbt-issues-conservative-judaism.

Human Rights Campaign. 2018b. "Stances of Faiths on LGBTQ Issues: Eastern Orthodox Church." July 24, 2018. https://www.hrc.org/resources/stances-of-faiths-on-lgbt-issues-eastern-orthodox-church.

Human Rights Campaign. 2018c. "Stances of Faiths on LGBTQ Issues: Islam—Sunni and Shi'a." August 1, 2018. https://hrc.org/resources/stances-of-faiths-on-lgbt-issues-islam.

Human Rights Campaign. 2018d. "Stances of Faiths on LGBTQ Issues: Orthodox Judaism." August 1, 2018. https://hrc.org/resources/stances-of-faiths-on-lgbt-issues-orthodox-judaism.

Human Rights Campaign. 2018e. "Stances of Faiths on LGBTQ Issues: Reform Judaism." August 1, 2018. https://hrc.org/resources/stances-of-faiths-on-lgbt-issues-reform-judaism.

Human Rights Campaign. 2018f. "Stances of Faiths on LGBTQ Issues: Roman Catholic Church." August 1, 2018. https://hrc.org/resources/stances-of-faiths-on-lgbt-issues-roman-catholic-church.

Iceland Magazine. 2018. "Icelanders Abandon National State Church, As Old Pagan Ásatrú Continues to Grow." European Congress of Ethnic Religions, October 26, 2018. http://ecer-org.eu/icelanders-abandon-national-state-church-as-old-pagan-asatru-continues-to-grow/.

Iceland Magazine. 2019. "11 Things to Know about the Present Day Practice of Ásatrú, the Ancient Religion of the Vikings." January 22, 2019. https://icelandmag.is/article/11-things-know-about-present-day-practice-asatru-ancient-religion-vikings.

International Orthodox Theological Association. 2019. "Women in the Orthodox Church Group." https://iota-web.org/women-orthodox-church-group/.

Iqbal, Nosheen. 2018. "Raise Your Gaze: 'Islamic Feminism Is Overlooked in the Mainstream.'" *The Guardian*, September 16, 2018. https://www.theguardian.com/world/2018/sep/16/new-radicals-2018-raise-your-gaze-muslim-feminists-mosque.

Kvennakirkjan. n.d. "The Women's Church." Accessed July 24, 2019. https://www.kvennakirkjan.is/home-version-4/english/.

LGBTI Equal Rights Association for Western Balkans and Turkey. 2016. "Bosnia and Herzegovina." June 1, 2016. https://www.lgbti-era.org/content/bosnia-and-herzegovina.

Lidia, Lidia. 2018. "Why Don't We Consider Violence against Women and Girls Terrorism?" Feminist Current, July 19, 2018. https://www.feministcurrent.com/2018/07/19/dont-consider-violence-women-girls-terrorism/.

Lipka, Michael. 2015. "The Continuing Decline of Europe's Jewish Population." Pew Research Center, Fact Tank: News in the Numbers, February 9, 2015. https://www.pewresearch.org/fact-tank/2015/02/09/europes-jewish-population/.

Lipka, Michael, and David Masci. 2019. "Where Europe Stands on Gay Marriage and Civil Unions." Pew Research Center, October 28, 2019. https://www.pewresearch.org/fact-tank/2019/10/28/where-europe-stands-on-gay-marriage-and-civil-unions/.

Lutheran World Federation. 2018. "Evangelical Lutheran Church of Saxony Takes Up Message of Twelfth Assembly." November 29, 2018. https://www.lutheranworld.org/news/participation-women-and-men-theological-issue.

Maguire, Daniel C., and Sa'Diyya Shaikh, eds. 2007. *Violence against Women in Contemporary World Religion: Roots and Cures.* 1st ed. Cleveland, OH: Pilgrim Press.

McClain, Lisa. 2018. "Pope Francis Won't Support Women in the Priesthood, but Here's What He Could Do." The Conversation, March 5, 2018. https://theconversation.com/pope-francis-wont-support-women-in-the-priesthood-but-heres-what-he-could-do-91555.

Methodist Church. 2014. "Methodist Church Celebrates 40 Years of Women's Ordination." June 17, 2014. https://www.methodist.org.uk/about-us/news/latest-news/all-news/methodist-church-celebrates-40-years-of-women-s-ordination/.

Miller Llana, Sara. 2017. "Europe's Female Imams Challenge Muslim Patriarchy—and Fight Islamophobia." Christian Science Monitor, July 19, 2017. https://www.csmonitor.com/World/Europe/2017/0719/Europe-s-female-imams-challenge-Muslim-patriarchy-and-fight-Islamophobia.

Monaghan, Jennifer. 2015. "Domestic Violence in Russia: Optimism as Country Faces Up to the 'Silent Crisis.'" *The Independent*, May 10, 2015. https://www.independent.co.uk/news/world/europe/domestic-violence-in-russia-optimism-as-country-faces-up-to-the-silent-crisis-10239053.html.

Mustillo, Michael. 2018. "Latvia Bristles against the Istanbul Convention Combating Violence against Women." *Baltic Times*, February 28,

2018.   https://www.baltictimes.com/latvia_bristles_against_the
_istanbul_convention_combating_violence_against_women/.

Nadell, Pamela. 2016. "Rabbi, Rabba, Maharat, Rabbanit: For Orthodox
Jewish Women, What's in a Title?" University of Chicago Divinity
School, January 28, 2016. https://divinity.uchicago.edu/sightings
/rabbi-rabba-maharat-rabbanit-orthodox-jewish-women-whats-title.

New Europe. 2007. "Church of Norway Ready to Ordain Same-Sex Priests."
November 24, 2007. https://www.neweurope.eu/article/church-norway
-ready-ordain-same-sex-priests/.

Noack, Rick. 2015. "Map: These Are the World's Least Religious Countries."
Washington Post, April 14, 2015. https://www.washingtonpost.com
/news/worldviews/wp/2015/04/14/map-these-are-the-worlds
-least-religious-countries/.

O'Connell, Gerard. 2019. "Pope Francis Says Commission on Women Deacons Did Not Reach Agreement." America: The Jesuit Review, May
7,   2019.   https://www.americamagazine.org/faith/2019/05/07/pope
-francis-says-commission-women-deacons-did-not-reach-agreement.

Pariona, Amber. 2017a. "Countries with the Most Orthodox Christians."
WorldAtlas, April 25, 2017. https://www.worldatlas.com/articles
/countries-with-the-most-orthodox-christians.html.

Pariona, Amber. 2017b. "Religious Beliefs in the United Kingdom (Great
Britain)." WorldAtlas, April 25, 2017. https://www.worldatlas.com
/articles/religious-beliefs-in-the-united-kingdom-great-britain.html.

Parliament of the World's Religions. 2016. "Inija Trinkuniene, Krive of
Lithuania's Romuva Religion, Addresses 2015 Parliament Indigenous Plenary." YouTube, January 29, 2016. https://www.youtube
.com/watch?v=_0pXMOVLC6A.

Patheos. n.d.-a. "Religion Library: Anglican/Episcopalian." Accessed July
20, 2019. https://www.patheos.com/library/anglican/ethics-morality
-community/gender-and-sexuality.

Patheos. n.d.-b. "Religion Library: Conservative Judaism." Accessed July
20,   2019.   https://www.patheos.com/library/conservative-judaism
/ethics-morality-community/gender-and-sexuality.

Patheos. n.d.-c. "Religion Library: Eastern Orthodoxy." Accessed July 12,
2019.   https://www.patheos.com/library/eastern-orthodoxy/ethics
-morality-community/gender-and-sexuality.

Patheos. n.d.-d. "Religion Library: Islam." Accessed July 12, 2019. https://
www.patheos.com/library/islam/ethics-morality-community
/gender-and-sexuality.

Patheos. n.d.-e. "Religion Library: Lutheran." Accessed July 20, 2019. https://www.patheos.com/library/lutheran/ethics-morality-community/gender-and-sexuality.

Patheos. n.d.-f. "Religion Library: Orthodox Judaism." Accessed July 20, 2019. https://www.patheos.com/library/orthodox-judaism/ethics-morality-community/gender-and-sexuality.

Patheos. n.d.-g. "Religion Library: Reform Judaism." Accessed July 20, 2019. https://www.patheos.com/library/reform-judaism/ethics-morality-community/gender-and-sexuality.

Patheos. n.d.-h. "Religion Library: Roman Catholicism." Accessed July 12, 2019. https://www.patheos.com/library/roman-catholicism/ethics-morality-community/gender-and-sexuality.

People of the United Methodist Church. 2019. "Timeline of Women in Methodism." February 22, 2019. http://www.umc.org/who-we-are/timeline-of-women-in-methodism.

Pew Research Center. 2011. "Regional Distribution of Christians." December 19, 2011. https://www.pewforum.org/2011/12/19/global-christianity-regions/#europe

Pew Research Center. 2015. "The Future of World Religions: Population Growth Projections, 2010–2050." April 2, 2015. https://www.pewforum.org/2015/04/02/religious-projections-2010-2050/.

Pew Research Center. 2016. "The Gender Gap in Religion around the World." March 22, 2016. https://www.pewresearch.org/wp-content/uploads/sites/7/2016/03/Religion-and-Gender-Full-Report.pdf.

Pew Research Center. 2017a. "Orthodox Christianity in the 21st Century." November 8, 2017. https://www.pewforum.org/2017/11/08/orthodox-christianity-in-the-21st-century/.

Pew Research Center. 2017b. "Religious Belief and National Belonging in Central and Eastern Europe." May 10, 2017. https://www.pewforum.org/2017/05/10/religious-belief-and-national-belonging-in-central-and-eastern-europe/.

Pew Research Center. 2018. "Eastern and Western Europeans Differ on Importance of Religion, Views of Minorities, and Key Social Issues." October 29, 2018. https://www.pewforum.org/2018/10/29/eastern-and-western-europeans-differ-on-importance-of-religion-views-of-minorities-and-key-social-issues/.

Piggot, Robert. 2008. "Turkey in Radical Revision of Islamic Texts." BBC News, February 26, 2008. http://news.bbc.co.uk/go/pr/fr/-/2/hi/europe/7264903.stm.

Religion Facts. 2016a. "Asatru." November 22, 2016. www.religionfacts
.com/asatru.

Religion Facts. 2016b. "Presbyterian Churches." November 18, 2016.
http://www.religionfacts.com/presbyterianism/branches.

Religious Tolerance. n.d. "Female Ordination: Ordaining Female Priests
in the Church of England." Accessed August 17, 2019. http://www
.religioustolerance.org/femclrg15.htm.

Ruck, Damian. 2018a. "Religious Decline Was the Key to Economic
Development in the 20th Century." The Conversation, July 24,
2018. https://theconversation.com/religious-decline-was-the-key-to
-economic-development-in-the-20th-century-100279.

Ruck, Damian. 2018b. "Secular Countries Can Expect Future Economic
Growth, Confirms New Study." Science Daily, July 18, 2018. www
.sciencedaily.com/releases/2018/07/180718143103.htm.

San Martín, Inés. 2015. "Vatican Backs Spanish Bishop in Vetoing Transgender Man as a Godfather." Crux: Taking the Catholic Pulse, September 2, 2015. https://cruxnow.com/church/2015/09/vatican-backs
-spanish-bishop-in-vetoing-transgender-man-as-a-godfather/.

Save the Children Federation, Inc. 2015. "The Urban Disadvantage: State
of the World's Mothers 2015." https://www.savethechildren.org
/content/dam/usa/reports/advocacy/sowm/sowm-2015.pdf.

Sawe, Benjamin Elisha. 2017. "Religious Demographics of Bosnia and Herzegovina." WorldAtlas, April 25. https://www.worldatlas.com/articles
/religious-demographics-of-bosnia-and-herzegovina.html.

Sawe, Benjamin Elisha. 2018. "European Countries with the Largest Muslim Populations." WorldAtlas, May 24. https://www.worldatlas.com
/articles/european-countries-with-large-muslim-populations
.html.

Sherwood, Harriet. 2018. "Christianity as a Default Is Gone: The Rise of a
Non-Christian Europe." *The Guardian*, March 21, 2018. https://www
.theguardian.com/world/2018/mar/21/christianity-non-christian
-europe-young-people-survey-religion.

Simons, Ilana, and Dan Simons. 2016. "Same Old Chuppah, Brand New
Ceremony." Masorti Judaism, February 3, 2016. https://masorti
.org.uk/newsblog/newsblog/news-single/article/same-old-chuppah
-brand-new-ceremony.html#.XSeldHdFw2w.

Sutherland, Scott. 2019. "10 Fundamentals of Religion in Sweden." Sweden, April 16, 2019. https://sweden.se/society/10-fundamentals-of
-religion-in-sweden/.

Tarjanyi, Judy. 2001. "Female Priest Tells Her Story." The Blade, July 14, 2001. https://www.toledoblade.com/news/religion/2001/07/14/Female-priest-tells-her-story/stories/200107140032.

Taylor, Lin. 2018. "Islam Shows Its Female Face with Rise of Women Mosques." Thomson Reuters Foundation, September 5, 2018. https://www.reuters.com/article/us-denmark-women-mosque/islam-shows-its-female-face-with-rise-of-women-mosques-idUSKCN1LL1FK.

Tschannen, Rafiq A. 2019. "Swiss 'Woman's Bible' Offers Feminist Theology for #Metoo Moment." Muslim Times, January 7, 2019. https://themuslimtimes.info/2019/01/07/swiss-womans-bible-offers-feminist-theology-for-metoo-moment/.

UN Women. 2016. "Global Database on Violence against Women." http://evaw-global-database.unwomen.org/en/countries.

United Church of Christ. 2002. "Global Trend: World's Oldest Protestant Churches Now Ordain Gays and Lesbians." June 1, 2002. https://www.ucc.org/global-trend-worlds-oldest.

U.S. News & World Report. 2019. "Best Countries for Women." https://www.usnews.com/news/best-countries/best-women.

Wiginton, Patti. 2019. "How Do Pagans Feel about Homosexuality?" Learn Religions, March 31, 2019. https://www.learnreligions.com/homosexuality-in-paganism-and-wicca-2561720.

Women's Ordination Worldwide. 2019. "About Us." http://womensordinationcampaign.org/aim-and-mission.

World Congress: Keshet Ga'avah. 2017. "Our History." http://glbtjews.org/our-history/.

World Council of Churches. 2019. "Evangelical Lutheran Church of Iceland." https://www.oikoumene.org/en/member-churches/evangelical-lutheran-church-of-iceland.

Yahmid, Hadi. 2008. "Europe's First Woman Imam." euro-islam.com. October 25. www.euro-islam.info/2008/10/25/europes-first-woman-imam/.

Yle. 2012. "Transgender Vicar Allowed to Keep Job." May 25, 2012. https://yle.fi/uutiset/osasto/news/transgender_vicar_allowed_to_keep_job/6121218.

Zaimov, Stoyan. 2016. "Church of Norway Approves Gay Marriage after 20 Years of Internal Debate." Christian Post, April 12, 2016. https://www.christianpost.com/news/church-of-norway-approves-gay-marriage-after-20-years-of-internal-debate-161479/.

Žemaitis, Augustinas. 2018. "Religion in Lithuania: An Introduction." TrueLithuania.com. http://www.truelithuania.com/topics/culture-of -lithuania/religions-faiths-in-lithuania.

Zezulin, Lena. 2017. "Is the Russian Orthodox Church Pushing Battered Women into Feminism?" Public Orthodoxy, February 17, 2017. https://publicorthodoxy.org/2017/02/27/is-the-russian-orthodox -church-pushing-battered-women-into-feminism/.

FOUR

North Africa and the Middle East

Hanan Hammad and Amina Zarrugh

WOMEN IN THE RELIGIONS OF THE MIDDLE EAST AND NORTH AFRICA

North Africa and the Middle East share important sociopolitical characteristics; both are predominantly Muslim and Arab, and they are culturally distinguished in ways that influence the relationship between gender and religion in the region. The Middle East and North Africa (MENA) is an expansive region that incorporates parts of three continents, Asia, Africa, and Europe, and accounts for approximately 6 percent of the world's population. Stretching from Iran in the east to Morocco in the west, the region includes nineteen countries.

Although many countries of the MENA region are predominantly Arab or Muslim, MENA is different from the Arab and Muslim worlds. For example, MENA does not incorporate Somalia, South Sudan, Mauritania, and Marcius—four African countries that are members of the Arab League. MENA also includes Iran, a predominantly Muslim but not an Arabic-speaking country. The Muslim world includes many predominantly Muslim countries in Central and Southeast Asia, such as Afghanistan, Pakistan, Malaysia, and Indonesia, but these countries are not considered Middle Eastern states.

Notwithstanding the arbitrary utilization of terms such as the Middle East, Near East, Greater Middle East, and North Africa, in this chapter, we discuss women in the nineteen MENA countries combined: Algeria, Bahrain, Egypt, Iran, Iraq, Israel, Jordan, Kuwait, Lebanon, Libya, Morocco,

Oman, Palestine (West Bank and Gaza), Qatar, Saudi Arabia, Syria, Tunisia, the United Arab Emirates (UAE), and Yemen. Although Turkey has always been part of the Middle East's history and politics, it is not discussed here because it is included in chapter 3, on Europe.

The MENA states are home to more than 455 million people. Egypt is the most populated country, with more than 100.3 million people, followed by Iran, with more than 82.9 million people. Geographically, North Africa is sometimes referred to as the *Maghreb*, which derives from the Arabic word meaning "the West." In this sense, it is geographically defined in relation to the Middle East and the westward expansion of the Islamic empire in the seventh and eighth centuries. From east to west, the countries of Libya, Tunisia, Algeria, and Morocco define the Maghreb, where a little under 100 million people live (World Bank 2018). Arab countries in the East Mediterranean are known as *Mashriq*, from the Arabic word meaning "East," and include the Fertile Crescent (Syria, Lebanon, Jordon, Iraq, Israel, and Palestine). Culturally, the region includes a wide variety of ethnic groups, languages, cultural traditions, and religious practices.

Although Arabic is the dominant language in MENA, the region is home to many ethnic-linguistic groups. The Kurdish people, a non-Arab Muslim population, live in northern Iran and Iraq, Syria, and eastern Turkey. The region also incorporates the Jewish state of Israel, whose official language is Hebrew, but Arabic is also widely spoken there, particularly among the Palestinians inside Israel. Persian is the official language of Iran, although the country enjoys a linguistic mosaic that includes Azari Turkish, Lori, Balush, and Kurdish, in addition to Arabic. The predominant ethnic group in North Africa is Arabs, but Indigenous communities, referred to as Amazigh or Tamazigh communities, reside across the borders of Maghreb countries as well as in Mauritania, Mali, and Niger. These ethnic communities have historically been referred to as *Berber* communities, a term that derives from the Greek "barbarous" or "barbarian." In contrast, the term *Amazigh* refers to "free man," and along with Tamazigh, these terms are preferred to describe these ethnic and linguistic communities.

While their population sizes vary across the Maghreb and are difficult to estimate given census administration in North African states, Amazigh communities influence social, cultural, and political life in significant ways, especially in Morocco, Algeria, and Libya, where there have been recent efforts to recognize the linguistic heritage of these communities. As the home of major ancient civilizations and the origin of the Abrahamic religions (Judaism, Christianity, and Islam), the Middle East has enjoyed a variety of religious and cultural traditions. Muslims make up 91.8 percent of the Middle Eastern population, making Christians and Jews minorities at 3.7 percent and 1.7 percent, respectively. The Maghreb enjoys small Jewish communities, and small Christian communities reside in Maghreb states, which are largest in Algeria and Morocco.

Islam started in Arabia in the seventh century, and before his death in 632, the Prophet Muhammad unified Arabia in one state. Under the political leadership of his successors, the Muslim state expanded rapidly and controlled territories encompassing Iberia in Europe, North Africa, and the Middle East, forming a strong global empire in its heyday in the ninth century. Yet, Islam did not become the religion of the majority of the population in the Muslim-ruled territories before the twelfth century. Currently, Islam, with its two major sects, Sunni and Shi'a, is the predominant religion in most states of the region. Sunni Islam is predominant in Egypt, Jordan, Kuwait, Oman, Palestine (West Bank and Gaza), Qatar, Saudi Arabia, Syria, and the UAE. All Maghreb states have a majority of Sunni Muslim populations, accounting for approximately 98 percent of the population. Ja'fari (Twelver) Shi'a Islam is predominant in Iran and is the religion of the majority in Iraq, Bahrain, and Lebanon. The Zaidi sect, a branch of Shi'a Islam, is predominant in Yemen. There are sizeable Shi'i communities in Saudi Arabia and Syria.

Christianity and Judaism also have their origins in the region. Throughout history, Jewish communities thrived throughout MENA countries. However, those communities have shrunken rapidly during the second half of the twentieth century and even vanished from most Arab states. Israel, established in 1948, is a predominantly Jewish state, but more than 20 percent of its population is Arab Muslims and Christians. All Maghreb states have small Jewish communities, including a particularly long Jewish history on the island of Djerba in Tunisia. There is still a sizeable Jewish community in Iran, although it witnessed a drastic reduction in its number in the last few decades. Iran was the birthplace of the young religions Babi and Bahá'í, which branched off and then separated from Shi'ism in the nineteenth century. The majority of both communities have left Iran since the Iranian Revolution in 1979. Iran was also the birthplace and is still home to one of the oldest religious communities, Zoroastrians, who mostly concentrate in the city of Yazd. Iraq is the indigenous home of other small monotheistic religious communities, including the Yazidis and Sab'ia. Christian communities from the three branches—Orthodox, Catholic, and

Protestant—are scattered in all MENA states except Saudi Arabia. The Eastern Orthodox churches include the Copts in Egypt and the Greek and Arminian Orthodox in the Levant (Syria, Lebanon, Palestine, and Jordan). Lebanon has a Middle Eastern Catholic sect known as the Maronites. Protestant churches in Egypt and the Levant are relatively new and were established by European and American missionaries in the region since the late nineteenth century.

Sunni and Shi'a Islam

The most widespread religion in the Middle East and one of the world's largest religions is Islam. More than 90 percent of the Middle East's population belong to Islam, but the Middle East's Muslim population accounts for about 20 percent of the world's Muslim population. Islam is a monotheistic Abrahamic religion, which is based on the belief of the oneness of God, and Muhammad (ca. 570–632 CE) was the last prophet sent by God. Islamic rituals and beliefs are based on the holy book the Qur'an and the documented practices and traditions of the Prophet Muhammad (Sunnah). The five pillars of Islam are *shahadah* (witnessing there is no God but Allah and that Muhammad is his prophet), *salah* (praying five times a day), *zakah* (alms), *sawm* (fasting during Ramadan, which is the tenth month in the Islamic lunar calendar), and *hajj* (pilgrimage once to Mecca).

Following the Prophet Muhammad's death, a group of Muslims rallied around his cousin and son-in-law, Ali ibn Abi Talib, calling for his right to succeed Muhammad as a political leader. That group became known as Shi'ite Ali, or Ali's party. The succession went to another close companion of Muhammad, Abi Bakr al-Sidiq. The political difference evolved during the following century to become a religious sect known as Shi'a Muslims. The rest of the Muslims became known as Sunni Muslims.

For Shi'is and Sunnis, the corpus of scholarship to canonize laws based on the interpretation of the Qur'an and Sunnah throughout the first four centuries of Islamic history is called Sharia, or Islamic, law. Most contemporary nation-states in the Middle East use Islamic law as the basis of their family and personal status legal system. Sharia makes the husband the sole provider for his wife and children. Sharia also recognizes the woman's full financial rights over her property and income from work. Muslim women can marry only Muslim men, but Muslim men can marry women from any Abrahamic religion. Sharia grants men the right to practice polygamy (up to four wives) and unilateral divorce. Because marriage in Islam is a contract rather than a sacrament, a wife has the option to make her husband waive his right to polygamy and to share her right to divorce herself. This option was readily available in the premodern state, where a marriage contract was drafted for each case.

Since the rise of the modern state, the prototype marriage contract became a rigid formula and overlooked the possibility of adding conditions or alterations (Kholousy 2010, 55). Shi'a Islam allows contractual *sygheh*, or temporary marriage, a form of marriage that allows the couple to determine the period after which the marriage becomes annulled. Socially, *sygheh* marriage has been controversial and uncommon among Shi'is (Haeri 2014, 35). Many consider *sygheh* a masked form of prostitution that exploits women's bodies to satisfy men's desires, mainly because men mostly practice it during the pilgrimage to shrine towns. On the other hand, some defend *sygheh*, maintaining that the marriage contract provides women with some protection, including granting their children full recognition as legitimate. Muslim Sunnis do not acknowledge the temporary marriage. Some Sunni Arab Persian Gulf states, including Saudi Arabia, Iraq, and the UAE, allow *misyar*, ambulant marriage. The couple bases their relationship on contractual terms through which the husband visits his wife without setting up home with her, and the wife waives her rights to maintenance, accommodation, and cohabitation and accepts keeping the marriage secret (Welchman 2007, 55, 101).

Middle East Christianity

Christian minority communities vary in size throughout the Middle Eastern countries, and accurately estimating their numbers in each country is difficult due to problematic official census taking. Orthodox Christianity is the majority religion among Middle East Christian communities. Orthodox Christianity is extremely restrictive about divorce, even making women continue in marriage if they face extended abandonment or domestic violence. If divorce is obtained through the state's law, the church does not allow divorced women to get married again. Christian women in countries that base their personal and family laws on Sharia find themselves in some situations subject to Islamic law. For example, Christian women in Egypt are subject to the Islamic inheritance law that grants a woman half as much as a man's share. Christian women who choose to marry Muslim men, which is permissible according to Islamic law, cannot pass their religion down to their children; they can only follow the father's religion, according to the legal system. Those women also face stigmatization in society and are often shunned by their families and communities.

Judaism in the MENA

Historically, Jews had diverse communities throughout the region. In addition to Mizrahim, Middle Eastern and North African Jews, there were Sephardim, Jews who left Spain after the Catholic Reconquista in the fifteenth century. The Ottomans, the Muslim empire that ruled South Europe, North Africa, and the entire Middle East, except Iran, since the sixteenth century, incorporated multireligious, multiethnic, and multilinguistic populations. Jews in the empire, like all religious minorities, had autonomy in managing their communal religious affairs through their *millet* councils. Due to European imperialist intervention and the Ottoman's response through state-led modernization, the region attracted more European subjects to work and invest in different Ottoman provinces throughout the nineteenth century. Some of those Europeans were Ashkenazi Jews, adding to the already existing ethnoreligious diversity. Middle Eastern Jews did not experience the European ghettos. Jewish alleys in Middle Eastern cities were open to all other religious communities. Jews also lived outside alleys in neighborhoods inhabited by their class peers among Muslims and Christians.

Imperial decrees in 1839 and 1858 granted Jews, and all non-Muslim Ottoman minorities, equal rights to Muslims, particularly in regard to taxation and military service. However, Ashkenazi Jews enjoyed higher social status and did not mingle or intermarry with Mizrahim. That socio-sectarian division became a focal subject among reformist-minded Jews who contributed to the cultural renaissance (*Nahda*) of the Arab East late in the nineteenth century. In addition to restrictions on intersect marriage and social stigma on interfaith marriage, poor Jewish families suffered the burden of *dawta*, a sum of money paid to grooms. The inability to pay *dawta* made daughters of poor families miss opportunities for marriage.

The establishment of Israel in 1948 and the backlash that Jews in Arab societies faced forced many Jews to leave their Arab countries to go to Israel or elsewhere. While Jewish communities shrank and vanished from Arab states, the Mizrahim population of Israel increased. Mizrahim and African Jewish women faced discrimination in Israel, including the sterilization of women (Madmoni-Gerber 2009; Lavie 2014; Omer 2019, 79).

The Western Wall, one of the most sacred sites for Jews, is also a contested site. Women are segregated at the Wall, and they face restrictions on the religious garb they can wear. Women of the Wall is an organization that struggles for the right of women to wear prayer shawls, pray, and read from the Torah out loud at the Western Wall. (Felix Bensman/Dreamstime.com)

Nationalist sentiments mediate the influence of religiosity and, along with the minority group status, may encourage higher fertility to ensure group preservation and strength in numbers (Schellekens and Anson 2007). The particular position of Israel as a Jewish state surrounded by Muslim-majority states and the position of Palestinians living under the Israeli military occupation in the Palestinian territories and as a minority inside Israel overload Israeli and Palestinian women with the burden of reproduction and raising as many children as possible.

ISSUES OF RELIGION FOR WOMEN IN MENA

Concerning gender in a general sense, international indicators generally regard the region of the Middle East and North Africa (MENA) together. A common refrain is that the "region is at the bottom on many gender indicators" (Abbott 2017). However, key differences emerge between the Middle East and North Africa in terms of gender equality in areas such as educational attainment and labor force participation when they are considered separately. For instance, according to the United Nations Development Index, Tunisia (ranked 48th) and Libya (ranked 27th) have some of the smallest gaps between men and women in terms of women's empowerment (as measured by reproductive health, economic activity, and educational and political attainment) compared to 155 countries around the world. Key exceptions include Morocco, where illiteracy rates as well as maternal mortality rates are relatively high for women. However, even Morocco excels in terms of protection for women in the labor force and boasts paid maternity leave, equal pay protections, and prohibitions on pregnancy discrimination (Abbott 2017).

International indicators related to gender equality and empowerment clearly indicate that it is important to examine gender regionally but also to examine country-specific dynamics. While there are key social and cultural practices shared across the MENA states, women's experiences do vary across countries and within countries in the region. One of the most important causes of this variation relates to religion and, more specifically, how religious texts, which influence the daily lived experiences of men and women, have been interpreted by political elites and how gender attitudes have influenced and determined the rulings. The evolution of Islamic law was a complex process shaped by numerous cultural, historical, political, and social factors as well as scriptural sources, whose importance cannot be dismissed (Jalajel 2017). For Mernissi and other scholars, historical patriarchal interpretations of Islamic texts are responsible for the marginalization of women within society and law today. Alongside other intellectuals, her scholarship, which includes a detailed history of overlooked female leadership in Islamic history, set the foundation for rereading patriarchal interpretations of the Qur'an (Barlas 2002) and has influenced international social movement organizations, such as Women Living under Muslim Laws.

Women in Religious Leadership

A Muslim woman may lead women-only congregational prayers in a private space, but the majority of Muslims have regarded women serving as an imam or leading men in congregational prayers as impermissible.

Saudi Arabia regards women legally unqualified to hold high public offices, but its small neighbor state, Qatar, appointed its first woman judge in 2010 (United Nations Children's Fund 2010). On the other side of the Persian Gulf, the Islamic Republic of Iran has had women ministers and presidential advisers. Some MENA countries, such as Kuwait, allow women high public offices as ministers, Parliament members, and advisers, but not as a judge or positions that require the public guardianship of the community's common good. Conservative traditionalists rely on legal rulings and practices that prohibit women from assuming positions of leadership (Jalajel 2017, 1).

Over the last few decades, Muslim feminist scholars have challenged the assumption that barring women from public guardianship is an inevitable consequence of embracing the Qur'an and Sunnah as primary sources of law. They have argued that the patriarchal societies in which Islamic law developed and the male gender biases of the juristic community privileged the exclusive monopoly of men over the interpretation of the Qur'an and Sunnah. According to American Muslim scholar Amina Wadud, the interpretations of the textual sources and applications of those interpretations in laws, public policies, and institutions are based on male interpretive privilege. Wadud took the challenge in the early 2000s and led a mixed-gender congregation of prayers. She maintained that there are no Qura'nic verses banning women from leading the prayer and that the Prophet Muhammad himself assigned a woman to lead mixed-gender prayers (Al-Doualia 2011).

In practice, the small number of Muslim women who claimed the position of imam, all outside MENA, face considerable opposition from the broader Muslim community. Until today, there is no serious attempt to form a mixed-gender congregation under the leadership of a woman imam anywhere in MENA countries. In 2004, a forty-year-old woman disguised in male dress, a false beard, and mustache tried to deliver the Friday sermon (*Jum'ah khutbah*) on the last Friday of Ramadan in Bahrain. According to press reports, the congregation saw through her disguise and handed her over to the police (Udodiong 2018). Seven years later, religious authorities in Saudi Arabia allowed a woman named Madawi al-Talshan to lead a women-only congregation for the evening and the special Ramadan *Tarawih* prayer. Reports hailed the incident as an unprecedented event, although for a woman to lead a women-only congregation for prayer was anything but unusual in many Arab states. It is noteworthy that the prayer taking place in public after a Ramadan dinner banquet sponsored by a

Saudi princess and attended by wives of Arab and foreign diplomats made it a high-profile event.

The situation is not much better for non-Muslim women. Only Reform Judaism, which has limited significance in Israel, allows the ordination of female rabbis; women are not part of the Orthodox religious hierarchy. Israel's religious establishment does not recognize non-Orthodox streams. In sum, women rabbis ordained in the United States have no legal standing in Israel. No Jewish community in a MENA state has a woman in its religious leadership. The head of the Jewish community in Egypt is now a woman, but her position is nonreligious; she does not lead any congregation in prayer. The community itself is too small to consider having a woman in that position as a significant achievement for Egyptians or Jewish women.

Among Middle Eastern Christians, women are often excluded from serving in the highest church offices. Orthodox Christianity and Catholicism dismiss the possibility of women ordination as heresy. Protestants churches allow women in some leading positions, but not all communities are open to ordaining women as priests or pastors. Lebanon was the pioneer when the Presbyterian Church in Tripoli made history and ordained Rola Sleiman and Najla Kassab on February 26, 2017, as the first women to be ordained in a Middle Eastern church. The ordination followed a 23–1 vote of the Evangelical Synod of Syria and Lebanon. The synod first gave a preaching license to a woman in 1993, and since then, women are

---

WHAT IS SHEKINAH?

Shekinah (pronounced shuh-KINE-uh or shuh-KEEN-uh) is a manifestation of the divine presence on earth. Different faith traditions give it slightly different connotations.

The word does not appear in the Christian Testament; however, Christian theology describes Shekinah as an ungendered presence of light. In Judaism, Shekinah is associated with the Holy Spirit. Because Hebrew words are gendered, in the Kabbalah, this feminine noun is said to reflect a feminine aspect of the divine. Others identify Shekinah as a wisdom goddess similar to ancient Sumerian and Egyptian goddesses.

Recently, some people have begun to revive this word with its feminine connotations, either to bring back its ancient meaning or to incorporate a more feminine presence into modern worship.

Janet Lockhart

allowed to preach in the churches (Hosami 2017; Kadi 2017). Reverend Sleiman, who heads the Evangelical Church in Tripoli, in northern Lebanon, had technically been performing all the functions of a pastor, except for the sacraments of baptism and Communion, since 2007. The National Evangelical Church in Beirut ordained Reverend Rima Nasrallah on November 11, 2018; she became the third ordained woman minister in Lebanon and the Arab world. Yet, the Presbyterian Church is a minority in Lebanon, and the ordination of women remains an exception rather than the norm (Shebaya 2017).

The larger dominations of Catholic, Orthodox, and Coptic Churches in the region still consider priesthood a vocation is reserved exclusively for men. The Presbyterian Church in Egypt has delayed any decision in that respect until 2026 and did not give any recognition to one of its members who got ordained in the United States in May 2019. The ordination of an Egyptian/Arab woman in diaspora raised a considerable controversy in which those who opposed women's priesthood adopted extreme misogynistic and homophobic discourses. In all dominations, only men hold power and authority to run day-to-day business based on each church's interpretation of the Scriptures and their adherence to Holy Tradition.

The Middle East Council of Churches (MECC) took a step toward recognizing women's leadership of the Christian community when it elected Thuraya Bachaalani as general secretary in January 2018. Bachaalani was the first woman to reach that position since the establishment of in the council, which represents Oriental Orthodox, Coptic Orthodox, and Catholic Churches, since its establishment in 1974 (Homsi 2018). To confirm her endorsement by the Orthodox Church, the largest and most conservative branch of Christianity in the Middle East, the patriarch of the Syrian Orthodox Church of Antioch received Bachaalani in his patriarchate in Damascus, Syria, in December 2018.

Judiciary Positions

While no Muslim woman has claimed the position of imam yet, the acceptance of female leadership in teaching circles in mosques and religious seminaries and madrassas is a significant change from much historical practice, signaling the mainstream acceptance of some form of female Islamic authority in many places (Bano and Kalmbach 2011). Throughout MENA, a diverse range of female religious leadership has emerged over

An Iranian woman reads the Qur'an in the prayer hall of the Imamzadeh shrine in Yazd. Women's local pilgrimages to shrines enrich their lives socially and spiritually. (Vladimir Grigorev/Dreamstime.com)

the past thirty years in physical and virtual spaces. This gender shift of religious leadership and religious spaces has increased women's participation at public prayers and mosque lessons. Gendered restrictions in long-standing traditions limit the religious authority of those women, but many are still able to play essential roles in the social and religious lives of their communities. Women in many parts of the Islamic world publicly speak for Islam as preachers, teachers, and interpreters of religious text.

The ability of women to exercise various types of Islamic religious authority has increased significantly, especially during the last three decades (Bano and Kalmbach 2011). In the early 2000s, professor of *fiqh* (Islamic jurisprudence) Dr. Su'ad Salih became the dean of the College of Islamic Studies at Al-Azhar University in Egypt. Al-Azhar is widely recognized as the most important Islamic theology university in the Sunni Muslim world. Salih used her platform to counter the reactionary calls that advocated for polygamy as a venue to provide women with an opportunity for marriage. Salih contends that polygamy would break more homes and inflict more social injustice on women (Salih 2005).

Each country in MENA has a different history in allowing women access to judiciary positions. Saudi Arabia, the UAE, and Iraq still uphold the traditional interpretation that Sharia restricts the public guardianship—and thus the position of a judge—to males. Other countries have adopted a more liberal interpretation that acknowledges the shared responsibility between all community members and men and women and removed being a man as a prerequisite for becoming a judge. Syria was the earliest country to allow women (1953), followed by Morocco (1959), Lebanon and Tunisia (1968), Sudan 1970, and Jordan 1996. There are also women judges in Libya and Egypt. In some of these countries, being a woman judge has not been an issue; in Morocco, 22 percent of judges are women, in Tunisia 22.5 percent, in Sudan 18 percent, in Lebanon and Yemen 16 percent, and in Syria 11 percent (Al-Morshedy 2016).

In Egypt, the progress was much slower. Although 'Aisha Ratib was the first woman to apply for the judge position in 1949, Egyptian law did not recognize that right until Law No. 7 in 2003 and the presidential decision that year to appoint Tahani al-Gibali as the first woman in the Supreme Constitutional Court, the highest degree of the judiciary (Al-Dirbi 2011). In February 2010, the General Assembly of the State Council's Judges eventually voted in support of appointing women in judicial positions in the State's Council. The National Council of Women demanded that the State Council respect women's right to serve in the council according to a previous decision (Al-Dilingawi 2011). In August 2018 (only two years ago), the first woman chaired an Egyptian court. Sudan became the first Arab Muslim country to appoint a woman as a chief justice. In October 2019, the Sovereignty Council of Sudan appointed the Supreme Court judge Nemat Abdallah per the Draft Constitutional Declaration.

Israeli women became judges in the 1950s, and in 1961, Miriam Ben-Porat (1918–2012), a judge in the Jerusalem District Court, became the first woman appointed to the Israeli Supreme Court (Kalman 2012.) Generally speaking, Israel has a high ranking in the Gender Inequality Index (GII); it was 24th out of 162 countries in the 2018 index. In Israel, 27.5 percent of parliamentary seats are held by women, and 87.8 percent of adult women have reached at least a secondary level of education compared to 90.5 percent of their male counterparts (United Nations Development Programme 2019, 6).

Meanwhile, Israeli feminists have serious concerns about what they consider a "rise of misogynistic religious conservatism impacting public policies" (Sztokman 2014). Ultra-Orthodox parties, which are increasingly becoming major players in politics, do not allow women to run for office or to become religious leaders. They emphasize their belief that women's place is outside of the public eye. Only Orthodox is recognized by the state, which led to exclusive male control over the state religious councils, and no woman has ever been appointed as a minister or deputy minister of religion or as a director of the rabbinic courts.

In Israel, the rabbinical courts, the Sharia courts, and the church authorities of the various denominations determine the personal law of Jews, Muslims, and Christians, respectively. Those religious courts have exclusive jurisdiction over matters of personal status (such as marriage and divorce) that excludes women, and no women serve as rabbinical judges, Sharia judges, or priests with judicial authority in the various religious courts. This priority of religious values incorporates and endorses a patriarchal concept of women's role in the family and excludes women from full participation in the public sphere while subordinating them to male authority in the private sphere (Halperin-Kaddari 2004).

Gendered Religious Practices

Colonialism was a world historical event in that it fundamentally reshaped geographic borders, cultures, psychologies, and economies around the world, particularly in Africa (Fanon 1961). A central, though often overlooked, aspect of colonialism is the use of gender and women's status as a justification for colonialism. For instance, British and French colonial officers argued that women's gendered religious practice of donning the veil in North Africa was a sign of their oppression and backwardness. This oppression, colonial officers argued, further justified the colonization of North African and Middle Eastern societies. Leila Ahmed (1992) refers to the justification of colonialism in terms of feminism, or liberating women from oppression, as "colonial feminism." She states that "an intrinsic connection existed between issues of culture and the status of women, and in particular that progress for women could be achieved only through abandoning the native culture" (Ahmed 1992).

The veil became a politically contested symbol of women's status, cultural integrity, modernity, and relationship to civility and progress (Samman 2011). The emphasis on the veil as a gendered religious practice during the colonial period was particularly salient in Algeria, where French colonial officers sought to "unveil" women from the "*haik*." The *haik* is a type of veil historically worn by women in Algeria that consisted of a long cloth that women drew over their bodies and heads and a handkerchief that fell over the nose and mouth, allowing only the eyes to be seen. It closely resembled a garment worn today by some Muslim women called the niqab. The veiling of women symbolized the extent to which the colonial force had acquired control of the colonized population. As Fanon, an anti-colonial intellectual and scholar from Martinique writes, "Every veil that fell, every body that became liberated from the traditional embrace of the haik, every face that offered itself to the bold and impatient glance of the occupier, was a negative expression of the fact that Algeria was beginning to deny herself and was accepting the rape of the colonizer" (Fanon 1965).

Women's bodies and their religious comportment thus became for both European colonizers *and* the colonized populations in the Maghreb a sign of cultural integrity and political power. Women's bodies were regarded as a "sign of the times" and reflected whether a given society was regarded as civilized or backward.

The early politicization of gendered religious practice in the form of veiling continues to influence debates about veiling in the Maghreb and the broader Middle East today. While contemporary Maghreb states do not have state laws mandating veiling or rendering it illegal, as we observe historically in Iran or Turkey, colonial discourses about veiling still influence gendered religious practices of veiling. For instance, in Tunisia, the postcolonial president Habib Bourguiba, who led the country from 1956 to 1987, regularly "denounced the veil as a 'dish rag' unsuitable for school, and claimed that 'without female evolution, no progress is possible'" (Marshall and Stokes 1981). The influence of these state positions on veiling is evident today, as around 89 percent of recently surveyed Muslim Tunisians argue that it should be women's choice whether or not to veil (Pew Research Center 2013). In addition, Tunisia recently became one among a wave of countries to ban "full-face" veils (Blaise 2019).

Similarly, anti-colonial resistance to French colonialism in Algeria further politicized women's donning of the veil. Since the postindependence period in Algeria, debates regarding the veil, specifically the hijab as a form of head covering, have influenced public and political discussions. From one perspective, the veil has come to represent cultural integrity and nationalism. Contrary to colonial prescriptions that deemed the veil to be oppressive, many Algerian women have found the veil to be an important mode of transgressing masculine space, creating new opportunities for women. As Islamist university students argued, "The *hijab* forces a rear-rangement of the male public sphere to make room for the presence of women. It is a badge of religious and political allegiance. . . . Women who wear the *hijab* escape the male gaze and are therefore exempted from the dominant male group's ability to control social space by means of sexual harassment or sexual objectification of females" (Slyomovics 1995). From this perspective, women in the region view the veil as an important resource that *facilitates*, rather than hinders or limits, their navigation of public space and commands them respect from male colleagues and peers. Similar dynamics have unfolded in Morocco and Libya, where the veil has become a fault line or "a *marker* of the boundaries between the 'authentic' Muslim woman and the alienated other" (Salime 2011). In this sense, the veil is not only a form of gendered religious embodiment but is also a political gesture.

The focus on the veil, from the colonial era to the present, as a sign of Muslim women's oppression or liberation is especially paradoxical given the prevalence of the veil as a common form of embodied religiosity for women of other religions as well. Female head coverings among Jewish women have, like Islamic head coverings, "been largely related to sexual modesty" (Chico 2000). In the Maghreb specifically, Jewish women often performed religious expectations of covering their heads, which in Europe took the form of three-cornered scarves or wigs, by donning similar garments to those of Muslim women (Chico 2000). In other Jewish communities, such as in Libya, women emphasize that they enjoyed a wider range of dress than Muslim women in the country, though they found little space to attend the local synagogue, which was an exclusively male space until a new synagogue was erected in the mid-twentieth century (Roumani, Meghnagi, and Roumani 2018).

It is also important to emphasize that the gendered modes of head covering apply to Jewish men in Maghreb societies as well. For Jewish men, "headpieces have served as constant reminders of men's relationship to God" (Chico 2000). These modes of religious observation have also endured periods of sanction, particularly in Europe, where anti-Semitic statutes regarding religious dress prevailed for several centuries. Gendered religious expression and comportment, as symbolized by ongoing debates regarding veiling, remain a key site in contemporary resistance movements in MENA. The region of North Africa, in particular, has been at the forefront of intellectual debates regarding the role of Islam in interpreting women's rights in the political sphere.

There is an implicit understanding of women's sexuality as a source of agency, rather than passivity, in the MENA region. While early Islamic scholars interpreted women's sexuality within strictly patriarchal understandings that characterized pre-Islamic Arabia, women's sexuality was understood as dynamic, and the significance of women's sexual fulfillment was recognized in hadiths (Mernissi 1991). The notion of women's sexuality as a source of agency—and therefore a threat to a patriarchal order—is embedded within policy across several countries (Mernissi 1991; Ilkkaracan 2008a). Depicting women's sexuality as a threat and the need to bring women's bodies under the patriarchal order runs strongly in mosques, Orthodox churches, and ultra-Orthodox Jewish communities. Most mosques are strictly segregated, and Muslim women are veiled and spend their time in the mosque, invisible, in women-only sections.

The Coptic Orthodox Church imposes strict segregations and forbids women from leaving their section to go where the Mass prayers are

Coptic Christians are found mostly in Egypt, North Africa, and the Middle East. Copts believe the church was founded in Egypt by Mark, who arrived there shortly after the time of Jesus. Coptic women do not have official leadership roles in the church. (Sergio Di Pasquale/Dreamstime .com)

IS FEMALE GENITAL CUTTING A RELIGIOUS REQUIREMENT?

Many associate female genital cutting (FGC), which is also called female genital mutilation (FGM) or female circumcision, with Muslims; however, some Jews and Christians also practice it. Different forms of FGC—cutting, scraping, or stitching a girl's or woman's external genitalia—are practiced in many countries in Africa, the Middle East, and Southeast Asia.

Many Muslim laypeople believe that FGC is compulsory; however, Qur'an experts say that although it has cultural and traditional roots, it is *not* required in Islam. In fact, some mention the Qur'an's injunction against self-mutilation.

FGC leads to emotional, mental, and physical trauma. Therefore, international rights groups label it a human rights violation and recommend an end to this unnecessary and harmful practice.

Janet Lockhart

---

performed. Women can receive Communion only at their section, and they must cover their hair. Women are encouraged to keep their head veiling everywhere inside the church, although they do not wear head veiling outside the church. Orthodox literature explicitly considers women a source of temptation, and the woman is responsible for protecting men from the distraction (Al-Maskin 1980). Israel still has dozens of gender-segregated bus lines, particularly in Orthodox communities (Ilan 2015). Religious conservatism went further in Israel and claimed that religious modesty rules required banning all female voices from the air. Recently, an Israeli district court fined a radio station owned by ultra-Orthodox Jews 1 million shekels, or about $280,000, for its long-standing refusal to allow women to speak on its programs (Chabin 2018).

LGBTQ People and Issues in Religions

In 2002, the Women's Working Group on the Turkish Penal Code demanded publicly that the code recognize discrimination based on sexuality. Although the revision ultimately failed owing to claims by the minister of justice that the reform was redundant because "the term sexual orientation was similar to the term sex, which is mentioned in Article 10 of the Turkish Constitution on equality," the debate brought to the fore a robust network of LGBTQIA organizations active within Turkey and the broader MENA region (Ilkkaracan 2008a).

The debate also raised the question of what sexualities exist within the region outside of a heterosexual framework. While many scholars study this question from within a heterosexual/homosexual binary, it is important to recognize that such distinctions are themselves reflections of Western cultural constructions; many societies do not define sexuality in such binary terms. According to Massad (2007), international human rights advocacy organizations around gay and lesbian rights have played a large role in defining sexuality politics in the MENA region and have often ignored a long history of same-gender sexual relationships in the region for centuries.

The penal code in the majority of MENA countries, aside from Saudi Arabia and Iran, does not include any explicit criminalization against private, noncommercial, or nonfraternal homosexual relations between consenting adults. However, sexualities outside of heterosexuality are increasingly subject to policing and surveillance in several states throughout the MENA region. In Iraq, since the fall of Saddam Hussein's regime, the lack of security and order unleashed gender-based violence, including social violence against gay men. Homosexual Egyptians face violence and prosecution by the state's institutions. Police and prosecutors have expanded the use of Law 10/1961, which vaguely criminalizes any practices against societal norms. The Egyptian Initiative for Personal Rights documents escalation in targeting people whose sexualities or sexual practices, actual or perceived, differ from those considered normative in Egyptian society. Police harass transgender persons (Abdel Hamid 2017). Under the fear of social stigmatization and state criminalization, LGBTQ people in the MENA region live without spiritual or religious guidance from within. In addition to the media discourses that dehumanize homosexuals, some religious institutions target them for conversion therapy in churches and televised sex therapy programs.

In Tunisia, gay men, in particular, have been targeted by the state for arrests for engaging in "homosexual acts." The state has mobilized sodomy laws to punish men suspected of homosexuality and subjected men to "anal tests" to determine whether they regularly engage in anal sex (Human Rights Watch 2018). This scrutiny has ironically emerged alongside the extension of individual freedoms in Tunisia following the revolution in 2011 that overturned the decades-long dictatorship of Zine El Abidine Ben Ali. Since the revolution, Tunisia has been consistently praised for its expansion of individual rights, as enshrined in its new post-revolutionary Constitution in 2014. Most recently, Mounir Baatour, who is an openly gay lawyer and leader of an LGBTQIA+ organization called Shams, announced his candidacy for Tunisian president in September 2019. His candidacy was met with support and also substantial critique, including from other Tunisian LGBTQIA+ organizations concerned about the politics of Shams and of Baatour himself.

Modern Muslim jurists consider sex change permissible in Islam. In response to a transwoman's plea in 1984, the supreme leader of the Islamic Republic of Iran, Ayatollah Khomeini, reissued a statement in support of the same opinion. Thus, transsexual became a religio-state-sanctioned category, and the state has permitted and partially subsidized sex reassignment surgery. This liberal standing toward transsexuality did not make a dent but might have increased the modern stigmatization of homosexuality. According to Najmabadi, sex reassignment surgeries were performed coercively on Iranian homosexuals by the government. The rise of transsexuality is because it is impossible to accept or to eliminate homosexuality (Najmabadi 2014).

The LGBTQ+ community in Israel has become more visible during the last decade. Israeli law grants official recognition to marriage established through religious rituals performed between persons of the same religious communities inside Israel. The state also registers couples married in ceremonies performed abroad. Through that venue, same-sex couples can marry abroad and then register their marriage and enjoy similar benefits the state offers to couples married by Orthodox rabbis inside Israel, including inheritance rights and division of marital property (Weiss and Gross-Horowitz 2013). The most significant development was the ordination of an openly gay man as a rabbi by a prominent Orthodox rabbi in Jerusalem last year. That ordination departed from a long-standing taboo against homosexuality in the Orthodox community (Sokol 2019).

Women at the Intersection of Religion and Politics

To understand the contemporary influence of religion as it relates to the everyday life experiences of men and women in North Africa and the Middle East, it is important to recognize the role of politics in the region. Politics and the state remain a key site for the codification of gendered rights, roles, and responsibilities as well as the specific role of religion within the political community. Contemporary women's rights are a direct reflection of how colonialism unfolded across the region and the role of kin groups and elites in interpreting Islamic jurisprudence (Charrad 2001).

Throughout the region, women's rights within the family are codified in legislation that is widely regarded as "family law." Family law governs issues related to marriage, divorce, child custody, and inheritance. In any family law legislation, there "contains a concept, an image, a normative model of the individual, the family, the society, and the relationships among them [and] family law by definition embodies an ideal of the family and social relationships" (Charrad 2001). Family law, sometimes referred to as personal status codes, is important in discussions regarding gender and religion because it represents how interpretations of the Qur'an and Sunnah vary across states and reflect differences in the social and political groups that have had the power to govern in each postcolonial setting. In addition, family law changes over time in some countries, which demonstrates dynamic and ongoing social and cultural debates about the role of religion in contemporary society.

Across the region, there is significant variation in the interpretation of religious texts, which produces different outcomes for family law in the region. In general, there are four major Sunni schools of law practiced: the Hanafi, mostly practiced in the Arab Middle East; the Hanbali, practiced in Saudi Arabia; Maliki, most dominant in North Africa and in small regions of the eastern Arabian Peninsula; and the Shafii school, practiced in southern Arabia. Iran, which is the largest Muslim Shi'a state in the region, follows the Ja'fari Shi'i school of law. Even where one school of law is predominant, states recognize the other three Sunni schools. In some cases, Sunni states, as in Egypt, recognize, at least theoretically, the Shi'i jurisprudence. Shi'a Islam differs slightly from Sunni Islam in that certain religious scholars (Mujtahid) enjoy supreme rights as religious interpreters of religious rules.

In other words, there is no one type of "Islamic law" or "Sharia." Nevertheless, the shared jurisprudence produces similar interpretations of women's rights as it relates, in particular, to inheritance. Across MENA states, women possess an unassailable right to inheritance with the exception in some states that their inheritance, in the absence of a written will to the contrary, is to be half the shares of a male relative. This common interpretation is based largely on Qur'anic scripture, which is rather unequivocal in specifying the shares of inheritance to be apportioned to men and women, respectively. Sunni jurisprudence grants shares of inheritance to extended family members in case no male children survive the deceased. In some circumstances, Shi'i jurisprudence adopts a more liberal approach and grants women, wives and daughters, a larger share of the inheritance.

Muslim women's rights to inheritance date from the inception of Islam as a religion in the eighth century. It departed in significant ways from the pre-Islamic era, when "only men were assured the right of inheritance in Arabia, and women were usually part of the inherited goods" (Mernissi 1991). In addition, Muslim women's rights to inheritance preceded by several centuries the legal right of women in much of the world, including Western Europe and colonial America, to inherit property and wealth as women.

Despite sharing in common guidelines regarding inheritance, which have been the site of contestation in some states, other aspects of women's rights vary across the region. Tunisia is widely recognized as having the most liberal family law throughout the entire region of the Middle East and North Africa and regularly ranks high on indices of women's empowerment in the region (Abbott 2017). A key reason for Tunisia's reputation as it concerns women's rights is its family law, which in Tunisia is called the Code of Personal Status. Promulgated in 1956, this code was distinctive in North Africa because it privileged women's autonomy over that of the family or kin group. Kin groups, sometimes called tribes, were an important source of political and social power across the Maghreb in the mid-twentieth century. Kin groups consisted of large extended families— such as fathers, mothers, aunts, uncles, and cousins—and important decisions within families were often decided by patriarchs within the kin group. Most schools of Islamic law, including the Maliki school, "sanction the control of women by their own kin group [and] sanctions the cohesiveness of the extended patrilineal kin group" over the nuclear family (Charrad 2001).

In Tunisia, kin-based groups, which are fewer in number compared to neighboring Algeria and Morocco, had comparatively little power to influence political elites in the postcolonial era. Accordingly, urban political elites in Tunisia departed from prevailing interpretations of Maliki Islamic jurisprudence and offered new interpretations that enhanced women's autonomy. For instance, gendered privileges of divorce changed in significant ways. Prior to the passage of the Code of Personal Status, prevailing interpretations of Islamic jurisprudence in the region allowed for the possibility of men to divorce their spouses by simply stating, "I repudiate thee," in a type of divorce called unilateral repudiation. The new code abolished this gendered male privilege and, instead, pronounced that divorce could only take place within the courts, and it was the privilege of both men and women to initiate divorce (Charrad 2001). This new interpretation granted significant power to women to negotiate the terms of their marriage in new ways.

Recent reforms in family laws have activated the Islamic principle of *Khul'* divorce, thus practically enabling women with the ability to dissolve her marriage when her husband refuses to grant the divorce. Egypt's Law No. 1 in 2000 granted women the right of the *Khul'* divorce if the woman gives up all the money, property, and gifts she had received and relinquishes her right to alimony. Similarly, the Moroccan Code of Personal Status, known as *Mudawanna*, allowed *Khul'* divorce in 2004 through mutual consent, and if the husband refuses, the wife can get the *Khul'* through the court. The Algerian legal code implements a similar procedure according to Article No. 54 of the Family Law.

Other key reforms included raising the legal minimum age of marriage for both men and women and outlawing polygamy in Tunisia, which had previously been a privilege afforded to men. Morocco revised its personal code by raising the minimum age for marriage to eighteen, requiring a judge's authorization for polygamy, and equal rights in divorce and community, and it has permitted mothers to ask for child custody. Similar changes to family law unfolded in Libya, where minimum ages for marriage were established, which departed from Maliki jurisprudence that stipulated "that consummation of the marriage cannot take place until after the woman reaches puberty, the determination of which is left open to the families" (Barger 2002). Additionally, education raised the marriage age among women throughout MENA. In Egypt, those who had not received an education married at age eighteen; those who received a secondary education or higher married at age twenty-three (Brotman et al. 2008). A more conservative interpretation of Sharia validates a woman's marital contract or decision to marry only with permission from male family members. In the Sunni Saudi Arabia and Shi'i Iran, women must obtain written permission from her father to marry, while men are not subject to the same obligation (Brotman et al. 2008). In countries following Hanafi law, women do not need any permission if they are legally an adult or were previously married.

Reproductive health and birth control have been part of the sociopolitics of the contemporary Middle East. These issues always intersect with religious beliefs, gender policies, and sociocultural customs as well as with development plans. The Qur'an does not address the question of contra-ception or birth control in any clear verse. Muslim jurists discussed *'azl*, coitus interruptus, as a method for birth control in the eleventh century. One opinion considered *'azl* lawful in all circumstances, a second opinion considered it unlawful in all circumstances, a third thought it was lawful with the consent of one's wife, and a fourth thought it was lawful in the case of female slaves but not in the case of free women (Rippin and Knappert 1986). In practice, MENA has encouraged reproduction or birth control based on practical needs rather than textual arguments. For example, the Islamic Republic of Iran, established after the Iranian Revolution in 1979, made contraceptives less accessible in the 1980s as part of the regime's so-called Islamic Cultural Revolution to create an abundant pious Islamic society. When the population growth rate jumped to 4.21 percent in 1983, the regime faced the challenges of rapid overpopulation. The regime had to promote birth control and a smaller family size, and the annual population growth sharply declined to 1.25 percent.

Women's Resistance to Religious Oppression

The passive and submissive images we often consume of Muslim women in the Middle East and North Africa are contradicted by a long history of women's deep engagements in activism. From the colonial period to the present, women have been at the center of politics and actively mobilized to oppose colonialism and support national independence, especially in Algeria. Despite their important contributions to independence efforts, women's bodies remained the site for disputes about whether societies were progressive or backward, modern or traditional, and civilized or barbaric. Nationalists, responding to colonial claims that the veil was a sign of oppression, made counterclaims to cultural integrity and arguments about the merits of veiling. In the process, women's autonomy continued to be influenced by male elites: "We observe the problematic notion that women's bodies and mind[s] are the most important sites through which the nation stamps its journey [to modernity], and it is [women] that are expected to discipline their bodies and minds" (Samman 2011).

In recent decades, social movements mobilizing under the rubric of Islam have argued for a greater role for Islam in political governance. Some activists have developed political parties, called Islamist parties, to seek representation in government. Islamist activists and politicians were deeply repressed in several North African states, many of which operated as dictatorships in the postcolonial period, and adopted negative colonial views on Islam as a religion, limiting its role in governance. Citizens in states such as Tunisia and Libya, in particular, faced the possibility of jail time or being forcibly disappeared by the state to undisclosed locations under the mere suspicion that they had advocated for a greater role of religion within the state. While many of the individuals targeted for imprisonment were men, the consequences often extended to women. For example, in Tunisia, women were tortured, humiliated, and sexually violated, often to send a message to male relatives regarded by the state as part of the political opposition: "Abuse was used as a systematic and institutionalized form of torture, often directed at women for no other reason than that they were married or related to a member of the opposition" (Gall 2015). The state deliberately orchestrated sexual violence as a tool of state violence because of the known stigma that such violence would carry for the women who endured it.

Violence against women in several MENA states was brought to light in the aftermath of the Arab uprisings (Arab Spring), a series of protests and revolutions that unfolded throughout North Africa and the Middle East in 2011. North Africa was a key catalyst in these uprisings, which began in Tunisia following the self-immolation of a Tunisian man in protest of the Tunisian state's harassment and extortion because he lacked appropriate permits to sell groceries as a street vendor. In response to his self-immolation, several states across North Africa and the Middle East organized "Days of Rage" to contest the authoritarian states in which they lived. Their grievances were many, including a lack of political and social freedom, economic insecurity, and state violence. The impact of the uprisings was particularly dramatic in North Africa, where heads of state resigned in Tunisia and Egypt, and the Libyan dictator Moammar Gaddafi was killed in August 2011. In each of these states, women were engaged as organizers, protestors, and political leaders. Women ran for election in the postrevolutionary contexts of Tunisia, Egypt, and Libya, and, once again, women's status became a key debate as states in North Africa developed new constitutions.

One important example of the multiple roles women have played in debates about gender and religion is the controversy surrounding Article 28 of a newly proposed constitution in Tunisia after the 2011 uprisings. One of the first political initiatives in postrevolutionary Tunisia was the development of a new constitution, which was initially drafted by the

Constituent Assembly, whose members were popularly elected following the revolution in 2011. The draft, released in 2013, contained a proposed article that stated, "The state shall guarantee the protection of the rights of women and shall support the gains thereof as true *partners* to men in the building of the nation and as having a role *complementary* thereto within the family. The state shall guarantee equal opportunities between men and women in the bearing of various responsibilities. The state shall guarantee the elimination of all forms of violence against women" (Charrad and Zarrugh 2014; emphasis added). The term "complementary" was particularly controversial among some women, who mobilized independently and as part of organizations such as the Democratic Women's Association, La Ligue Tunisienne des Droits et l'Homme (LTDH), and Association des Femmes Tunisiennes pour la Recherche sur le Développement (AFTURD) to protest the new constitution. The women also argued for the protection of the Code of Personal Status, the liberal family law that was promulgated in the postcolonial period and was feared to be under threat by Islamist political parties.

Many Islamist women politicians argued in favor of the article, suggesting that the language of complementarity is consistent with equality and acknowledges the importance of partnership between men and women in public and private life. Despite the support among some women for Article 28, the controversial article was ultimately removed from the final draft of the constitution. This change was undeniably influenced by the large number of women who vehemently protested the article and expressed concern about how the language, however inclusive it was intended to be, could be instrumentalized in the future to circumscribe women's rights.

Similar debates around the Mudawanna, or family law, in Morocco have unfolded in the years prior to and since 2011. At issue, in particular, is how the Qur'anic text is interpreted in gendered ways, and on both sides of the issue, women have been active participants in advocating for a greater or lesser role of particular interpretations of Islamic law to shape everyday life (Salime 2011). Morocco has been especially important in the development of intellectual movements around reinterpreting the Qur'an from gender-egalitarian perspectives. Moroccan sociologist Fatima Mernissi was at the forefront of these contributions and is credited with developing the intellectual foundation for Islamic feminism, an intellectual and social movement to interpret Islamic texts from nonpatriarchal perspectives. According to Mernissi,

ASSIA DJEBAR

Assia Djebar was an Algerian novelist, playwright, and activist. She was born in 1936 in Algeria as Fatima-Zohra and was the only Muslim woman in her college and the first Algerian and Muslim woman to be educated in France's elite schools. She taught at the University of Algiers and New York University and was elected to the Académie Française in 2005.

Djebar's work exemplified writing as resistance as she explored the lives of Muslim women in Arab and Berber cultures. In her novels, she addressed critical issues of women's oppression, religion, patriarchy, education, violence, and terrorism. She called readers to look past the colonial-era assumptions of "oriental Islam," to push back against rising Islamic fundamentalism, and to look to Muhammad to reform Islam from within. In 1979, she highlighted the inability of Muslim women authors to be published in Arabic with her French film *La Nouba des femmes du Mont Chenou.*

Shannon Garvin

One of the frontiers I crossed is actually the act of analyzing the memoir and the religious text and the historical text and how history is made and framed and produced and packaged. And I just by looking and doing that—I mean, reading history for myself—I discovered, first of all, that the Prophet is a wonderful person, and any Muslim woman could claim it as an inspiring model. . . . And on the other hand, that I showed that—and the real mistake of women was to let the memoir, the collective, the history, space of producing history—*to let it in the hands of men.* (NPR [1993] 2015; emphasis added)

Collectively, the active social movement activism among women in the MENA and the contributions of North African and Middle Eastern scholars are responsible for transforming debates and legal structures that influence women's and men's experiences of religion throughout not only the region but within Muslim communities around the world.

FURTHER READING

Abbott, Pamela. 2017. "Gender Equality and MENA Women's Empowerment in the Aftermath of the 2011 Uprisings." Arab Transformations Working Paper 10. University of Aberdeen.

Abdel Hamid, Dalia. 2017. *The Trap: Punishing Sexual Difference in Egypt*. Cairo, Egypt: Egyptian Initiative for Personal Rights.

Ahmed, Leila. 1992. *Women, Gender, and Islam: Historical Roots of a Modern Debate*. New Haven, CT: Yale University Press.

Al-Dilingawi, 'Uthman. 2011. *Misr 2010: Ahwal Watan*. Cairo, Egypt: Kitab al-Jumhuriyya.

Al-Dirbi, 'Abd al-'Al. 2011. *Al-Iltizamat al-nashi'a 'ann al-mawathiq al-'alamiyya: Huquq al-insan: dirasa muqarana*. Cairo, Egypt: al-Markaz al-Qawmi lil-isearat al-qanuniyya.

Al-Doualia. 2011. "Imra 'ah ta'um al-nisa' fi al-Sa'udia liawwal marra" [A Woman Leads Women in in Prayer in Saudi Arabia for the First Time]. August 13, 2011. https://www .doualia .com /2011 /08 /13 / امرأة تؤمُ النساء في السعودية لأول مرة/.

Al-Maskin, Matta. 1980. *Al-Mar'a: huququha wa wajibatuha fi al-haya al-ijtima'iyya wa al-diniyya fi al-kanisa al-ula*. Wadi al-Natrun, Egypt: Dayr al-Qidis Anba Maqqr.

Al-Morshedy, Amal. 2016. "Dirasa muqarana hawla tawliayat al-mar'a al-qada." [A Comparative Study on the Accession of Women to the Judiciary]. Mohamah.net, August 16, 2016. https://www.mohamah.net/law دراسة مقارنة تولية المرأة القضاء/.

Bano, Masooda, and Hilary Kalmbach. 2011. *Women, Leadership, and Mosques: Changes in Contemporary Islamic Authority*. Leiden, Netherlands: Brill.

Barger, John. 2002. "Gender Law in the Jamahiriyya: An Application to Libya of Mounira Charrad's Theory of State Development and Women's Rights." *Journal of Libyan Studies* 3 (1): 30–41.

Barlas, Asma. 2002. *"Believing Women" in Islam: Unreading Patriarchal Interpretations of the Qur'an*. Austin: University of Texas Press.

Blaise, Lilia. 2019. "Tunisia Bans Full-Face Veils for Security Reasons." *New York Times*, July 5, 2019. https://www.nytimes.com/2019/07 /05/world/africa/tunisia-ban-veil-niqab.html.

Brotman, Sam, Emma Katz, Jessie Karnes, Winter West, Anne Irvine, and Diana Daibes. 2008. *Implementing CEDAW in North Africa and the Middle East: Roadblocks and Victories*. March 3. https://pages .uoregon.edu/aweiss/intl421_521/CEDAW_Report_MENAf.pdf.

Chabin, Michele. 2018. "Israeli Court Fines Ultra-Orthodox Radio Station for Banning Women from the Air." Religion News Service, September 21, 2018. https://religionnews.com/2018/09/21/israeli-court

-fines-ultra-orthodox-radio-station-for-banning-women-from-the
-air/.

Charrad, Mounira M. 2001. *States and Women's Rights: The Making of Postcolonial Tunisia, Algeria, and Morocco.* Berkeley: University of California Press.

Charrad, Mounira M., and Amina Zarrugh. 2014. "Equal or Complementary: Women in the New Tunisian Constitution after the Arab Spring." *Journal of North African Studies* 19 (2): 230–243.

Chico, Beverly. 2000. "Gender Headwear Traditions in Judaism and Islam." *Dress* 27 (1): 18–36.

Fanon, Frantz. 1961. *The Wretched of the Earth.* New York: Grove Press.

Fanon, Frantz. 1965. *A Dying Colonialism.* New York: Monthly Review Press.

Gall, Carlotta. 2015. "Women in Tunisia Tell of Decades of Police Cruelty, Violence and Rape." *New York Times*, May 28, 2015. https://www
.nytimes.com/2015/05/29/world/africa/women-in-tunisia-tell-of
-decades-of-police-cruelty-violence-and-rape.html.

Haeri, Shahla. 2014. *Law of Desire Temporary Marriage in Shi'i Iran.* Syracuse, NY: Syracuse University Press.

Halperin-Kaddari, Ruth. 2004. *Women in Israel: A State of Their Own.* Philadelphia: University of Pennsylvania Press.

Homsi, Hala. 2018. "al-mr'a al-ula fi hadha al-mansib: Thuraya Bachaalani tatawalla Majlis Kanai's al-Sharq al-Awsat" [The First Woman in This Position . . . Soraya Bashaalani Takes Over the Middle East Council of Churches]. An-Nahar, January 29, 2018. https://www
.annahar.com/article/743730-بشعلاني تتولى مجلس. كنائس الشرق الأوسط
المرأة الأولى في هذا المنصب ثريا

Hosami, Nada. 2017. "How Rola Sleiman Became the First Arab Female Pastor." Aljazeera, April 16, 2017. https://www.aljazeera.com
/indepth/features/2017/03/rola-sleiman-arab-female-pastor
-170330073956533.html.

Human Rights Watch. 2018. "Tunisia: Privacy Threatened by 'Homosexuality' Arrests." November 8, 2018. https://www.hrw.org/news/2018
/11/08/tunisia-privacy-threatened-homosexuality-arrests.

Ilan, Shahar. 2015. "An Ultra-Orthodox Woman Who Refuses to Sit at the Back of the Bus." Haaretz, July 16, 2015. https://www.haaretz.com
/.premium-gender-segregation-on-buses-lingers-on-1.5305320.

Ilkkaracan, Pinar. 2008a. "How Adultery Almost Derailed Turkey's Aspirations to Join the European Union." In *Deconstructing Sexuality in the Middle East: Challenges and Discourses*, edited by P. Ilk-karacan, 41–64. Burlington, VT: Ashgate.

Ilkkaracan, Pinar. 2008b. "Introduction: Sexuality as a Contested Political Domain in the Middle East." In *Deconstructing Sexuality in the Middle East: Challenges and Discourses*, edited by P. Ilkkaracan, 1–16. Burlington, VT: Ashgate.

Jalajel, David Solomon. 2017. *Women and Leadership in Islamic Law: A Critical Analysis of Classical Legal Texts*. New York: Routledge.

Kadi, Samar. 2017. "Ordination of Female Lebanese Pastors Marks Prec-edent for Arab Christians." *Arab Weekly*, April 16, 2017. https://thearabweekly.com/ordination-female-lebanese-pastors-marks -precedent-arab-christians.

Kalman, Aaron. 2012. "Miriam Ben-Porat, First Female Supreme Court Justice and Crusading State Comptroller, 94." *Times of Israel*, July 26, 2012. https://www.timesofisrael.com/miriam-ben-porat-1918 -2012-first-female-supreme-court-justice-and-crusading-state -comptroller/.

Kholousy, Hanan. 2010. "Interfaith Unions and Non-Muslim Wives in Early Twentieth-Century Alexandrian Islamic Courts." In *Untold Histories of the Middle East: Recovering Voices from the 19th and 20th Centuries*, edited by Amy Singer, Christoph Neumann, and Selcuk Aksin Somel, 54–70. New York: Routledge.

Lavie, Smadar. 2014. *Wrapped in the Flag of Israel: Mizrahi Single Moth-ers and Bureaucratic Torture*. Rev. ed. Lincoln: Nebraska Univer-sity Press.

Madmoni-Gerber, Shoshana. 2009. *Israeli Media and the Framing of Internal Conflict: The Yemenite Babies Affair*. New York: Palgrave Macmillan.

Marshall, Susan E., and Randall G. Stokes. 1981. "Tradition and the Veil: Female Status in Tunisia and Algeria." *Journal of Modern African Studies* 19 (4): 625–646.

Massad, Joseph A. 2007. *Desiring Arabs*. Chicago: University of Chicago Press.

Mernissi, Fatima. 1991. *The Veil and the Male Elite: A Feminist Interpre-tation of Women's Rights in Islam*. New York: Basic Books.

Najmabadi, Afsaneh. 2014. *Professing Selves, Transsexuality and Same-Sex Desire in Contemporary Iran*. Durham, NC: Duke University Press.

NPR. (1993) 2015. "Remembering Islamic Feminist Fatema Mernissi." December 10, 2015. https://www.npr.org/2015/12/10/459223430 /remembering-islamic-feminist-fatema-mernissi.

Omer, Atalia. 2019. *Days of Awe Reimagining Jewishness in Solidarity with Palestinians.* Chicago: Chicago University Press.

Pew Research Center. 2013. *The World's Muslims: Religion, Politics and Society.* Washington, DC: Pew Research Center. https://www .pewforum.org/wp-content/uploads/sites/7/2013/04/worlds -muslims-religion-politics-society-full-report.pdf.

Rippin, Andrew, and Jan Knappert, eds. 1986. *Textual Sources for the Study of Islam.* Chicago: University of Chicago Press.

Roumani, Jacques, David Meghnagi, and Judith Roumani. 2018. *Jewish Libya, Memory & Identity in Text & Image.* Syracuse, NY: Syracuse University Press.

Salih, Su'ad. 2005. "Ta 'addud al-zawjat la yahil mushkilat al-'unusa" [Professor of Islamic jurisprudence at Al-Azhar University, Souad Saleh: Polygamy Does Not Solve the Problem of Spinsterhood]. Al-Qabas, July 12, 2005. https://alqabas .com /article /55695 ‫منوعاتأستاذة الفقه الإسلامي في جامعة-‬.

Salime, Zakia. 2011. *Between Feminism and Islam: Human Rights and Sharia Law in Morocco.* Minneapolis: University of Minnesota Press.

‫تعدد الزوجات لا يحل مشكلة العنوسة. :أستاذة الفقه الإسلامي في جامعة الأزهر سعاد صالح‬ July 12, 2005. https://alqaba s .com /article /55695-‫الإسلامي في جامعة‬ ‫منوعاتأستاذة-الفقه‬.

Samman, Khladoun. 2011. *The Clash of Modernities: The Islamist Challenge to Arab, Jewish, and Turkish Nationalism.* Boulder, CO: Paradigm Publishers.

Schellekens, Jona, and Jon Anson. 2007. *Israel's Destiny: Fertility and Mortality in a Divided Society.* New York: Taylor & Francis.

Shebaya, Halim. 2017. "Arab World's First Ordained Female Pastor Is Historic." HuffPost, March 3, 2017. https://www.huffpost.com/entry /arab-worlds-first-ordained-female-pastor-is-historic_b _58b732b1e4b0563cd36f643e.

Slyomovics, Susan. 1995. "'Hassiba Ben Bouali, If You Could See Our Algeria': Women and Public Space in Algeria." *Middle East Report* 192: 8–13.

Sokol, Sam. 2019. "First Openly Gay Orthodox Rabbi Ordained in Jerusalem." Jewish Telegraphic Agency, May 27, 2019. https://www.jta.org

/2019/05/27/israel/first-openly-gay-orthodox-rabbi-ordained
-in-jerusalem.

Syrian Orthodox Patriarchate of Antioch. 2018. "Meeting with the Acting
General Secretary of the MECC—Damascus." December 9, 2018.
https://syriacpatriarchate.org/2018/12/meeting-with-the
-general-secretary-of-the-mecc-damascus/.

Sztokman, Elana Maryles. 2014. *The War on Women in Israel: A Story of
Religious Radicalism and the Women Fighting for Freedom.*
Naperville, IL: Sourcebook, Inc.

Udodiong, Inemesit. 2018. "5 Countries Where Muslim Women Have Led
Friday Prayer." Pulse.ng, February 6, 2018. https://www.pulse.ng
/communities/religion/female-imams-5-countries-where-muslim
-women-have-led-friday-prayer/j6rms4f.

United Nations Children's Fund (UNICEF). 2010. "Qatar MENA Gender
Equality Profile: Status of Girls and Women in the Middle East
and North Africa." https://www.unicef.org/gender/files/Qatar
-Gender-Eqaulity-Profile-2011.pdf.

United Nations Development Programme. 2019. "Human Development
Report 2020 The Next Frontier: Human Development and the
Anthropocene Briefing note for countries on the 2020 Human
Development Report Israel." http://hdr.undp.org/sites/all/themes
/hdr_theme/country-notes/ISR.pdf.

Weiss, Susan M., and Netty C. Gross-Horowitz. 2013. *Marriage and
Divorce in the Jewish State: Israel's Civil War.* Waltham, MA:
Brandeis University Press.

Welchman, Lynn. 2007. *Women and Muslim Family Laws in Arab States:
A Comparative Overview of Textual Development and Advocacy.*
Amsterdam: Amsterdam University Press.

Wing, Joel. 2013. "Iraqi Women before and after the 2003 Invasion, Interview
with Prof Nadje Al-Ali." *Musings On Iraq* (blog), December 23, 2013.
https://musingsoniraq.blogspot.com/2013/12/iraqi-women-before
-and-after-2003.html.

World Bank. 2018. "Data for Algeria, Morocco, Libya, Tunisia: Population, Total." https://data.worldbank.org/?locations=DZ-MA-LY-TN.

FIVE

Sub-Saharan Africa

Mary-Antoinette Smith

WOMEN IN THE RELIGIONS OF SUB-SAHARAN AFRICA

With close to a billion people in its fifty-four countries, Africa ranks second in both size and population among the continents of the world. The Sahara Desert separates the eight countries of North Africa from the forty-six sub-Saharan countries. Most North Africans are Muslims; however, sub-Saharan Africa is "a region of massive religious complexity and vigorous and multifaceted social change" (Agadjanian 2015, 982). It includes a "vast mosaic of ethnic religions that are usually called 'traditional'" (Isichei 2004, 4) that existed long before other faith traditions came to the continent. By the turn of the twenty-first century, Christianity and Islam were the two predominant religions in most sub-Saharan countries, but long-standing ethnic, Indigenous, and traditional African spiritual customs are incorporated into the practices of both religions.

Across the sub-Saharan region, Christians account for 64 percent of the population, Muslims 31.4 percent, folk religions 3.2 percent, unaffiliated people 3 percent, Hindus 0.2 percent, other 0.2 percent, Buddhists less than 0.1 percent, and Jews less than 0.1 percent. The countries with the highest percentage of Christians in the region are São Tomé and Príncipe (97 percent), the Democratic Republic of the Congo (95.8 percent), Angola (95 percent), Rwanda (93.6 percent), Seychelles (93.1 percent), Equatorial Guinea (93 percent), Lesotho (90 percent), Namibia (90 percent), Swaziland (now called Eswatini) (90 percent), and Zambia (87 percent).

Nigeria and Ethiopia rank among the countries with the largest total number of Christians in the world. Nigeria also ranks among the top ten Muslim countries in the world. While approximately 30 percent of the world's Muslims live in Africa, and the continent surpassed all other countries in 2019 in having the largest number of Christians in the world, it is also true that "the religious scene in sub-Saharan Africa is characterized by radical pluralism" (Chitando 2013, 111). This includes what are called "immigrant religions," such as Judaism, Hinduism, Sikhism, the Parsee religion, Jainism, Chinese religions, Buddhism, the new esoteric religions, the Bahá'í religion, and African American religions (Chitando 2013, 111), but their overall representation across the region is minimal compared to the large number of Muslims and Christians.

While statistics are informative, what is most significant about religion in the region is its integration into all aspects of African life—home and hearth, tribal culture, and local and national politics—with women playing the largest roles on the domestic and community levels. Although faith and worship are central in the lives of sub-Saharan Africans—from the twentieth century forward, Christianity and Islam increased more than seventyfold and twentyfold, respectively—there is also the "way of the ancestors," and sacred ancestral connections play deeply interrelated roles in African traditional religions (ATRs).

Despite the fact that these Indigenous spiritual practices are frequently dismissed as "superstitious, magic, idolatry, and a host of other condescending labels" (Chitando 2013, 109), they remain central in the lives of sub-Saharan Africans, who revere community and hold tenaciously to the passing down of oral traditions, including stories about ancestral worship, creation myths, folktales, trickster stories, mystical and herbal healing, witchcraft, and animal (and sometimes human) sacrifices. African theologian John Mbiti notes that, despite the influences of Christianity and Islam, sub-Saharan Africans "don't take off their traditional religiosity. They come as they are. They come as people whose worldview is shaped according to African religion" (Burleson 1986, 3784).

It is significant that "more than anywhere else in the world, Christians and Muslims mix freely in daily life in every field of human endeavor, be it in the marketplace, at the office, in business, in political parties, in schools and other institutions of learning" (Von Sicard 1993, 273). Overall, there is little evidence of "widespread anti-Muslim or anti-Christian hostility" (Pew Research Center 2010) in the region, except in Nigeria, where tensions between these two groups run higher than in other sub-Saharan countries. There is a paucity of documented evidence regarding the roles Christian and Muslim women play in promoting the peaceful coexistence between practitioners of both religions, but research suggests they carve out opportunities to engage in peacemaking and peacekeeping through activities within their respective faith communities and by making interfaith connections when opportunities arise.

Women and Religion in Sub-Saharan Africa

The vastness of continental sub-Saharan Africa prevents covering all aspects of women and religion in each country, but there are some common experiences and realities. Historically, in the religious sphere, African women's contributions have either "been regarded as negligible, exceptional and infrequent, or irretrievable" (Berger, White, and Skidmore-Hess 1999, xxxi), and available information tends to be so fragmentary that a full story of sub-Saharan women's presence in the religious realm remains elusive. Where information does exist, evidence suggests that participation in churches, mosques, and spiritual communities may be "a source of power for women, or a source of subordination, or both" (Berger, White, and Skidmore-Hess 1999, xxxv).

Using available information, we can see that women have resisted subordination and demonstrated strength, agency, and empowerment. African women's value is reflected in their past, present, and future-oriented maintenance of Indigenous religious rites and cultural practices. This includes their matrilineal importance in family life as well as their moral, economic, political, and cultural influences in their communities. As participants in Christian, Muslim, and traditional African religions, their leadership opportunities may be limited because of long-standing patriarchal prohibitions (more so for African Muslim women than African Christian women), but across time, they have demonstrated conscious efforts to increase these opportunities.

Christianity

The Holy Bible is the central scriptural text for Christians, which Protestants and Catholics use as their basis for living moral, faith-based lives. The Portuguese first introduced Christianity to the sub-Saharan region during the fifteenth century, but most Africans continued to practice traditional and Indigenous religions until white Europeans brought great change to the continent four hundred years later. Colonizers wanted to rule as masters of land and people, and missionaries wanted to end transatlantic slavery while converting and educating the "illiterate" tribal masses. Colonization took place rapidly, but Christian evangelization moved more slowly, as the missionaries initially learned the languages and customs of the African communities with whom they were living. The missionaries held that African ways of life and Indigenous religious practices were harmful and lacked true spiritual value; their conversion efforts targeted the erasure of African traditional religions and adoption of "civilized" Western Christian ways of life. Missionaries established Westernized mission schools that many Africans now believe had devastating consequences. As one Nigerian scholar has lamented, "The greatest and most effective weapon used by Christian missionaries to disrupt traditional beliefs was Western education. As the missionaries claimed that they were working for spiritual salvation of the people, so also did they claim to be working for their material well-being. All new converts were taught in the mission houses and were encouraged to look down on their culture. . . . In this way, traditional life was deeply undermined, and the family structure was disrupted" (Awolalu 1991, 113–114).

Opinions vary as to the degree of harm done by missionary zeal; some argue it was undermining and disruptive, while others assert that "Africans have gained greatly in the secular as well as in the religious spheres from the work and therefore the presuppositions of the missionaries" (Hastings 1966, 129).

These controversial concerns are reflected in many countries, including the most "Westernized" sub-Saharan country: South Africa. This country exemplifies the many tensions and challenges associated with Christian evangelizing in general as well as the particular effects on women. For example, beginning in the 1820s, missionaries settled in South Africa among the Tswana, Xhosa, Zulu, Sotho, and Pedi peoples, and by the 1880s, they had made substantial advancements. As the number of converts increased, African males began to assume leadership roles as teachers and pastors. The influence of Christianity combined with British and American Victorian-era cultural values resulted in the religious domestication and cultivation of African girls as "future spouses of Christian men, mothers of Christian children, makers of Christian homes" (Walker 1990, 255).

These female-focused Christian values were encouraged among the peoples of the Transvaal province of South Africa under the stewardship of two white Methodist women, who also helped an African clergyman's wife found the African Women's Prayer Union in 1907. Their formative document defined the roles of the ideal Christian African wife: to evangelize women, to emphasize the importance of Christian homes, to raise girls as Christians, and to cultivate morals such as industry, honesty, truthfulness, cleanliness, and kindness into their homes (Burnet 1913, 251).

Although these aims are time- and place-specific, they reflect the crux of Christian missionary zeal. They also demonstrate that although missionaries brought Western education to sub-Saharan Africans, they also brought Victorian gender divisions. As a result, access to learning was granted almost exclusively to African men; their mothers, wives, and daughters were relegated to the domestic sphere.

Although many sub-Saharan women had previously held leadership roles, the Westernized worldviews of the missionaries prevented them from seeing African women in religious and political leadership, with debilitating consequences for their socioreligious advancement. However, the resilience of traditional and Indigenous religions, and women's empowered places within them, have been shields against the total Christianization of Africa. Appropriating relevant Christian principles and merging them with African religious practices has created a hybridized Africanization of Christianity that resists attempted erasures.

Islam

The central scriptural text for Islam is the Qur'an (or Koran), which Muslims believe to be divine revelations from God; it is the basis for living faith-based moral lives. Muslims introduced Islam to the sub-Saharan region during the mid-seventh century. During the eighth century, it became prominent along the East African coast, and by the nineteenth century, it was established across a third of the continent. Initially met with resistance by ancient, deeply embedded African religious practices, Islam took hold by indigenizing some of its practices and inserting elements of itself into existing aspects of African life.

Although Islam successfully merged with African cultural customs, Muslims live according to divine law—Sharia—distinct to their faith tradition. Drawn directly from the Qur'an, Sharia specifies that Muslims live all aspects of their lives (including prayers, fasting, and giving alms to the poor) by these laws. Historically, the religion has been dominated by men

About one-eighth of the population of Uganda is Muslim. These women have gathered outside the Kibuli Mosque in Kampala City. Completed in 1951, the mosque also offers a nursery, primary and secondary schools, and a nursing school. (Dvrcan/Dreamstime.com)

holding high-ranking positions as imams (as these leaders are referred to by Sunni Muslims) of communities and mosques. Men are also the traditional leaders of *salat*—the Muslim practice of engaging in prayer five times throughout the day; it is very rare for a Muslim woman to be allowed to lead ritual *salat*.

Lack of access to education also restricts Muslim women, who, like male Muslims in the region, are more than twice as likely as Christians to have no formal schooling (McClendon 2016). Historically, this high rate of illiteracy has limited women's ability to access educational, leadership, and advancement opportunities, and this reality remains typical for twenty-first-century African Muslim women.

There have been exceptions. For example, Nana Asma'u bint Shehu Usman dan Fodiyo, a nineteenth-century Northern Nigerian writer, intellectual, and activist, "offer[ed] an alternative to the popular stereotype that the Qur'an and the teachings of the Prophet Muhammad have historically sanctioned the abuse and low social status of women throughout the

---

THE MESSAGE OF MAMA KIOTA

In 2017, a Sufi Muslim known as "Mama Kiota" received the Global Humanitarian Citizen Award. For more than fifty years, she has been working within her faith for the advancement of Muslim women, especially rural women.

In the 1960s, Saïda Oumulkhairy Niasse (her full name) founded Jamiyat Nassirat Dine (JND), a Muslim women's association in Niger and other West African countries. JND empowers Muslim women by mentoring female leaders, promoting religious tolerance, educating girls and women, and increasing financial opportunities for them.

The award recognizes that her work at local, national, and international levels promotes peace and is a vital part of the global feminist movement, of which many influential leaders are now African women.

Janet Lockhart

Muslim world" (Azuonye 2006, 54). She was the daughter of the great Islamic reformer Shaykh 'Uthman b. Muhammad Fodiye, who was educated to value women's capabilities by his mother, Hawa, and grandmother, Ruqaya. Nana Asma'u was a beneficiary of her father's support and an education in Qur'anic studies.

She used her knowledge and influences to establish the *Yan Taru*, a "network of itinerant female educators, who were granted the title *Jaji*" (Chahrouk 2016). These women traveled to rural villages, spreading her religious messages. Nana Asma'u always managed to conform to the "traditional feminine roles recognized both by Islam and by her own non-Islamic West African heritage" (Azuonye 2006, 63–64). She was a rare feminist presence during her time, and although Islam has remained patriarchal, she serves as a testament to what is possible for Muslim women's agency, educational abilities, and leadership potential.

Indigenous Religions

Sub-Saharan Indigenous religions have existed for thousands of years, and they represent spiritual forces central to the lives of peoples long before the "Hebrew people gave birth to the Abrahamic faiths—Judaism, Christianity, Islam" (Thomas 2005, 1). The many variants of Indigenous religions, also known as African traditional religions (ATRs), have beliefs and traditions specific to individual tribes while also sharing common elements. They are holistic by nature; profess allegiance to a single, genderless Creator; and have rites and symbols that inform all aspects of communal life from birth to death. Ancestral worship, sacrificial rites, witchcraft, sacred offerings to restore and maintain cosmic balance (cosmology), divination, symbolism, mediums and modes of revelation, and varied tribal cultural rituals are vitally important because they are "premised upon the idea of harmony. . . . Any breech in the order among the Creator, divinities, ancestors, and nature must be avoided at all costs" (Thomas 2005, 9). Sub-Saharan Africans reflect the reality of a human community, which involves participating in the community's religious observances. "A person cannot detach himself from the religion of his group. . . . African peoples do not know how to exist without religion" (Mbiti 1990, 2–3).

Through this holistic emphasis, Indigenous religions embrace an intricate mixture of feelings, experiences, and rites; the existence of both a visible and an invisible world based on the belief in a Creator; and a firm belief in the ancestral oral wisdom passed down from one generation to the next. Significant symbolic elements of these religions include "clan initiation, spirit initiation, communion in feasting and the blood pact, rites of purification, confession and reconciliation, marriage ceremonies, rites concerned with death, [and] investiture rites" (Mulago 1991, 124).

Despite the community-based nature of these religious practices, there is little gender equity among them. Male priests and pastors are at the helm of the churches and religious circles. In their high-ranking positions, they are turned to by people who are sick, confused, unhappy, or otherwise in need, as "their services have full cultural meaning and satisfaction" (Olupona and Nyang 2013, 19). Rare exceptions include such cultures as the Shona and Chewa of Malawi, which "have always recognized the leadership potential of women in their religio-political spheres" (Mapuranga 2016, 155).

Typically, women are relegated to such subservient roles as ritual assistants and suppliants, but they can also be powerful contributors as spirit mediums, medicine women, herbal healers, mystics, diviners, fortunetellers, and cultural counselors. Women are especially venerated as fertility resources, valued for their vital reproductive and regenerative roles in childbirth and food production.

Groups that put special emphasis on fertility include the Nyakyusa people of Tanzania, the Yakö and Yoruba of Nigeria, the Mende of Sierra

Leone, the Ganda of Uganda, the Lemba of Zimbabwe, the Bemba of Zambia, and the Swazi of Southern Africa. Powerful and "diverse spiritual beings are considered to control these sources of fertility," which include deities, heroes, royal ancestors, clan fertility spirits, the Supreme Being, and ancestor spirits (Kilson 1976, 136).

In many cultures, such as the Igbo in Nigeria, water goddesses and other spirits "embody the female element crucial for creation, procreation, birth, life, death, reincarnation, and the perpetual cycle of time" (Jell-Bahlsen 1998, 105). This further reinforces the importance of fertility as the starting point for all phases of African life, culture, and religious practice.

Determined to forge their viability beyond their fertility-related importance, sub-Saharan women have stretched the boundaries of their influence more broadly beyond the confines of home and hearth, but their prominence and influence may not be wide-ranging in churches across the region.

New Religious Movements

Although they did not flourish until the twentieth century, both Christian and Islamic new religious movements arrived with the influx of colonial and missionary presence in Africa and were developed as intentional "defenders of cultural capital" (Clarke 2012, 302). The impetus behind these movements—which have been characterized as resistance movements, revivalist movements, healing movements, and embryonic forms of feminism (Clarke 2012, 303)—has always been a firm commitment to the preservation of African cultural and religious practices. There are many new religious movements (NRMs), including African independent churches (AICs), and they all typically blend African and Christian spiritual practices. They generally reflect what has been termed a "new synthesis . . . [but] the degree of synthesis depends on the sway of dogma of individual churches, whether they lean more toward African or Christian culture" (Sackey 2006, 1).

Most important to recognize about NRMs is that they are deeply committed to sustaining African cultural and religious customs so as not to be subsumed by Western religious ideologies. The establishment of AICs has been particularly beneficial for sub-Saharan women, who have been at the forefront of leadership, although AICs remain largely male dominated and women have typically not received adequate credit for their services and contributions.

Nevertheless, in AICs, women have consistently reclaimed empowerment as the primary sustainers of significant aspects of African life and culture, which otherwise would risk erasure by pervasive Christian constructs. This is particularly true in West Africa, where women are integral to "the complex whole of social institutions, including religion, economics, and politics. This social importance has traditionally permitted female leadership" (Sackey 2006, 199).

Sub-Saharan women have been key in preserving and incorporating established religious customs into their contemporary churches. These include traditional African drumming and cultural music, the promotion of kinship, and addressing sociopolitical issues in church operations. Although distinct as individual churches, AICs share common features and practices, such as "healing, prophesying, solving social problems—especially marital problems—and helping women to become economically self-sufficient" (Sackey 2006, 1).

Across tribal cultures, the *sofo* (prophetess) is a highly regarded healing role in independent churches, where they "command both affection and respectful obedience . . . because of the wide range of their specialized knowledge." They divine illness, act as midwives, conduct healing rituals, minister to their patients' physical needs, and frequently serve as counselors (Breidenbach 1979, 108).

As practitioners of both African and Christian traditions, women across the region adeptly interweave the life and work of Jesus Christ into all aspects of their cultural lives. For them, "the Christ controls evil and is a wonder-worker. In times of crisis, the Christ is expected to intervene directly on the side of the good, for God is the giver of Good. In the Gospels, the Christ is seen as a healer, an exorcist, and a companion" (Oduyoye 2012, 152).

The full integration of this spiritual view ensures that sub-Saharan AICs continue to thrive in the twenty-first century. Interestingly, even as more women assume prominent roles, they actually may join the church for help with a health or financial problem rather than the intent to lead. "Nevertheless, the small number of women in leadership has encouraged and sensitized gender cohesion, stimulating a general acceptance of female leadership in these churches and the wider society" (Sackey 2006, 201).

In addition to their gradual leadership success in independent churches, women are claiming varying degrees of religious authority in Pentecostal,

Charismatic, Apostolic, and Zionist churches. Although their progress may be slow from a global perspective, some are hopeful that males at the helm of sub-Saharan religious institutions may come to "think of women's entry into leadership positions and greater acceptance of that leadership as two mutually reinforcing processes" (Agadjanian 2015, 1002).

ISSUES OF RELIGION FOR WOMEN IN SUBSAHARAN AFRICA

The Impact and Legacy of Christian Missionaries on the Colonial Project

Opinions vary as to whether the long-term legacy of the Africa-meets-West encounter has been positive or negative. While all sub-Saharan Africans have been affected, the status of women and their religions have seen adverse changes.

African religions were well established prior to intrusion of colonial and missionary influences. "This, of course, is contrary to exotic accounts by European Christians who invented the myth of Africa as a 'dark continent'" (Njoh and Akiwumi 2012, 3). It was believed that Africans were pagans, cannibals, spirit worshipping, godless people with few redeeming religious values and customs, and early Christian missionaries evangelized with a fervor founded on this premise. Although at first the missionary goals ran counter to colonialist enterprises, the agendas of both groups gradually merged into complementary profiteering arrangements.

Historians refer to such European imperialistic ventures as the quest for "God, Gold, and Glory": "God" reflected missionary zeal for spreading Christianity; "Gold" represented mercantile interests, such as the highly profitable African slave trade; and "Glory" referred to thirsts among monarchs for expansion, acquisition, and dominance. As a popular anonymous African oral story reveals, "when the white man came to our country, he had the Bible and we had the land. The white man said to us, 'let us pray.' After the prayer, the white man had the land and we had the Bible" (Mofokeng 1988, 34).

Botswanan feminist theologian Musa Dube has added the word "gender" to these "unholy three" (Dube 2012, 111). Via her four "Gs" of "God, gold, glory, and gender," she says European arrivals justified their travels into African lands, painted themselves as superior and the colonized peoples as in need of salvation or corrections, and "used gender representations to construct their claims" (Dube 2012, 117).

MUSA DUBE

Musa W. Dube, a professor of the New Testament at the University of Botswana, writes on HIV/AIDS, violence, and African indigenous values. She describes Western interpretations of the Bible as patriarchal and oppressive to non-Westerners.

Her book *Postcolonial Feminist Interpretation of the Bible* emphasizes the colonial aspects of the biblical interpretation often missed by mainstream scholars as well as white feminists. Another book, *HIV/AIDS and the Curriculum*, urges that Christian theological education include HIV/AIDS information in ministerial preparation as well as lay education.

Dube was awarded an honorary doctorate by Stellenbosch University of South Africa in recognition of her work as "a prime example of socially engaged scholarship" (University of Botswana n.d.).

Janet Lockhart

University of Botswana. n.d. "Stellenbosch University Honours UB Professor." Accessed December 31, 2019. https://www.ub.bw/news/stellenbosch-university-honours-ub-professor.

A case in point is the Yoruba people of Nigeria. Christian conversion apparently had some positive effects, such as the abandonment of human sacrifice, and the benefits of Western educations, improved health care, electricity, and railroads. Gradually, however, these advancements came under suspicion by Muslim and Yoruba leaders, who viewed themselves as the custodians of long-standing traditions threatened by Western influences. These leaders encouraged their religious communities to resist adoption of European ideologies advanced under the slogan "Christianity, Commerce, and Civilization" As African Christians sought to maintain their traditional religious customs across the region, others in countries such as Senegal, Yoruba-speaking areas of Nigeria, and the northern parts of Ghana adopted Islam "as a means to assert alternative forms of identity. Islam provided access to different resources of moral power and legitimacy that had long been a component of their societies and challenged the coercive colonial hierarchies of secular power and authority" (Gore 2002, 209).

As these conflicting influences played out across the region, women were especially challenged. Prior to European contact, women in many African cultures held political, decision-making, and religious leadership roles, but the colonial enterprise thwarted women's empowerment by imposing Western gender perceptions and stratification upon them. In general, Europeans could not conceive of women holding significant socioreligious and advisory roles, and this was especially true in their perception of sub-Saharan women. According to Nigeria's first published female playwright, Zulu Sofola, "The first level of damage was done when the female lines of authority and sociopolitical power were destroyed and completely eliminated by the foreign European/Arabian male-centered systems of authority and governance. That was the first deathblow to our psyche and the beginning of the *dewomanization* (impotence) of African womanhood" (Sofola 1998, 61). These reductions limited many women to the domestic sphere, restricted their access to literacy and educational opportunities, and lessened their previously held religious leadership roles. There were exceptions, however: a group of converted sub-Saharan Christian women, known as Biblewomen, traveled around the region to proselytize, convert, and establish women's scripture study sessions in remote rural areas. But these were rarities; overall, the colonial encounter marginalized women within circles where they once held high positions as chiefs, queens and empresses, and religious leaders within churches, mosques, and shrines.

Female presence in the religious realm also included revered goddesses, such as Adoro, a powerful Nigerian goddess among a pantheon of deities worshipped by the Igbo, who was so threatening to twentieth-century Christian missionaries that they attempted to demolish her shrine; Abonada, a Ghanaian goddess of justice and protectress of women and children worshipped by the people of Accra; Asase Yaa, an Asante goddess worshipped as a source of truth; Dzivaguru, a Zimbabwean earth goddess; and one of the most popular and ubiquitous goddesses, Mami Wata (Mammy Water), a water spirit worshipped by Western, Central, and South Africans.

Beyond the significant presence of female goddesses and spirits, there have been female prophets such as Alinesitoué Diatta (ca. 1920–1943), a Senegalese prophetess of the Dioula tribe who claimed the supreme being, Emitai, had spoken directly to her. She used her empowered position to fight French colonialism and facilitate access to religious authority for women and young men in her community. Because of her influence and large following, she was arrested in 1942 and later starved to death in Timbuktu.

More than two dozen female prophets have followed in her wake. Diatta's legacy reflects that, despite challenges to women's agency, acceptance, and access to religious leadership, sub-Saharan women have filled religious leadership roles. Some have reclaimed dormant religious roles from the past, while others have forged prominent new roles. Given that Africa is rapidly becoming the largest Christian continent, with increased access to literacy, education, and global connections, women will have more access to religious leadership opportunities.

Women in Religious Leadership

Although women make up a high percentage of participants in religious communities, they continue to be relegated to the margins. Religious leadership opportunities for Muslim women are minimal, and while women in Christianity may play more prominent roles within their churches, opportunities for full agency remain limited. And, as previously mentioned, while women within African traditional religions may have roles that give them degrees of status, these are highly prescribed and stratified. Compared to other countries, documented evidence of women's religious

Mapostori are part of the African Independent Churches, churches established by Africans themselves rather than foreign missionaries. While women are mostly excluded from formal leadership, they actively participate through testifying and singing. The sect is recognizable by its white robes and outdoor meetings. (Kevspics/Dreamstime.com)

leadership in Islam, Christianity, and traditional African religions is sparse, particularly with regard to Muslim women. However, there are examples across time of both Muslim and Christian women forging opportunities in religious circles.

The pioneering work of women's leadership has found traction in Ghana, largely because its "history and culture open[s] up to women not only religious positions such as that of priestess, healer, or ritual expert, but also as female *ohene* and *ohenma* or queen mother" (Sackey 2006, 199–200). For example, as a young woman, Maame Harris Grace Tani (ca. 1870/80s–1958) of the Nzema people established a reputation as an herbalist and healer, and one with a special talent for spirit possession, before meeting Liberian prophet William Wadé Harris. The charismatic Harris has been called the "most extraordinary one man evangelical crusade that Africa has ever known" (Hastings 1976, 10), and it was under his influence that Maame Tani converted to Christianity. She rose in prominence, becoming a chief priestess to a river deity known as Nana Tano, and the first ever Black prophetess. Maame Tani cofounded the first-known African-initiated church in Ghana along with Papa Kwesi John Nackabah, which they named the Twelve Apostles Church.

As its first convert, Maame Tani was considered the "owner of the church" by Papa Nackabah. He supported her leadership role, and "because she was a woman, he took her as his mother" (Breidenbach 1979, 591). She was instrumental in incorporating her own traditional beliefs, principles, customs, and practices into the Twelve Apostles Church, which differed from Harris's practice of encouraging African Christian converts "to reject their traditional beliefs, especially with regard to the concept of plurality of deities and 'magical' objects" (Sackey 2006, 30).

The main tenets of Maame Tani's faith focused on casting out evil spirits, healing the sick and infirm, and seeking secure, prosperous lives, and these remain part of the church. The two most important sacred artifacts of the church continue to be the African dancing gourd-rattle, which is used as an accompaniment to spiritual singing and dancing, and the Bible, which is primarily used as an object for warding off evil or as a pillow for the infirm. The fact that all church members possess these objects in their homes demonstrates Maame Tani's long legacy, as does its use of *sunsum edwuma* (spiritual work), a healing water ritual using basins developed by her in the 1920s.

More recently, Mercy Amba Oduyoye became an iconic African women's religious leader and feminist theologian. She was born in Ghana in

1933 to a Methodist minister father and a strong-willed mother, who encouraged her to seek answers to the query, "What about the women?" Her role as a feminist religious leader was "informed by her location and position as a woman within the West African context and its Christian church" (Oredein 2016, 154). Over her decades-long career, she has authored many books and held numerous influential theological positions. Through it all, she has been an indefatigable advocate in seeking recognition and equality for women within the Christian Church in Africa, giving "voice to African women as valued contributors in Christian theological discourse" (Oredein 2016, 154).

Oduyoye also advocated tirelessly for women's rights, powerfully blending the familiar tradition of African cultural storytelling with the tenets of Christian doctrine. Fondly known as the "mother of our stories," she continues to be lauded for sharing stories of African people's struggle to comprehend the divine, recasting mythical stories as stories of healing, and affirming African women as valuable contributors to and sustainers of the long heritage of African spiritual and cultural traditions.

Although African Muslim women have few opportunities to demonstrate leadership, contemporary Muslim women are increasingly finding inspiration and support from their Christian women counterparts. For example, the Federation of Muslim Women's Associations of Ghana (FOMWAG) was established with the support of local African Christian women's groups and with allies of the Federation of Muslim Women's Associations of Nigeria (FOMWAN). Motivated by social and religious considerations, FOMWAG was launched with goals to increase women's knowledge of Islam, encourage them to enter public service, create leadership role models for girls, and help women help their daughters choose careers, "to lift the Muslim woman from her hitherto downtrodden status to one of recognition" (Samwini 2006, 138).

Though inevitably limited by the male-dominated realities of Islam, the FOMWAG constitution promotes Ghanaian women's opportunities through the propagation of Islam, raising the level of awareness and the need for education among Muslims, promoting unity among Muslim women in Ghana, and raising the social status of Muslims in Ghanaian communities (Samwini 2006, 138). In keeping with their aims, FOMWAG advocates for women at all levels of society, whether they are literate, illiterate, rich, poor, rural, urban, Indigenous, or foreign. The synergistic ways in which organizations such as FOMWAG and Christian women's fellowship groups work together supports interfaith connections and fosters their development as leaders in their religious communities.

LGBTQ People and Issues

The history of queer issues in sub-Saharan countries is complicated; progress toward acceptance and inclusion has been fragmented and fraught with tension. Historically, many Africans have believed that homosexuality is nonexistent in their various cultures and that Europeans introduced it when they colonized the continent. Because of these deeply rooted beliefs, many Africans who identify as homosexual hide their identities, feeling isolated and fearful amid long-standing heterosexual traditions. One African lesbian wrote of her search for community and companionship in 1990s Lesotho just before "the president of nearby Zimbabwe, Robert Mugabe, himself mission-educated, declared moral war on homosexuality as a 'Western' phenomenon imported into Africa by the colonists" (Kendall 1999, 157).

This "war" was launched during the Zimbabwean International Book Fair (ZIBF) in August 1995, "the historical event that triggered the public debate on homosexuality and put it on the political agenda" (Aarmo 1999, 256). In his address at the fair, President Mugabe overtly condemned homosexuality as "abominable and destructive" (Dunton and Palmberg 1996, 9–10). High-ranking officials of other sub-Saharan countries echoed similar sentiments. Vice-President Seretse Ian Khama, for example, upheld Botswana's official position on the issue before Parliament, stating, "Human rights are not a licence to commit unnatural acts which offend the social norms of behaviour. . . . The law is abundantly clear that homosexuality, performed either by males or females, in public or private is an offence punishable by law" (Dunton and Palmberg 1996, 9–10). Namibian president Nujoma proclaimed, "Homosexuals must be condemned and rejected in our society" (BBC News 2001).

Government officials and media sources expressed violent antigay rhetoric throughout the region with such statements as "Homosexuals, lesbians, gays, you homosexuals, go home, who needs you?" (Long, Brown, and Cooper 2003). Aligning themselves with these secular viewpoints, Christian churches were overwhelming in support of the presidents of their respective countries. Their tenets held that, from a procreational standpoint, homosexuality is against the laws of God, man, and nature and that LGBTQ persons are possessed by evil spirits; "rituals must be performed to make the person conform to the norms" (Aarmo 1999, 265).

Amid these hostilities, members of LGBTQ communities lived in fear and isolation. As religious studies scholar K. Limakatso Kendall observed of her three-year experience in Lesotho, she encountered no women who identified as lesbian. What she discovered from this experience were the ways female sexualities manifest and express themselves in African cultures. She found that even though lesbians in Lesotho may experience social constraints, they cultivate ways to develop close bonds while engaged in their conventional roles of wives and mothers. Similar paradoxes are found in the vibrant interactions of poor urban Ghanaian lesbians, who "flirt, gesture, communicate, and act upon same-sex passions within their informal networks on the one hand, and on the other hand maintain the invisibility of same-sex desire" (Dankwa 2009, 193). Such silence around LGBTQ issues reinforces the colonial influences of the past and the perpetuation of political antigay positions of the present. Kendall ultimately concludes for herself and other sub-Saharan lesbians that "love between women is as native to southern Africa as the soil itself, but that homophobia, like Mugabe's Christianity, is a Western import" (Kendall 1999, 157).

Twenty-first-century queer activist Bisi Alimi has noted the irony of those who use Western religion to disparage homosexuality while also claiming it was brought to Africa by Westerners. "When I have challenged people who are anti-gay, many have said that it is not our culture. However, when you probe further, they argue that homosexuality is not in the Bible. But the Bible is not our historical culture. This shows there is real confusion about Africa's past" (Alimi 2015). This confusion continues to be divisive, and, as Alimi argues, "As long as the notion that homosexuality is un-African persists, [Kenyan president] Kenyatta will receive applause, Mugabe will win elections, and parliaments across the continent will reintroduce harmful laws" (Alimi 2015).

In 2013, for example, Nigerian president Goodluck Jonathan implemented the Same Sex Marriage Prohibition Act, which states, in part, that if two persons of the same sex enter into a civil union or marriage contract, they face up to fourteen years in prison. Nationwide support of this law has caused many LGBTQ persons to flee Nigeria, and its region-wide support reflects the degree to which popular perpetuation of homophobia poses dangers for LGBTQ persons.

To adopt more inclusive attitudes toward and acceptance of queer persons, it seems prudent to follow Alimi's wise counsel: "We need to start by re-telling our history and remembering our true African culture, one that celebrates diversity, promotes equality and acceptance, and recognises the contribution of everyone, whatever their sexuality" (Alimi 2015).

Women at the Intersection of Religion and Politics

The sub-Saharan region yields a wealth of information about "the public aspects of women's lives as farmers and mothers, traders and wives, spiritual figures and daughters" (Stichter and Hay 1995, 189). Women's "political" empowerment in the region has best been witnessed through their involvement in Christian, Muslim, and long-standing African traditional religions, which have characterized sub-Saharan life and culture in terms of "the varieties of religious experience and its links with politics and the 'public sphere(s)'" (Abbink 2014, 83). The degree of women's political placement and agency has changed over time; there have been disappointing downward trends in their leadership opportunities ever since colonial intrusion came to the continent.

Prior to the arrival of Europeans, "women's political positions varied extensively across Africa's multiple ethnic and tribal groups; in some societies women exercised extensive authority" (Stichter and Hay 1995, 189). In many sub-Saharan cultures, women governed kingdoms as queens or singular leaders or in tandem with a king. Empowered women leaders also founded states and cities, participated in military conquests, and played other prominent sociopolitical and religious leadership roles. As imperial values were imposed, however, women's traditional bases of power were undermined, and they gradually "became politically and economically subordinated and marginalized. . . . Thus, today, women in Africa remain politically underrepresented and economically disadvantaged" (Stichter and Hay 1995, 189).

The political sphere remains highly patriarchal and persists in barring women from prominent leadership roles, but limitations are not necessarily to the same degree. A comparative analysis of Muslim women in Nigeria and Senegal, for example, indicates that because Nigeria has been less "Westernized" than Senegal, "northern Nigeria today secludes women and bars them from public life, whereas Senegalese social and religious norms are less discriminatory" (Gerhart 1995, 158). Because of social conservatism and patriarchal customs, Northern Nigerian Muslim women have few opportunities for advancement unless gender equality is promoted through

Islamic law (Sharia) reforms. Senegalese Muslim women, however, "have achieved at least a toehold in the modern sector, and a feminist agenda is supported by a nascent women's movement" (Gerhart 1995, 158). However, Muslim fundamentalists in both countries use Sharia law to oppose women's equality. These realities are seen across the pluralistic sub-Saharan landscape.

The gradual loss of agency over time may account for differing contemporary perspectives on democratic governance across the region, where statistics indicate that more men (74 percent) than women (66 percent) believe that democracy is preferable to any other kind of government (García-Peñalosa and Konte 2014, 104). The continued intermingling of Indigenous and monotheistic traditions may lead to increased subordination of women "by excluding them from the exercise of formal or ritual authority and regulating them to supportive, gender-specific positions" (Banchoff and Wuthnow 2011, 134–135). The controlled, oppressive, and subordinate positionings of women have gradually limited their access to political leadership. For example, "Africa had no democratically elected female heads of state, and only three monarchs" in the twentieth century (Mama 2013, 148).

In addressing the contemporary global underrepresentation of women in politics, the Inter-Parliamentary Union has stated that "the inclusion of the perspectives and interests of women is a prerequisite for democracy and good governance" (Inter-Parliamentary Union 2008, 6). This coincides with the fact that "during the first decade of the twenty-first century, several of Africa's 54 nations [saw] dramatic increases in the number of women in politics" (Mama 2013, 147). This included its first elected female head of state, Ellen Johnson Sirleaf, the twenty-fourth president of Liberia (2006–2018).

While tremendously important, this remains unusual. At present, the overall percentage of female elected representatives remains low at just under 25 percent (Inter-Parliamentary Union 2008), and this confirms the degree to which "most African women feel ignored, persecuted, and powerless. They have no interest in politics or politicians because no government officials—male or female—addresses issues relevant to their daily experience" (Stichter and Hay 1995, 203).

Considering such despairing viewpoints, it is understandable that in countries with relatively high numbers of women in legislative positions, women's movements are concerned that they actually do focus on the "the delivery of gender-just policies—that is, policies that lead to real advances in the lives and prospects of society at large" (Mama 2013, 149). It is important to recognize the tendency to focus "on a small number of success stories, most notably post-apartheid South Africa, post-1989 Uganda, and post-genocide Rwanda" (Mama 2013, 14). Data from other countries is often excluded. However, acknowledging this does not diminish the fact that more prominent sub-Saharan countries continue to focus on what it will take to make women "more effective political actors in political institutions" (Mama 2013, 148–149).

Though progress is slow, it is encouraging that women's political representation in some sub-Saharan countries has dramatically increased since the 1960s; governmental gender quotas were adopted, encouraged by opportunities offered to women by political transitions, pressures from elite women's movements, and the spread of international and regional norms regarding the incorporation of women into the political sphere (Barnes and Burchard 2013, 769).

As the twenty-first century proceeds, progress is made, and women politicians grow in numbers and representation. It will be important for interested parties to remember that gender perspectives are varied. Sub-Saharan women may be "more interested in social issues and men in the political decision making process" (García-Peñalosa and Konte 2014, 116). Women, then, may be less interested in the political system itself than in how their sociopolitical agendas are informed by Christian, Muslim, and African traditional values.

Religious Violence against Women

Gender-based violence is common and includes domestic, physical, emotional, and sexual violence. This last is the most underreported form, in part because it "is met with silence or defined as part of a socially acceptable range of behavior" (Joseph and Nağmābādī 2003, 126). However, domestic violence is the most common form and includes all the other types of violence. It is most common "where the social structure favors male power and the dominant ideology legitimates women's subordination" (Joseph and Nağmābādī 2003, 125–126). Given these realities, sub-Saharan Africa is an ideal site for the perpetuation of violence against women. Studies in Kenya, South Africa, and other African countries have all documented high levels of abuse against women by their intimate partners (Takyi and Lamptey 2020, 27).

Controversially, research indicates that opinions about abuse vary across the region. In some Senegalese Muslim communities, for example, both women and men believe female battering by males runs counter to Islamic precepts, but others view it as permissible "under the label of 'correcting' wives who misbehave" (Joseph and Naǧmābādī 2003, 126). This broad range of perspectives reflects the paradoxical reality that, while behaving abusively, many African Christians and Muslims simultaneously "identify with a religious organization, attend church or mosque on a regular basis, or report that religion is salient to their lives" (Takyi and Lamptey 2020, 27).

Religion plays an especially prominent role in the lives of people in Ghana and South Africa; yet, both countries reported high incidents of violence against women. In Ghana, for example, indicators of high levels of violence include "ideologies that support wife abuse, the nature of [the] decision-making process at the household level, and [the] husband's use of alcohol" (Takyi and Lamptey 2020, 27). In South Africa, which has a high percentage of religious adherents, approximately one in four women are in abusive relationships. Further, although women may turn to their religious leaders for help, "perpetrators use easily misinterpreted scriptures, religious teachings and cultural practices to support abusive behaviour" (Petersen 2016, 50).

In South Africa, a commodity-driven cultural practice known as *lobola* (in which the groom and his family give a gift or money to the bride's family) leads many men to believe they "own" their wives and thus have unlimited rights to discipline and abuse them. Such bridewealth traditions, along with patriarchal institutions that foster unequal power between men and women, "provide the catalyst for some African men to abuse their partners" (Takyi and Lamptey 2020, 30).

While violence against women (whether secular or religious) typically takes place behind closed doors, South Africa is "faced with the enormous problem of gender-based violence against women in intimate relationships and public spaces because of the intricacies of [w]hite supremacy and patriarchy" (Petersen 2016, 50). However, it is also a country where multifaith nongovernmental organizations (NGOs) such as the South African Faith and Family Institute (SAFFI) have been established to address the religious aspects of violence against women and to "be a resource to religious leaders and faith communities in advancing culturally informed strategies and interventions that promote equal and more loving relationships between intimate partners" (Petersen 2016, 50).

As a pioneering NGO committed to redressing violence against South African women, SAFFI is a role model for the establishment of new resources, and it demonstrates that faith-based organizations, governments, and NGOs can work together to change "behavior[s] that have the potential to affect women's life experiences (rights, health, etc.)" (Takyi and Lamptey 2020, 29). As more activist agencies such as NGOs emerge, it has been cautioned that they "must draw on existing cultural resources while working to transform economic, political, and legal contexts in which African women live" (Joseph and Naǧmābādī 2003, 127).

NGOs are not the sole option to combat female abuse in the region: women have launched collaborative organizations from within and on behalf of their own communities. Two Zimbabwean women founded the Musasa Project (1988) to seek solutions for ending sexual and domestic violence against women; it "works with individual women to help them to confront the problems they face, and provides legal and counseling services to the survivors of violence" (Njovana and Watts 1996, 51). As faith-based and secular sister organizations, governmental agencies, and NGOs communicate, collaborate, and combine their efforts as allies, they will increase the pace by which violence against women is overcome.

THE SOUTH AFRICAN FAITH & FAMILY INSTITUTE (SAFFI)

The South African Faith & Family Institute (SAFFI) partners with faith leaders, institutions, and faith communities to challenge patriarchal traditions that encourage violence against women and children. Recognizing that intimate partner violence destroys the dignity of the women who are violated as well as the men who commit rape, assault, and murder in the name of religion, SAFFI offers opportunities for truth telling, healing, and possible restoration.

As South Africa experiences intimate partner murder at five times the global rate, SAFFI challenges the men and women of South Africa to engage their faith traditions in ways that honor one another and make supportive unions. The recent rapes, killings, and hanging of South African women Tshegofatso Pule, Nadeli Phangindawo, and Sanele Mfaba as well as Trevor Noah's account of his mother's shooting at the hands of his stepfather have brought the violence against South African women to the forefront of the international news.

SAFFI continues to partner and expand its work in South Africa to engage men and women and to raise up boys and girls who can live out their faith in healthy relationships and personal safety.

Shannon Garvin

Proactive religious leaders are also becoming advocates for gender equality. Christian and Muslim leaders in Liberia are countering violence by "re-examining teachings and passages from the Bible and the Koran, re-evaluating their messages about dignity, responsibility and respect between men and women" (Radtke and Khan 2018). They provide hotlines for victims of sexual violence, establish safe houses, and involve police and government service providers as assistants in the process. There has been a sixfold reduction in violence countrywide (Radtke and Khan 2018). These promising results suggest that if secular leaders were to follow suit, there could be demonstrable decreases in violence against women across the region. In time, sub-Saharan women would see advancements in their well-being, livelihoods, economic status, and access to educational opportunities.

Women's Resistance to Religious Oppression

Traditionally, Islam and Christianity have both been male-dominated religions, but in recent years, more African women are asserting forms of feminist resistance that question and counter sexist traditions within their churches and mosques. To "critically [assess] the status of women in Africa and to examine the role of religion and culture in shaping their lives and destinies" (Hinga 2002, 79), in 1989, eighty women participated in a convention at Trinity College in Accra, Ghana, which marked a turning point in African theology (Hinga 2002, 79). In her keynote address, Ghanaian Methodist theologian Mercy Amba Oduyoye observed, "For many years African women had been treated as if they were dead. They had been discussed, analyzed, and spoken about and on behalf of by men and outsiders as if they were not subjects capable of self-naming and analysis of their own experiences" (Hinga 2002, 80). Motivated by the desire to change these oppressive gendered realities, convention delegates named themselves the Circle of Concerned African Women Theologians, and they developed a seven-year plan designed to elevate women's theology through research, publications, dialog, and inclusion in higher education (Hinga 2002, 81).

As sub-Saharan women advance in their communities, churches, and mosques, they also bring their concerns into government circles. "In this way, women in religion are brought into the high echelons of decision-making bodies. Some women members are directly involved in political decision-making in their capacity as Assembly (Parliament) Members, negating the common idea that women are generally apolitical" (Sackey 2006, 5).

While progress has been slow, it is important to recognize that women have, in fact, been active participants and holders of prominent roles in Indigenous and African traditional religions for thousands of years. By embracing and integrating Christian and Muslim traditions into their divergent spiritual practices, they have created hybrid traditions that enrich the religious lives of their communities. As opportunities for their religious leadership steadily increase, the future bodes well for the promotion of African women's agency and activism in the religious realm.

FURTHER READING

Aarmo, Margrete. 1999. "How Homosexuality Became 'Un-African': The Case of Zimbabwe." In *Female Desires: Same-Sex Relations and Transgender Practices across Cultures*, edited by Evelyn Blackwood and Saskia E. Wieringa, 255–280. New York: Columbia University Press.

Abbink, Jon. 2014. "Religion and Politics in Africa: The Future of 'The Secular.'" *Africa Spectrum* 49 (3): 83–106.

Agadjanian, Victor. 2015. "Women's Religious Authority in a Sub-Saharan Setting: Dialectics of Empowerment and Dependency." *Gender & Society* 29 (6): 982–1008.

Alimi, Bisi. 2015. "If You Say Being Gay Is Not African, You Don't Know Your History." *The Guardian*, September 9, 2015.

Awolalu, Joseph Omosade. 1991. "The Encounter between African Traditional Religion and Other Religions in Nigeria." In *African Traditional Religions in Contemporary Society*, edited by J. K. Olupọna, 111–118. St. Paul, MN: Paragon House.

Azuonye, Chukwuma. 2006. "Feminist or Simply Feminine? Reflections on the Works of Nana Asmā'u, a Nineteenth-Century West African Woman Poet, Intellectual, and Social Activist." *Meridians* 6 (2): 54–77.

Banchoff, Thomas, and Robert Wuthnow, eds. 2011. *Religion and the Global Politics of Human Rights*. New York: Oxford University Press.

Barnes, Tiffany D., and Stephanie M. Burchard. 2013. "'Engendering' Politics: The Impact of Descriptive Representation on Women's

Political Engagement in Sub-Saharan Africa." *Comparative Political Studies* 46 (7): 767–790.

BBC News. 2001. "Gays 'Fearful' in Namibia." March 20, 2001. http://news.bbc.co.uk/2/hi/africa/1231732.stm.

Berger, Iris, E. Frances White, and Cathy Skidmore-Hess. 1999. *Women in Sub-Saharan Africa: Restoring Women to History.* Bloomington: Indiana University Press.

Breidenbach, Paul S. 1979. "The Women on the Beach and the Man in the Bush: Leadership and Adepthood in the Twelve Apostles Movement of Ghana." In *The New Religions of Africa: Priests and Priestesses in Contemporary Cults and Churches*, edited by Bennetta Jules-Rosette, 108–109. Norwood, NJ: Ablex Publishing Corp.

Burleson, Blake Wiley. 1986. "John Mbiti: The Dialogue of an African Theology with African Traditional Religion." PhD diss., Baylor University.

Burnet, Lilian. 1913. "The Transvaal Native Women's Prayer Union." *Foreign Field* 10: 251.

Callaway, Barbara, and Lucy E. Creevey. 1994. *The Heritage of Islam: Women, Religion, and Politics in West Africa.* Boulder, CO: Lynne Rienner.

Chahrouk, Rima. 2016. *Do You Know about Nana Asmā'u, the Early Islamic Feminist Icon?* Mvslim, June 24, 2016. https://mvslim.com/know-nana-asmau-early-islamic-feminist-icon/.

Chitando, Ezra, ed. 2013. *Prayers and Players: Religion and Politics in Zimbabwe.* Harare, Zimbabwe: Sapes Books.

Clarke, Peter. 2012. "New Religious Movements in Sub-Saharan Africa. In *The Cambridge Companion to New Religious Movements*, edited by Olav Hammer and Mikael Rothstein, 303–320. Cambridge, UK: Cambridge University Press.

Coles, Catherine M., and Beverly B. Mack. 1991. *Hausa Women in the Twentieth Century.* Madison: University of Wisconsin Press.

Dankwa, Serena Owusua. 2009. "'It's a Silent Trade': Female Same-Sex Intimacies in Post-Colonial Ghana." *NORA—Nordic Journal of Feminist and Gender Research* 17 (3): 192–205.

Dube, Musa W. 2012. *Postcolonial Feminist Interpretation of the Bible.* St. Louis, MO: Chalice Press.

Dunton, Chris, and Mai Palmberg. 1996. *Human Rights and Homosexuality in Southern Africa.* Current African Issues 19. Uppsala, Sweden: Nordic Africa Institute.

Edwin, Shirin. 2006. "We Belong Here, Too: Accommodating African Muslim Feminism in African Feminist Theory via Zaynab Alkali's the Virtuous Woman and the Cobwebs and Other Stories." *Frontiers: A Journal of Women Studies* 27 (3): 140–156.

Ellis, Stephen, and Gerrie Ter Haar. 1998. "Religion and Politics in Sub-Saharan Africa." *Journal of Modern African Studies* 36 (2): 175–201.

García-Peñalosa, Cecilia, and Maty Konte. 2014. "Why Are Women Less Democratic Than Men? Evidence from Sub-Saharan African Countries." *World Development* 59: 104–119.

Gerhart, Gail. 1995. "The Heritage of Islam: Women, Religion, and Politics in West Africa." (Book Review). *Foreign Affairs* 74 (4): 158.

Gore, Charles. 2002. "Religion in Africa." In *Religions in the Modern World: Traditions and Transformations*, edited by Linda Woodhead, Christopher Partridge, and Hiroko Kawanami, 235. New York: Routledge.

Hastings, Adrian. 1966. "Christianity and African Cultures." *New Blackfriars* 48 (559): 127–136.

Hastings, Adrian. 1976. *African Christianity: An Essay in Interpretation*. London: Geoffrey Chapman.

Hinga, Teresia. 2002. "African Feminist Theologies, the Global Village, and the Imperative of Solidarity across Borders." *Journal of Feminist Studies in Religion* 18 (1): 79–86.

Inter-Parliamentary Union. 2008. "Women in National Parliaments." http://archive.ipu.org/wmn-e/world.htm.

Isichei, Elizabeth Allo. 2004. *The Religious Traditions of Africa: A History*. Westport, CT: Praeger.

Jell-Bahlsen, Sabine. 1998. "Female Power: Water Priestesses of the Oru-Igbo." In *Sisterhood, Feminisms, and Power: From Africa to the Diaspora*, edited by Obioma Nnaemeka, 101–132. Trenton, NJ: Africa World Press.

Joseph, Suad, and Afsāna Nağmābādī, eds. 2003. *Encyclopedia of Women & Islamic Cultures: Family, Law and Politics*. Vol. 2. Leiden, The Netherlands: Brill. 125–128.

Kaoma, Kapya. 1989. "Unmasking the Colonial Silence: Sexuality in Africa in the Post-Colonial Context." *Population and Development Review* 15 (2): 185–234.

Kaoma, Kapya. 2017. *Christianity, Globalization, and Protective Homophobia: Democratic Contestation of Sexuality in Sub-Saharan Africa*. New York: Springer.

Kaoma, Kapya John. 2006. "African Religion and Colonial Rebellion: The Contestation of Power in Colonial Zimbabwe's Chimurenga of 1896–1897." *Journal for the Study of Religion* 29 (1): 57–84.

Kendall, K. Limakatso. 1999. "Women in Lesotho and the (Western) Construction of Homophobia." In *Female Desires: Same-Sex Relations and Transgender Practices across Cultures*, edited by Evelyn Blackwood and Saskia E. Wieringa, 157–181. New York: Columbia University Press.

Kilson, Marion. 1976. "Women in African Traditional Religions." *Journal of Religion in Africa* 8 (2): 133–143.

Kotzé, Elmarie. 2013. "Boitumelo and the Cultural Practice of Lobola: A Counseling Example from South Africa." *Journal of Systemic Therapies* 32 (2): 17–29.

Kouvouama, Abel, and Jean Burrell. 1999. "Some New Religious Movements in Sub-Saharan Africa." *Diogenes* 47 (187): 62–70.

Kraemer, H. 1938. *The Christian Message in a Non-Christian World*. New York: Harper.

Lanman, C. 2007. "Mercy Amba Ewudziwa Oduyoye: Mother of Our Stories." *Studia Historiae Ecclesiasticae* 33 (1): 187–204.

Levtzion, Nehemia, and Randall Lee Pouwels. 2000. *The History of Islam in Africa*. Athens: Ohio University Press.

Long, Scott, A. Widney Brown, and Gail Cooper. 2003. "The Spread of Homophobic Rhetoric in Southern Africa." In *More Than a Name: State-Sponsored Homophobia and its Consequences in Southern Africa*. New York: Human Rights Watch.

Mama, Amina. 2013. "Women in Politics." In *Routledge Handbook of African Politics*, edited by Nicholas Cheeseman, David Anderson, and Andrea Scheibler, 147–162. London: Routledge.

Mapuranga, Tapiwa Praise. 2016. "Religion and the Participation of Women in Politics in Zimbabwe: Changing Identities and Perspectives (1960s–2014)." In *Being and Becoming: Gender, Culture and Shifting Identity in Sub-Saharan Africa*, edited by Chinyere Ukpokolo, 153–170. Denver, CO; Bamenda, Cameroon: Spears Media Press.

Mbiti, John S. 1990. *African Religions & Philosophy*. Portsmouth, NH: Heinemann.

McClendon, David. 2016. "Muslims in Sub-Saharan Africa Are Twice as Likely as Christians to Have No Formal Education." Pew Research Center, Fact Tank: News in the Numbers, December 14, 2016.

https://www.pewresearch.org/fact-tank/2016/12/14/muslims-in
-sub-saharan-africa-are-twice-as-likely-as-christians-to-have-no
-formal-education/.

Merritt, Nikki. 1994. "Nana Asmā'u, Her Elegies and the Possibility of 'Insider Alternatives.'" *African Languages and Cultures* 7 (2): 91–99.

Mofokeng, Takatso. 1988. "Black Christians, the Bible and Liberation." *Journal of Black Theology* 2 (1): 34–42.

Mulago, Vincent. 1991. "Traditional African Religion and Christianity." In *African Traditional Religions in Contemporary Society*, edited by J. K. Olupọna, 119–134. St. Paul, MN: Paragon House.

Njoh, Ambe J., and Fenda A. Akiwumi. 2012. "The Impact of Religion on Women Empowerment as a Millennium Development Goal in Africa." *Social Indicators Research* 107 (1): 1–18.

Njovana, Eunice, and Charlotte Watts. 1996. "Gender Violence in Zimbabwe: A Need for Collaborative Action." *Reproductive Health Matters* 4 (7): 46–55.

Nnaemeka, Obioma, ed. 1998. *Sisterhood, Feminisms, and Power: From Africa to the Diaspora*. Trenton, NJ: Africa World Press.

Oduyoye, Mercy Amba. 2002. "Jesus Christ." In *The Cambridge Companion to Feminist Theology*, edited by Susan Frank Parsons, 151–170. Cambridge, UK: Cambridge University Press.

Ogunbado, A. F. 2012. "Impacts of Colonialism on Religions: An Experience of Southwestern Nigeria." *IOSR Journal of Humanities and Social Science* 5 (6): 51–57.

Olupọna, J. K., ed. 1991. *African Traditional Religions in Contemporary Society*. St. Paul, MN: Paragon House.

Olupona, J. K., and S. S. Nyang, eds. 2013. *Religious Plurality in Africa: Essays in Honour of John S. Mbiti*. Vol. 32. Berlin, Germany: Walter de Gruyter.

Oredein, Oluwatomisin. 2016. "Interview with Mercy Amba Oduyoye: Mercy Amba Oduyoye in Her Own Words." *Journal of Feminist Studies in Religion* 32 (2) (Fall): 153–164.

Parratt, J. 1995. *Reinventing Christianity: African Theology Today*. Grand Rapids, MI: Wm. B. Eerdmans Publishing.

Petersen, Elizabeth. 2016. "Working with Religious Leaders and Faith Communities to Advance Culturally Informed Strategies to Address Violence against Women." *Agenda* 30 (3): 50–59.

Pew Research Center. 2010. "Tolerance and Tension: Islam and Christianity in Sub-Saharan Africa." April 15, 2010. https://www.pewforum

.org/2010/04/15/executive-summary-islam-and-christianity-in-sub
-saharan-africa/.

Radtke, Rob, and Anwar Khan. 2018. "Religion Is Blamed for Violence against Women. We Are Christian and Muslim Leaders Who Fight It—Together." *Newsweek*, November 20, 2018. https://www .newsweek.com/religion-blamed-violence-against-women-we-are -christian-muslim-leaders-fight-1224771.

Rakoczy, Susan. 2004. "Religion and Violence: The Suffering of Women." *Agenda: Empowering Women for Gender Equity* 18 (61): 29–35.

Ranger, T. O. 1986. "Religious Movements and Politics in Sub-Saharan Africa." *African Studies Review* 29 (2): 1–70.

Robinson, D. 2004. *Muslim Societies in African History*. Vol. 2. New York: Cambridge University Press.

Sackey, Brigid M. 2006. *New Directions in Gender and Religion: The Changing Status of Women in African Independent Churches*. Lanham, MD: Lexington Books.

Samwini, Nathan. 2006. *The Muslim Resurgence in Ghana Since 1950: Its Effects upon Muslims and Muslim-Christian Relations*. Vol. 7. Münster, Germany: LIT Verlag.

Shank, David A. 1986. "The Legacy of William Wadé Harris." *International Bulletin of Missionary Research* 10 (4): 170–176.

Sheldon, K. 2016. *Historical Dictionary of Women in Sub-Saharan Africa*. Lanham, MD: Rowman & Littlefield.

Sofola, Zulu. 1998. "Feminism and African Womanhood." In *Sisterhood, Feminisms, and Power: From Africa to the Diaspora*, edited by Obioma Nnaemeka, 51–64. Trenton, NJ: Africa World Press.

Stichter, Sharon, and Margaret Jean Hay, eds. 1995. *African Women South of the Sahara*. London: Longman Scientific & Technical.

Sudarkasa, Niara. 1986. "'The Status of Women' in Indigenous African Societies." *Feminist Studies* 12 (1): 91–103.

Takyi, Baffour K., and Enoch Lamptey. 2020. "Faith and Marital Violence in Sub-Saharan Africa: Exploring the Links between Religious Affiliation and Intimate Partner Violence among Women in Ghana." *Journal of Interpersonal Violence* 35 (1–2): 25–52.

Thomas, Douglas E. 2005. *African Traditional Religion in the Modern World*. Jefferson, NC: McFarland & Company, Inc., Publishers.

Trimingham, J. S. 1980. *The Influence of Islam upon Africa*. London: Longman.

Tripp, Aili Marie. 2017. "Women and Politics in Africa." In *Oxford Research Encyclopedia of African History*, edited by Thomas Spear. Oxford, UK: Oxford University Press.

Ukpokolo, Chinyere, ed. 2016. *Being and Becoming: Gender, Culture and Shifting Identity in Sub-Saharan Africa*. Denver, CO: Spears Media Press.

Von Sicard, Sigvard. 1993. "Christian-Muslim Relations in Africa." In *Religious Plurality in Africa: Essays in Honour of John S. Mbiti*, vol. 32, 273–283, edited by Jacob K. Olupona and Sulayman S. Nyang. Berlin, Germany: Walter de Gruyter.

Walker, Cherryl, ed. 1990. *Women and Gender in Southern Africa to 1945*. Claremont, South Africa: New Africa Books.

West, Gerald, Charlene Van der Walt, and Kapya John Kaoma. 2016. "When Faith Does Violence: Reimagining Engagement between Churches and LGBTI Groups on Homophobia in Africa." *HTS Theological Studies* 72 (1): 1–8.

SIX

Central and East Asia

Suzanne E. Schier-Happell

WOMEN IN THE RELIGIONS OF CENTRAL AND EAST ASIA

Central and East Asia are incredibly diverse in terms of culture, language, history, politics, gender norms, and religion. Central Asia is composed of five former Soviet republics—Kazakhstan, Kyrgyzstan, Tajikistan, Turkmenistan, and Uzbekistan—and Afghanistan. East Asia includes China, Hong Kong, Japan, Macau, Mongolia, North Korea, South Korea, and Taiwan (Republic of China).

The dominant religion in Central Asia is Islam, though the Russian Orthodox Church also plays an important role in the region, even though Orthodox Christians make up a small minority of the population. Before the widespread introduction of and conversion to Islam throughout Central Asia in the eighth century CE, the religious landscape was incredibly diverse, with significant populations of Buddhists, Zoroastrians, and Hindus (especially those dedicated to the god Shiva).

Buddhism is the most populous religion throughout East Asia, though Protestantism and Catholicism also have well-established minority presences throughout the region, in large part because of Christian missionary activity over many years. Islam has a small but significant presence throughout East Asia as well.

In Central Asia, the religious landscape is completely different from that of East Asia. Islam is the dominant religion in Afghanistan and among the Central Asian republics, with hardly any of the population identifying as religiously unaffiliated (Pew Research Center 2012). Meanwhile, large percentages of the population in East Asia self-identify as unaffiliated, with over half the populations of China, Japan, North and South Korea, and Hong Kong claiming no religious identity at all (Pew Research Center 2012).

However, a distinction must be made between overt religious affiliation (actively identifying with a specific religion) and deeply embedded religious influence. For example, although many people living in China may not consciously see themselves as religious, the culture in which they live has historically been deeply shaped by Buddhism, Taoism, and Confucianism. As such, women's lives are also shaped by these traditions, though such influence may be taken for granted as a natural part of culture and society. Similarly, in Japan, Shinto beliefs and rituals permeate the culture so completely that many people in Japan do not see them as religious in nature; instead, they just seem like a normal part of Japanese culture and daily life. As such, the impact of religion on women's lives in East Asia is stronger than any self-reported data will indicate.

Folk traditions also play a significant role in religious life throughout East Asia. These are beliefs and practices that are unique to each geographical region. Folk religions often date back to before the introduction of formal religious and philosophical systems, such as Buddhism, Taoism, or Confucianism, between the sixth and third centuries BCE. Folk religions typically include a belief in spirits, Indigenous healing systems, storytelling or mythic traditions, significant figures (deities, heroes, saints, etc.) who are worshipped or highly respected, philosophical worldviews, and rituals meant to bring about good fortune or other desired outcomes in both the material and spiritual worlds.

There are many people throughout East Asia who identify as practitioners of folk religions, but even for people who do not think of themselves in this way, including people who identify with other religions, such as Christianity or Islam, the social and cultural influences of folk traditions remain strong, even though these influences may be taken for granted.

The influence of folk religion is significant for women in these societies because folk traditions often include beliefs and practices that include and even empower women in ways that many formal religions do not. For this reason, many women throughout present-day East Asia are finding a renewed interest in folk religions and are assuming leadership roles in those traditions at a growing rate (Sang-Hun 2007; Nishide 2014).

To fully understand the significance of religion in the everyday lives of women in Central and East Asia, it is important to consider not only individual beliefs and experiences but also how seriously people take religion in general in each geographical region. The importance people give to religion in Central Asia is very different from East Asia. While religion plays a critical role in the lives of most people in Central Asia, East Asia has some of the least religious nations in the world.

For example, in a 2018 report, the Pew Research Center for Religion and Public Life found that in the Central Asian country of Afghanistan, 92 percent of the population said that religion was "very important" to them. Conversely, in South Korea, only 16 percent of the population deemed religion to be very important; in Japan, only 10 percent considered religion to be very important; and in China, this percentage dwindles to a mere 3 percent (Pew Research Center 2018)—the lowest in the entire world! It is also notable, however, that China is also ranked as one of the most highly restrictive countries in the world in regard to religion (Pew Research Center 2019).

A large number of people in Afghanistan say they identify with a specific religion, and most people there also believe that religion is important. In contrast, China and Japan both have very low rates of formal religious affiliation, and a low percentage of the people find religion important (Pew Research Center 2018). The Central Asian republics, however, show a different pattern altogether. They report extremely high formal affiliation rates, but the percentage of the population that considers religion to be "very important" is surprisingly small: 50 percent in Tajikistan, 47 percent in Kyrgyzstan, 29 percent in Uzbekistan, and only 22 percent in Kazakhstan (Turkmenistan was not included in the dataset) (Pew Research Center 2018). Where governments are concerned, however, the Pew Research Center identifies Kyrgyzstan as "high" and Uzbekistan, Turkmenistan, Tajikistan, and Kazakhstan as "very high" regarding restrictions on religion. In the same report, Afghanistan received a ranking of "high" for government restrictions (Pew Research Center 2019).

These numbers are important in the consideration of how religion impacts women in these regions. For example, Islamic beliefs about women's status in Afghanistan have the power to carry tremendous weight because of how highly the overall population values Islamic tradition, whereas the same beliefs among Muslims in China would have a much smaller effect on women overall. Religious beliefs of any kind about women's status in China may have a much smaller effect in the lives of Chinese women due to the overall low importance of religion to the general population.

However, in highly religious areas, a common challenge for women in these regions is trying to negotiate traditional roles and gender norms with the desire for their own empowerment and social equality (Washington 2018; Urbaeva 2019). Like many places throughout the world, male privilege defines most Central and East Asian cultures and religions, so women who value religion may struggle to balance their desire to respect tradition with wanting to fully participate in the social and religious life of their communities as equals.

Women in Buddhism in the Region

Buddhism has a wide presence throughout East Asia, making up modest percentages of the population in Mongolia (55.1 percent), Japan (36.2 percent), South Korea (22.9 percent), Taiwan (21.3 percent), China (18.2 percent), Macau (17.3 percent), and Hong Kong (13.2 percent) (PewResearch Center 2012).

While Buddhism tries to avoid focusing on physical distinctions or the material world, male bias remains present in many aspects of Buddhist tradition, partially because of the deep influence of a culture that privileges masculinity but also because of the way sacred texts and traditions get interpreted by practitioners.

Most Buddhist traditions in East Asia fall within the category of Mahayana Buddhism, which means "the Great Vehicle." In Mahayana Buddhism, practitioners think it is possible for human beings to reach enlightenment in this lifetime, and they also believe enlightenment is accessible to laypeople (people who are not monks or nuns), including laywomen (Smith and Novak 2004). Buddhist women can either become nuns or remain laypeople.

In contrast, Theravada Buddhist traditions include the belief that it is more difficult for women to become enlightened than men. While not impossible, women are believed to have more obstacles to overcome on the path to awakening. One such obstacle is that their bodies are biologically tied to the physical world through menstruation, pregnancy, and childbirth (Harris 1999). On the other hand, a woman who is able to overcome such obstacles and become enlightened is deemed to be worthy of great respect because she has had to work harder than a man to reach the same goal.

Zen Buddhism, which is a subset of Mahayana, has a strong presence in East Asia. Zen playfully flips social norms upside down, rejecting the

In Buddhism, worshippers such as these at the Beidi Temple in Shenzhen, China, burn incense as an offering to the Buddha or other deities. Many Buddhists also believe incense dispels evil and purifies the space. (Sansan67/Dreamstime.com)

many powerful—but false—ideas that keep us stuck in the impermanent material world. As such, through spiritual practice, many Zen practitioners declare freedom from restrictive societal conventions. For some Zen Buddhists, that includes rejecting ways of thinking and doing that discriminate against women. Many women seeking monastic life have found Zen Buddhism to be a particularly hospitable tradition because of its openness and transcendent philosophy.

Buddhist nuns have been a key driver of education for women throughout East Asia, making a valuable contribution to women's advancement. Buddhist nuns also contributed to the early growth and success of Buddhism in East Asia. Female monasticism thrived as Buddhism spread, and nuns enjoyed high status and broad opportunity overall during this time. During the rise of Buddhism in Japan in the late sixth through eighth centuries, almost half of all Buddhist monastics in Japan were nuns, and in the eighth century, a governmental initiative pushed for a convent (as well as a monastery) to be built in every single province in Japan (Meeks 2014).

The availability of monasticism as a potential life choice for East Asian Buddhist women has expanded their opportunities beyond socially pre-scribed roles, both then and now. Ding-hwa Hsieh writes that in China during the Sung period (960–1279 CE), "the nunnery indeed offered women a respected social role other than that of mother and wife; entrance into the monastic life provided career-minded women the opportunity to gain fame and publicity" (Hsieh 2000, 65).

Becoming nuns also enabled women to sidestep unsatisfying or oppres-sive life circumstances. For example, the twelfth-century Korean text the *Samguk sagi* ("The History of the Three Kingdoms") describes the regu-lar practice of high-status women taking vows to become Buddhist nuns when they became widows (Meeks 2014), thereby avoiding the precarious-ness and social stigmatization of widowhood in the surrounding society. In the Sung period, Chinese women who remained unmarried past a cer-tain age often became nuns (Hsieh 2000) rather than incur the family bur-den and individual social fallout of supposed "spinster" status. Monasticism gave women an alternate path, and it still does in many ways today.

Women in Christianity in the Region

Although not a majority religion in any part of Central or East Asia, Christianity still has a notable presence in the region. In East Asia, there are Christian populations in South Korea (29.4 percent), Hong Kong (14.3 percent), Macau (7.2 percent), Taiwan (5.5 percent), China (5.1 percent), Mongolia (2.3 percent), North Korea (2.0 percent), and Japan (1.6 percent). In Central Asia, there are Christian minority populations in Kazakhstan (24.8 percent), Kyrgyzstan (11.4 percent), Turkmenistan (6.4 percent), Uzbekistan (2.3 percent), and Tajikistan (1.6 percent) (Pew Research Cen-ter 2012).

Central Asia

The Russian Orthodox Church remains a key Christian presence in the Central Asian republics in the post-Soviet era. Christians in Central Asia face a number of social challenges, especially as religious fervor grows among certain parts of the population. Conservative Muslims in Kyrgyz-stan have heavily targeted Christians for violence and discrimination. This is especially true for people who convert from Islam to Christian Baptist affiliation, a Protestant branch of Christianity that has recently been heavily targeted. Churches have been burned down, and converts have been harassed, beaten, and even killed. Uzbekistan and Kazakhstan have also experienced beatings of recent converts from Islam to Christianity (Botobekov 2017).

East Asia

Evangelical Protestant Christianity has found success in China, especially following the Cultural Revolution, when all religion was heavily suppressed under Maoist rule. In present-day Communist China, Protestantism and Catholicism are both officially sanctioned as permitted religions by the Chinese government. However, only churches that register with the state and operate within rather strict guidelines are recognized by the government as legitimate. There is also a thriving underground Protestant Christian movement whose members primarily meet in homes and other venues outside the recognized churches. Because the government only counts officially registered churches in the total numbers, it is difficult to get a true estimate of the number of people in China who self-identify as Christian. However, it is surely far higher than the official counts indicate.

Anglican Priesthood

Women have been formally approved for ordination as priests in the Anglican Communion, also known as the Church of England, in three East Asian countries: Korea, Japan, and Hong Kong. Although Hong Kong did not receive official approval to fully ordain women until 1971, such an ordination actually happened there far earlier. In 1944, Florence Li Tim-Oi became the first woman ever to be ordained as an Anglican priest—not just the first in Asia but in the entire world!

Florence Li Tim-Oi was serving as a deacon at a settlement in Macao filled with Chinese refugees during World War II, where she assisted the priest charged with caring for the community. As a woman, she was unable to celebrate the Eucharist and depended on a priest to travel to Macao to officiate over the sacraments. However, when Japanese occupation prevented the priest from traveling, he remotely conferred upon Tim-Oi the authority to preside over the Eucharist, which she did faithfully for three years. Then, in January 1944, Bishop R. O. Hall of Hong Kong formally ordained Tim-Oi—an act that he believed merely confirmed the gifts she already had (Li Tim-Oi Foundation n.d.).

However, because her ordination was not formally approved by authorities before it was performed, her priestly status was not immediately recognized by church officials despite multiple appeals. Tim-Oi voluntarily gave up her priest's license in 1946, wanting to stem the conflict, but she did not give up her Holy Orders. She continued to practice as a priest in China and then later in Canada after retirement.

Women in Hinduism in the Region

While Hinduism enjoys a strong presence throughout South and Southeast Asia, it is a less common religious affiliation in Central and East Asia. Historically, Hinduism had a strong presence in pre-Islamic Afghanistan, with Hindus numbering in the tens of thousands, but those numbers fell to just a few thousand Hindus after Afghanistan came under Islamic rule between and seventh and tenth centuries CE. That number was further reduced following the Taliban's rise to power in the mid-1990s.

When the Taliban sought to separate Afghan Hindus from the Islamic-majority population, Hindu women were affected by being forced to wear hijabs and conform to the same restrictive social expectations the Taliban had of Muslim women (Rashid 2001). These and other discriminatory policies caused many Afghan Hindus to migrate to India, where there is a Hindu majority, and today only around one thousand Hindus remain in Afghanistan around Kabul.

Women in Islam in the Region

Central Asia

Islam plays a critical role in Central Asia: there are significant Muslim populations in the former Soviet Central Asian states: Tajikistan (96.7 percent), Uzbekistan (96.7 percent), Turkmenistan (93.0 percent), Kyrgyzstan (88.0 percent), and Kazakhstan (70.4 percent). Likewise, Afghanistan is 99.7 percent Muslim (Pew Research Center 2012). It is important to note that Islam in Central Asia is extremely diverse, with many unique branches of Islam represented throughout the region. These include Ismaili, Twelver, and Zaidi Muslims, all of which are subgroups of Shi'a Islam. Sufism, a tradition build around Islamic mysticism, is also prevalent in the region.

The Islamic traditions throughout Central Asia also have many regionally unique characteristics due to the influence of local folk traditions, resulting in various forms of folk (or vernacular) Islam. Beliefs and practices under the category of folk Islam may include specialized devotional practices, showing reverence to saints or other important figures, and the inclusion of sacred sites for use as shrines or pilgrimage destinations. Importantly, folk Islamic traditions can create space for women's greater participation in the religious life of the community (Mills 2005).

East Asia

Muslims make up an extremely small minority of the East Asian population. For example, only 3.2 percent of Mongolia, 1.8 percent of China, and 1.8 percent of Hong Kong identify as Muslim (Pew Research Center 2012). There are a number of unique features of Chinese Islam, both presently and historically. In China, the tradition of women's mosques dates back to 1820, and they still remain in service in the provinces of Henan, Shanxi, and Hebei. By having a dedicated women-only mosque, women were able to assume leadership roles and enjoy more active participation, with the mosque serving as the "heart of a community" (Lim 2010). The predecessors of women-only mosques were the Qur'anic schools for girls established in Central China toward the end of the seventeenth century.

Women's mosques were formed and administered "by women for women" (Lim 2010). They were often established by highly educated Muslim women who were prepared to be theological teachers and leaders. In many cases, women were able to become imams—Islamic worship leaders and spiritual guides—to their congregations in these mosques. China is the only country with such a long-standing tradition of having female imams. While they cannot officiate over certain funeral rituals, female imams play a vital role in the spiritual lives of the women in their mosque communities (Lim 2010). Although there have always been some Chinese Muslims who oppose women-only mosques, women's mosques have enjoyed a long history of independence, honorable status, and strong community participation in Central and Eastern China for many years.

However, in Western China, the social and political landscape changes dramatically, and women enjoy no such elevated status. This part of China is home to the Uighur Muslim community, which has regularly experienced marginalization by the local Han Chinese majority population. In Xinjiang province, there are laws banning Islamic face veils, criminalizing the display of certain Islamic symbols or wearing traditional Islamic dress, and prohibiting fasting during Ramadan—a ritual tradition that is required of Muslims in the Five Pillars of Islam. Bethany Allen-Ebrahimian reports, "To enforce the ban, schools and work units are required to monitor the behavior of Muslim students and employees to ensure they are eating" (Allen-Ebrahimian 2015).

A critical issue for Uighur Muslim women in Xinjiang is their ability to worship and pray together. In Uighur tradition, only men are allowed to pray in the mosque, so women must pray elsewhere. To accommodate this restriction, Uighur women have commonly gathered at one another's homes for religious activities instead. However, because only certain mosques are sanctioned by government officials and thereby allowed to operate, the home-based religious meetings were deemed illegal by authorities and were actively suppressed.

In 2017, China legally banned the burqa and headscarves in Xinjiang, with the articulated reasoning being that this was an effort to fight religious extremism (Dearden 2017). By 2019, discriminatory policies and practices expanded beyond Xinjiang and are now affecting Muslims throughout China. Some of these more widespread initiatives include the banning of Arabic script, the destruction of mosques with distinctly Arabian features (e.g., minarets), a prohibition against organizing kindergartens, and the elimination of Islamic financial systems (Myers 2019). Uighur Muslims have also experienced an increase in suppressive policies and actions. The future status of Islam in China remains uncertain.

Women in Judaism in the Region

Although the present-day Jewish population is small—but present—throughout Central and East Asia, for many centuries, waves of Jewish refugees have fled to this region to escape persecution. The following are some examples:

- A unique Jewish community was established in Uzbekistan following the destruction of the First Temple in Jerusalem during the sixth century BCE.

- Jewish refugees facing forced conversion in Persia fled to Afghanistan during the nineteenth century CE. Russian Jewish refugees fleeing the Russian Civil War settled in Mongolia around 1920 (World Jewish Congress 2020).

- During World War II, European Jewish families fleeing the Holocaust found safe haven in China, with nearly thirty thousand Jewish refugees settling in Shanghai (Guang n.d.).

Central Asia

One of the oldest ethnic groups in Central Asia is the Isro'il, more commonly known as Bukharan Jews. They speak a unique language called Bukhori, a hybrid of Persian and Hebrew languages in a Tajik dialect. This community traces its own roots of settlement in the region back to the seventh century BCE during a time of exile. While some Jewish migrants continued moving eastward to settle in China, many remained in Central Asia to establish Bukharan communities throughout the region.

Until Islamization occurred around 700 CE, Central Asia was predominantly of the Zoroastrian religion. The small Bukharan Jewish community was largely accepted by the majority population and was treated well by both Zoroastrian and Islamic regional authorities. This changed when Uzbek rulers assumed power; they persecuted the Bukharan Jewish community. Bukharan Jews had to pay special taxes and wear different clothes than the general population (Carr n.d.). The clothes were drab and uniform in contrast to the colorful traditional dress.

Bukharan Jewish communities differed from many others through their colorful clothes and lively customs. For example, Bukharan women's customary dress is described as follows: "The Bukharan Jewish woman's costume of that period included a loose-fitting ikat silk gown in shades of rose or violet, over which was worn an elaborately-embroidered coat with kimono sleeves, called a kaltshak. Head-covering was either an embroidered cap or tulle scarf with a jeweled forehead ornament. Other jewelry included bracelets, earrings and coin necklaces" (Carr n.d.).

Eventually, many Bukharan Jews converted to Islam. Others left the region and settled elsewhere in the world. Meanwhile, many Jewish people from Russia also either migrated to or were banished to the region, joining the Bukharan Jewish community that remained. This movement in and out of the community permanently changed the face of Bukharan

Judaism, including a strong Russian influence thanks to the influx of Russian Jewish refugees and exiles (Carr n.d.). Today, most Bukharan Jewish people speak both Bukhori and Russian in addition to any other regional languages.

Bukharan Jewish communities experienced further repression under Soviet rule because of the antireligious stance of the Soviets. Following the end of this repressive era in the late 1980s, the Bukharan Jewish community largely dispersed from Central Asia and primarily exists today in diaspora throughout the world. Only a very small Bukharan Jewish population remains in Central Asia. Many migrated to Israel, but the second-largest Bukharan Jewish population in the world, outside of Israel, is in Queens, New York, where the Bukharan Jewish population numbers around fifty thousand (Benaim 2017).

Bukharan Jewish gender relationships, even between romantic or marriage partners, are traditionally conservative and restrained. Parents must approve of potential marriage partners, who should also be members of the community, and men and women do not live with one another until after marriage (Schoenberg 2006). After marriage, Bukharan women traditionally wear clothing with high necklines and long skirts and cover their hair with a headscarf (Schoenberg 2006).

However, "traditional" Bukharan culture also privileges men over women, a dynamic that was established and supported within a larger patriarchal Central Asian culture. In marital relationships, husbands assumed dominant roles within the household. In diaspora, however, the patriarchal order is often challenged by a different set of social norms and compounded by other stressors.

As such, one issue that some Bukharan Jewish women face in diaspora is domestic abuse. In an article about Bukharan community family violence, Joseph Berger writes, "Rabbi Nisanov, who was raised in a suburb of Samarkand in Uzbekistan and came here as a boy, said, 'We always have this problem, but now the women are speaking out, the rabbis are speaking out and we're not just shoving it under the rug like we did before'" (Berger 2003).

Indeed, domestic abuse is being actively tackled within diasporic Jewish communities *by* women and *for* women who are affected by abuse. The Shalom Task Force (STF), based in New York, is an organization that conducts workshops to "teach young women and men about forging healthy relationships and avoiding abusive ones" (Shalom Task Force 2018). Within STF, Beit Shalom serves the Bukharan Jewish community, providing education, free legal services, and a domestic violence hotline.

Jewish Marriage in China

Jewish marriage has historically been endogamous, meaning people found marriage partners within their own community. Endogamy is an important practice in Judaism because of the way Jewish identity transfers from one generation to the next. Traditionally, Judaism is matrilineal—meaning Jewish identity is passed down through the mother's bloodline. Maintaining endogamous marriage customs ensures that future generations will retain ancestral Jewish identity.

However, following the wave of Jewish refugee resettlement in China following World War II, the practice of endogamy relaxed somewhat, given the small size of the Jewish community. Intermarriage between Jewish and non-Jewish Asian partners has complicated the way identity is passed down and understood for many East Asian blended Jewish families. The children born from these half-Jewish intermarriages often struggle to understand their multilayered, multiethnic Jewish and Asian identities as they live a life between two different cultures.

This is especially complex for Jewish Asian women. Gen Slosberg writes about her experience growing up in China as the child of such a blended marriage: "I became defined by things I did not choose. . . . As a young teenager, I attracted hollers of 'wa! Gui mui! Hou leung! (wow, foreign girl, how pretty)!' from men before I was even ready to embrace my womanhood. To be mixed [Jewish and Chinese] and a woman meant my appearance was of the utmost importance to everyone around me" (Slosberg 2018). While descendants of Jewish Asian partnerships may question identity and belonging, regardless of gender, the social objectification of women's bodies that Slosberg describes reveals a particularly complex experience for Jewish Asian women.

Women in Indigenous Religions

There are many Indigenous spiritual beliefs and practices throughout East Asia that are widely observed but may not be recognized by the local population as overtly religious, mainly because the line between religion and culture is blurred. They are so deeply embedded in the regional culture that it is easy for people who observe such traditions to take them for granted. Such traditions are often referred to as *folk religions*.

In East Asia, folk religions often include ethical guidelines, belief in spirits, medical/healing systems, and rituals that often punctuate daily life. They may also include forms of divination or communication between humans and spirits.

Chinese folk religions have a strong presence, with 21.9 percent of the population practicing these traditions. Hong Kong reports 12.8 percent, and in North Korea, 12.3 percent of the population practices folk religions as well. Macau has the highest percentage of folk religion practitioners, with an incredible 58.9 percent, though Taiwan (Republic of China) is not far behind with 44.2 percent (Pew Research Center 2012).

Women have historically been associated with healing practices and shamanism (a shaman is a ritual expert who can communicate with the spirits) in East Asian folk traditions, broadly speaking. Women still serve as traditional shamans in some parts of East Asia, especially in Japan and South Korea. In China, however, shamanic spiritual roles for women have declined as patrilineal ancestor veneration took the place of shamanism over time (Nelson 2008).

In Japan, there is a uniquely Japanese, culturally embedded spiritual system that is commonly called Shinto—literally "the Way of the Gods."

WU IN CHINESE FOLK RELIGION

The practice of Chinese folk religion was widespread in ancient China and Taiwan. Practitioners of folk religions venerated forces of nature and ancestors, and they believed humans, as well as spirits and gods, can influence the universe.

In Chinese folk religion, the role of a shaman or spirit medium was to repair breaches in nature and to heal people. Women shamans are called *wu* (men are called *xi*). The *wu* and *xi* "represent the voice of spirits, repair the natural dis-functions, foretell the future based on dreams and the art of divination" (Chirita 2014). As intermediaries with the spirits, *wu* healed people, made rain, interpreted dreams, and exercised political power.

Confucianists challenged women's public political and religious power, attempting to relegate them to service roles to maintain male power. Despite these attempts and efforts by the Chinese government to discourage religious practice, folk religions persist across the region, and women shamans persist in local practice.

Susan M. Shaw

Chirita, Andreea. 2014. "Antagonistic Discourses on Shamanic Folklore in Modern China." *Analele Universitatii Crestine Dimitrie Cantemir, Seria Stiintele Limbii, Literaturii si Didactica predarii* 1 (1): 22–34.

It is a tradition that dates back to approximately the second century CE. As with other folk religions, many people who observe Shinto rituals or beliefs may not view them as "religious." However, this spiritual belief system includes many features commonly associated with religion: temples and shrines, priests, ritual practices, rules regarding purity and pollution, ethical guidelines, belief in nature and ancestor spirits, and ways of communicating with those spirits.

During the initial rise of Shinto in Japan, women served as priests and shamans, whose primary role was communicating with the spirits. In Japanese culture, women have traditionally been seen as having a stronger connection to the spirits (Nelson 2008). Therefore, women fulfilled a critical duty in the ongoing spiritual life of the community, as they bridged the connection between the human and spirit worlds (Haruko 1993).

The active role of women in the priesthood experienced a decline as Shinto traditions became more structured and formalized over time. However, in the present day, women's participation in the Shinto priesthood has experienced a modern revival and is now steadily on the rise (Nishide 2014).

ISSUES OF RELIGION FOR WOMEN IN EAST AND CENTRAL ASIA

The Impact of Christian Missionaries on the Colonial Project in East and Central Asia

Women's Education

The presence of Christian missionaries had a significant impact on educational opportunities for East Asian women. Until 1920, 80 percent of the colleges and universities in China were missionary colleges; in Korea, there were almost eight hundred Christian missionary schools by 1910, with more schools for girls than boys (Hong 2019). Christian missionaries established schools throughout East Asia that were accessible to women, often either displacing local educational systems or providing new opportunities where few previously existed.

Jeesoon Hong writes, "In China, missionaries ran 38 mission schools for girls in 1877 and educated more girls relative to boys than did government schools. American Protestant missionaries founded the first college for women 13 years before the government university admitted its first female student" (Hong 2019, 4).

These schools were largely founded by Christian women from the United States, who traveled to East Asia to become missionaries as representatives of different women's foreign missions societies. Women dominated the missionary field in East Asia at the turn of the century, with women outnumbering men more than two to one in the East Asian mission field by 1919 (Hong 2019). As such, Christian women's colleges were largely founded by women, for women, and were therefore deeply influential both in direct instruction and in modeling Western norms and values.

Missionary-established Christian women's colleges affected the way the women saw themselves and their social roles. These schools intentionally sought to replace Confucian values in exchange for American, Protestant, middle-class values regarding women's roles and prescribed behaviors both in public and in the home (Hong 2019). Although government-sponsored schools replaced missionary schools in China and Japan in the mid-twentieth century, the influence of missionary education on East Asian views of womanhood has been long lasting.

Decline and Revival of Shamanism

Christian missionaries opposed many religious practices associated with folk traditions, especially those that involved consulting spirits or performing animal sacrifice, which many Christian missionaries viewed as demonic. As a result, such local traditions were actively suppressed by missionaries.

Because women commonly served in roles of spiritual authority as shamans (ritual experts who mediate between the human and spirit worlds) in folk religions, the suppression of local spiritual traditions was accompanied by the loss of a source of power, status, and opportunity for women.

In Korea, shamanism was condemned not only by Western Christian missionaries but also by Japanese colonial forces and postwar military governors, who saw such practices as superstitious and regressive (Sang-Hun 2007). Such powerful opposition forced Korean shamans to practice in secret or in some cases to abandon their work altogether.

However, today, shamanism is building a new popularity among Korean women. This resurgence began when shamanism was finally recognized again by authorities as a tradition of cultural significance and a valuable symbol of Korean history (Sang-Hun 2007). Because shamanism is regaining public respect, fewer women who practice as shamans feel the need to hide, and more women are answering the call to become new practitioners.

Women in Religious Leadership

Traditional Shamans in South Korea

Korean shamanism has seen a revival in popularity in recent years, as more people seek shamans to ask the spirits for healing or good luck or for help in overcoming obstacles (Sang-Hun 2007). For example, someone may ask for a good score on an upcoming exam, a successful job interview, or a quick recovery from recent illness for themselves or someone they love. Women who serve as shamans in South Korea perform work that is highly respected, and this shamanic tradition is thriving in this region today (Nelson 2008).

Shinto Priests in Japan

In early Shinto tradition, many temples had both male and female priests, as they managed different aspects of spiritual life. However, as Shinto became more formalized over time, the role of women changed. The focus on local deities declined in exchange for a more unified national Shinto identity and practice—an initiative sponsored by political authorities as Shinto became a state-sponsored tradition. With increasing formalization, the role for male priests grew while that of female priests declined (Haruko 1993). The dynamic world of shamanism—a world of openness and unpredictability—gave way to the more structured, regimented, and predictable work of male priests.

The Shinto priesthood remained dominated by men until after World War II, when women were openly welcomed back into the priesthood, but this time carrying the same status and duties as male priests. Women who are priests do face a unique challenge in that they must manage the perceived pollution associated with menstruation in Shinto beliefs, an idea that is locally reinforced by widely influential Buddhist beliefs as well (Haruko 1993).

Shinto women's participation in the priesthood has been steadily rising following an initial decline. At the end of 2012, Japan had 667 female chief Shinto priests, which was about 7 percent of all chief priests (Nishide 2014)—a small minority but a growing one nonetheless.

Mikos, who serve at Shinto shrines, were once shamans who actively participated in religious rites. Now, their roles are significantly reduced, although they may be involved in some ceremonies, such as weddings, funerals, and festivals. (Checco/Dreamstime.com)

Catholic Leadership in China

Catholic missionary activity in China started with Dominican missionaries in the Fujian province during the 1600s. They actively recruited Chinese women into authoritative roles as beatas, who took vows of spiritual service to God and church. Then, in the early 1700s, Catholic missionaries from France recruited women into leadership roles—with Rome's approval—as consecrated virgins (Leung and Wittburg 2004).

Women in these roles enjoyed high esteem and relative social power. However, when Christianity was banned in China in 1724, Christian communities went underground and had to meet in secret without the benefit of priests to guide them. Under these circumstances, consecrated virgins stepped in to lead congregations, actively teaching others and leading worship services with authority and independence.

This status continued until European missionaries returned to China during the 1800s. Although the missionaries tried to bring the consecrated virgins back under church control/authority so that male priests could resume their liturgical roles, the virgins had already become so important that they ultimately were able to continue preaching, teaching, and evangelizing throughout China.

This significant Christian leadership role for Chinese women flourished well into the twentieth century, with consecrated virgins numbering over three thousand by 1948. However, when Mao Zedong came to power in 1949, the antireligious agenda of communism ended the consecrated virgin tradition.

Gendered Religious Practices: Feminine Deities

One form of innovation that is common in East Asian spiritual traditions is the formation of devotional cults around particular mythic or religious figures, including figures from outside the host country. In such cases, the figure undergoes a process called *indigenization*, which is the act of transforming something foreign to adapt it to the local culture. Two popular examples of such devotional cults are those focused on Guanyin and Mazu.

Mahayana Buddhism incorporates spiritual figures called *bodhisattvas*, or compassionate ones dedicated to relieving the suffering of all beings, into their ritual and belief systems. Bodhisattvas are believed to have special powers, and they function in a way that is similar to saints or deities in other traditions. The most well-known female bodhisattva in this region is Guanyin (also called Quan Am, Kuan Yin, Kuan Shih Yin, and Kannon), a powerful feminine deity. Her name means "she who hears the cries of the world." Guanyin is popular throughout East and Southeast Asia, with devotees in China, Hong Kong, Japan, Korea, and Vietnam. There are images of her in almost every Chinese temple, and there are practitioners devoted to her in Buddhist, Taoist, and folk traditions alike (Davis 2019). Eight of the fifteen largest Buddhist statues in the world are of Guanyin (Luekens n.d.).

Although Guanyin has Buddhist roots, the contemporary devotional movement surrounding her is not an exclusively Buddhist phenomenon. She represents a distinctively East Asian indigenized version of an Indian deity called Avalokiteshvara, who made its way to China with merchants traveling along the Silk Road. Avalokiteshvara, the bodhisattva of compassion, is represented in masculine form. Gaining increasing popularity in China, Avalokiteshvara was slowly indigenized between the seventh and eleventh centuries, taking on a female form and a distinctly East Asian appearance to become the deity Guanyin. She conformed to local aesthetics and grew to represent core values and principles that were reflective of the surrounding culture. As such, Guanyin now enjoys broad regional popularity that is unconstrained by her Buddhist roots.

Pictures and sculptures of Guanyin show her with many faces pointing in all directions, seeing the suffering of all beings, and with thousands of arms reaching outward from her body to embrace all who suffer. Other images show her as a beautiful woman holding a willow branch and an upturned vase, symbolizing healing and purification (Luekens n.d.). She is sometimes depicted cradling an infant, showing maternal associations with her as well. As a mother figure, she is seen as a great protector of all beings, available to devotees in times of trouble, and people often feel like they can approach her as they would approach a loving mother (Kurtz 2015).

An example of Guanyin as protector took place at the Hung Hom Kwun Yum Temple (built in 1873) in Hong Kong, which is a famous temple to Guanyin. During World War II, when the area was being bombed by the Japanese, there were heavy casualties and destruction in the area, including at the school right next to the temple. However, all the people who took shelter in the temple remained unharmed, which her devotees see as a miracle sent by Guanyin to bless the faithful (Chinese Temples Committee 2019).

Women in Sacred Texts in the Region: Buddhism

The most dominant religion in East Asia is Buddhism, and Buddhist sacred texts are complex in the area of gender. Early Buddhist traditions did allow opportunities for women to choose lives of religious dedication by becoming nuns, demonstrating that women's spiritual practices and devotion were valued in the tradition overall. However, some sacred texts do not address women's status in an equal way.

An overwhelming majority of canonized Buddhist texts were written by male authors for an audience of primarily male practitioners. As a result, many texts show not only an overt male bias but also a more pervasive bias reflecting patriarchal social norms of the time in which they were written. Women's bodies are often equated with lust and death in Buddhist tradition (Young 2004), both of which must be conquered to achieve spiritual growth and awareness. Women are sometimes presented as less pure than men due to the polluting impact of menstruation and childbirth. The attention demanded by menstruation also forces premenopausal women to focus on their impermanent material bodies, tying them to the physical realm of samsara and the burdensome cycle of rebirth, whereas men can more easily transcend their physical bodies to focus on the eternal (Harris 1999).

In this view, the lower status of women does not merely have a spiritual or cultural basis but rather a biological one: women's bodies and their uncontrollable functions make women less suited for spiritual discipline than men—or so this logic suggests. However, there are also texts that claim that because women face more obstacles than men on their path to enlightenment, any woman who manages to overcome these obstacles to become enlightened must have greater spiritual strength than a man who reaches the same goal and is therefore worthy of great respect (Harris 1999). Even within this seemingly positive framework, though, women's bodies are still presented as problems that need to be overcome.

Women's bodies are problematized in other ways as well. In some texts, women are depicted in a sexualized way, characterized as a temptation and a distraction to men who can easily be swayed from the path to enlightenment by desire. In fact, this idea plays a key role in the Buddha's life story. When the Buddha was seated in meditation under the Bodhi Tree, at the very brink of attaining enlightenment, the Lord of Death promptly sent three temptations up from the underworld to sway the soon-to-be Buddha from his path to liberation. The first of these temptations was a harem of beautiful women who danced around him in an attempt to distract him from his meditation with lust and desire. Importantly, these women serve a symbolic purpose, as they are a representation of the way that the sexualized bodies of women can become barriers to the spiritual advancement of men (Young 2004).

To avoid this potential distraction, and to reinforce the principle of impermanence, a text called the *Mahadukkhakhanda Sutta*, dating back to around 20 BCE, uses the female body as a teaching tool. Men are advised to imagine a beautiful, young woman of age fifteen or sixteen, and then they are told to imagine her now at age ninety, growing older and unattractive. She is "crooked as a rafter, bent, leaning on a stick, going along palsied, miserable, youth gone, teeth broken, hair thinned, skin wrinkled, stumbling along, the limbs discolored" (Harris 1999). Then they are to imagine her dying and decomposing, her body breaking down into a pile of bones, blood, and pus. In so doing, lustful men may be freed from their sexual desires (Smith and Novak 2004). However, this is not the *beautiful* female body *resisted* in service to men's spiritual progress; rather, this is the *repulsive* female body *broken* in service to the same.

However, there is one Buddhist text that adds an interesting twist. A Chinese Buddhist text called the *Lung-hsing fo-chiao pien-nien t'ung-lun*, written in 1164 CE, chronicles the life of a princess named Miao-shan. Her father, the king, desperately wants her to marry so that he can have an heir, but Miao-shan wants to follow a life of spiritual vocation instead. Responding to her father's command that she find a husband soon, Miao-shan has this dialogue with the king:

The king asked: "What do you mean by 'three misfortunes'?"

[Miao-shan] said: "The first is this: when the men of this world are young, their face is as fair as the jade-like moon, but when they grow old, their hair turns white and their face is wrinkled; in motion or repose they are in every way worse off than when they were young.

The second is this: a man's limbs may be lusty and vigorous, he may step as lithely as if flying through the air, but when suddenly an illness befalls him, he lies in bed without a single pleasure in life.

The third is this: a man may have a great assembly of relatives, may be surrounded by his nearest and dearest, but suddenly one day it all comes to an end [with his death]; although father and son are close kin they cannot take one another's place.

If it can prevent these three misfortunes, then you will win my consent to a marriage. If not, I prefer to retire to pursue a life of religion. When one gains full understanding of the original mind, all misfortunes of their own accord cease to exist." (Columbia University n.d.)

The tale of Miao-shan is one of fierce independence, spiritual devotion, selfless sacrifice, and radical forgiveness.

There are numerous Buddhist texts that are favorable toward women, including many more Chinese Buddhist texts. For example, the Chinese text the *Biqiuni zhuan*, written by the monk Baochang in the sixth century, is a collection of the biographies of sixty-five Buddhist nuns who lived between 317 and 557 CE. The purpose of this text was to present the nuns as examples to others, serving as role models to people who seek a life of virtue. Baochang celebrated them "not only for their virtue and filial piety, but also for their intelligence, aptitude for learning, administrative skills, and meditation abilities" (Meeks 2014, 319).

Baochang also provides evidence of the great social status these early nuns carried in East Asian society: "He also describes some nuns as having attracted large numbers of disciples, both lay and monastic, and he portrays many as having earned the personal devotion of emperors, empresses. princes, royal ladies, governors, and other elites. He says that some were invited to the palaces of royalty to give lectures on the sutras, to have been treated as the teacher of an emperor, and even to have performed rituals for members of the royalty" (Meeks 2014, 319–320).

The picture of women painted here differs dramatically from the negative image presented in the Theravada texts previously mentioned. Rather than being associated with lust, greed, and death, women are depicted as incredible spiritual teachers, leaders, and guides to all strata of society.

LGBTQ People and Issues in Religions in the MENA

East Asia

The heavy influence of Confucianism throughout East Asia, and especially in China, creates challenges for integrating LGBTQ persons into the traditional social order. For example, Confucianism centers on respecting long-established family relationships and honoring patrilineality (ancestry traced down through the male bloodline) as a means of creating virtue and preserving social harmony. The perceived challenge to "traditional" family structures posed by LGBTQ relationships complicates the Confucian social order that so deeply depends on a hierarchical set of duties and predetermined relationships.

However, in some places, attitudes are shifting. For example, in Taiwan, the percentage of the population supporting same-sex marriage increased from 12 percent in 1991 to 59 percent in 2012, reflecting the liberalizing norms and values of younger generations as they replace their more conservative elders (Cheng, Wu, and Adamczyk 2016). Some religious groups, such as the Alliance of Taiwan Religious Groups for the Protection of Family, oppose LGBT rights and same-sex marriage, but, in May 2019, Taiwan became the first place in Asia to officially legalize same-sex marriage. On the day of the legislature's historic vote, Taiwan's president, Tsai Ing-Wen, tweeted: "Good morning Taiwan. Today, we have a chance to make history & show the world that progressive values can take root in an East Asian society. Today, we can show the world that #LoveWins" (@ iingwen).

Japan is similarly in a time of transition regarding LGBTQ rights. Shinto, the dominant religion in Japan, does not condemn homosexuality but sees it as unnatural. Still, attitudes are changing. In a 2018 survey, 78.4 percent of the population supported same-sex marriage; however, the same survey also found that among LGBTQ respondents, 50.7 percent did not feel comfortable coming out in the workplace, and only 21.1 percent indicated that they did feel comfortable (Dentsu Inc. 2019). In other words, while ideas may be shifting among the population, the social and cultural norms that have supported less accepting attitudes still impact the LGBTQ community and their quality of life.

Central Asia

The prevalence of Islam in Central Asia combined with the long-standing influence of Russia, which takes a notoriously anti-LGBTQ stance, makes this a rather inhospitable region for LGBTQ persons. In Uzbekistan and Turkmenistan, gay male relationships are against the law (a holdover from Soviet law), though there is no reference in the law to sex between women. In Uzbekistan, in September 2019, the violent murder of a man who had just come out as gay on social media (Bacchi 2019) serves as a reminder of the discriminatory social environment LGBTQ people face throughout Central Asia.

Following the adoption of a similar policy in Russia, Kyrgyzstan introduced a bill in 2014 to outlaw any materials that normalize same-sex relationships. The bill moved forward to additional readings in 2015 and 2016, but it was suspended shortly thereafter. However, following the heavy publicity these initiatives received, anti-LGBTQ violence—some of it severe—surged in the region.

Following these anti-LGBTQ policy initiatives, in the capital city of Bishkek, violent attacks increased by 300 percent against the LGBTQ community (Fershtey and Sharifzoda 2019). There are also reports of police officers making false profiles on dating websites to entrap LGBTQ people seeking partners and then demanding money upon meeting the victim, threatening to publicly reveal their sexual identity unless they get paid (Fershtey and Sharifzoda 2019). In Tajikistan, the approximately thirty thousand LGBTQ people there also face discrimination and harassment. They report feeling unsupported and unsafe, worrying that they will lose their jobs or other status due to anti-LGBTQ social attitudes. Parents regularly disown LGBTQ children, and anti-LGBTQ violence is also a problem (Fershtey and Sharifzoda 2019).

Kazakhstan has the most favorable climate of the Central Asian republics, but discriminatory attitudes still exist. Anti-LGBTQ "propaganda" bills, similar to those of Kyrgyzstan, have been proposed here as well, though they have been ruled unlawful by the Constitutional Council. Other common forms of anti-LGBTQ bias, such as violence, bullying, and discrimination in schools and the workplace, are also ongoing problems (Fershtey and Sharifzoda 2019).

However, the Central Asian LGBTQ community is not passive. In Kyrgyzstan, Labrys is an organization that works on behalf of the LGBTQ community, self-described as a "grassroots platform for advancement and protection of the human rights of LGBTIQA people in Kyrgyzstan and Central Asia," with the goal of "empowering and giving voice to our communities, through protection of our rights and freedoms founded on common human values" (Labrys Kyrgyzstan n.d.).

On March 8, 2019—the regional Women's Day holiday—activists assembled in Bishkek, Kyrgyzstan, to march on behalf of women's rights and "equality for all." This is being called Central Asia's first Gay Pride March, as among the participants were members of the LGBTQ community carrying rainbow flags (Baumgartner 2019). The reaction from the public, including several parliamentarians, was swift and scathing. Overt threats of violence were even publicized from elected officials. However, others praised and defended their actions, and participants were largely undeterred.

March participant Bektour Iskander made this statement on Radio Free Europe: "I think it's very cool that the LGBT community came on the march, because this is also related to the rights of women if we are talking about lesbians and transgender girls who face tremendous violence in Kyrgyzstan. . . . This is part of the women's rights movement—it's impossible to separate them. And I'm very proud of Kyrgyzstan that this has become possible here" (Baumgartner 2019).

Women at the Intersection of Religion and Politics in the Region

Throughout East and Central Asia, women have been front and center in regard to many political conflicts, especially Muslim women. In fact, authorities have strategically used women as a means by which they have communicated and consolidated their power. The Soviets used the improved status of women under their rule as a means by which they justified their occupation of the region to the rest of the world (Chenoy 1996). The Taliban used the apparent control of women as an indicator of the Taliban's strength, power, and dominance of the region. China's criminalization of the burqa communicates a sociopolitical ideology that leaves no room for religious fervor in general or for Islam in particular. In all of these examples, a particular version of masculine authority is being verified using women's status (or lack thereof) as an index of male power. Jildyz Urbaeva refers to this phenomenon as "public patriarchy," with "the main representation of public patriarchy being the subordination of women in the public domain" (Urbaeva 2019, 208).

On the other hand, movements dedicated to women's rights in both East and Central Asia often carry a recognition that women's rights are inextricably linked to the rights of other marginalized groups. In Kyrgyzstan, the fight for women's equality is linked to LGBTQ rights.

The Hong Kong Women Christian Council was founded in 1988 as a means by which to work for social justice and gender equality both within and through the Christian church. Their stated mission includes promotion of Christian women's education, development opportunities, social participation, and networking. They also explicitly state a concern for "the social-political development in Hong Kong and the renewal of the Church" (Hong Kong Women Christian Council n.d.). They have organized political action and responses to issues ranging from the #MeToo movement and sex abuse by priests to standing with other marginalized communities in solidarity and advocacy.

Religious Violence against Women: Burqa Laws

The practice of wearing a veil, which is called a *hijab*, is a common practice among Muslim women. This may range from wearing a simple scarf to cover the hair to wearing a full-face veil and head-to-toe robe. It is important to note that some Muslim women choose not to wear a hijab at all and that expectations and social norms regarding veiling and modesty in different places vary widely. Many customs related to wearing the hijab, including the specific type of hijab that is worn, are also extensions of regional culture and history, not just religious beliefs.

The quality of life for women under fundamentalist Taliban rule was a major point of contention post-9/11. Narrow interpretations of Islamic social and behavioral norms supported patriarchal dominance and the disempowerment of women—a departure from the status women enjoyed in Afghan society before the Taliban enforced their politicized version of Islam upon the population. One of the Taliban's most visible restrictions against Afghan women was making the burqa mandatory for all women. The burqa is uniquely affiliated with Afghanistan and other parts of Central Asia. It consists of a loose robe that hides the body and a full-face veil that leaves only a mesh screen covering the eyes.

Malika Rasuli, the deputy head of the women's section of the Afghan Independent Human Rights Commission (AIHCR), has referred to this forced wearing of the burqa as an "expression of gender violence" (Barikzai 2016). Afghan women are no longer required to wear the burqa under current laws, but many women still wear it for a variety of reasons, including bowing to family or other social pressure or feeling protected from male harassment in public spaces. Both of these justifications, however, still place women in the passive role of victimhood, being forced by social circumstances, if not the law, to cover themselves.

This depiction of Afghan women as universal victims can be problematic. Offering a different point of view, Tonita Murray at the Middle East Institute writes, "Wearing the veil on the other hand is an Islamic symbol of modesty, worn to conceal the outer beauty in order to show the inner. While it is regarded as a symbol of repression by Western feminists, recently Muslim feminists have returned to wearing it as a protest against

---

THE MEANING OF MODESTY

Many religious traditions emphasize the importance of "modest" dress, especially for women. Women are often encouraged to cover their bodies, which are considered the source of sin and temptation. The type and amount of coverings differ—hair, face, wrists, ankles, or whole body—but the goal is to conceal their sexuality.

Conservative religions say dressing modestly protects women and girls, keeps them pure, and makes them more pleasing to God. Social justice movements say it gives them an unhealthy body image, inhibits their natural sexual expressions, and keeps them subordinate and helpless.

In what ways could being covered be empowering, and in what ways could it be oppressive? Why might being covered make women safer? From whom? Are there other ways to ensure women's safety?

Janet Lockhart

prevailing Western colonialist attitudes. It proclaims that they can be Muslim and equal to men at the same time" (Murray 2012).

Women's Resistance to Religious Oppression

Central Asian Republics

Before the Soviet era, the five Central Asian states—Kazakhstan, Kyrgyzstan, Tajikistan, Turkmenistan, and Uzbekistan—had strongly patriarchal societies that were divided into tribal factions or clans. Women had limited rights, little social autonomy, and few educational opportunities.

As the Soviet authorities began outlawing sociocultural practices that caused women harm (e.g., forced marriage, child marriage) and established new laws that favored women's rights and gender equality, Central Asian women began forming "women's clubs" that met in special red tents, where they learned to read and write, sought medical care, received training in skilled trades, and learned about their legal rights in this newly minted society (Chenoy 1996). By the 1980s, women had achieved universal literacy and made up half of all employees and university students (Urbaeva 2019).

Capitalizing on their newfound empowerment, Central Asian women participated in the "red scarf movement," in which they rejected formerly restrictive Islamic face veils in exchange for a simple red scarf worn over the head. Significantly, they were not renouncing Islam nor the denying the value of modesty. They did not throw off the scarves altogether! Rather, theirs was a revisionist movement. Their goal was to reinterpret, not reject, Islamic tradition in a way that they perceived to be more progressive. Because the red scarf movement operated in opposition to male privilege and religious authority, the women who participated in this movement were sometimes subject to violent backlash. Many women died or were harmed in service to this movement (Chenoy 1996).

Afghanistan

After September 11, 2001, an ever-present symbol of religious oppression was the Afghan woman, who was deemed by observers to be suffering under repressive Islamic rule in endless, universal victimhood (Murray 2012). Afghan women were pictured in the media and the popular imagination alike as leading lives of endless violence; they were forced into burqas by religious tyrants, abused by family members, forced into unwanted relationships, denied education, and deprived of basic human rights. While Afghan women have certainly had their share of challenges, indignities, and both individual and communal violence, this cannot, and does not, define them. The following list appeared in a United States Institute of Peace publication in March 2019:

- "Millions of women have voted in local and national elections. Of parliament's 320 members, 63 are women, while women hold 18 seats as ministers or deputy ministers and four serve as ambassadors.
- "Schools and universities employ more than 68,000 women instructors including 800 university professors in both private and public institutions.
- "More than 6,000 women serve as judges, prosecutors, defense attorneys, police and army personnel.
- "Government data counts about 10,000 women among the country's doctors, nurses and health professionals.
- "Female journalists number 1,070, working throughout Afghanistan.
- "Some 1,150 women entrepreneurs have invested $77 million in their businesses, providing job opportunities for 77,000 Afghan women and men" (Ahmadi 2019).

These are all truths about women in Afghanistan. These stories are just as important as the ones of oppression and struggle. They all must be told.

In her TED talk "The Danger of a Single Story," Chimamanda Ngozi Adichie warns us against allowing any story—especially negative stories—to be the defining story of any place or people: "The single story creates stereotypes. And the problem with stereotypes is not that they are untrue, but that they are incomplete. They make one story become the only story" (Adichie 2009).

Consider the stories presented in this chapter as not defining any place, people, or identity group; rather, they are a mosaic that, when viewed alongside one another, can provide a small glimpse into the rich textures of the lives women live—and have lived—in diverse places, in ever-changing circumstances, over not just hundreds but *thousands* of years. For every story shared here, there are countless other that remain untold.

SAKENA YACOOBI

Saken Yacoobi founded the Afghan Institute of Learning (AIL) in 1995, recognizing the need for education, especially for girls, following decades of conflict and war in Afghanistan. She also founded the Professor Sakena Yacoobi Private Hospital in Herat and the Professor Sakena Yacoobi Private High Schools in Kabul and Herat.

Her vision is informed by her Muslim faith. She says, "I really believe that Islam says that education is a must for both men and women. . . .The Quran tells us to be good, and education gives you critical thinking skills that are essential for ethical decision-making" (HuffPost 2014).

The AIL provides teacher training for women, supports education for boys and girls, and offers women and children health education. After the Taliban closed girls' schools in the 1990s, AIL supported eighty underground home schools for three thousand girls. AIL now also provides free legal services for women through a legal clinic, and it hosts peace conferences around Afghanistan.

Susan M. Shaw

HuffPost. 2014. "50 Powerful Women Religious Leaders to Celebrate on International Women's Day." March 8, 2014. https://www.huffpost.com/entry/women-religious -leaders_n_4922118.

FURTHER READING

Adichie, Chiamanda Ngozi. 2009. "The Danger of a Single Story." Filmed July 2009 at TEDGlobal, TED video, 18:34. https://www.ted.com /talks/chimamanda_ngozi_adichie_the_danger_of_a_single_story /transcript.

Agha-Jaffar, Tamara. 2005. *Women and Goddesses in Myth and Sacred Text*. New York: Pearson.

Ahmadi, Belquis. 2019. "Afghanistan Talks: No Women, No Peace." United States Institute of Peace, March 1, 2019. https://www.usip .org/publications/2019/03/afghanistan-talks-no-women-no-peace.

Allen-Ebrahimian, Bethany. 2015. "China: The Best and the Worst Place to Be a Muslim Woman." Foreign Policy, July 17, 2015. https:// foreignpolicy.com/2015/07/17/china-feminism-islam-muslim -women-xinjiang-uighurs/.

Bacchi, Umberto. 2019. "Gay Man's Murder Raises Questions over Uzbek Human Rights Reforms." Reuters, September 27, 2019. https://

www.reuters.com/article/us-uzbekistan-lgbt-rights-analysis/gay
-mans-murder-raises-questions-over-uzbek-human-rights-reforms
-idUSKBN1WC1Z4.

Barikzai, Naqiba. 2016. "Afghan Women Still Bound by Burqa." Institute
for War & Peace Reporting, February 12, 2016. https://iwpr.net
/global-voices/afghan-women-still-bound-burka.

Baumgartner, Pete. 2019. "Rainbow Rage: Kyrgyz Rail against LGBT
Community after Central Asia's 'First' Gay-Pride March." Radio
Free Europe/Radio Liberty, March 16, 2019. https://www.rferl.org
/a/rainbow-rage-kyrgyz-rail-against-lgbt-after-central-asia-s-first
-gay-pride-march/29825158.html.

Benaim, Rachel Delia. 2017. "Now Americans, Bukharian Jews Face New
Set of Challenges." *Times of Israel*, April 19, 2017. https://www
.timesofisrael.com/now-americans-bukharian-jews-face
-new-set-of-challenges/.

Berger, Joseph. 2003. "Old Ways Bring Tears in a New World; Immigrants
Face Family Violence." *New York Times*, March 7. https://www
.nytimes.com/2003/03/07/nyregion/old-ways-bring-tears-in-a-new
-world-immigrants-face-family-violence.html.

Botobekov, Uran. 2017. "The Kyrgyz Baptists: A Case Study in Religious
Persecution in Central Asia." *The Diplomat*, February 6, 2017.
https://thediplomat.com/2017/02/the-kyrgyz-baptists-a-case-study
-in-religious-persecution-in-central-asia/.

Carr, Donna L. n.d. "The History of Bukharan Jews." Partnership in Academics and Development. Accessed January 8, 2021. https://www
.bukharacity.com/jews.htm.

Cheng, Yen-hsin Alice, Fen-Chieh Felice Wu, and Amy Adamczyk. 2016.
"Changing Attitudes toward Homosexuality in Taiwan, 1995–
2012." *Chinese Sociological Review* 48 (4): 317–345. https://doi.org
/10.1080/21620555.2016.1199257.

Chenoy, Anuradha M. "Islam, Women, and Identity in Contemporary
Central Asia." *Economic and Political Weekly,* 31 (9): 516–518.

Chinese Temples Committee. 2019. "Administered Temples: Kwin Yum
Temple, Hung Hom." Chinese Temples Committee. http://www.ctc
.org.hk/en/directcontrol/temple12.asp.

Columbia University. n.d. "Chinese Cultural Studies: The Legend of
Miao-Shan." Columbia Department of East Asian Languages and

Cultures. Accessed April 30, 2020. http://ccnmtl.columbia.edu
/services/dropoff/china_civ_temp/week05/pdfs/legend.pdf.

Davis, Hana. 2019. "The Many Legends of Guanyin—or Kwun Yum—the
Goddess of Mercy Revered in Hong Kong and around the World."
South China Morning Post, June 29, 2019. https://www.scmp.com
/news/hong-kong/society/article/3016496/many-legends-guanyin
-or-kwun-yum-goddess-mercy-revered-hong.

Dearden, Lizzie. 2017. "China Bans Burqas and 'Abnormal' Beards in
Muslim Province of Xinjiang." *The Independent*, March 30, 2017.
https://www.independent.co.uk/news/world/asia/china-burqa
-abnormal-beards-ban-muslim-province-xinjiang-veils-province
-extremism-crackdown-freedom-a7657826.html.

Dentsu Inc. 2019. "Dentsu Diversity Lab Conducts 'LGBT Survey 2018.'"
January 10, 2019. https://www.dentsu.co.jp/en/news/release/pdf
-cms/%EF%BC%8B2019002-0110en.pdf.

Fang, Tony. 2012. "Yin Yang: A New Perspective on Culture." *Manage-
ment and Organization Review* 8 (1): 25–50.

Fershtey, Anastassiya, and Khamza Sharifzoda. 2019. "Life in the Closet:
The LGBT Community in Central Asia." *The Diplomat*, January
29, 2019. https://thediplomat.com/2019/01/life-in-the-closet-the-lgbt
-community-in-central-asia/.

Guang, Pan. n.d. "Shanghai: A Haven for Holocaust Victims." The Holocaust and the United Nations Outreach Programme. Accessed January 15, 2020. https://www.un.org/en/holocaustremembrance/docs
/pdf/chapter6.pdf.

Hao, Zhidong. 2011. *Macau History and Society.* Pokfulam: Hong Kong
University Press.

Harris, Elizabeth J. 1999. "The Female in Buddhism." In *Buddhist Women
across Cultures*, edited by Karma Lekshe Tsomo, 49–65. Albany:
State University of New York Press.

Haruko, Okano. 1993. "Women and Sexism in Shinto." *Japan Christian
Review* 59: 27–31.

Hong, Jeesoon. 2019. "Christian Education and the Construction of Female
Gentility in Modern East Asia." *Religions* 10 (467): 1–14. https://
doi.org/10.3390/rel10080467.

Hong Kong Women Christian Council. n.d. "Home Page." https://hkwcc
.org.hk.

Hsieh, Ding-hwa. 2000. "Buddhist Nuns in Sung China (960–1279)."
Journal of Song-Yuan Studies 30 : 63–96.

Ing-Wen, Tsai (@iingwen). 2019. "Good morning #Taiwan. Today, We Have a Chance to Make History & Show the World That Progressive Values Can Take Root in an East Asian Society. Today, We Can Show the World that #LoveWins." Twitter, May 16, 2019, 9:44 p.m. https://twitter.com/iingwen/status/1129200931642302465.

Kortunov, Andrei. 1998. "Unlocking the Assets: Energy and the Future of Central Asia and the Caucasus." James A. Baker III Institute for Public Policy of Rice University, April. https://www.bakerinstitute .org/media/files/Research/628a73a2/russia-and-central-asia -evolution-of-mutual-perceptions-policies-interdependence.pdf.

Kurtz, Lester R. 2015. *Gods in the Global Village: The World's Religions in Sociological Perspective.* Los Angeles: Sage Publications.

Labrys Kyrgyzstan. n.d. "About Labrys." Accessed April 1, 2020. https:// www.labrys.kg/about.

Leung, Beatrice, and Patricia Wittburg. 2004. "Catholic Religious Orders of Women in China." *Journal for the Scientific Study of Religion* 43 (1): 67–82.

Li Tim-Oi Foundation. n.d. "Li Tim-Oi's Story." Accessed January 8, 2021. https://www.ltof.org.uk/litimoi-story/.

Lim, Louisa. 2010. "Female Imams Blaze Trail amid China's Muslims." National Public Radio, July 21, 2010. https://www.npr.org/2010/07 /21/128628514/female-imams-blaze-trail-amid-chinas-muslims.

Luekens, David. n.d. "Quan Am, the Bodhisattva of Compassion, in Vietnam." Travelfish. Accessed April 1, 2020. https://www.travelfish .org/beginners_detail/vietnam/9.

Meeks, Lori. 2014. "Nuns and Laywomen in East Asian Buddhism." In *The Wiley Blackwell Companion to East and Inner Asian Buddhism*, edited by Mario Poceski, 318–339. Malden, MA: John Wiley and Sons.

Mills, Margaret. 2005 "Folk Religion: Folk Islam." In *Encyclopedia of Religion*, edited by Lindsay Jones, vol. 5: 3161–3164. Detroit, MI: Macmillan Reference.

Murray, Tonita. 2012. "The Oppressed Women of Afghanistan: Fact, Fiction, or Distortion." Middle East Institute, April 23, 2012. https:// www.mei.edu/publications/oppressed-women-afghanistan-fact -fiction-or-distortion.

Myers, Steven Lee. 2019. "Mosque Demolitions across China Raise Fears over Escalating Persecution of Uighur Muslims." *The Independent*, September 22, 2019. https://www.independent.co.uk/news

/world/asia/china-uighur-muslim-persecution-mosque-demolition
-xi-jinping-regime-islam-a9115431.html.

Nelson, Sarah Milledge. 2008. *Shamanism and the Origin of States: Spirit, Power, and Gender in East Asia*. New York: Routledge.

Nishide, Takeshi. 2014. "Women's Entry into Shinto Priesthood Is on the Rise." *Japan Times*, March 6, 2014. https://www.japantimes.co.jp /life/2014/03/06/lifestyle/womens-entry-into-shinto-priesthood-is -on-the-rise/#.Xjs-uC3MxE4.

Pew Research Center. 2012. "Religious Composition by Country." https:// www.pewforum.org/2012/12/18/table-religious-composition-by -country-in-percentages/.

Pew Research Center. 2018. "The Age Gap in Religion around the World: How Religious Commitment Varies by Country among People of All Ages." June 13, 2018. https://www.pewforum.org/2018/06/13 /how-religious-commitment-varies-by-country-among-people-of -all-ages/.

Pew Research Center. 2019. "A Closer Look at How Religious Restrictions Have Risen around the World." July 15, 2019. https://www .pewforum.org/2019/07/15/a-closer-look-at-how-religious -restrictions-have-risen-around-the-world/.

Pye, Michael. 2018. "New Religions in East Asia." *In The Oxford Handbook of New Religious Movements*, edited by James R. Lewis, 1–22. Oxford, UK: Oxford University Press. https://doi.org/10.1093 /oxfordhb/9780195369649.003.0022.

Rashid, Ahmed. 2001. "Taliban Will Force Hindus to Wear Marks on Clothing." *The Telegraph*, May 23, 2001. https://www.telegraph.co .uk/news/worldnews/asia/afghanistan/1331382/Taliban-will-force -Hindus-to-wear-marks-on-clothing.html.

Sang-Hun, Choe. 2007. "In the Age of the Internet, Korean Shamans Regains Popularity." *New York Times*, July 6, 2007. https://www .nytimes.com/2007/07/06/world/asia/06iht-shaman.1.6527738 .html.

Schoenberg, Shira. 2006. "Bukharian Jews in U.S. Cope with New World." Jewish Telegraphic Agency, January 10, 2006. https://www.jta.org /2006/01/10/lifestyle/bukharian-jews-in-u-s-cope-with-new-world

Shalom Task Force. 2018. "Battling Domestic Abuse in the Orthodox Home." Shalom Task Force, October 22, 2018. https://www .shalomtaskforce.org/single-post/2018/10/22/Battling-Domestic -Abuse-in-the-Orthodox-Home.

Slosberg, Gen. 2018. "How I Finally Learned to Accept Both My Chinese and Jewish Identities." HuffPost, May 23, 2018. https://www.huffpost.com/entry/im-chinese-and-jewish-and-always-wanted-to-claim-one-identity_n_5b044e95e4b0740c25e5e2af.

Smith, Huston, and Phillip Novak. 2004. *Buddhism: A Concise Introduction.* San Francisco: Harper Collins.

Urbaeva, Jildyz. 2019. "Opportunity, Social Mobility, and Women's Views on Gender Roles in Central Asia." *Social Work* 64 (3): 207–215.

Valussi, Elena. 2008. "Female Alchemy and Paratext: How to Read 'Nüdan' in a Historical Context." *Asia Major* 21 (2): 153–193.

Washington, Garrett L. 2018. "Introduction." In *Christianity and the Modern Woman in East Asia*, 1–13. Leiden, Netherlands: Brill.

World Jewish Congress. 2020. "Communities." https://www.worldjewishcongress.org/en/about/communities.

Young, Serenity. 2004. *Courtesans and Tantric Consorts: Sexualities in Buddhist Narrative, Iconography, and Ritual.* New York: Routledge.

SEVEN

South and Southeast Asia

Shannon Garvin

WOMEN IN THE RELIGIONS OF SOUTH AND SOUTHEAST ASIA

South and Southeast Asia comprise approximately 15 percent of the globe and 7 percent of its landmass. On the Asian continent, it includes all the countries east of Europe, south of Russia and the former Soviet countries, west of the Pacific Ocean, and north of the Indian Ocean. It also includes several island nations in the Indian Ocean that share genetic similarities to the Javanese and Malay peoples.

Indigenous Asian Religions

Hindu and Buddhist beliefs developed in early India as Daoist and Confucian beliefs developed in China. Early traders, settlers, and religious practitioners began moving east and south from India and China into the undeveloped river plains and coastlines of Bangladesh, Thailand, Myanmar (Burma), Cambodia, Laos, Malaysia/Singapore, and Vietnam. They set sail for the islands of Sri Lanka, Indonesia, Malaysia, Brunei, East Timor, the Maldives, and the Philippines, bringing a variety of basic understandings of philosophy and religion. They also spread north into the mountainous regions of Nepal, Bhutan, Afghanistan, and Pakistan. The older Indigenous Asian religions of Buddhism, Hinduism, Confucianism,

Women take part in a ceremony as part of the annual Black-Necked Crane Festival in Bhutan. The festival generates awareness of the endangered crane and promotes its conservation. The story holds that the crane is a reincarnation of two deities who guard the valley where the festival is held. (Antonella865/Dreamstime.com)

and Daoism mixed with local tribal beliefs as they crossed ethnic groups (Nyitray 2004).

Confucianism

Confucianism, as a civil religion, wielded the largest influence across South and Southeast Asia, as its emphasis on community order and tranquility was adopted and promoted by leaders to support their authority. Today, Confucianism undergirds the social structures in all of the South and Southeast Asian countries, binding particular "religions" to particular ethnic groups. Confucianism is not a separate religion but rather the belief in specific cultural values that bind a community together as they practice their religion. Confucianism affirms it is the responsibility of women to create and maintain this social harmony (Berling n.d.).

Buddhism

Buddhism began in India, but as monks and nuns traveled, Buddhist teachings spread across all of South and Southeast Asia to the extent that most people today practice Buddhism or Buddhist beliefs alongside other religions. Cambodia (96.93 percent), Laos (64.72 percent), Myanmar (89.87 percent), Sri Lanka (70.10 percent), and Thailand (93.58 percent) contain majority Buddhist populations. Bangladesh (0.62 percent), Brunei (7.83 percent), India (0.77 percent), Indonesia (0.72 percent), Malaysia (19.84 percent), the Maldives (1.33 percent), Nepal (9.04 percent), the Philippines (0.03 percent), Singapore (33.26 percent), Timor-Leste (0.07 percent), and Vietnam (9.31 percent) record minority populations (UNdata n.d.). However, none of these countries or any Buddhist governments allow the official ordination of women as Buddhist nuns.

A statue of Guanyin, goddess of compassion and mercy, venerated by East Asian Buddhists. This statue is in Wat Plai Leam Buddhist Temple in Thailand. One legend says that Guanyin vowed not to rest until she freed all beings from reincarnation. (Tomas Ciernik/Dreamstime.com)

Daoism

Forming in China, parallel to Buddhism in India, Daoism offered women the opportunity to become mediums, nuns, priests, prophets, local healers, and shamanic travelers or to start their own movements as they sought to obtain immortality. Because Asian thinking allows for an integration of belief systems into a "workable whole," Daoism, like Buddhism, is practiced by the majority of people even when they do not label themselves as Daoist. Outside Singapore (10.92 percent), solo practitioners account for only 1–3 percent of local populations, but the ideas of Daoism and reverence for the cosmic order and balance heavily influence people (UNdata n.d.). Women continue to be the primary practitioners, writers, and leaders of Daoism.

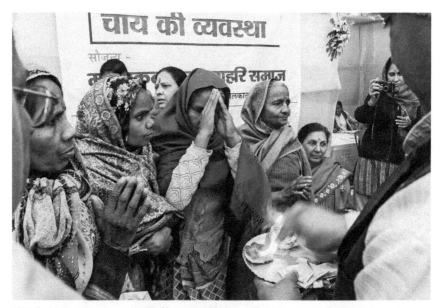

Hindu devotees pray in Kolkata while on pilgrimage to Gangasagar. Every year on January 14, hundreds of thousands of Hindus dip themselves in this holy place at the confluence of the Ganges and Bay of Bengal to cleanse their souls. (Rudra Narayan Mitra/Dreamstime.com)

Hinduism

Hinduism, as a category of all the beliefs that come from the Vedas, specifically does not make a distinction between philosophy and religion (Arvind 2004), which is why the Hindu gods point to a single divine presence that can take form in "endlessly diverse ways" (Murphy n.d.). India (80.46 percent) and Nepal (81.34 percent) contain the highest Hindu populations, but Bangladesh (9.33 percent), Indonesia (1.69 percent), Malaysia (6.27 percent), the Maldives (2.53 percent), Myanmar (0.5 percent), Pakistan (0.67 percent), Singapore (5.08 percent), Thailand (0.06 percent), and Timor-Leste (.03 percent) also record Hindus (UNdata n.d.). Women are central to Hindu stories and the primary deities, but they remain marginal in their ability to worship in their own temples or to lead as gurus. In rural areas less centered on Sanskrit liturgy from the Vedas, women can work as healers and artists near temples in service to the deities (Arvind 2004). They also tell the stories of the Hindu deities in singing and folk dance (Arvind 2004).

Jainism

Jainism originated in western India and originally taught gender equality, but its beliefs were deeply immersed in a fear of female sexual power and quickly became intermingled with Hinduism and could not shake its influence (Conway 2017). Over four million Jain live and practice in their native India (0.41 percent), and there is a small population in Nepal (0.01 percent) (UNdata n.d.). Women create the backbone of Jain practice because of the time and care taken to prepare food in a way that is not harmful to the environment.

Sikhism

Guru Nanel Dev (1469–1539) developed Sikhism in the Punjab region of northern India as a way of life in contrast to the oppressive caste and gender systems he saw rising within Hinduism. He focused on developing teachings and practices that affirm the worth and value of all people, regardless of gender, finances, profession, or age. Today, the Sikh number nearly twenty million, primarily in the Punjab region, with significant diaspora populations in Singapore (0.35 percent) and Malaysia (0.35 percent) (UNdata n.d.). Sikh women, while afforded the opportunity to practice their faith freely by their beliefs, increasingly feel pressured by local Hindu and Muslim cultural norms to avoid leadership and to practice their faith privately in their homes.

Transnational Religions and Women in South and Southeast Asia

The transnational Abrahamic religions of the Middle East, Islam and Christianity, were brought by early Christian monks and Muslim traders centuries before Europeans brought Catholic and Protestant Christianity (Andaya 2006). They found the local people friendly, the rulers open to beneficial new religious ideas, and some communities willing to intermarry. While early Christianity "became widespread around the littoral of the Indian Ocean" and "east to the Pacific," it was eventually stamped out in all areas except southern India, leaving only its influence on burgeoning religions (Jenkins 2008).

Islam

Scattered tribes across the Malay and Indonesian islands adopted and melded Indigenous practices with relaxed Islamic teachings, practices, and law brought by early traders and influenced by early Christian beliefs (Chaudhuri 2004). Traditionally, South and Southeast Asian Muslim women throughout the centuries have practiced a faith compatible with both their Indigenous Asian relational understanding of existence and their belief in Allah. Today, South and Southeast Asian countries face enormous pressure from more militant forms of Middle Eastern Islam and outspoken clerics. Oil-rich Muslim countries and governments, such as the Sultanate of Brunei (78.80 percent), Indonesia (87.18 percent), Malaysia (61.32 percent), and the Maldives (93.93 percent), afford women more opportunities for state-sponsored education and careers. Poor Muslim countries, notably Afghanistan (99.97 percent) and Pakistan (96 percent), afford little opportunity for women, who are often married off as child brides in arranged marriages and face dire circumstances, including female genital cutting (FGC), honor killings, and dowry deaths (UNdata n.d.). Traditionally, the primary duty of all Muslim women is to honor Allah by obeying their husband and by raising a new generation of Muslim children. A handful of Islamic scholars today are pressing for men and women to look past the Hadith and back to the Qur'an and Muhammad's wives to lead and practice theology.

Sufism

Sufism developed within Islam as mysticism similar to Eastern Christianity, complete with monks, saints, pilgrimages, and rites (Jenkins 2008), and found popularity among the mystical ideas and traditions of South and Southeast Asia (Malik 2006), as it supported the spiritual ambitions of women as well as men (Andaya 2006). Sufi Islam is not a sect but a mystical order within Islam primarily practiced by Sunni Muslims but sometimes by Shi'a Muslims as well.

Christianity

In the 600s, in China, rulers during the Tang dynasty embraced early Christianity (Jingjiao or "luminous teaching") at the same time Buddhism was first reaching Tibet. Christianity's existence alongside Buddhism, Daoism, and Confucianism in China influenced the beliefs and politics developing across South and Southeast Asia (Jenkins 2008). Christian missionaries translated their scriptures into local languages as they moved east from the Indus Valley and Asia Minor (Jenkins 2008) and encultured beliefs alongside Indigenous practices. Syriac Christians and Jews settled in southern India, which still records a significant population of twenty-four million Christians (2.34 percent) (UNdata n.d.). European missions brought distinctly Roman Catholic and Protestant belief systems that were not open to enculturation and sometimes even at odds with the ancient forms of the same faith. Bangladesh (0.31 percent), Brunei (8.69 percent), Cambodia (0.37 percent), Laos (1.73 percent), Malaysia (9.24 percent), the Maldives (1.59 percent), Myanmar (6.31 percent), Nepal (1.42 percent), Pakistan (0.63 percent), and Thailand (1.20 percent) all record marginal populations of Christians. Timor-Leste and the Philippines are the only countries that consider themselves to be Christian. Roman Catholics make up 94.46 percent of the population in Timor-Leste (with 2.24 percent

Protestant) and 80.27 percent of the population in the Philippines (with 8.09 percent Protestant). Several countries record significant Christian populations: Indonesia (2.91 percent Catholic, 6.96 percent Protestant), Singapore (18.33 percent Christian, 7.06 percent Catholic, 11.27 percent Protestant), Sri Lanka (6.19 percent Catholic, 1.43 percent Protestant), and Vietnam (6.7 percent Catholic, 0.54 percent Protestant) (UNdata n.d.).

Zoroastrianism

Zoroastrianism survived the fall of Persia but never found wide acceptance past its early ascendancy (600 BCE–650 CE). India and Pakistan record marginal populations of practitioners, primarily around Mumbai and Karachi (UNdata n.d.). Each woman's s ability to practice and worship is primarily influenced by the beliefs of the larger culture in which these remaining Parsi women are located.

Indigenous Religions

Most traditional Indigenous belief systems are practiced alongside imported religions across South and Southeast Asia in a manner consistent with Asian ways of thinking. Myanmar (0.81 percent), the Philippines (0.24 percent), and Timor-Leste (0.79 percent) record significant Indigenous religious groups. The Kirati in Nepal, a Sino-Tibetan ethnic group, maintain their own religious practices among their several tribes, which number over eight hundred thousand and make up a little over 3 percent of the population (UNdata n.d.).

Local Syncretist Religions

Southern Vietnam is home to two of the most common syncretic faiths incorporating several faith traditions. Established in 1926 in Tây Ninh and numbering around 850,000 adherents, the Cao Đài combine Buddhist, Christian, Daoist, Confucian, and Islamic ideas. Established in 1939 by Buddhist reformer Huỳnh Phú Sổ, the Đạo Hòa Hảo practice a modified Buddhism that focuses on following Buddha (học phật) and self-improvement (tù nhân). Followers number between one and two million (UNData n.d.).

Transnational Religions and Women in South and Southeast Asia

Across South and Southeast Asia, outside the strict centers of Hinduism in India and Confucianism in China, women were valued as significant and secure members of their local tribes (Andaya 2006). Many tribes were matrilineal, and women inherited property alongside the men, ensuring their financial stability and future ability to care for children and their elders (Stange, Oyster, and Sloan 2011). Temporary marriages existed alongside traditional marriages, affording travelers and traders the opportunity to live in a community seasonally. Women in these marriages held all the advantages of custody, communal property, and inheritance, and the men were socially responsible to their wife's relatives (Andaya 2006). Women held valued places as shamans, healers, midwives, and communicators with the spirits not inhabiting human form (Chaudhuri 2004). All the early forms of these religions found acceptance among the spiritually minded Asian peoples (Malik 2006). Local shrines and temples gathered worshippers, and people dwelled in constant exchange with powerful local spirits in mountains, rivers, and the ocean (Andaya 2006).

Women could escape marriage and childbearing by joining the Buddhist or Daoist nuns and seeking, in a limited manner, their own spiritual actualization. In Vietnam, Buddhism developed a prominence of feminine deities, "holy mothers," "formidable dames," and powerful female-led monasteries. Chinese military incursions into the North Vietnam Empire enforced Confucianist desires to repress the disruptive influence of female imagery and their power in Buddhist practices and social structures (Nyitray 2004, 282). Some women who publicly practiced other faiths (generally Islam) continued to pass on their traditional Christian beliefs and became the primary keepers of holy days and worship from the safety of their homes up to the nineteenth century (Jenkins 2008). The reality of these "crypto-Christians" is possible because Asian ways of thinking allow for multiple integrated and concurrent sets of religious beliefs that are brought into a kind of workable harmony with each other dependent on outside political and legal influences (Jenkins 2008). Together, the highly migratory peoples of South and Southeast Asia melded and merged unique cultures and religions with a distinctly Asian understanding of the nature of the cosmos, woman's creative power, and man's need to control that power to form the basis for the vast and colorful array of religions we see today.

ISSUES OF RELIGION FOR WOMEN IN SOUTH AND SOUTHEAST ASIA

The Impact of Christian Missionaries on the Colonial Project

The arrival of the European colonial powers and Catholic and Protestant missionaries on the mainland and islands of South and Southeast Asia changed the fundamental place and role of women in their communities (Gandhi 1988). From the 1500s until World War II, England, Portugal, France, Spain, the Netherlands, and later the United States all maintained and developed a colonial presence and civil power to bring the spices, textiles, and industrial resources of hardwood and rubber to their expanding economies. Religious missionaries, their practices and teachings, also supported and enhanced the political and economic agendas of foreign rulers and the powerful trading companies representing those rulers (Chaudhuri 2004). Where migratory peoples had once lived in relative peace alongside each other for 1500–2500 years with distinct and combined local traditions, colonial powers imposed new civil laws, outlawed temporary marriages, declared sacred sites "sinful," and forbade communication with "spirits" (Andaya 2006). Additionally, Catholic missionaries clashed with the remnants of the ancient Christians and sought to bring their distinctive theologies and practices within the control, influence, and authority of the papal church (Jenkins 2008).

Britain colonized the majority of the Indian subcontinent during a time of strict "noninterference" policy. Local laws reminiscent of ancient Persian "millet" laws were established to separate and protect the rights of each religious population: Hindu Indians, Confucian/Buddhist Chinese, and Muslim Malay tribes (Gandhi 1988). The British example of separate rules for separate peoples set the stage for the largest influences on women and the greatest obstacles to freedom in religion today: (1) people of a certain ethnic group are assumed/required to be a certain religion (Stivens 2010); (2) religious groups have their own "common law" courts in each village (Stange, Oyster, and Sloan 2011); (3) individuals cannot seek legal protection outside their local religious courts (Samuel and Rozario 2010); and (4) the authority of local courts is protected under constitutional law, which ultimately usurps the power of the federal government and any national civil courts (Minority Rights Group International 2005).

The legacy of colonialism and the hierarchal teachings of transnational religions have combined with the ancient Asian philosophies and teachings of women as objects of fear rather than respect to create an increasingly unstable and violent place for women across South and Southeast Asia. Where women once held places of honor as respected leaders, economic providers, healers, and shamans connecting the relationships of this world to the cosmos (Andaya 2006), women across South and Southeast Asia are now relegated to places of subservience, primarily in the home, and subjected to culturally accepted FGC, child marriages, honor killings, and dowry deaths (Stange, Oyster, and Sloan 2011). As a result, the women of South and Southeast Asia face unparalleled challenges accessing education, health care, family planning, legal rights, and living wage jobs (Gandhi 1988). Influenced by Hindu teachings and practices, Buddhist monks across South and Southeast Asia have refused to ordain and recognize ordained nuns for over one thousand years (Paudel and Dong 2017), and women in parts of India, Bangladesh, Thailand, and Nepal continue to be banned from temples and rituals due to the assumed impurity of menstruation (Stange, Oyster, and Sloan 2011). Women in the Philippines and East Timor, as predominantly Catholic countries, cannot access adequate health care and family planning because of the influence of the Vatican against any form of contraception (Gandhi 1988). Women in Islamic countries face local common law courts where they can be punished for being raped. Disadvantages faced by women due to "structural and socio-cultural factors" that marginalize them in early life become even more pronounced with the aging process (Devasahayam 2014). While historians traditionally viewed the women of South and Southeast Asia as more free and respected than their counterparts in Europe or Africa, those claims can no longer be made today in the face of rising fundamental Islam from the Middle East (Brunei, Malaysia, Singapore, the Maldives, Indonesia, and East Timor) and Buddhist reactions to rising Muslim power (Thailand and Myanmar).

Colonization reduced and eliminated the civil and economic power of women. It marginalized women, building on the traditional fears of the creative power of women and the social hierarchies of Confucianism. Prior to colonization, religious influences came from a progression of empires from the Persians to the Romans, the Mongols, and the Ottomans, who focused on the Silk Road trading routes (Jenkins 2008) but stopped short of ruling the low-lying areas of South and Southeast Asia. When European trading company ships first arrived in South and Southeast Asian ports in the 1500s, they returned home with the promise of vast tropical riches, uneducated peoples, and the potential for religious converts. Social structures were changed by European governments when local practices impeded economic progress. Catholic missionaries collided with ancient and locally encultured early Christian practices (Jenkins 2008). European laws and courts established men as superior in position and value to women (Niner and Loney 2019). Interactions and relationships between the sexes were no longer defined by local customs and beliefs but by laws where women and minorities were sidelined and silenced.

European traders neither sought to understand nor appreciated the depth and breadth of an Asian way of thinking, where existence is bound to living respectfully within the earth's resources and the cosmos and in relationship to the spirits that exist in noncorporeal form. The Orang Asli Bidor in Malaysia believed that women bind humanity to the land. In the same way that the blood a woman sheds during childbirth falls and seeps into the soil, the bodies of those who die are buried and become intermingled with the ground (Thambiah, Chopil, and Lian 2018). The matrilineal cultures in Sri Lanka, where men moved into their wives' homes, disappeared, and co-ownership of property in India between spouses was outlawed (Gandhi 1988). From Vietnam to the Philippines, local elders incorporated new Catholic images and beliefs. Many resisted total assimilation by maintaining traditional religious beliefs or practices in private or by appropriating foreign concepts or activities to suit local needs (Molnar 2005; Bovensiepen and Rosa 2016).

Women who once held secure positions in society with legal rights of landownership and inheritance (Andaya 2006) as well as options for permanent or temporary marriages replete with custodial rights and sexual fulfillment (Chaudhuri 2004) lost their financial independence and security as colonial rulers transferred landownership to men and outlawed temporary marriages and women's rights of inheritance (Andaya 2006). Chinese businessmen quickly realized that financially displaced women were a perfect match for sex-starved sailors and civil workers. Foreigners realized it was easier to buy women to work as slaves than to bother with the social and financial responsibilities of a "wife" and her relatives (Andaya 2006). Women and children quickly found themselves caught in an expanding web of prostitution and slavery (Chaudhuri 2004). The booming sex trade advanced the notion that South and Southeast Asian women were promiscuous and willing to sell themselves for anything (Andaya 2006). Nearly five centuries later, South and Southeast Asia remains the sex trafficking center of the world.

Constitutions across South and Southeast Asia, written after World War II and influenced by colonial noninterference policies and, later, legal reforms, "protect the religious nature of family laws" in relation to Hindus, Buddhists, and Muslims, disempowering national civil courts. These common law courts primarily dispense judgment on matters related to women without benefit of evidence or codified laws in matters of marriage age, divorce, child support, guardianship, polygamy, rape, and landownership (Gandhi 1988). Postcolonial citizenship rights are tied to one's religious group rather than the country in which one is born. In most Buddhist and Muslim countries, women cannot be citizens or only hold citizenship via a husband of the same faith (Sugiyama 2006). In most of South and Southeast Asia, the rights of a woman and her children are secondary to the rights and importance of maintaining good family relationships in a community. If police officers in Timor-Leste are related to a man accused of abuse, the woman will be sidelined by a family decision before the matter goes to court. Likewise, in India, Pakistan, and Bangladesh, the financial pressures involved with paying a dowry and the view that the husband owns his wife make her an easy target for an honor killing or a dowry death. Women in Malaysia, Indonesia, and the Philippines who are Indigenous and not part of the ruling religious group face a double discrimination (Stange, Oyster, and Sloan 2011).

Today, women are commonly victims of gender violence and easier prey for human traffickers, especially in Laos, Cambodia, and Vietnam. Outside the oil-rich countries of Malaysia, Brunei, and Singapore, which offer universal education, girls are often kept home for economic reasons (Timor-Leste, Laos, Cambodia) or "fear of impurity" (Nepal, Bangladesh, Pakistan, Afghanistan, Bhutan). The seclusion of women has become more prominent in the modern era, which has reinforced gender rhetoric in every arena (Mahat 2018).

Women in Religious Leadership

Women across South and Southeast Asia struggle to hold a legitimate and lasting place of leadership in any religion, whether Indigenous or transnational, that is substantially different from their ability to be practitioners (Andaya 2006). With the exception of Catholic and Protestant Christianity and Sikhism, the role of women is to support their husband's spiritual attainment. Excepting Islam, Christianity, Sikhism, and ancient

Daoism, women can only hope to live well enough to return in the next life as a man and then pursue their own spirituality.

Traditionally, local practices allowed older women, as possessors of community history and the wisdom and experience of childbirth and the curative powers of local herbs, to hold revered positions as local shamans and healers (Despeux and Kohn 2003). They functioned as a kind of interpreter between various people, spirits, and deities. They offered sacrifices and made healing cures and supplications for local residents in an ongoing effort to harmonize the physical existence of the local people with the existence of the cosmos and the physical environment, with its powerful deities and spirits taking plant or animal rather than human form (Paudel and Dong 2017). These various living parts of the cosmos existed in relationship within a continuous cycle of exchanges (Arvind 2004). Gifts needed to be given and received to keep the cycle of human and cosmic life and death in perpetual balance (Andaya 2016). Traditionally, women and "third-gender" people, who challenge gender norms, have mediated between the various entities that make up the rhythms and flows of cosmic life (Jones 2012). Since colonial times, an increasing number of men have taken over these shaman duties. In some places, the traditional oral stories of women are virtually lost (Thambiah, Chopil, and Lian 2018).

Leadership as a Nun

Traditionally, across the Buddhist and Hindu cultures of South and Southeast Asia, the only way for women to escape the inevitability of marriage and childbearing has been to take up an ascetic lifestyle and to become a nun. Becoming a nun allowed a woman the opportunity to learn, sometimes to teach, and, ultimately, to pursue her own spiritual destiny. As Buddhism spread, it developed into three distinct traditions. Only one of these, Theravada Buddhism, prevalent in South and East Asia but not Southeast Asia, still allows women to be ordained as practitioners. Vajrayana Buddhism, practiced across the Indian subcontinent, and Mahayana Buddhism, practiced in the northern Himalayan countries of Nepal and Bhutan, do not allow ordination and severely restrict lay recognition of female practitioners. Although Buddhists believe in a "nonessentialist view of the self," they practice a strict gender binary (Langenberg 2018).

Buddhist and Daoist nuns traditionally engaged in a cloistered life as very young women or in midlife after being widowed and raising a family

---

THERAVADA NUNS

Although the Buddha preached equality of men and women and created orders of both monks (bhikkhus) and nuns (bhikkhunis), in fifth-century BCE India, women had a harder time reaching Nirvana (enlightenment). Women's monastic life had less social and financial support (although many laywomen did support them with money and food), and they were expected to be subordinate to the monks.

The bhikkhunis' independence and freedom flourished for several centuries. However, their numbers were reduced by wars, being forced into other work by secular leaders, and the lack of the required ten monks *and* ten nuns for ordination. Today, there are a small number of Theravada nuns, a larger number of female lay Buddhists, and some called "Dasa-Sil-Maniyo," who follow the monastic vows but are not ordained. Although they claim the Buddha preached the monastic life, not ordination itself, they still have trouble being validated.

Shannon Garvin

---

as the only way to seek their own enlightenment. Devotees can remain lay practitioners (*sāmaṇeri* or *sāmaṇera*) or they can work and study full time to join the Sangha as ordained nuns (*bhikkhunī*) and monks (*bhikkhu*) (Jutima 2002). Nuns today still must rely on monks for ordination, education, permission to travel, and the resolution of legal disputes (Despeux and Kohn 2003). In short, women are not theologically or practically believed to contain the desire or ability to achieve their own enlightenment while possessing a female body (Paudel and Dong 2017). Across South and Southeast Asia, their only practical option is to return as a man and reach enlightenment in a male body.

Buddhist practices forbid monks and nuns to work for a wage, so they must live off donations given to them by laypeople. Traditionally, local villages supported their own monks and nuns, but, today, Buddhist governments provide allowances that pay for food, education, and health care. However, because only male monks are recognized as ordained by the Buddhist governments, nuns are left without provision or a means to provide for themselves without breaking their vows. Across South and Southeast Asia, nuns, who cannot be ordained, can neither work (according to their beliefs) nor collect an allowance (according to their government). In Burma, the ideal of *thilashin*, with its emphasis on humility, moral purity, and service, is now seen in opposition to the desire to pursue full monastic life. Becoming a nun is still the only wholly acceptable adult female role outside the home in Nepal, even though a nun cannot be ordained (Langenberg 2018). In Thailand, influenced by Hinduism, Buddhist women are still banned from temples during their menses (Stange, Oyster, and Sloan 2011).

Buddhist Nuns and Feminist Ideas

Today's Buddhist nuns acknowledge and wrestle with Western ideas of feminism as they lead, teach, and serve their communities. Western feminism not only assumes a Greek idea of the distinct nature of a created human form, but it also seeks to bring full independence to that form. The desire of Buddhist enlightenment is to pursue the inward way until a full merging with the cosmos. The work of Buddhist nuns today toward ordination, while a seemingly feminist idea, does not take a Western feminist form in belief or practice. In fact, it can appear in contradiction with the basic tenets of independent women. Buddhist nuns do not seek separation from others but rather an understanding pure enough to pass back into the cosmic dharma. The feminist ideas of equality, autonomy, and women's liberation do not correlate to the Buddhist ethical self-understanding of Karma as a remerging of a person with the cosmos. For example, Sri Lankan nuns focus on the problems of *dukkha* (suffering) and *nibbana* (search for liberation from rebirth) rather than on the "oppression" of women (Langenberg 2018). The international Sakyadhita community brings together women from all the Buddhist traditions and seeks to create an international Buddhist recognition, promotion, and education of female ordained life (Jutima 2002). The various Buddhist councils of monks in South and Southeast Asia reject this movement, but the nuns who attend continue to appeal to Buddha's teaching that enlightenment is only contingent upon the mind, which is genderless (Langenberg 2018).

Daoist Nuns

Historically, a third of Daoist ordained practitioners have been women. Women commonly brought their daughters into the communal life with them, and so a tradition of family-based lineage also became standard for Daoism, such as the Nuns of Complete Perfection. Daoists lived and practiced as both celibates and in mixed-gender cloisters with children. Nuns could ascend to "Celestial Immortality" and conduct holy rites and lead meditations. Daoist nuns today, while few in number, continue to show that "religious women who claimed their independence created a strong counterweight to the more unfavorable images of women and dispelled the idea that all females are empty-headed and only good for secondary tasks" (Despeux and Kohn 2003).

Female Hindi Gurus

Hinduism does not include an organized ordained order in its beliefs and practices. Female gurus today, while small in number compared to the men, engage in profound social and community work. Guru Amma Amritanandamayi Devi, known as the "hugging saint," lives in Alappad, India. Every day, she hugs hundreds of people to show them their value. Her nonprofit projects have combined spiritual awareness with humanitarian service that addresses social, medical, financial, and educational needs across India and around the world. Guru Maayi Chidvilasananda leads the international Siddha Yoga path. Together, Guru Amma and Guru Maayi counter the rigid Hindu interpretation of women, their genetic nature, and their socially sanctioned roles and responsibilities (Stange, Oyster, and Sloan 2011).

In contrast to the Hindu teachings that women cannot attend religious ceremonies for the first four days of menses or cannot worship at many Hindu temples until menopause, the religious orders of Brahmakumaris, the Daughters of God, established in 1961, with branches internationally, promote social peace and harmony through their feminine Hindu lives. Women gurus today live both single and married lives with children, creating new models for Hinduism in society (Stange, Oyster, and Sloan 2011). Recently, women in India have been engaged in legal court battles to obtain regular access to their own temples and to raise awareness of the manner in which traditional Hindu teachings regarding sexuality have created an environment that bans them from their own religious sites and promotes rape and murder as religiously acceptable behaviors.

The Subordination of Nuns in Jainism

Jainism teaches a strict ascetic environmental lifestyle to both women and men as traveling renunciants. Nuns and monks remain scrupulously loyal to the *pancha mahavratas*, or the five great vows undertaken at *diksha* (initiation): *ahimsa* (absolute nonviolence), *satya* (absolute truthful-ness), *asteya* (absolute nonstealing), *brahmacharya* (absolute celibacy), and *aparigraha* (absolute nonattachment and nonpossession) (Sethi 2009). While Jainism has traditionally been hailed as a woman-friendly religion, the foundational teachings of Jainism are grounded in the sexuality of women and, as a result, nuns are kept strictly subordinate to men to control their creative sexual power. They cannot walk to get food or even use the toilet without a male escort. Nearly 80 percent of Jain ascetics are nuns (Sethi 2009).

Sikhism as Equality in Contrast to Hinduism

Sikhism developed in the northern area of the Indian subcontinent in the Punjab region. Guru Nanel Dev (1469–1539) was appalled at the caste system that had been created under Hinduism and labeled women impure. In an effort to counteract the powerful and socially destructive forces of the Hindu caste system, including *purdah* and *sati*, he not only taught social equality, but he also established practices to reinforce that foundational equality in Sikhism to create a place where all genders and classes could worship equally. Women adopt the surname *Kaur* and men *Singh*, signifying equality and royalty. For Sikhs, the work of humanity is a transformation of spirit. All people come from the same source, and so men and women alike should be treated with equal respect and with nothing called impure (Kaur and Gill 2018). The Sikh do not have an ordained clergy, but individuals can become leaders by fully committing to the Sikh teachings and lifestyle during the Dastar Bandi ceremony.

While women are accorded the same position and authority as men, Sikhism has been greatly affected by the male dominance of Islam and the Brahmanism of Hinduism in the Punjab region. Today, woman can no lon-ger worship at many sacred Sikh sites in Punjab. Sikh women in Malaysia are pressured to live subservient to Sikh men within the larger Islamic culture. In some communities, in defiance of Sikh beliefs of equality, women are banned from serving by their local religious congregations (Kaur and Gill 2018) or from attending gatherings during menses (Stange, Oyster, and Sloan 2011), as current Sikh practices accommodate men and a warrior mentality.

Making Space for Leadership in Islam

Islam teaches that men and women are equally valued, but it emphasizes the distinct and contained roles for each gender (Abdul Rahman 2014). Women are the primary educators of their children. In Islam, women must actively teach and pass on their religion both by their words and in their daily examples. Women, however, are not allowed to teach men. Women cannot lead or teach in mosques or gender-mixed workplaces; they can only lead in women-only organizations (Hamzah et al. 2016).

South and Southeast Asian Muslim women have traditionally been seen by Westerners to be in a "better" condition than their Arab sisters because of access to health care, education, employment, advancement, social activities, and less restrictive dress codes (Andaya 2006). Mosque instructors in some parts of Indonesia now use their influence to resist the rise of politicized and fundamentalist Islamic teaching and practices from the Middle East and Pakistan, such as forced marriage and restricting women to the home—showing them to be cultural rather than from Islamic texts (Stange, Oyster, and Sloan 2011). Amina Wadud helped found the Sisters of Islam in Malaysia in the 1990s to teach interpretations of Islam that "support gender equality in order to halt the spread of conservative Islamic teachings and practices in Malaysia" (Stange, Oyster, and Sloan 2011), which see the female body and sexuality as a "potentially dangerous dimension of the everyday world," requiring veiling, polygamy, and child-rearing as "acts of piety" intended to reap rewards for the husband and self with Allah (Tong and Turner 2008).

Although South and Southeast Asian Muslim women have traditionally not attended mosque (Pew Research Center 2012), women in some areas are now using the mosques to hold classes for women in areas of personal and cultural value, such as picking a good husband, learning to be a good wife, and engaging in personal spiritual development (Stange, Oyster, and Sloan 2011). In a culturally Muslim way, these women are acting as leading forces of internal resistance against powerful fundamental forces as they gather, observe, and experience other women speaking and leading in their own mosque. Women Muslim scholars, such as Paskistani-American Asma Barlas, are increasingly publishing works detailing the conditions of Muslims in their communities and doing hermeneutical work on the Qur'an by examining passages that affirm the role of women to speak and

---

KUMARI: FEMALE DEITY IN HUMAN FORM

In Nepal, Indigenous, Hindu, and Vajrayana Buddhist beliefs combine in the worship of a Kumari: a prepubescent local girl, who is worshipped until she begins to menstruate. The goddess Taleju, or Durga, is believed to inhabit her body and make her a living virgin goddess.

The most famous is the Kumari Devi in Kathmandu. Buddhist priests select a girl based on the thirty-two perfections of a goddess, including hair, eyes, and voice. She must pass a series of tests to see whether she remains calm in darkness and fear. She is then cleansed and lives in a temple in the center of town, where she is worshipped until she reaches puberty or bleeds excessively from an injury. When she bleeds, she becomes a mortal again, and a new Kumari is found.

Shannon Garvin

---

lead in the Muslim community and to resist the politization of their faith (Stange, Oyster, and Sloan 2011).

Gendered Religious Practices

The strictly gendered practices of all the religions of South and Southeast Asia, except Sikhism, make it challenging for women not only to rise to leadership but also to access and practice their faith in meaningful ways in their daily lives. With the exception of some Sikhism and Daoism, one thread of Buddhism and one of Jainism, and the marginal communities of Christians, the women of South and Southeast Asia cannot live as their own spiritual agents. That is, they cannot help to determine their own spiritual destiny (Sethi 2009). The best they can hope for is adding to their husband's eternity or returning as a man to pursue their own spirituality (Arvind 2004). Becoming a nun or actively teaching in the mosque are acts of internal resistance to the constraints of each faith system. When marriage is assumed to be the ultimate destiny of any human in a woman's body, unconscious assumptions work to create preferred access to education, health care, employment, and civil leadership for men. In distinctly Asian ways, women have quietly incorporated less rigid local practices and sought to hold Indigenous beliefs alongside imported ones in an attempt to temper the hard confines of male-dominated religions and to engage the spiritual world. It is difficult to imagine the number of times personal religious practices have been reimagined by women under new governments and rulers, powerful and influential monks, and colonial powers with economic agendas (Andaya 2006).

Living with the Influence of Confucianism as a Civil Religion

Organized as a social and ethical philosophy to establish social values and institutions, the transcendent ideals of Confucianism created the common binary system we see in Asia: inner/outer, principal/subordinate, ruler/people, men/women, and adult/child. Each holds a superior or inferior position to affirm the authority, ultimately, of the Chinese emperor (Nyitray 2004), and they were later reinforced by colonial rulers and laws (Andaya 2006). Chinese migrants were the first to encounter the small native populations of South and Southeast Asia, and they brought their sense of order as well as an inherent desire to remain connected to their familial structures in China (Fielding 2016). Today, women remain burdened with the responsibility to maintain this social order, even while it exempts them from leadership (Arvind 2004).

Blending Confucianism, Daoism, and Buddhism

Daoists, understanding the yin and yang to be the complementary forces of the universe and recognizing the yin as more powerful with its creative energy, freely admitted women as priests, nuns, lay adepts, recluses, and warrior heroes (Despeux and Kohn 2003). The Daoist harmony of nature focuses on health and vitality, including diet, massage, and exercise. As Confucianism rose under the auspices of the Chinese emperors and provided civil order, Daoism continued to develop, incorporating a private religious life in which women led family worship at a home altar, visited local temples and sacred sites, and studied from other women (Despeux and Kohn 2003). Today, a handful of pure Daoist women practice their faith as nuns, but the majority practice Daoism inside and alongside Confucianism and Buddhism in a melded Asian way of life.

Buddha created a strictly gendered system so that monks could oversee and control every facet of a nun's life. In doing this, he established the assumption of gendered practices within all of Buddhism (Langenberg 2018). Combined with the Buddhist understanding of cyclical life, the role of women became to support men in their achievement of enlightenment

(Nyitray 2004). As Buddhism from India merged with Confucianism from China, this process was systemized and ordered in support of the social functioning of the whole community (Nyitray 2004). Buddhists seek to withdraw from life and live internally, but monks are also drawn into supporting the power structures of the civil governments. While early Syriac Christianity influenced early Buddhism (Jenkins 2008), that influence is lost today under the civil dominance of Confucianism. Contemporary women who actively seek enlightenment in the Buddhist traditions also maintain Confucian family obligations and Daoist practices.

Working for a Husband's Eternal Future

Hindu practices, which are centered on powerful female deities, often confine women to the home and the duties as wife and mother. Women worship separately from men. They are not allowed into some temples during the years they menstruate and are not allowed into other temples at all (Stange, Oyster, and Sloan 2011). Women often celebrate festivals in the village together, while the men celebrate at the local temple. Rituals are important to Hinduism as reenactments of ancient stories and ideas, but women, while required to be present and to participate so that their husbands will earn Karma, must sit in silence in one place while the stories are reenacted around them by men (Arvind 2004).

A Hindu woman lives to procreate sons so that her husband can pay off his debts to his ancestors, and she performs rituals to collect enough merit, or Karma, for her husband to be reunited with the deities upon death. "The primary moral and religious duty of a married woman is pativratadharma: those actions that are directed towards the welfare of her husband and all that is related to him—his home, kin group and the performance of his duties towards his ancestors and deities" (Sethi 2009). She can work toward returning as a man in a higher caste in her next life, but she cannot attain or fulfill dharma in her female form.

Pre-Vedic stories and writings testify to the presence of early guru women, but the Codes of Manu (200 BCE), written by a male sage, systemized the caste and gender systems of Hinduism we see in history and today (Andaya 2006). Women continued to lose social standing from 200 BCE on and were eventually forced into purdah, sati, isolation, dowry systems, and child marriages (Stange, Oyster, and Sloan 2011). While some Hindu women in India may work outside the home, others still endure violence in the home from hierarchical positioning and the financial and relational pressures of dowries (Johnson 2015). Women in Nepal, where Hinduism has combined with Buddhism, are relegated to menstruation huts with their young children, where their diet is limited to rice and beans; they commonly die from exposure during the frozen winter months.

Understanding Allah's Will for Men and Women

Muslim women in South and Southeast Asia do not traditionally worship at the local mosque, even though all mosques include partitioned areas for women and young children (Andaya 2006). Muslim women are more supportive of women's rights than the men. Outside sub-Saharan Africa, there is general agreement that women should make their own choice about whether to wear a veil, but most women do believe they should obey their husbands (Pew Research Center 2013). Until recently, South and Southeast Asian Muslims did not practice veiling. Under the influence of wealthier Arab states, Islam is rapidly changing, causing women to become the visible barometer of local Islamic beliefs (Stange, Oyster, and Sloan 2011). Moderate and hybrid South and Southeast Asian forms of Islam face increasing pressure and influence from oil-rich Arab Islam to conform to religious extremes, which mainly affect women's bodies—a kind of "glorious Islam in the abstract," where women become "the symbolic bearers of how the abstract should be translated into reality" (van Doorn-Harder 2016). Countries that include Indonesia, India, and Singapore have banned veiling in an effort to limit the influence of the fundamentalist ideas promoted by Wahhabism and extremist groups influenced by the "militant and puritanical" writings of Ibn Taymiyyah (Jenkins 2008; Pew Research Center 2016).

Muslim women in the wealthier and urban countries of Malaysia, Singapore, and Brunei enjoy access to education and health care, and they work in private and government jobs while overseeing their home or caring for their family (Anaman and Kassim 2006). The increased practice of veiling is met with concern and harsh criticism from Western ideas of equality, but it also has to be engaged and read within the relevant social, political, economic, and religious contexts of where it is practiced (Stange, Oyster, and Sloan 2011). Some women choose to veil their heads to show they follow Allah and to publicly show that not all Muslims are extremists, while others are forced to veil. Muslim beliefs and practices in poorer and rural Afghanistan and Pakistan force women to remain at home with little to no access to education or health care. Honor killings and dowry deaths are frequent, and women endure high levels of domestic violence (Stivens 2010). Gendered cultural norms are taught as religious beliefs, in which women are purchased with dowries and owned by men (Stange, Oyster, and Sloan 2011). Muslim women in Bangladesh and Myanmar live in areas of conflict where Muslim men are seen as sexually powerful in contrast to humble Buddhist monks—even when those monks actually wield great civil power. The current Rohingya crisis in Myanmar began with a rape, but it is fueled by a distinctly Thai cultural understanding of the "prestige" of Buddhist men (Walton, McKay, and Mar Mar Kyi 2015) and the fear of the "other" (i.e., a Muslim) who holds different beliefs and practices.

Women in Sacred Texts

The ancient sacred texts of every Asian and transnational religion include the stories of powerful and influential women with agency over their own physical and spiritual destiny. Later revisions and interpretations undercut these stories, adding comments by men on the fickle, tempestuous, or mindless ways of women (Sethi 2009). Male sages and scholars, true to the misogynistic cultures surrounding them, presented women in the way they commonly understood them (Arvind 2004). Women, without access to literacy and education in male-dominated cultures, found their voices squeezed out, reinterpreted, and drowned out (Andaya 2006). Scholars today are working to reclaim the ancient stories and places of women as actors and agents in their own cosmic dramas by intentionally looking for the voices and legacies of women and minority groups and by searching for silences that indicate the loss of voices from an era. "A gender-oriented study should do more than put women into history. . . . It should also throw light on the history—male as well as female—into which women are put," even though "documentation pertaining to women is limited and is largely the work of men" (Andaya 2006).

Buddhist texts across South and Southeast Asia record goddesses and powerful women engaged with divine forces. In Vietnam, Quan Am, the locally worshipped female form of Buddha, pours healing water on her devotees (Andaya 2016). Early pagodas dedicated to the female form of Buddha challenged the idea that only males could seek enlightenment. In Laos, all six goddesses in *Nangsu nithan Urangkhathat*, the *Chronicle of the Stupa and the Breast-Bone Relic of the Buddha,* from pre–fourteenth century CE, live beside ponds or marshes (Andaya 2016). One of the most powerful Theravada Buddhist deities is the earth goddess, who drowned the armies of the evil Mara by wringing the water out of her hair (Andaya 2016).

Ancient pre-Confucian texts, written before Confucianism was system-ized and ordered, include stories of women actively engaged in their own lives. Early Christian texts and scriptures were translated into the vernacu-lar in China around 600 CE and taught that women were equal to men before God (Jenkins 2008), but the unmarried, male, early Christian monks held no personal stake in promoting the engagement of women in forming Indigenous theologies, thus allowing Confucianist hierarchical values to take root.

Ancient Daoist texts were written by both men and women. The women, seen as the "pure cosmic force of yin, necessary for the working of the universe" and even superior to the yang (Despeux and Kohn 2003), recorded stories and thoughts as nuns and leaders of their own orders, including the *Kunning Jing,* the *Scripture of Female Peace,* and the *Zheny-ijing,* the *Scripture of Perfect Unity* (Despeux and Kohn 2003).

Sikh writings reflect a strict adherence to the belief that men and women of all castes hold the highest levels of intrinsic worth and value. Guru Granth Sahib, the main Sikh scripture, does not describe the differences between men and women or compare and contrast them; rather, it brings them together. As both men and women are taught to live as the soul "wife" of God, gentleness, acceptance, nurture, and unconditional love are "not exclusive to females as they are equally valid and essential to the male species" (Kaur and Gill 2018). Sikhs believe that without actively and intentionally tending to these practices and values, men will naturally become misogynistic. Current Punjabi and diasporic practices of translat-ing the mutually/fully gendered Sikh God into the male pronouns *he* and *lord* have undermined the egalitarian nature of God and each person's faith and pushed women into the margins of Sikhism.

Caught within a fearful obsession of the power of women's sexuality, Hindu texts both point to powerful goddesses coming from the earth and the destructive nature of those goddesses. Early Vedic texts recount how Gārgī, a woman philosopher from 800 BCE, sat in dialogue with Phil Yājñavalkya. Rather than keep silence, she argued that all in the nature of reality is interconnected until he was convinced and agreed. While later interpretations insist that it was not a female philosopher but rather the spirit of Braham, early texts speak to the integral role of women in the formation of Asian philosophy (Arvind 2004). Vedic hymns from the early pre-Upanishadic construct the worldview on the goddess principle. Devi-sukta of Rgveda, the goddess Vac, daughter of the sage Ambhrna, sees the entire reality as a connected whole. Other texts argue that all existence, including the very nature of Brahman (the distinctly male emanation from the creator god), are all simply manifestations of the goddess (Arvind 2004). Original Upanishadic texts suggest women could be scholars (Arvind 2004). In fact, early texts state that salvation is available to all who sincerely follow commands and seek knowledge and renunciation.

Manusmrti, the classic Hindu treatise on duty, says a husband is to honor his wife on all festivals and holidays and affirms there is no difference between a virtuous wife and the goddess of fortune: "Devotion is offered to the Divine Feminine in her most supreme aspect, through the medium of any number of chosen goddess image or image clusters" (Arvind 2004). The most pervasive image during Hindu festivals is of the Cosmic Mother, "creatix, nourisher, and nurturer of the world or the regal warrior goddess Durgā" (Arvind 2004). Hinduism has one of the "historically richest traditions regarding feminine perceptions and embodiments of the Divine, whether conceptualized as the ultimate divine power or energy of Shakti pulsating through the cosmos and life, or in its myriad, celebrated goddesses, or in its awesome metaphysical concept of the Great Goddess or Mahadevi" (King 2004).

Jain texts record the lives of chaste women whose chastity grants them miraculous powers. Sixteen Mahasatis, whose lives and deeds are recorded in the canonical texts, transitioned from pious laywomen to nuns. Of these, Rajimati and Chandanbala are the most popular and subjects of dramas during festivals (Sethi 2009). Chandanbala is the first woman to take ordination under Mahavira, and her life is a model for renunciation. Facing Jain obsession with sexuality and Digambaras who deny women can even attain Nirvana after this life, male and female renunciants tell these stories differently today. For Jain nuns, "storytelling becomes an act invested with their agency" (Sethi 2009).

The Qur'an freely records the wives of Muhammad as leaders. Khadija was a thriving businesswoman and onetime employer of the Prophet. Aisha was a scholar renowned for her foresight and advice as well as a "great authority on Islamic jurisprudence" (Hamzah et al. 2016). Umm Salama advised the Prophet on a peace proposal, and he followed her counsel (Sikand 2006). Later writings in the Hadith, the collected interpretations of the Qur'an, devalue the place and role of women. Scholars today, including Sadiq, a Shi'ite scholar in India, are using the Qur'an to sort through the later Hadith texts to verify whether they are internally harmonious and were written by the Prophet or his close disciples or whether they were later additions justifying cultural values of hierarchy rather than the original words and teachings of the Prophet. Sadiq weaves social values and responsibilities into his messages, especially addressing the place and devaluation of women and the need to respect and work with those of other faiths (Sikand 2006). He reminds Muslims that the Qur'an records how both genders were created at the same time from the same substance and with the same spirit. He believes more women need to become Islamic scholars, like the wives of the Prophet, and effectively challenge the majority voices of men seeking to deny them their rights and value as Muslim women (Sikand 2006).

LGBTQ People and Issues in Religion

In the same way that Asian philosophy informs the nature of being in Asian religious, it also informs the nature of being gendered and sexual. South and Southeast Asia commonly gives "third-gender" people specific and honored roles as shamans and ritual practitioners (Andaya 2006). This third gender does not imply eunuchs or androgynous people; rather, it commends those who leave gender roles behind and fully embrace their new role as shaman either by choice or because they have reached menopause and the creative power of blood no longer flows through them (Stange, Oyster, and Sloan 2011). Traditionally, Asian ideas of gender are fluid between races—complex, multiple, and shifting (Chaudhuri 2004).

The idea of a gay person "coming out" to establish an identity is a very Western way of asserting an independent identity not only in comparison to but often in conflict with the community and others. Disembodied spirits can take on either gender as needed (Thambiah, Chopil, and Lian 2018), so Asians come from a philosophical understanding of a more fluid nature of gender. In Asia, sexual orientation does not define a person. Rather, it is simply part of a person who is still defined by the roles and relationships around him or her. Hijras in India are considered third gender, and women can be intimate with other women in parts of Indonesia but are not defined as lesbians. "The globalization of LGBTQ does not determine how on a local level gender and sexuality is done" (Stange, Oyster, and Sloan 2011).

KINNAR AKHARA: A TRANSGENDER CONGREGATION

The Hindu pantheon includes a large number of deities—female, male, and transgender. Hindu scriptures also contain references to transgender people.

Despite their presence in Hindu religion and in society, transgender people in India have often been rejected and discriminated against. Although transgender was legally recognized as a third gender beginning in 2014, they still struggle for acceptance.

The Kinnar Akhara is a male-to-female transgender Hindu congregation working for acceptance. For several years, they were excluded from the Khumbh Mela, a major Hindu celebration, but participated without permission. In 2019, they were welcomed by crowds of enthusiastic devotees, and in 2020, they gained approval to participate from the Juna Akhara, the largest of the congregations in the celebration.

Janet Lockhart

While none of the Indigenous great Asian religions or the transnational religions encourage or make space for queer sexuality or gender, local Indigenous beliefs and practices informed by fluid gender spirits make creative space for gender in the local variations of those religions. In contrast to varied local beliefs, based on his own former licentious lifestyle as a prince, Buddha viewed sexuality as core to a person. As a result, Buddhist law forbids the ordination of anyone who is not biologically male or female.

Within the thousands of local interpretations of the Hindu deities, the pantheon includes the dual-gendered Ayyappa, composite deities, and Bhagiratha, who was born of two women (Andaya 2006). Among the Hijra community across the Indian subcontinent, from India to Tibet and Pakistan to Bangladesh, Hijras, or eunuchs in Urdu, are men who dress as females. They serve as psychic channels for female goddesses and play parts at weddings and festivals. Eunuchs and third genders are not commonly accepted across Hinduism, but Hijras are introduced in the Kama Sutra (chapter IX). Local interpretations show how the Hindu pantheon makes space for gender and sexual identity outside the prescribed norms.

Homosexuality is illegal under Muslim law and comes with prescribed punishment. It has only begun to gain acceptance and legal rights among some Christian communities. In 2019, the small Muslim sultanate of Brunei replaced the civil courts with Sharia courts. Powerful and rich individuals across the world as well as corporations from Christianized cultures threatened to boycott and remove funding from Brunei. As the absolute ruler, the sultan announced a moratorium on the prescribed stoning of individuals for sexual offenses, including homosexuality.

The *bissu* in Indonesia employ androgynous Islamic shamans in a professional role for community rituals and healings. This does not imply a biological identity but reinforces the idea that their power lies in their embodiment of all genders (Jones 2012). The Bugis, also in Indonesia, traditionally recognize five genders: male, female, male/female (*calabai*), female/male (*calalai*), and *bissu*. The calabai are men who take on the social roles and work of a woman. Likewise, the calalai are women who take on the social roles and work of a man. The bissu leave gender behind, live as celibates, and work as the local shaman and ritual healer.

Women at the Intersection of Religion and Politics

While women in South and Southeast Asia have traditionally held more rights associated with economic stability, they have rarely held positions of civil authority. Across South and Southeast Asia, persistent migratory patterns of traders, settlers, and people displaced by Chinese military aggression or natural disasters and seasonal flooding created an "extensive mixing of 'races,' cultures and religions" within most immediate family circles (Andaya 2006). As a result, women have always worked as interpreters of cultural values and creative agents incorporating Indigenous beliefs with new religious ideas (Jenkins 2008). Women maintain this work today in South and Southeast Asian countries as national identities continue to form in the wake of the colonial project and the British policy of noninterference which both (1) separated minority groups from each other socially and (2) legally affirmed majority status as powerful and minority status as unnecessary or intolerable (Minority Rights Group International 2005).

Even the idea of citizenship is based more on family of origin than on a specific location (Sugiyama 2006). In Brunei, women cannot hold citizenship at all, and in Laos, a woman is not an adult until she has borne children (Stange, Oyster, and Sloan 2011). While men are free in all the major religions to work and marry, women are culturally and religiously tasked with the work of raising children and tying competing cultural demands into a workable rhythm of daily life. As a result, "the discourses and structures of feeling developing around gender, parenting and family relations have formed and continue to form important symbolic and actual sites for the working through of religious/national/ethnic struggles" (Stivens 2010).

Across South and Southeast Asia, women are rarely seen at the intersection of religion and politics. This is a man's domain, where the decisions of men affect the everyday lives of women, even in areas where men have no knowledge or experience. Women are instructed by Confucianism to maintain the social order by playing out certain roles and identities as mothers, sisters, wives, and grandmothers (Andaya 2006). Women are instructed by Hinduism on the cosmic power that resides in their menses but also constrains them to live under the fearful watch of their male relatives. Women are instructed by Daoism that their yin reflects the creative and life-giving power, which they can redirect into the cosmos. Women are instructed by Buddhism that they should desire enlightenment but are not likely to attain it in this life. Women are instructed by Islam that their proper place in the universal order pleasing to Allah is to serve as wife and mother, raising another generation of young people. Women influenced by early Christians did not benefit from a faith encultured by both genders but inherited one taught by unmarried monks. Women are promised by local faith practices and ancient words and stories passed down from their mothers and grandmothers that the rivers and streams and trees and oceans are filled with life that works together with them as women to bring forth life upon the earth, growing the crops needed to feed their families and the herbs needed to heal sickness and ensure safe delivery of babies. In the middle of all these religious traditions, women navigate the practical application of marriage, bearing babies, feeding children, cooking meals, harvesting crops, working outside the home, and seeking ways to achieve immortality or reunion with the cosmic forces or creator without the benefit of civil or political power.

Despite all this, women today encourage each other and their daughters to pursue education, learn to read and write, work a paying job outside the home, seek out the power to inherit and own property and retain custody of their children, and engage in civil and political discussions locally and globally with an Asian understanding of human rights, citizenship, the challenges of migration, gender inequalities, and interfaith dialogues. Many South and Southeast Asian countries influenced by Confucianism, such as Singapore and Malaysia, have implemented countrywide organizational schemes to keep public order. People of various ethnic backgrounds must practice certain religions, citizenship is inherited only through the father or to certain religious groups, and temporary and permanent migrants are barred from landownership and even from practicing their religion in the same mosques or buildings as those the local citizens use.

As a moderate Islamic modern country with well-educated women, Malaysia is a laboratory for creative resistance to the rising pressure of fundamental teachings from Arab countries. The rising tide of Islamic nationalism, which is proved by the manner in which local women dress and deport themselves, is challenged by women professors and government ministers, who address issues of child marriages, polygamy, domestic abuse, custodial rights, and access to women's health care. Buddhist, Hindu, or Muslim common law courts have replaced civil courts in nearly every South and Southeast Asian nation (Stange, Oyster, and Sloan 2011). Muslim women are frequently finding themselves "deployed as boundary markers of religious identity in global, national and communal struggles" (Stivens 2010). Male and female Qur'anic scholars are formulating arguments for women's rights from the inside of Islam by using the Qur'an, because any defense of women originating from the West or outside the Qur'an is immediately suspect and dismissed.

In Jakarta, India, the Rahima, a Muslim NGO with leaders from middle-class backgrounds, stresses piety through action for social justice in antithesis to the increasing "global Islamic revival for women's politic subjectivity" (Samuel and Rozario 2010). In Nepal, the Peace Grove community offers families an alternative to marrying off child brides for fear their purity will be compromised before they come of age. Girls of all faiths are welcomed to come and live in dorms, continue their education through primary and secondary school, learn the meditative practices of Buddhism, play together, and visit with their families in a safe communal living space (Langenberg 2018).

The United Nations and Australia continue to give leadership and substantial financial aid to address the higher infant and maternal mortality rates in places where women have no education or access to health care much less civil leadership. International groups continue to challenge the Vatican's ban on family planning and contraceptives in Catholic areas, such as the Philippines and Timor-Leste. Republicans in the United States have reinstated the global gag order on health-care centers receiving U.S. aid (January 2017), and the president has rescinded World Health Organization (WHO) funding (April 2020). Women remain the clearest victims and recipients of national and religious agendas both from their own nations and from religious-political interference or advocacy by other nations.

Whether existence is understood in an independent Western sense or within the family relationships around a person in the Asian sense, women, as humans, need access to basic health care, education, and legal rights regardless of the religion they practice or the place in which they live. The United Nations and various NGOs are actively working together to help women move into positions of civil power where they can retain their distinct religious voices and find creative solutions to regional issues of oppression through funding health care and micro industries and education for literacy and understanding legal rights (UN Women n.d.).

Religious Violence against Women

Religious violence against women can take two primary forms. The first is physical, emotional, verbal, or spiritual violence that can be taken against another person in defense of or in the name of a religion. The second is violence that occurs as a result of the pressure to live between competing religious and cultural demands and the inability to find a workable place of resolve. In this case, stress and pressure can often lead to violence as a kind of pressure valve release. The results of the violence do not improve the situation, but they expend emotional and physical energy. Women and children are almost exclusively the recipients of both forms of religious violence, primarily because they are culturally and religiously positioned as the most powerless and least educated. Women in South and Southeast Asia are often unaware of their personal rights or legal protections (Stange, Oyster, and Sloan 2011). Sometimes they do know but do not have economic access, or they perceive the relational cost will be too great.

Civil governments and local religious communities can easily create self-enforcing circles that condone religious domestic violence and enforce the feminization of poverty (Andaya 2006), but women and men can create opportunities for women to seek help and for men to learn new behaviors and attitudes. Across South and Southeast Asia, some countries are raising the marriage age for girls to protect them from becoming child brides, but in many countries, exceptions are allowed for Muslims when men point out that the Qur'an does not contain a specific age. When governments are run by men, they are more likely to listen to the complaints of men who feel their religious "rights" are being threatened than they are to consider the welfare of a girl who is exposed to sex and pregnancy within months of her first menses when she should still be in school.

Today, scholars such as K. H. Muhammad Ali Yafie (Indonesia, 1900s), who saw education for both men and women as the secret to his country's future success, are quoted and reimagined for Islam in this century (van Doorn-Harder 2016). Groups from the United Nations and Australia as well as various NGOs are attempting to bring greater access to health care in Timor-Leste, but when the celibate Catholic priests without families whose livelihood is paid for by the Church continue to deny women access to family planning and health care, they speak from ignorance and continue to doom women and children to generational poverty and continued high mortality rates. When governments such as Brunei sign the UN Convention to end FGC but practice female circumcision, even though it is not prescribed in the Qur'an, they continue to condemn girls and women to lives of increased pain, disease, and early mortality (Stange, Oyster, and Sloan 2011).

Across South and Southeast Asia, all the traditional Asian religions and the imported transnational religions practice destructive traditions not included in their ancient texts that place women at risk. Buddhism, Hinduism, Islam, and, increasingly, Sikhism condone individual male and family violence against women. Unlike in the West, religion, culture, and civil law can rarely be separated (Johnson 2015). Women are considered property, and the men who "own" them have the right to decide their fate (Andaya 2006). In collectivist cultures, family is more important than an individual (Stange, Oyster, and Sloan 2011). Hindu women in India and Bangladesh and Muslim women in Pakistan and Afghanistan face the highest risk of maiming or murder by their male relatives in honor killings (to restore "family honor")—*karo kari* (Sindhi: کارو کاري; Urdu: کاروکاری)—or dowry deaths (financial stress–related killing). Rape, abuse, and disfigurement by acid or removal of the ears or nose are also common. In 2006, Pakistani law was amended to prosecute rape victims instead of the perpetrators. Violence is also on the rise in Nepal. Dowry deaths from 1999 to 2016 accounted for 40–50 percent of female homicides. In 2010, 8,391 dowry and honor killing deaths were reported in India and 2,000 in Pakistan, meaning 1.4/100,000 women in India and 2.45/100,000 women in Pakistan were killed by a family member or forced to kill themselves. "Bride burning" is most common in Hindu and Sikh villages. Experts agree the deaths are widely underreported or disguised as "stove burns" (16/100,000 women in Pakistan). Although both India and Pakistan have banned dowries since 1961, the law was declared unconstitutional in Pakistan, where 95 percent of marriages include a *Jahez* (dowry), and it is generally ignored in India or disguised. In Bangladesh, *Joutak* (dowry) compelled men to victimize 7.2/100,000 brides in 2013. Civil unrest and the #MeToo movement in India have not effected change in violence against women. Police collude with perpetrators and families when registering crimes and undermine enforcement of national laws designed to protect women (Johnson 2015). Increasingly, in Pakistan and Bangladesh, women see suicide as the best option to escape their circumstances (Samuel and Rozario 2010).

Violence remains high in both Afghanistan and Pakistan toward girls who attempt to attend school, as the world saw in the shooting of Mahala Yousafzai (2014 Nobel Peace Prize) and the 192 attacks on Afghan schools in 2018. The United Nations and WHO are increasingly concerned with the health and welfare of women isolated in their homes during SARS-CoV-2/COVID-19 (UN Women 2019). As religion will continue to play a central role in the lives of women and men in South and Southeast Asia, nuanced and culturally and religiously aware approaches that understand women to be positioned within an extended family and community for their economic livelihood and friendships are vital to addressing the specific needs of women and children caught in religious violence (Gandhi 1988).

Women's Resistance to Religious Oppression

The United Nations defines *discrimination* as "any distinction, exclusion or restriction made on the basis of sex which has the effect or purpose of impairing or nullifying the recognitions, enjoyment or exercise by women, irrespective of their marital status, on the basis of equality with men, of human rights and fundamental freedoms in the political, economic, social, cultural, civil or any other field" (UN Women 2019). The primary question that haunts South and Southeast Asia is who holds the authority to establish "rights" for people—the national civil government or the local religious group to whom an individual/family belongs? Westerners steeped in Greek democracy automatically answer that civil government is the only place that can guarantee the safety of religious plurality.

But Asians, coming from their own worldview and living in a postcolonial power vacuum, invariably end up conceding power to local religious groups. Further muddying the waters, Asian-influenced cultures, unlike Greek-influenced cultures, do not view religious conversion as "wholesale transformation" of a "mutually exclusive package of ideas and practices." Religion is not like a piece of clothing one puts on or takes off. Culturally, this puts modern Islamic, Catholic, and Protestant religious assumptions in conflict with the indigenized Asian philosophies and practices of Buddhism, Daoism, Islam, Sufism, and early Christianity, which all made "imaginative use" of "older beliefs, incorporating them into their own systems" (Jenkins 2008).

International groups and some local religious groups are attempting to create religiously appropriate curriculum to use in schools and to teach children how to live in dialogue with each other's beliefs (Minority Rights Group International 2005). Women and men use their oldest texts to speak into the dialogue on what is acceptable behavior and to seek to bring lasting change from within their own faith traditions (Stange, Oyster, and Sloan 2011). Creative individuals engage in video and photographic projects online, such as the Kaur project (http://www.kaurcollective.com/).

Muslim women in Singapore have decided to reclaim the mosque as the gathering place of women as well as men. Today, young women are holding classes and overnight activities in the mosques on topics pertinent to Muslim women in an effort to show a "credible female religious authority" and to "temporarily re-shape the spatiality of the mosque" from a man's domain to a Muslim gathering place. These classes have the potential to subvert overtly masculine interpretations of Islam by emphasizing complementary roles but not endorsing misogynistic interpretations (Jamil 2016). Whereas any external change to Muslim law is seen as an inherent threat to Islam, a reinterpretation from within can gain traction. A growing number of Muslim scholars are attempting to discern between meaningful and relevant traditions and the eternal, universal, and absolute values of Islam. As Islam dominates the governments of South and Southeast Asian countries, they acknowledge that dogmatism leads to "clinging to selective traditions" at the expense of "improving human lives in concrete forms" (Abdul Rahman 2014).

In Bangladesh, Muslim piety is encouraged by some to purge Hindus from the community and by others to open up safe places of meaningful dialogue between Muslim and Hindu women neighbors. A few communities in Bangladesh have sought to bring together the voices and stories of

Muslims, Hindus, and Catholics in creative ways that are opposed by outside forces but which make space within the communities for each religion to practice its own beliefs and rituals. Women along the Pakistan-India border continue "popular practices" that transcend their Sikh, Muslim, and Hindu religions. They are commonly dismissed as women being more civil than religious, but their actions and attitudes give a powerful example for understanding religious identity and how communities can offer belonging to more than one religion (Samuel and Rozario 2010). Scholars in some Christian traditions are highlighting and exploring evidence that faith systems mold, shape, and influence each other over time without threatening the legitimacy of the faith itself as well as showing how beliefs system die, go underground, and are reborn (or not) over time (Jenkins 2008).

FURTHER READING

Abdul Rahman, Noor Aisha Binte. 2014. "Convention on the Elimination of Discrimination against Women and the Prospect of Development of Muslim Personal Law in Singapore." *Journal of Muslim Minority Affairs* 34 (1): 45–65.

Anaman, Kwabena A., and Hartinie M. Kassim. 2006. "Marriage and Female Labour Supply in Brunei Darussalam: A Case Study of Urban Women in Bandar Seri Begawan." *Journal of Socio-Economics* 35 (5): 797–812.

Andaya, Barbara Watson. 2006. *The Flaming Womb: Repositioning Women in Early Modern Southeast Asia*. Honolulu: University of Hawai'i Press.

Andaya, Barbara Watson. 2016. "Rivers, Oceans, and Spirits: Water Cosmologies, Gender, and Religious Change in Southeast Asia—Erratum." *TRaNS: Trans-Regional and -National Studies of Southeast Asia* 4 (2): 239–263.

Arvind, Sharma. 2004. *Goddesses and Women in the Indic Religious Tradition*. Leiden, Netherlands: Brill.

Berling, Judith A. n.d. "Confucianism." Asia Society. Accessed August 29, 2019. https://asiasociety.org/education/confucianism.

Bovensiepen, Judith, and Frederico Delgado Rosa. 2016. "Transformations of the Sacred in East Timor." *Comparative Studies in Society and History* 58 (3): 664–693.

Chaudhuri, Nupur. 2004. "Clash of Cultures: Gender and Colonialism in South and Southeast Asia." In *A Companion to Gender History*, edited by Teresa A. Meade and Merry E. Wiesner-Hanks, 430–443. Malden, MA: Blackwell Publishing.

Conway, Timothy. 2017. "Women of Jainism." Enlightened Spirituality. https://www.enlightened-spirituality.org/Women_of_Spirit_Chapter_Three_Jainism.html.

Despeux, Catherine, and Livia Kohn. 2003. *Women in Daoism*. 1st ed. Cambridge, MA: Three Pines Press.

Devasahayam, Theresa W. 2014. "Growing Old in Asia: What Do We Know about Gender?" In *Gender and Ageing*, edited by Theresa W. Devasahayam, 1–32. Singapore: Institute of Southeast Asian Studies.

Fielding, Tony. 2016. *Asian Migrations: Social and Geographical Mobilities in Southeast, East, and Northeast Asia*. London; New York: Routledge.

Gandhi, Nandita. 1988. "Impact of Religion on Women's Rights in Asia." *Economic and Political Weekly* 23 (4): 127–129.

Hamzah, Siti Raba'ah, Azimi Hamzah, Jamilah Othman, and Sharmila Devi. 2016. "Impact of Islamic Values on the Leadership Style of Muslim Women Academics in Malaysia." *Advances in Developing Human Resources* 18 (2): 187–203.

Jamil, Nurhaizatul. 2016. "'You Are My Garment': Muslim Women, Religious Education and Self-Transformation in Contemporary Singapore." *Asian Studies Review* 40 (4): 545–563.

Jenkins, Philip. 2008. *The Lost History of Christianity: The Thousand-Year Golden Age of the Church in the Middle East, Africa, and Asia—and How It Died*. New York: HarperOne.

Johnson, Andy J., ed. 2015. *Religions and Men's Violence against Women*. New York: Springer.

Johnson, Jean. n.d. "Shakti: The Power of the Feminine." Asia Society. Accessed August 29, 2019. https://asiasociety.org/education/shakti-power-feminine.

Jones, Carla. 2012. "Review of Gender Diversity in Indonesia: Sexuality, Islam and Queer Selves, by Sharyn Graham Davies." *Asian Studies Review* 36 (4): 585–586.

Jutima, Ani. 2002. "Full Ordination for Nuns Restored in Sri Lanka." *Insight Journal* (Spring). buddhistinquiry.org/article/full-ordination-for-nuns-restored-in-sri-lanka/.

Kaur, Charanjit, and Sarjit S. Gill. 2018. "Sikh Women Diaspora in Malaysia: The Reality of Their Role and Status in the Religious Domain." *Millennial Asia* 9 (1): 40–65.

King, Ursula. 2004. "Religion and Gender: Embedded Patterns, Interwoven Frameworks." In *A Companion to Gender History*, edited by Teresa A. Meade and Merry E. Wiesner-Hanks, 70–85. Malden, MA: Blackwell Publishing.

Kohn, Livia. 2008. "Sexual Control and the Daoist Cultivation." In *Celibacy and Religious Traditions*, edited by Carl Olson, 241–264. Oxford, UK; New York: Oxford University Press.

Langenberg, Amy Paris. 2018. "An Imperfect Alliance: Feminism and Contemporary Female Buddhist Monasticisms." *Religions* 9 (6): 190.

Mahat, Ishara. 2018. "Women, Religion and Spirituality in South Asia 'One Does Not Have to Be a Man in the Quest of Truth.'" *Anthropology and Ethnology Open Access Journal* 1 (2): 1–3.

Malik, Jamal. 2006. "Madrasah in South Asia." In *The Blackwell Companion to Contemporary Islamic Thought*, edited by Ibrahim M. Abu-Rabi', 105–121. Malden, MA: Blackwell Publishing.

Minority Rights Group International. 2005. "Key Issues for Religious Minorities' Rights in Asia." https://www.refworld.org/pdfid/469cbfa90.pdf.

Molnar, Andrea K. 2005. "Religion: Catholicism and Ancestral Cults." http://seasite.niu.edu/EastTimor/religion.htm.

Murphy, Anne. n.d. "The Religions of South Asia," Asia Society. Accessed August 29, 2019. https://asiasociety.org/education/religions-south-asia.

Niner, Sara Louise, and Hannah Loney. 2019. "The Women's Movement in Timor-Leste and Potential for Social Change." *Politics & Gender* 16 (3): 874–902. https://doi.org/10.1017/S1743923X19000230.

Nyitray, Vivian-Lee. 2004. "Confucian Complexities: China, Japan, Korea, and Vietnam." In *A Companion to Gender History*, edited by Teresa A. Meade and Merry E. Wiesner-Hanks, 273–284. Malden, MA: Blackwell Publishing.

Paudel, Archana, and Qun Dong. 2017. "The Discrimination of Women in Buddhism: An Ethical Analysis." *Open Access Journal* 4 (4): 18.

Pew Research Center. 2012. "The World's Muslims: Unity and Diversity." August 9, 2012. https://www.pewforum.org/2012/08/09/the-worlds-muslims-unity-and-diversity-executive-summary/.

Pew Research Center. 2013. *The World's Muslims: Religion, Politics and Society*. Washington, DC: Pew Research Center.

Pew Research Center. 2016. "Restrictions on Women's Religious Attire." April 5, 2016. https://www.pewforum.org/2016/04/05/restrictions -on-womens-religious-attire/.

Samuel, Geoffrey, and Santi Rozario. 2010. "From Village Religion to Global Networks: Women, Religious Nationalism and Sustainability in South and Southeast Asia." *Women's Studies International Forum* 33 (4): 301–304.

Sethi, Manisha. 2009. "Chastity and Desire: Representing Women in Jainism." *South Asian History and Culture* 1 (1): 42–59.

Sikand, Yoginder. 2006. "An Islamic Critique of Patriarchy: Mawlana Sayyed Kalbe Sadiq's Approach to Gender Relations." In *The Blackwell Companion to Contemporary Islamic Thought*, edited by Ibrahim M. Abu-Rabi', 644–656. Malden, MA: Blackwell Publishing.

Sprenger, Guido. 2016. "Dimensions of Animism in Southeast Asia." In *Animism in Asia*, edited by Kaj Århem and Guido Sprenger, 31–54. London; New York: Routledge.

Stange, Mary Zeiss, Carol K. Oyster, and Jane Sloan. 2011. *Encyclopedia of Women in Today's World*. 4 vols. Thousand Oaks, CA: Sage Reference.

Stivens, Maila. 2010. "Religion, Nation and Mother-Love: The Malay Peninsula Past and Present." *Women's Studies International Forum* 33 (4): 390–401.

Sugiyama, Takashi. 2006. "Gay and Lesbian Youth Research: An East Asian Perspective." *Journal of Gay & Lesbian Issues in Education* 3 (2–3): 119–120.

Thambiah, Shanthi, Tijah Yok Chopil, and Rosalind Leong Yoke Lian. 2018. "Reclaiming the Eclipsed Female in the Sacred: Semai Women's Religious Knowledge and Its Connection to Their Rights to the Land, in Malaysia." *Journal of the Humanities and Social Sciences of Asia and Oceania* 174 (2–3): 264–290.

Tong, Joy Kooi-Chin, and Bryan S. Turner. 2008. "Women, Piety and Practice: A Study of Women and Religious Practice in Malaysia." *Contemporary Islam* 2 (1): 41–59.

UN Women. 2019. "Convention on the Elimination of All Forms of Discrimination against Women." https://www.un.org/womenwatch /daw/cedaw/text/econvention.htm#article1.

UN Women. n.d. "The 2030 Agenda for Sustainable Development." Accessed February 5, 2021. https://www.unwomen.org/en/what-we -do/2030-agenda-for-sustainable-development.

UNdata: A World of Information. n.d. "Population by Religion, Sex and Urban/Rural Residence." United Nations Statistics Division. Accessed July 15, 2020. https://data.un.org/Data.aspx?d=POP&f=tableCode%3A28.

van Doorn-Harder, Nelly. 2016. "Indonesian Muslim Feminists: Islamic Reasoning, Rumah Kitab and the Case of Child Brides." Key Issues in Religion and World Affairs, January 29, 2016. https://www.bu.edu/cura/files/2016/02/Boston-University-presentation-January-29-2016-van-Doorn-2.pdf.

Walton, Matthew J., Melyn McKay, and Daw Khin Mar Mar Kyi. 2015. "Women and Myanmar's 'Religious Protection Laws.'" *Review of Faith & International Affairs* 13 (4): 36–49.

EIGHT

Oceania

Karen G. Massey

WOMEN IN THE RELIGIONS OF OCEANIA

Oceania is a vast region consisting of thousands of islands in the tropical Pacific Ocean. Oceania includes many island nations in Micronesia (Palau, Nauru, the Federated States of Micronesia, the Marshall Islands, and Kiribati), Melanesia (Papua New Guinea, the Solomon Islands, Vanuatu, Fiji, and New Caledonia), and Polynesia (Tuvalu, Tokelau, Samoa, Tonga, the Cook Islands, the Society Islands, the Marquesas Islands, and others) as well as Australia and New Zealand. Home to over thirty-four million people, Oceania includes a wide variety of cultural traditions, languages, ethnic groups, Indigenous groups, and religious practices (Misachi 2017).

Christianity is currently the majority religion in Oceania (Misachi 2017). In 1992, 95 percent of the people in Oceania identified with some Christian tradition (Swain and Trompf 1995, 192). By 2015, the percentage of Christians in Oceania had dropped to 81 percent due to the increase of other faith traditions in the region (Association of Religion Data Archives 2015), and it is predicted that the percentage will continue to decrease because of an increase in persons claiming no religious affiliation at all (known as "nones").

In Oceania, Christianity is represented by Catholicism and Protestantism. Protestants make up approximately 44 percent of the population (Central Intelligence Agency 2019), and this group includes Baptists, Methodists, Anglicans, Lutherans, Presbyterians, Churches of Christ, and Seventh-day Adventists. Protestant Christianity can be found on all the major island

countries of Oceania, and it is the largest tradition on Tuvalu, Samoa, Vanuatu, and the Marshall Islands (Central Intelligence Agency 2019). Nontraditional religious groups, such as Mormons and Jehovah's Witnesses, make
up a very small yet growing percentage of the population in Tuvalu, Tonga,
Samoa, and the Marshall Islands (Central Intelligence Agency 2019).

Twenty-six percent of the people in Oceania identify as Roman Catholic (Central Intelligence Agency 2019). Catholicism is practiced by a large
percentage of the population on all the major islands of Oceania, except
Tuvalu. Palau, Papua New Guinea, and Kiribati have the largest percentages of Catholics (Central Intelligence Agency 2019).

Besides Christianity, two other monotheistic religions are practiced in
Oceania. Although it is present in much smaller numbers, Islam is growing in Palau, Papua New Guinea, and Australia. The largest Muslim population is on Fiji (Central Intelligence Agency 2019). Judaism is practiced in
New Zealand and Australia, where it comprises less than one-half of 1
percent of the population.

Other religions, such as Buddhism, Bahá'í, and Sikh, are practiced by
less than 3 percent of the population in any given country. A large Hindu
population (27.9 percent) can be found on Fiji, making it the second-largest
religion in that country (Central Intelligence Agency 2019). Although situ-
ated mostly in Fiji, Tuvalu, Papua New Guinea, New Zealand, and Australia, a variety of Indigenous religions are practiced throughout Oceania,
holding a common worldview that encompasses the spiritual and natural
worlds (Patheos n.d.). In New Zealand (38.5 percent) and Australia (30.1
percent), the percentage of "nones" is greater than any one religious tradition (Central Intelligence Agency 2019).

Women in Religions in Oceania

Because Oceania contains thousands of islands, researching the relationship between women and religion is a challenging endeavor. Each
island and country has its own history, traditions, religions, and ideologies
that affect women. However, looking at examples from various countries
can provide a general understanding of women in religion in the region.
For example, in some regions of Papua New Guinea, there have never
existed any "ideologies of male superiority and female inferiority." Males
and females both lead in agricultural, economic, and ritual practices. As a
result, it has been easier for women to naturally assume religious roles in

---

PAYAME IMA: FEMALE SPIRIT, HELPER OF MEN

Payame Ima lives in the highland forests of Papua New Guinea and is specifically associated with helping men. She manifests in waters such as pools,
rivers, rain, and underground lakes.

She is a shape changer with many powers: healing the sick, contacting the
dead, preparing boys for initiation, directing game toward hunters, and possessing women and men, which allows her to identify witches (which she may
use either for or against them).

Even after the arrival of Christianity, Payame Ima still finds expression.
Because she protects the environment, she is invoked in gaining restitution
from harm done by corporations. Ballads are sung of her support of young
men in their heroic endeavors.

Janet Lockhart

---

some of the Protestant denominations in the region. In other regions of
Papua New Guinea, where there are very clear leadership roles for males
and women are in submission to men, the conservative theology of some
Protestant traditions has flourished. Men are heads of churches, and
women are submissive to their husbands and church structures.

Another complicating factor in understanding the role of women in religion is the male bias that pervaded the observations of early missionaries
and colonial officials in the Pacific. Most of the earliest anthropological
studies were also done by men, who, because of cultural norms, were not
allowed access to the religious practices of Pacific women. It was not until
pioneering anthropologist Margaret Mead studied male and female identity in several island cultures that the way was paved for more studies to be
conducted with a feminist perspective.

Also, at the beginning of the twenty-first century, the majority of the
people of Oceania were Christian, thus influencing the religious practices
of women with Christian values and biases. In Australia, for example, some
conservative Christian denominations embraced a mistrust of feminism
that grew in the 1980s. While Australian society empowered women, conservative Christianity taught women, based on scriptural and theological
obligations, to submit to male authority at home and at church. At the same
time, many young people born in rural settings moved to urban centers for
education and work, and their conservative views of women, derived from
Indigenous religions and Christianity, became more progressive.

Protestantism

Protestantism first made its way to Oceania in the late 1700s after several naval expeditions by the British Captain John Cook. In 1770, Cook reached and charted New Zealand and the Great Barrier Reef of Australia (Villiers 2020). Stirred by his "discoveries," church leaders back in England awakened to the possibility of evangelizing the Pacific Islands. In 1797, the London Missionary Society (LMS), an interdenominational group composed of Anglicans, Congregationalists, Methodists, and Presbyterians, traveled to Polynesia (Encyclopedia.com n.d.).

While Protestantism is the majority religion in most of Oceania, it has often been viewed as being critical of and adversarial to the traditions of the native islanders. Early Protestant missionaries were very much affected by the doctrine of "the depravity of Man." Sharing the Gospel included processes for not only saving souls but also for "civilizing" the natives. It was believed the islanders exhibited "barbaric" behaviors, such as public nudity, tattoos, and sacrifices, and missionaries were convinced that

Women leaving a Sunday service at a Cook Islands Christian Church. The CICC is the largest religious denomination in the islands. The church does not ordain women. (Rafael Ben Ari/Dreamstime.com)

Christianity could be the principal instrument for "the civilizing and improvement of islander societies" (Irving-Stonebraker 2019, 228). Among some native societies, such as in Micronesia, many Indigenous religious practices were lost. Among other societies, the islanders found ways to integrate their cultural religious practices with Christianity. For example, many societies in Oceania celebrate marriages by employing cultural traditions, such as an exchange of wealth between the families of the couple, followed by a traditional Christian wedding ceremony.

In the nineteenth and twentieth centuries, education and literacy were added to the already established goals of sharing the Gospel and teaching ethical behavior based on biblical principles. Protestantism's emphasis on both education and biblically based ethical behavior has been a double-edged sword for women in Oceania. On one hand, the emphasis on education has allowed them to form church groups that provide opportunities for fellowship, Bible study, and charitable acts, giving women some sense of agency. These groups have provided space for women to ask questions, participate in community activities outside the home, engage in leadership roles, and expand their knowledge. In a surprising and subversive way, many of these groups have become the basis for networking, income generation, social activism, and women's empowerment.

In Papua New Guinea, in the 1960s, a women's group known as Wok Meri accumulated money and made exchanges with other women's groups, protesting men's wastefulness in using money to buy beer and play cards. The women showed their own economic competence and set a moral example for both women and men.

Another strong women's group, the Presbyterian Women's Missionary Union (PWMU), was formed in Vanuatu in 1945. At the time, women in Vanuatu enjoyed limited freedom, so the founders set out to establish a fellowship program that women would be allowed to attend. It soon moved beyond fellowship and became a place for women to develop sewing and weaving skills, learn English, and improve their knowledge of personal hygiene and nutritional cooking. Learning these skills helped improve the living conditions in the members' households, and because of this, the women wanted to make a difference in the lives of others outside their communities. Eventually, the PMWU developed a community-wide focus on climate change, agriculture, and health (Clarke and Halafoff 2016).

While Protestantism has often provided women with a sense of agency in the larger community, its conservative attitudes about proper behavior and women's roles continue to diminish women's authority in the home and church, requiring them to be submissive to their husbands and church leadership.

Catholicism

Catholicism is practiced in all the major countries of Oceania, with the largest numbers in Palau, Papua New Guinea, and Kiribati (Central Intelligence Agency 2019). Catholicism was introduced by Europeans as early as the sixteenth century with the arrival of Spanish explorers and Jesuit missionaries (Ernst and Anisi 2016, 591). Over the next 150 years, Catholic missionaries frequently visited the Pacific Islands and established missions and churches in various locations.

Like their Protestant counterparts, Catholic missionaries were guided by the desire to preach the Gospel to all nations. Unlike them, Catholic missionaries were more sensitive to Indigenous Oceanic cultures. An important task of Catholic missionary work was "the recovery of insights about the divine which had been suppressed by savage cultures" (Swain and Trompf 1995, 197). This focus came from St. Augustine, the fourth century Catholic bishop from North Africa, who taught the theological concept of original sin: the belief that all people are contaminated by sin inherited from Adam. But Augustine also argued there was something in all people not contaminated by original sin: the image of God (*imago Dei*). Since all people possessed this image, rather than eliminating cultural practices, missionaries attempted to uncover the divine in the traditions of Oceania (Swain and Trompf 1995, 197).

This sensitivity gave rise to situations in which women functioned as religious leaders. For example, in Papua New Guinea in the 1940s, a prophetess and medium, Philo of Inawai'i, had revelations from Mary, the mother of Jesus. Philo believed Mary was calling her to work for the renewal of faith in her Catholic community (Fergie 1977, 163). Part of her message was that traditional values and Christianity were not incompatible. Philo was respected by both within her Indigenous religion and by the Catholic missionaries.

In the 1980s, the God Triwan movement began in Papua New Guinea. It was characterized by divination, prophecy, and a deep devotion to Mary. Followers were known as "spirit women," and they committed themselves

MARY IN OCEANIA

Many Catholics venerate the Virgin Mary, who may seem especially com-
forting. People in Oceania have incorporated her worship into their faith practices in unique ways.

Traditional Catholics in New Zealand, Vanuatu, and New Caledonia celebrate the Assumption of Mary into heaven with a mandatory mass, followed
by food, music, and dancing.

On Pollap, in Micronesia, Mary is seen, like Pollapese women, as a provider, breadwinner, and ultimate nurturer. The Feast of the Immaculate Conception emphasizes women's role as producers of food, especially taro, an
arduous task reserved for them.

Mary's names include Our Lady Help of Christians in Australia, Our Lady of
Camarin in Guam, Our Lady of Fatima, and Our Lady Star of the Sea in Samoa
and elsewhere.

Janet Lockhart

to spiritual practices and deep soul searching. They also served as spiritual mediums and guides for others (Lohmann 2003, 53–54).

Despite this apparent openness to women in religious roles in certain
contexts, the Catholic Church still predominantly holds to traditional values about gender and sexuality. Although Augustine had acknowledged
that women possessed *imago Dei*, he also believed that females were
guilty for the fall of humanity into sin and therefore must be submissive to
male authority. For Augustine, women could never represent God (Ruether
2006). Based on this view, the Catholic Church teaches that women cannot be ordained as priests or deacons.

Catholic women who feel called to ministry and service may serve as
nuns. In a 2011 Catholic World Report, there were approximately 1,012
Catholic sisters in Oceania serving in a variety of religious orders (Ziegler
2011). Their work focuses on such social issues as health care, poverty,
education, and personal safety. For example, the Sisters of St. Joseph in
Australia work to improve Indigenous health care, calling it the most
pressing justice issue in Australia today (Agenzia Fides 2006). In the diocese of Bereina, in Papua New Guinea, the Sisters of Jesus the Good
Shepherd work to alleviate poverty, illiteracy, and child abuse (Agenzia
Fides 2019b).

Islam

Although small numbers of Muslims are scattered throughout Oceania, the largest populations can be found in Australia, New Zealand, and Fiji. It is believed that Islam first came to some parts of Oceania in the seventeenth century, when sea merchants from China and the Malay Empire brought trade to New Guinea. Other parts of Oceania, such as Fiji, felt the presence of Islam at the end of the nineteenth century, when Muslim migrants were brought as indentured laborers from India to work on sugarcane farms.

The Qur'an, the Muslim sacred text, teaches that women and men are spiritually equal in the eyes of God, but Islam also teaches that wives should obey their husbands, women must be modest in their dress, only males may inherit, and men and women must worship separately. Like most monotheistic religions, Islam can be both an encourager and an oppressor of women. However, attitudes toward women and gender issues are often influenced by the social and political contexts in which Muslims live. In Australia, for example, where women's rights are encouraged and supported, Muslim women have found their voices and are using their faith to articulate their rights. Despite the misconception that Islam condones violence against women, Muslim women leaders have enlisted the help of leading imams (Muslim clerics) to spread the message that Islam does not permit abuse of women (Krayem 2013). Because of this collaboration, a support center and refuge for Muslim women escaping domestic violence now operates in Australia.

In less progressive regions of Oceania, traditional Muslim beliefs are finding compatibility with traditional cultural values. For example, Papua New Guinea is the new frontier for the growth of Islam in Oceania (Agenzia Fides 2013). Islam is growing rapidly in Melanesia because it is believed that Islamic practices are more compatible with Melanesian values and traditional customs. For example, they cite the acceptance of polygamy, the separation between men and women, and the authority assigned to husbands over their wives (Agenzia Fides 2013).

Hinduism

Hinduism is primarily found on Fiji. It is practiced by approximately 30 percent of Fiji's population, primarily among the Indo-Fijians. These are descendants of either indentured laborers brought to Fiji from what are

A woman worships at the Sri Siva Subramaniya Hindu temple in Nadi, Fiji. It is the largest Hindu temple in the Pacific. An old temple had long existed at this site, but the new temple was dedicated in 1994. Divided into three parts, it is dedicated to Murugan, the god of nature; Ganesh, the deity of intellect and wisdom; and Meenakshi, a warrior goddess, and her husband Shiva, the protector and destroyer. (Rafael Ben Ari/Dreamstime .com)

now India, Bangladesh, Pakistan, Nepal, and Sri Lanka by the British in the 1800s or immigrants who came to the island nation in the early twentieth century. Today, the Hindu communities of Fiji are thriving, and large and impressive temples are scattered across the country.

Family is central to Hinduism, and women's primary role is as keeper of the household. In sacred scripture, women are presented as a duality of benevolence and malevolence, endowing them with great contrasting powers (Rodrigues 2008): "In times of prosperity she indeed is Lakshmi (goddess of wealth), who bestows prosperity in the homes of men; and in times of misfortune, she herself becomes the goddess of misfortune, and brings about ruin" (Wadley 1977, 113). Because of this changing power, men feel a need to control women. Thus, the roles of women are very clearly defined in Hinduism to "keep her in her place": running the household, raising the children, and serving as an assistant to her husband while he performs various religious rituals (Rodrigues 2008).

Indigenous Religions and Syncretistic Religions

Indigenous Oceanic religions encompass a variety of beliefs and practices, but some commonalities exist among them. Oceanic traditions tend to be polytheistic (many gods), with a worldview encompassing the spiritual and natural worlds. Rituals are not only seen as religious practices that appease or honor the gods but are also thought to have specific consequences in the natural world. For example, practicing certain rituals can influence whether a war is won or determine the sex of a baby. Spirits are believed to inhabit objects such as rocks, sticks, plants, and animals and have a hand in everything that happens in the natural world. Many believe that humans have supernatural powers that can be increased or decreased based on their behaviors. Respect for ancestors is highly favored because it is believed that ancestors can become spirits who can positively or negatively influence life. And for many, certain spaces are considered sacred, including burial grounds, ceremonial grounds, and battlefields (Guiart 2005).

Among the variations in Indigenous Oceanic religions, local tribal members in Papua New Guinea believe in evil spirits, known as *masalai*, who are responsible for all sorts of malicious activity in the world, including disease, injury, misfortune, and death (Illsley 2018). In Australia, many Indigenous people believe rituals must be observed to maintain cosmic balance by increasing scarcity or decreasing overabundance in daily life (Swain and Trompf 1995, 25). For example, a ritual may be performed to increase the fall harvest so that all may have enough food. Or, a ritual may be performed the next year to decrease the harvest so that food does not go to waste. In Tonga, it is believed that tribal chiefs are the only persons with spirits and are the only ones who go on to an afterlife when they die (Echolls 2019).

Men play important roles in performing rituals and ceremonies, but there is a strong female presence among the spirits. Female spirits can be both good and bad. They can positively influence events in the world, such as marriage, fertility, healing, and the change of seasons, and they can be the cause of death, disease, bad luck, and natural disasters. Among the Duna tribe in Papua New Guinea, a female spirit known as Payame Ima is associated with ecological care, human welfare, and witchcraft. She can possess men and women and grant them the power to heal, to predict the future, and to identify witches.

Among the Indigenous religions of Oceania, women's roles vary. However, women are often subordinate to men and have very defined roles in religion and day-to-day life. In daily life, women give birth, raise children, and collect and prepare the vast majority of foodstuffs consumed in the family. In religious life, women engage in rituals that have significance to their bodies. For example, to some extent, a girl's first period announces her coming of age, and she undergoes an initiation ritual to celebrate her womanhood. Childbirth is also a ceremonial occasion; ancestral songs are sung to make for an easy delivery and prevent complications (Swain and Trompf 1995, 33).

Among some Polynesian tribes, power can be described in two ways: *mana* (supernatural) and *tapu* (sacred). *Mana* is mainly used in reference to gods and tribal chiefs. *Tapu* can also be translated as "forbidden" and is often used in reference to female roles. For example, the "sacred maid" is a chief's daughter or niece who is responsible for leading a group of unmarried girls in hosting visitors to the village. Unlike other unmarried women in the village, the sacred maid is expected to remain a virgin until marriage. The prestige and admiration of the village depend on her.

Most of the region's Indigenous people had been converted to Christianity by the mid-1800s. Many of the converts gave up their Indigenous religions altogether, while others found ways to blend their Indigenous religions with Christianity. In Samoa, for example, Siovili is a syncretistic (blended) religion that combines traditional *taula aitu* activity (spirit possession) with Christian preaching. Christian religious practices, such as being filled with the spirit and speaking in tongues, felt familiar to the native people; therefore, it was easy to blend *taula aitu* with Christianity (Gibbs 2005). In Tuvalu, the largest Christian denomination, the Church of Tuvalu, bases its beliefs on the Apostle's Creed, but it also blends the Tuvaluan language and use of Indigenous musical traditions, such as dance, native instruments, and songs, into its Christian worship services. These examples of blending provided greater opportunities for women to participate in religious rituals and practices. The belief that all people can be filled with the Spirit gives women, along with men, the opportunity to speak a word from God. Including traditional dances, instruments, and songs in Christian worship provides a way for women to express themselves in public worship through movement, rhythm, and music.

New Religious Movements

The most influential religious movements in Oceania today developed in the twentieth century. Some were strongly influenced by Indigenous cultural forms, some arose in opposition to Christianity, and others developed as offshoots of Christian churches.

Cargo Cults

After World War II, anthropologists discovered that an unusual religion had developed in the South Pacific. It focused on the concept of *cargo*, which the islanders believed to be the Europeans' and Americans' source of wealth and power. This religion maintained that if the proper rituals were performed, shipments of riches would be sent from some heavenly place. It was all very logical to the islanders, who saw that they worked hard but were poor, whereas the Europeans and Americans did not work. Instead, they wrote their wants down on paper, and, in due time, a shipment of supplies, food, clothing, and luxuries would arrive (Trompf 2015, 5–15).

The islanders developed their own rituals with the hope of receiving the special cargo. They built replicas of airplanes out of twigs and branches and made the sounds associated with airplanes to try to activate the shipment of cargo, or they built a hut in the forest and left money inside in the expectation that the money would multiply. (Unfortunately, the money was often stolen from the hut.) Government and law officials discouraged participation in the cargo cults because they diverted people away from productive and rewarding activities in the present and toward an unrealistic future. In most cases, the men and women who joined the cargo cults became even poorer than they were before (Trompf 2015, 5–15).

Independent Churches

During the twentieth century, there was a movement to reconnect with various native traditions and incorporate them into Christian worship. In many instances, conflicts arose between the leaders of the native traditions and Christian denominations. As a result, the native leaders broke away and formed their own independent churches, which began popping up throughout the region.

In the Solomon Islands, for example, the Christian Fellowship Church broke away from the Methodist Church in 1960. The founder, Silas Eto, believed that the Holy Spirit had visited his people through the *taturu* phenomenon of mass enthusiasm, which included crying out, drumming, and involuntary movements during worship. The church still exists today and has several thousand followers. Its theology is still basically Methodist, but even though Silas Eto has died, the members still believe that he guides their worship by appearing to members through visions (Gibbs 2005).

By the early 1900s, most of the Maori (the Indigenous people of New Zealand) had been converted to Christianity. In 1928, an Indigenous religious leader, Tahupotiki Ratana, arose. Ratana believed that God had given him gifts as a visionary and faith healer. News of his extraordinary gifts spread, and Maoris from all parts of New Zealand came to hear him preach his doctrines of moral reform and the existence of the one God of the Bible. Support for him from the mainstream churches was strong until the Anglican Church condemned him as a false prophet. He soon became isolated from the Christian churches and formed his own independent church, the Ratana Church. The Ratana Church has been very influential in both ecclesial and secular politics, motivating the Anglican Church to establish a Maori bishop in a New Zealand diocese and promoting four Maori seats in the New Zealand Parliament (Gibbs 2005). In 2018, the church had more than forty thousand members in New Zealand and Australia (Newman 2018).

Most independent churches hold very conservative values about women. Because they broke away from traditional Christian denominations, the independent churches tended to carry traditional beliefs and values with them. Also, many of the independent churches were started by an influential, powerful tribal chief who would often pass on tribal traditions that encouraged women to maintain their place in the home, not in church leadership.

Pentecostalism

Since the 1990s, one of the fastest-growing religious movements in Oceania is Pentecostalism. This is a Christian movement that emphasizes a personal relationship with God through baptism by the Holy Spirit. This enables a Christian to live a spirit-filled life and to acquire spiritual gifts, such as speaking in tongues, prophecy, discernment, and healing.

Pentecostals also believe in biblical inerrancy, strict moral behavior, and the imminent return of Jesus Christ.

Pentecostalism has been attractive to the people of Oceania because it seems to build upon familiar religious practices. Indigenous and tribal religions tend to be very expressive and emotive, including dancing, clapping, and shouting. Therefore, the expressive worship of Pentecostalism, which also includes many of these behaviors, is appealing. Pentecostalism provides a way for the people of Oceania to claim both their traditional roots and Christianity.

Pentecostalism has also been both an encourager and an oppressor of women. As Pentecostalism holds that anyone can be filled with the Holy Spirit, women are often the most receptive, raising their status within a congregation. Women are allowed to have ministry roles by reading and interpreting scriptures and by sharing their divine inspirations. In Australia, Pentecostalism railed against the feminist movement of the 1980s, but it encouraged and equipped women in ministry. In the earliest days of the movement, some of the churches were pioneered and pastored by women (Austin and Grey 2017, 204–206).

However, in areas of Papua New Guinea and the Solomon Islands, Pentecostalism took a more traditional view. Women were taught to be submissive to men; they were not allowed to be ministers and were limited in their roles of teaching and prophesying in the church. However, they found greater ministry roles within women's groups that met in homes, and they organized and led group meetings, which included prayer, the reading and interpretation of scripture, and prophecy.

ISSUES OF RELIGION FOR WOMEN IN OCEANIA

The Impact of Christian Missionaries on the Colonial Project

Since Christianity made its way to Oceania, its impact on the cultural integrity, language, local customs, and economy of the region has been profound. It must be noted, though, that much of what has been written about the missionary movement was published by the white European missionaries themselves. The story of Christianity in Oceania has not been written from the viewpoint of the islanders, thus leaving out complexities and perspectives that were overlooked, ignored, or unrecognized by the white missionaries. Considering this, the Christianization of Oceania has been both positive and negative.

Although the Christian missionaries arrived in Oceania with the proselytizing purpose of "preaching the Gospel to all nations," their evangelistic techniques were questionable. Mass conversions were precipitated through the conversion of tribal leaders, who, once converted, would, in turn, initiate ceremonies in which tribal members were "strongly" encouraged to convert to Christianity (Guiart [1987] 2005). On the one hand, this allowed for the conversion of more people. On the other hand, the conversion of the tribal leaders eventually set up a negative relationship with the colonial powers. European colonists officially recognized the tribal chiefs as the persons with whom they would trade and make business deals. Among the items traded were firearms. At first, the firearms were used to overcome local enemies but, over time, they were used against rival chiefs of different faiths. Religious wars erupted in Samoa, Tonga, and other Pacific Islands; many islanders, including women and children, lost their lives.

Intentionally or not, missions became a primary avenue for trade between Europe and the islands. Part of this desire came from the newly converted natives, who wanted access to European money and goods. The London Missionary Society, the Anglicans, and the Church Missionary Society leased ships to supply food to their converts in the islands and to establish chains of local trading posts. These posts prospered, and the missionaries began to acquire land for commercial potential. Much of the acquired land was taken from natives, and, as a result, they suffered economically (Guiart [1987] 2005). Many islanders lost their homes and had to migrate to other islands to find work.

Another technique used to evangelize the islanders was the establishment of programs to educate Indigenous children as future Christian leaders. The missionaries set up boarding schools to which the children were brought at an early age. They were separated from their parents for many years, and most of their time was spent being indoctrinated in beliefs and creeds rather than being educated in the faith. When the children grew up, the missionaries arranged Christian marriages for them, in which women often had little choice. This system of conversion and indoctrination was for the purpose of sending couples from island to island to establish Christian influence. However, this technique of rapid conversion was also a way of obtaining recognition and support from European powers (Guiart [1987] 2005).

Protestant missionaries tended to build village parishes around adult converts, deacons, and native male teachers. These teachers and their wives had been trained in Christian doctrines and beliefs and often replaced the missionaries who had performed the initial conversions. Many village parishes added strong women's Bible study groups and women's associations to this structure. Although Christian missionaries taught that women should be submissive, they were allowed to lead these Bible study groups and women's associations. Missionaries taught the women to read and write, enabling them to teach scripture in their native languages. They were also taught other skills that, in general, improved their home life. Unfortunately, the belief taught by missionaries that women should submit to their husbands only perpetuated the tribal belief that men could beat their wives when the wives "made" them unhappy.

European contact also brought many diseases to the islands, such as smallpox, measles, influenza, tuberculosis, and venereal diseases (sexually transmitted diseases). Western medicine had few remedies for tropical diseases and was not very successful at curing the illnesses brought by the Europeans. While the missionaries focused on saving souls, a large number of natives died (Guiart [1987] 2005). For example, gonorrhea was an ongoing problem that caused women's infertility and kept the islands' populations low for two centuries (Guiart [1987] 2005). Because of the devastation of diseases, missionary organizations eventually added trained doctors to their staffs and established the first modern hospitals in the region.

Women in Religious Leadership

Despite the progress made by women's movements and humanitarian organizations, religious women in Oceania are predominantly subordinated to men. Most Protestant denominations enforce this traditional view of women and do not allow women to be deacons or pastors. But within these traditional denominations, women have found ways to use their gifts. Most Protestant women's church groups provide opportunities, a sense of agency, and space for women to ask questions, expand their knowledge, and become leaders. In creative and subversive ways, women's church groups have become the basis for activism and empowerment.

While most of the Protestant denominations hold very conservative views of women and do not permit female ministers, some denominations permit women to be catechists and evangelists. More progressive denominations, such as the United Church of Christ, Methodists, and Presbyterians, permit women to serve as pastors and deacons. The Anglican Church, with members throughout Australia and New Zealand, permits women to be deacons, priests, and bishops. Women have been allowed to be Anglican bishops in New Zealand since 1990 and in Australia since 2008.

In the Catholic Church, women are not allowed to be deacons, priests, or bishops, but they have begun to find their voices through new religious practices and expressions. Some Catholic churches have been influenced by Pentecostalism in their worship services; women are often allowed to lead portions of the worship services by prophesying, reading and interpreting scripture, assisting with Holy Communion, or leading congregational singing.

Catholic women are also finding their voices through involvement in groups focused on human rights and women's empowerment. The efforts of numerous Catholic women's groups throughout Oceania are leading to significant changes. In Kiribati, for example, members of the Catholic Women's Association started a project to encourage young people to replant coconut trees on their own land as an investment in their future. In Papua New Guinea, the Catholic Women's Association plays a role in keeping peace between rival Indigenous tribes and providing food and safety for the women and children caught in the middle of the conflicts. Another women's group, the Council for Australian Catholic Women, provides advice to the Bishops' Commission for Church Ministry about women and their participation in the church. Finally, even though the numbers of Catholic sisters have declined since 2011, the work of religious orders continues to make a difference on social issues such as health care, poverty, and education.

In Islam, women are not allowed to be religious leaders. But, as has been noted, Muslims' attitudes toward women and gender issues are often influenced by the social and political contexts in which they live. In many parts of Oceania, Muslim women tend to follow traditional roles and practices. But in Australia, Muslim women are gradually finding their voices for change and empowerment because Australia has a progressive attitude about women and gender, and it is quite common for women to hold leadership positions. For example, there are several female bishops in the Anglican Church, 122 women are in Parliament, and a woman was elected as prime minister in 2011.

In Australia, Muslim women's organizations advocate for and empower women. There is the Muslim Women's National Network Australia (MWNNA), whose goals are to educate Muslim women and girls to know their rights, to advocate with government institutions on behalf of Muslim women and children, and to maintain good relations with Australians of other faith traditions. The MWNNA helped elect the first Muslim woman to Parliament in 2013 (Mercer 2013). Another active organization is the Muslim Women's Association, which provides visible and public opportunities for women to participate in and contribute to Australia's cultural and religious societies. This group represents their views and the contributions of women to the media, government organizations, and religious groups.

Gendered Religious Practices

Religious traditions and doctrines guide how women are treated in places of worship and in everyday life. In traditional Protestant churches, women are not allowed to serve as deacons and ministers, but they are allowed to serve as musicians, scripture readers, and ushers. Men are the heads of the household, and women are admonished to be submissive to their husbands.

In the more liberal Protestant churches, women may serve at all levels of leadership, such as deacons, pastors, priests, and bishops. Families are encouraged to worship together, and men and women share worship space. Marriage is considered a gift from God, and there is to be mutual love and respect between husbands and wives. Marriage roles tend to be more egalitarian, mutual, and shared. Marriage is intended to be lifelong, but divorce is allowed in most denominations.

Sexual expression varies across Protestant denominations. Traditional Protestantism limits sexual expression to monogamous heterosexual marriage. Sex outside of marriage and homosexual relationships are considered sinful, and unmarried people (straight and gay) are urged to remain celibate. In more liberal Protestant denominations, homosexual relationships are becoming more accepted. For example, some Presbyterian churches in New Zealand perform same-sex marriages and encourage LGBTQ persons to serve as worship leaders. In most Protestant traditions, family planning and contraception are acceptable forms of birth control; however, attitudes about abortion vary. Some traditions hold that abortion should be totally forbidden, others that it should be legal in all circumstances, and still others that it should only be legal in cases of rape or to save the life of the mother.

Although women's leadership roles are limited in the Catholic Church, women are allowed to be catechists (instructors in basic doctrine), musicians, and Communion servers. However, when serving Communion, women are not permitted to go behind the altar because that is where the male priest blesses the bread and wine for Communion, initiating the mystical act of transubstantiation (the bread and wine become the body and blood of Christ).

The Catholic Church considers marriage a sacrament, and it is intended to be lifelong. Catholics are forbidden to divorce, but marriages can be annulled (declared invalid) if there is proof of dishonesty or irreparable damage to the relationship. Divorced Catholics cannot remarry within the church as long as the former spouse is alive. Should a divorced Catholic remarry, he or she is not allowed to receive Communion.

Among Catholics, sexual expression is limited to monogamous heterosexual marriage. Sex outside of marriage, homosexual relationships, and some sex acts, such as masturbation, are forbidden by the church. The only contraception permitted is abstinence, which includes natural family planning (abstaining from sex during the time that a woman is ovulating). Abortion is forbidden in all cases, and a woman who has had an abortion may be excommunicated.

In Muslim tradition, women are not allowed to be religious leaders. Men and women worship separately, and women are not allowed in a mosque during menstruation or after childbirth. In daily life, Muslim women tend to maintain traditional identities. Being a homemaker and bearing children are highly valued, but women are not forbidden from having a job and earning money. Muslims believe that marriage is a contract between a man and a woman to live as husband and wife, and although it is not encouraged, divorce is permitted if a marriage is irrevocably broken. In most instances, men are allowed to initiate divorce, though waiting periods and witnesses are often required before a divorce is granted. If a woman initiates divorce (called *khula*), a waiting period is required to ensure she is not pregnant. Generally, divorced Muslims are permitted to remarry.

Muslims regard abortions as wrong and forbidden, but many accept that it may be permitted if continuing the pregnancy would put the mother's life in danger. Homosexuality is forbidden, and LGBTQ Muslims are expected to remain permanently celibate as a test from Allah (Jahangir 2016).

Women's roles may vary among Indigenous religions, but in general, they are responsible for child-rearing and household work. In religion, tribal chiefs are responsible for leading community rituals, and women engage in and lead rituals that have significance to their bodies. Unfortunately, in some of the most remote areas of Oceania, female bodies and their reproductive functions are feared. The ability to create new life is seen as a power that is threatening to men. In Papua New Guinea, female genital cutting (FGC), the cutting and sewing of female genitals, is on the rise (Zeid 2016). FGC is done to mark ethnic boundaries, preserve virginity, make girls more marriageable, and enhance male sexual pleasure. FGC is often performed by women as a religious ritual.

In some Indigenous religions in Papua New Guinea and Fiji, *polygyny* (marriage of one man to more than one woman) is still practiced, even though legislation has been passed to outlaw it (Organisation for Economic Co-Operation and Development 2013). While polygyny functions to enlarge a man's access to productive resources (e.g., more gardens, animals, children), it can also create jealousy, hostility, and violence between co-wives (Organisation for Economic Co-Operation and Development 2013).

In areas of Polynesia, such as Samoa, Tonga, and Tuvalu, sexual expression is encouraged: "Sensualism, eroticism, and a high level of sexual activity are actively cultivated throughout the area. Homosexuality is not stigmatized. Relations between men and women are relatively harmonious and mutually respectful" (Ortner 1981, 351).

Women in Sacred Texts

Most of the practices, beliefs, and experiences of the Indigenous religions of Oceania have been passed down through the spoken word. Stories about gods and goddesses, visitations by ancestor spirits who positively or negatively influence life, sacred spaces such as burial grounds and battlefields, and power found in relics and symbols all contribute to the oral history of Indigenous religions. Most of the understanding about the identities, roles, and relationships of men and women are communicated through myths and songs. For example, a long-held myth in Polynesia tells of a woman named Hina who lived long ago and who established women's activities, such as the making of tapa cloth. Hina fell in love with a handsome chief and ran away from home to marry him. This myth is told to communicate to women that marriage and domestic activities are important roles for them.

The Protestant and Catholic sacred text, the Bible, has been used to subordinate women to men and church leaders and to control their sexuality,

MUSIC AS SACRED TEXT

Music is another way of passing on the stories of Indigenous religions. Two music styles have been especially important. Clan songs tell about specific events in the life of a clan. These can include visitations from ancestor spirits, births, marriages, deaths, ecological disasters, and blessings from the gods. Clan songs pass on the history of a clan and distinguish its identity from neighboring clans.

The second style of music is called chant songs, which help establish the identity of each person within a clan. Each person is given a chant at the time of his or her birth, which belongs to that person; no one else can sing it. The lyrics of the chant song are words of blessing and hope for the child as he or she grows up. For a male, the lyrics may include blessings for good health, wealth, many children, and success in farming and fishing. For a female, the lyrics may reflect the hope for a husband, fertility, cooking and sewing skills, and a long life. The chants, in some ways, lay the foundation for who the child will become in the future.

Karen G. Massey

clothing, and behavior. In recent years, feminist theologians have stressed the importance of examining the biblical texts in historical context. By examining such factors as when, why, to whom, and by whom a text was written, one comes to understand that the text is a story about a particular time and place and not prescriptive for all times and places. This is particularly helpful to women because it gives a new perspective on texts that have often been used to oppress them.

To this day, most Christians in Oceania still hold tightly to the ways of reading and interpreting scripture taught to them by white European missionaries. Feminist and womanist theologians are encouraging Christians to "refresh" the Bible by identifying and paying attention to factors that can help scriptures become the "'scriptures *from* Oceania' rather than the Bible of the Christian missionaries" (Havea 2014, 3). These factors include paying attention to native and Indigenous voices, female voices, people with brown and Black skin colors, the effects of climate change on the land, and cross-cultural influences.

The Qur'an teaches that women and men are spiritually equal in the eyes of God, but it also teaches that wives should be subordinate to their husbands. In recent years, feminist Muslim scholars have encouraged fresh readings of the Qur'an that are liberating to women. For example, feminist scholars are encouraging a closer look at the women who are mentioned in the Qur'an. By studying and analyzing the stories of Eve, the mother of Moses, the Queen of Sheba, Anna (the mother of Mary), and Mary, women can find role models who exemplify the characteristics of equality, wisdom, virtue, and a nurturing spirit (Wadud 1999, 103). A closer reading of the Qur'an also shows evidence of many texts in which God values women, that God decisively and declaratively created men and women, and that men and women are equal when it comes to faith and believing.

Feminist Muslim scholars are also encouraging readers of the Qur'an to understand the significance of Islamic law and culture when interpreting the Qur'an. Depending on how a particular country interprets Islamic law and the cultural traditions of that country, the Qur'an may be interpreted through those lenses to empower or oppress women. According to some feminist Muslim scholars, the greatest challenges to Muslim women are the interpretations of Islamic law and the cultures in which they live.

Hinduism has a variety of sacred texts called the Vedas, and according to some texts, women are considered inferior to men. A woman has limited freedom. She is a dependent entity in a household dominated by male members. As a child, she lives under the protection of her father, and as a wife, she lives under the protection of her husband. Women are expected to be the caretakers of the household and children, while men are expected to be the providers for the family. In other texts, women are prohibited from hearing the Vedas, from performing religious ceremonies or rituals, and from holding positions of religious leadership. Because women's lives are dominated by men, Hindu women face many problems, such as domestic violence, parental interference in marriage, gender inequality in the treatment of children, and sex trafficking.

For as much as some Hindu texts denigrate women, there are also texts that provide a more positive image. Some texts describe a whole range of goddesses who serve as role models of virtue and morality. For example, Lakshmi is the model wife, the bringer of prosperity, and the embodiment of compassion. Another goddess, Parvati, is depicted as the model mother. Hindus worship many female deities and believe that women are embodiments of the pure energy of the Universal Mother (Jayaram 2019). Because women possess pure energy and are considered to be gifts from the gods, some religious texts prohibit men from harassing or neglecting the women in their household. It is a man's duty to protect his wife and take care of her until the end.

LGBTQ People and Issues in Religions

Attitudes of the major religious groups toward members of the LGBTQ community vary across Oceania. Generally, the Catholic Church and most Protestant denominations hold conservative views about LGBTQ persons, ranging from believing that homosexuality is a sinful and deviant behavior, to "loving the sinner but hating the sin," to welcoming LGBTQ persons to worship in the church but not allowing them to serve in ministry. These views are based on biblical texts such as Leviticus 18:22, Romans 1:26–27, and 1 Corinthians 6:9–10. Evangelical churches, Pentecostal churches, and the Catholic Church have established the strongest stance against LGBTQ persons and their rights, particularly in the areas of ordination to ministry and same-sex marriage.

The strong conservative views held by the Catholic Church and the Evangelical churches are reflective of Oceanic society in general. Seven countries still have laws against same-sex intimacy, with convictions resulting in three to fourteen years in prison (Admin76crimes 2016). As many as ten countries still have laws prohibiting same-sex unions and same-sex marriage (Admin76crimes 2016).

There is evidence of progress in Australia and New Zealand, which have some of the most liberal laws supporting LGBTQ rights. Both countries have laws prohibiting any form of discrimination based on sexual identity. Same-sex unions are recognized, and it is legal for same-sex couples to marry and adopt children. LGBTQ persons are also allowed to openly serve in the military (Admin76crimes 2016). The existence of such liberal human rights laws eventually has an effect on cultural traditions and religious practices. There is evidence that individual churches and dioceses are developing a welcoming and affirming attitude, even if this is contrary to the larger denomination. For example, in October 2019, the conservative Anglican archbishop of Sydney suggested that same-sex marriage supporters should leave the church (Taylor 2019). More progressive churches and dioceses, such as the Anglican Church in Southern Queensland and the Anglican Dioceses of Perth and Melbourne, rejected the archbishop's position and expressed their desire to be welcoming and safe churches for all people.

In Islam, homosexuality is forbidden, and LGBTQ Muslims are expected to remain permanently celibate. Most LGBTQ Muslims live in fear of being shunned by their families and forced to leave home with nowhere to go. Others live in fear of losing their lives because of the disgrace they are viewed as bringing to their families and communities. Yet, in some of the more progressive cities of Australia, there are glimmers of hope for LGBTQ Muslims. For example, in Melbourne, a gay imam (Muslim cleric) announced in 2018 that he was planning to open an LGBTQ-friendly mosque. The mosque would also provide affordable housing for LGBTQ teenagers who had been ousted by their families and communities (Beresford 2018).

In New Zealand, in 2018, the Catholic bishops acknowledged the church's shortcomings in providing love and care to groups such as the LGBTQ community, who have felt a very real sense of rejection from the church (Shine 2018). The bishops went further to say that positive statements are not enough to rectify the problem; concrete actions are needed to prove church leaders' commitment to becoming more inclusive (Shine 2018).

An interesting way in which some churches are taking the first step toward opening their doors to the LGBTQ community is through music and performing arts groups. For example, a Maori performing arts group was founded in Wellington for *takatapui*, an inclusive term that embraces all Maori who identify in ways other than heterosexual (Bird 2018, 437). The Glamaphones, an LBGTQ community choir, was formed in Wellington, New Zealand, in 2011. To demonstrate its intent to be inclusive of the LGBTQ community, St. Andrew's on the Terrace Presbyterian Church invited the Glamaphones to use their facilities for rehearsals and concerts. The choir's location in a church has provided an opportunity for reconciliation for those who have felt ostracized and hated, and the space has provided choir members with a place for spiritual reflection and ritual. The choir's presence in the church legitimizes St. Andrew's desire to be an LGBTQ-inclusive church (Bird 2018, 436–437).

Religious Violence against Women

According to findings from the 2014 *Federated States of Micronesia Family Health and Safety Study*, Oceania is one of the most dangerous places in the world for women. Two of every three women are impacted by domestic and gender-based violence, which is twice the global average.

Violence against women can take various forms. It can be verbal, physical, sexual, emotional, psychological, or economic, and it is most often rooted in religious beliefs and traditions.

In the countries of Oceania with the highest Protestant populations, violence against women is extremely high, partly because of the belief that women are to be submissive to men. Discrimination against LGBTQ persons is another frequent form of violence in these countries because of the belief that the Bible condemns homosexual behavior. For example, violence against women is frequent in Vanuatu, and women often do not report it for fear of possible backlash (Braunstein 2017). In Vanuatu, women also struggle to make their voices heard: the nation has a fifty-two-member Parliament with no female representation (Braunstein 2017).

In Tuvalu, the law prohibits discrimination based on race, color, and place of origin, with no mention of gender. In 2005, the High Court of Tuvalu stated that this omission was deliberate, resulting in no constitutional protection for sex discrimination (Admin76crimes 2016).

In the Marshall Islands, there is no current legislation on issues related to domestic violence. A 2017 report by Women United Together showed that 51 percent of women had experienced domestic violence, and more than half of the population believed that it was normal to commit violence against women within marriage (Gao 2018). Economically, in the Marshall Islands, "potential discrimination in job markets frequently restricts women from earning credits or managing businesses, which affects their economic independence" (Gao 2018). The unemployment rate for women is 10 percent higher than for men, and the annual wages for women are $3,000 less than for men in the same occupations.

In the countries with the highest Catholic populations, human rights for women are sadly lacking in many areas because of the belief that women are to be submissive to men and to church leadership. In Kiribati, for example, violence against women in the form of rape and spousal abuse is common. Although rape is a crime in the eyes of the law, the culture and the church urge women to take the route of reconciliation over reporting (Wattal 2017). Fear also prevents women from reporting spousal abuse because they are financially dependent on their husbands. Working is not an option because there are limited economic opportunities for women—a fact stemming from the domestic view of women (Wattal 2017). Although it is considered a criminal offense, sex trafficking among young girls is rampant. Fishermen visiting Kiribati are the primary participants in this illegal activity; it is widely known that girls' family members help organize "visits" with the fishermen in exchange for money, alcohol, and food (Wattal 2017).

In Papua New Guinea, police and prosecutors rarely pursue investigations or criminal charges against men who commit family violence, even in cases of bodily injury or repeated rape. Instead, they prefer to resolve such cases through mediation or payment of compensation (Human Rights Watch 2019). Women needing help after family violence face a severe lack of services such as safe houses, counselors, financial support, and legal aid. The law in Papua New Guinea outlaws consensual same-sex intimacy, which is punishable by up to fourteen years in prison (Human Rights Watch 2019). Although Papua New Guinea supports universal access to contraception, two of every three women and girls lack access due to economic, cultural, and religious barriers. Abortion is illegal, except in cases where the mother's life is at risk, and maternal death rates are among the highest in Oceania (Human Rights Watch 2019).

Palau is one of only seven countries in the world not to sign the Convention on the Elimination of All Forms of Discrimination against Women (UN Women 2019), and there is no legislation against sexual harassment, sex trafficking, or sex tourism. The definition of rape is limited to sexual intercourse, and spousal rape is still exempt from prosecution (UN Women 2019).

Depending on the cultural and political contexts and the interpretation of Islamic law, forced marriage, domestic violence, and polygyny are still practiced in some sects of Islam. However, according to Dr. Ghena Krayem, a lecturer at Sydney Law School, the greatest threat to Muslim women in the Pacific Islands comes from persons outside the Muslim community. Muslim women who wear a hijab (head cover) or a niqab (face cover) are visible representatives of the Muslim faith and are often victims of anti-Muslim slurs because they are seen as a threat to society. Their dress unfairly depicts them as followers of a fundamentalist or terrorist movement (Krayem 2013). For example, international news agencies reported a horrific anti-Muslim attack in 2019 in which a pregnant Muslim woman was beaten inside a restaurant in Sydney, Australia, simply because she was wearing a hijab (Assuncao 2019).

Most Indigenous religions of Oceania have either disappeared or combined with traditional religions to create new movements, but in some remote island regions, Indigenous religions still exist. In most of these, women and men have clearly defined and separate roles, and women are considered to be subordinate to men. It is also believed that women possess magical powers that can be both creative and destructive. Women have the power to create life, but if they are angered, they can unleash their destructive powers on crops, other persons, or the weather. These powers are both intriguing and frightening to men, so they often feel the need to control women. As result, many women are the subjects of violence.

In some remote parts of Papua New Guinea, violence in the form of female genital mutilation (FGM) is practiced. Polygyny is another common practice among the Indigenous religions, which can lead to emotional, psychological, and physical harm. A man can also find one or more of his wives no longer useful and break the marriage bond with her, leaving her to survive on her own, with no help or anywhere to go.

Violence also occurs between Indigenous groups. Many tribes are in conflict over land rights, tribal boundaries, or personal property. The conflicts frequently turn physically violent, and women and children get caught in the middle. For example, in the highlands of Papua New Guinea, in the summer of 2019, at least twenty women and children were massacred in a payback killing that was the result of a long-standing conflict between two rival communities (Kwai 2019).

Women's Resistance to Religious Oppression

The women of Oceania have not remained silent in the face of religious oppression. Depending on the resources available to them, women have found ways to make their voices heard and to encourage change. Some work within their own faith communities to advocate for more leadership roles for women on committees and councils and the inclusion of women in worship planning and leadership. Others collaborate with denominational or diocesan organizations to examine doctrine and policies that subordinate women and to encourage change within faith traditions. Still others work outside traditional faith institutions to create new religious organizations that empower women.

Feminist and womanist (Black feminist) theologians from some of the theological schools in Oceania have taken on the role of advocating for women in faith communities. They believe that one way to empower women is through education—not only through formal education but also through workshops, conferences, and written materials for laywomen. They insist that they can best advocate for women by working outside the institutional church. For example, the influential group Weavers was formed in 1989 as the women's advocacy arm of the South Pacific Association of Theological Schools. Their purpose is to support Pacific Islander women in their efforts to study theology and to advocate for their inclusion in theological institutions and faith communities in the region (Johnson and Filemoni-Tofaeno 2003, 12). Since their founding, one of the most important ways Weavers has helped to empower women is through publishing writings by women in the region. These are a way of putting the words, perspectives, and feelings of women in the hands of the public as well as those of clergymen and leaders who can help reform the church.

One of the largest Catholic women's organizations is the Council for Australian Catholic Women (CACW). In 1999, the Bishops Conference called for a balance between men and women in professional and leadership roles within ecclesial bodies (Agenzia Fides 2019a). This led to the formation of the CACW, whose purpose is to promote the participation of women in leadership, decision-making, and other ecclesial ministries in the church and to study theology in light of women's experiences and perspectives (Agenzia Fides 2019). Every three years, the council organizes a conference that promotes women's education and involvement. In February 2019, the conference Shaking the Waters: Catholic Women Responding to the Spirit invited participants to reflect on the involvement of women in the life of the church and to encourage them to continue to advocate for renewal and change in the church and its leadership (Agenzia Fides 2019a). While this organization is specific to Australia, there are similar organizations in other countries throughout Oceania.

For Muslim women, religious oppression comes from both inside and outside the religious community. They must work at maintaining healthy relationships within the faith community as well as overcoming obstacles in society. To do this, Muslim women engage at the local and national levels. For example, in a town in Australia, Muslim women recently enlisted the help of Muslim clerics to hold community-wide discussion groups for non-Muslims to learn about the Muslim faith and to ask questions about Islam's treatment of women. In New Zealand, Muslim women are actively involved in the Islamic Women's Council of New Zealand, a national organization that supports Muslim women's empowerment by encouraging women to gain the spiritual, social, and economic skills and knowledge that will enable them to overcome obstacles in their home life, religious life, and work.

Education is the most important tool for helping raise the awareness of Hindu women against oppression. As more and more Hindu girls and women are allowed to attend school, there are more opportunities for reflection and discussion about oppressive gender roles and religious practices. As a result, resistance to oppression tends to come from women at the community level. For example, in a small town outside Fiji's capital of Suva, a group of women argued over the importance of upholding menstruation taboos. Many of the older women insisted that all women must follow the Hindu laws for cleanliness in all circumstances, while some of the younger educated women believed that the laws should be adhered to when women enter the temple for sacred ceremonies but should be lifted when they meet in homes for prayer and the reading of religious texts (Trnka 2012).

Another example of Hindu women raising their voices against oppression can be found among women who are studying religion and theology in higher education. These women encourage clerics and teachers to undertake a feminist interpretation of religious texts as well as the many undocumented beliefs, practices, and spiritual traditions. They also encourage a stronger focus on the presence of the feminine in the Hindu religion, such as the various goddesses and feminine spirits in the pantheon of divine beings, and due attention to women of power, religious leaders, and feminine symbols of power. These women studying religion believe it is empowering to women when they see themselves in their religious traditions.

FURTHER READING

Admin76crimes. 2016. "Human Rights in Oceania—Lots of Work to Do." *Erasing 76 Crimes* (blog), May 1, 2016. https://76crimes.com/2016 /05/01/human-rights-in-oceania-lots-of-work-to-do/.

Agenzia Fides. 2006. "Josephite Sisters Says Plight of Indigenous Australians Is Most Pressing Social Issue, United Catholic Community Must Take Action." http://www.fides.org/en/news/8138.

Agenzia Fides. 2013. https://www.fides.org/em/news/33295.

Agenzia Fides. 2019a. "OCEANIA/AUSTRALIA—Catholic Women 'Responding to the Spirit': The Commitment to the Life of the Church." https://www.fides.org/en/news/65529.

Agenzia Fides. 2019b. "The Mission of the Sisters of Jesus Good Shepherd in the 'Land of the Unexpected.'" http://www.fides.org/en/news /67017-OCEANIA_PAPUA_NEW_GUINEA_The_mission_of _the_Sisters_of_Jesus_Good_Shepherd_in_the_"land_of_the _unexpected".

Association of Religion Data Archives. 2015. "Regional Profiles." https:// thearda.com/internationaldata/regions/.

Assuncao, Muri. 2019. "Pregnant Muslim Woman Viciously Punched, Stomped on Head by Man after Apparent Racially Motivated Random Attack in Australia." *New York Daily News*, November 23, 2019. https://www.nydailynews.com/news/world/ny-pregnant-muslim-woman-attack-stranger-sydney-racially-motivated-20191123 -f3dmoqlsh5capdnyszn5knfkfm-story.html.

Austin, Denise, and Jacqueline Grey. 2017. "The 'Outback Spirit' of Pentecostal Women Pioneers in Australia." In *Women in Pentecostal and Charismatic Ministry: Informing a Dialogue on Gender, Church, and Ministry*, edited by Margaret English de Alminana and Lois E. Olena, 204–206. Boston: Brill.

Beresford, Meka. 2018. "Gay Imam Announces Plans to Open LGBTQ-Friendly Mosque." PinkNews, January 9, 2018. https://www .pinknews.co.uk/2018/01/09/gay-imam-announces-plans-to-open -LGBTQ-friendly-mosque/.

Bird, Frances. 2018. "A Queer Relationship? The Construction of a New Zealand LGBTQ Community Choir and Its Host Church." *Culture and Religion* 19 (4): 435–450.

Braunstein, Adam. 2017. "Human Rights in Vanuatu." *Borgen Project* (blog), October 2, 2017. https://borgenproject.org/human-rights-in-vanuatu/.

Central Intelligence Agency. 2019. *The World Factbook*. https://www.cia .gov/library/publications/the-world-factbook/.

Clarke, Matthew, and Anna Halafoff. 2016. *Religion and Development in the Asia-Pacific: Sacred Places as Development Spaces*. London: Routledge.

Davidson, Steed, Margaret Aymer, and Jione Havea. 2015. *Islands, Islanders, and the Bible: Ruminations*. Atlanta, GA: SBL Press.

Echolls, Taylor. 2019. "Tongan Religious and Cultural Beliefs and Taboos." Classroom. https://classroom.synonym.com/tonga-religious-and -cultural-beliefs-and-taboos-12086267.html.

Encyclopedia.com. n.d. "London Missionary Society." *Encyclopedia of Western Colonialism since 1450*. Accessed December 25, 2020. https://www.encyclopedia.com/history/encyclopedias-almanacs -transcripts-and-maps/london-missionary-society-0.

Ernst, M., and A. Anisi. 2016. "The Historical Development of Christianity in Oceania." In *The Wiley Blackwell Companion to World Christianity*, edited by L. Sanneh and M. J. McClymond, 644–662. Chichester, UK: John Wiley & Sons.

Fergie, Deane. 1977. "Prophecy and Leadership: Philo and the Inawai'a Movement." In *Prophets of Melanesia*, edited by Garry Trompf, 147–173. Suva, Fiji: Institute of Papua New Guinea Studies.

Filemoni-Tofaeono, Joan. 2004. "Cracking the Silence: The Churches' Role in Violence against Women in Oceania." *Ministerial Formation* 103: 26–36. http://www.wcc-coe.org/wcc/what/education/mf103.pdf.

Gao, Xin. 2018. "Women's Empowerment in the Marshall Islands Needs Improvement." *Borgen Project* (blog), January 13, 2018. https://borgenproject.org/womens-empowerment-in-the-marshall-islands/.

George, Nicole. 2015. "'Starting with a Prayer': Women, Faith, and Security in Fiji." *Oceania* 85 (1): 119–131.

Gibbs, Philip. 2005. "Oceanic Religions: New Religious Movements." Encyclopedia.com, *Encyclopedia of Religion*. https://www.encyclopedia.com/environment/encyclopedias-almanacs-transcripts-and-maps/oceanic-religions-new-religious-movements.

Guiart, Jean. (1987) 2005. "Oceanic Religions: Missionary Movements." Encyclopedia.com, *Encyclopedia of Religion*. https://www.encyclopedia.com/environment/encyclopedias-almanacs-transcripts-and-maps/oceanic-religions-missionary-movements.

Guiart, Jean. 2005. "Oceanic Religions: An Overview." Encyclopedia.com, *Encyclopedia of Religion*. https://www.encyclopedia.com/environment/encyclopedias-almanacs-transcripts-and-maps/oceanic-religions-overview.

Hardin, Jessica. 2016. "Challenging Authority, Averting Risk, Creating Futures: Intersectionality in Interpreting Christian Ritual in Samoa." *Journal of Contemporary Religion* 31 (3): 379–391.

Havea, Jione. 2014. "Engaging Scriptures from Oceania." In *Bible, Borders, Belonging(s): Engaging Readings from Oceania*, edited by Jione Havea, David Neville, and Elaine Wainwright, 3–19. Atlanta, GA: Society of Biblical Literature.

Human Rights Watch. 2019. "Papua New Guinea: Events of 2018." https://www.hrw.org/world-report/2019/country-chapters/papua-new-guinea.

Illsley, C. L. 2018. "Religious Beliefs in Papua New Guinea." WorldAtlas, July 25, 2018. https://www.worldatlas.com/articles/religious-beliefs -in-papua-new-guinea.html.

Irving-Stonebraker, Sarah. 2019. "'Redeemed from Savagery': Sanctification and Civilization in the Accounts of Cook Islands Missionaries Aaron Buzacott and John Williams." *Missiology: An International Review* 47 (3): 226–239.

Jahangir, Junaid. 2016. "Unpacking 5 Muslim Beliefs on Homosexuality." HuffPost, *The Blog* (blog), July 25, 2016. https://www.huffingtonpost .ca/junaid-jahangir/islam-and _homosexuality_b_11174594.html.

Jayaram, V. 2019. "Traditional Status of Women in Hinduism." Hinduwebsite .com. https://www.hinduwebsite.com/hinduism/h_women.asp.

Johnson, Lydia, and Joan Filemoni-Tofaeno, eds. 2003. *Weavings: Women Doing Theology in Oceania*. Suva, Fiji: South Pacific Association of Theological Schools and Institute of Pacific Studies, University of the South Pacific.

Johnson, Todd M. 2005. "Christianity in Global Contexts: Trends and Statistics." Pew Forum on Religion & Public Life, July 5, 2005. https:// www.pewresearch.org/wp-content/uploads/sites/7/2005/05/051805 -global-christianity.pdf.

Krayem, Ghena. 2013. "The Challenges of Being a Muslim Woman in a Multicultural Society." Right Now, April 5, 2013. http://rightnow .org.au/opinion-3/the-challenges-of-being-a-muslim-woman-in-a -multicultural-society/.

Kwai, Isabella. 2019. "Papua New Guinea Massacre Kills Pregnant Women and Children, Police Say." *New York Times*, July 10, 2019.

Leon, Carlued and Eleanor S. Mori, 2014. "Federated States of Micronesia Family Health and Safety Study—A Prevalence Study on Violence against Women." Palikir, Pohnpei State. https://evaw-global -database.unwomen.org/en/countries/oceania/micronesia -federated-states-of/family-health-and-safety-study/family -health-and-safety-study-a-prevalence-study-on-violence-against -women.

Lohmann, Roger. 2003. "Glass Men and Spirit Women in Papua New Guinea." *Cultural Survival* 27 (2): 52–55.

MacDonald, Mary N. 2005. "Gender and Religion: Gender and Oceanic Religions." Encyclopedia.com. https://www.encyclopedia.com /environment/encyclopedias-almanacs-transcripts-and-maps/gender -and-religion-gender-and-oceanic-religions.

MacDonald, Mary N. 2015. "Religions of Oceania." In *Understanding the Religions of the World: An Introduction*, edited by Will Deming, 237–268. Chichester, UK: John Wiley &Sons, Ltd.

Mercer, Phil. 2013. "First Muslim Woman Will Enter Australian Parliament," Voice of America, April 23, 2013. https://www.voanews.com /east-asia/first-muslim-woman-will-enter-australian-parliament.

Miller, Elizabeth. 2016. "Women in Australian Pentecostalism: Leadership, Submission, and Feminism in Hillsong Church." *Journal for the Academic Study of Religion* 29 (1): 52–76.

Misachi, John. 2017. "What Is Oceania?" WorldAtlas, April 25, 2017. https://www.worldatlas.com/articles/what-is-oceania.html.

Newman, Keith. 2018. "Ratana Church—Te Haahi Ratana." Te Ara—The Encyclopedia of New Zealand, April 4, 2018. https://www.TeAra .govt.nz/en/ratana-church-te-haahi-ratana.

Organisation for Economic Co-Operation and Development. 2013. "Papua New Guinea." Social Institutions and Gender Index. https://www .genderindex.org/wp-content/uploads/files/datasheets/PG.pdf.

Ortner, Sherry. 1981. "Gender and Sexuality in Hierarchical Societies: The Case of Polynesia and Some Comparative Implications." In *Sexual Meanings: The Cultural Construction,* edited by Sherry Ortner and Harriette Whitehead, 359–409. Cambridge, UK: Cambridge University Press.

Patheos. n.d. "Religion Library: Oceania." Accessed December 26, 2020. https://www.patheos.com/library/oceania.

Rodrigues, H. 2008. "The Hijras." Mahavidya, June 23, 2008. http://www .mahavidya.ca/2008/06/23/the-hijras/.

Ruether, Rosemary Radford. 2006. "Contraception, Religion in Public Policy, Essay: Women, Reproductive Rights and the Church." Catholics for Choice. https://www.catholicsforchoice.org/issues _publications/women-reproductive-rights-and-the-church-2/.

Scheyvens, Regina. 2003. "Church Women's Groups and the Empowerment of Women in Solomon Islands." *Oceania* 74 (1): 24–43. https://doi.org/10.2307/40331918.

Shine, Robert. 2018. "New Zealand Bishops Acknowledge Church's "Shortcomings" on LGBT Inclusion." New Ways Ministry. July 24, 2018. https://www.newwaysministry.org/2018/07/24/new-zealand -bishops-acknowledge-churchs-shortcomings-on-lgbt-inclusion.

Sutton, Peter. 2010. "Aboriginal Spirituality in a New Age." *Australian Journal of Anthropology* 21 (1): 71–89.

Swain, Tony, and Garry Trompf. 1995. *The Religions of Oceania*. New York: Routledge Publishers.

Taylor, Josh. 2019. "Anglican Churches Reject Sydney Archbishop's Stance on Same-Sex Marriage," *The Guardian*, October 17, 2019. https://www.theguardian.com/world/2019/oct/17/anglican -churches-reject-sydney-archbishops-stance-on-same-sex -marriage.

Te Paa, Jenny. 2014. "Gender Based Violence in the Pacific." *Pacific Journal of Theology* 52 (2): 3–20.

Trnka, Susanna. 2012. "Cleanliness in a Caste-Less Context: Collective Negotiations of Purity and Pollution among Indo-Fijian Hindus." *Anthropological Forum* 22 (1): 25–43.

Trompf, Garry. 2015. "New Religious Movements in Oceania." *Nova Religio: The Journal of Alternative and Emergent Religions* 18 (4): 5–15.

UN Women. 2019. "Asia and the Pacific: Palau." https://asiapacific .unwomen.org/en/countries/fiji/co/palau.

Villiers, Alan John. 2020. "James Cook." *Encyclopaedia Britannica*, October 23, 2020. https://www.britannica.com/biography/James-Cook.

Wadley, Susan S. 1977. "Women and Hindu Tradition." *Signs* 3(1): 113–125.

Wadud, Amina. 1999. *Qur'an and Woman: Rereading the Sacred Text from a Woman's Perspective*. New York: Oxford University Press.

Wattal, Tanvi. 2017. "The State of Human Rights Violations for Women in Kiribati." Borgen Magazine, October 16, 2017. https://www .borgenmagazine.com/state-human-rights-violations-for-women-in -kiribati/.

Zeid, Ra'ad Al Hussein. 2016. "Female Genital Mutilation in Guinea on the Rise." United Nations Human Rights Office of the High Commissioner, April 25, 2016. https://www.ohchr.org/EN/NewsEvents /Pages/DisplayNews.aspx?NewsID=19869.

Ziegler, J. J. 2011. "Nuns Worldwide." Catholic World Report, May 12, 2011. https://www.catholicworldreport.com/2011/05/12/nuns-worldwide/.

Bibliography

Abu-Lughod, Lila. 2002. "Do Muslim Women Really Need Saving? Anthropological Reflections on Cultural Relativism and Its Others." *American Anthropologist* 104 (3): 783–790.

Al Wazni, Anderson Beckmann. 2015. "Muslim Women in America and Hijab: A Study of Empowerment, Feminist Identity, and Body Image." *Social Work* 60 (4): 325–333.

Ashcraft-Eason, Lillian, Darnise Martin, and Oyeronke Olademo. 2009. *Women and New and Africana Religions*. 1st ed. Women and Religion in the World. Santa Barbara, CA: ABC-CLIO.

Bano, Masooda, and Hilary Kalmbach. 2012. *Women, Leadership and Mosques: Changes in Contemporary Islamic Authority*. Women and Gender: The Middle East and the Islamic World, vol. 11. Leiden, Netherlands; Boston: Brill.

Bartel, Rebecca C. 2018. "Women & Christianity in Latin America." In *Encyclopedia of Women in World Religions: Faith and Culture across History*, edited by Susan de Gaia, 180–185. Santa Barbara, CA: ABC-CLIO.

Bender, Courtney, and Wendy Cadge. 2006. "Constructing Buddhism(s): Interreligious Dialogue and Religious Hybridity." *Sociology of Religion* 67 (3): 229–247.

Brooks, Joanna, Rachel Hunt Steenblik, and Hannah Wheelwright. 2016. *Mormon Feminism: Essential Writings*. Oxford, UK; New York: Oxford University Press.

Brooten, Bernadette J., and Jacqueline L. Hazelton, eds. 2010. *Beyond Slavery: Overcoming Its Religious and Sexual Legacies*. 1st ed. Black Religion, Womanist Thought, Social Justice. New York: Palgrave Macmillan.

Burack, Cynthia. 2014. *Tough Love: Sexuality, Compassion, and the Christian Right.* SUNY Series in Queer Politics and Cultures. Albany: State University of New York Press.

Bushman, Claudia L., and Caroline Esther Kline. 2013. *Mormon Women Have Their Say: Essays from the Claremont Oral History Collection.* Salt Lake City, UT: Greg Kofford Books.

Carr, Donna L. n.d. "The History of Bukharan Jews." Partnership in Academics and Development. https://www.bukharacity.com/jews.htm.

Cartier, Marie. 2014. *Baby, You Are My Religion: Women, Gay Bars, and Theology before Stonewall.* 1st ed. Gender, Theology and Spirituality. New York: Routledge.

Chestnut, R. Andrew. 2003. "Pragmatic Consumers and Practical Products: The Success of Pneumacentric Religion among Women in Latin America's New Religious Economy." *Review of Religious Research* 5 (1): 20–31.

Clarke, Colin. 1983. "Review: Colonialism and Its Social and Cultural Consequences in the Caribbean." *Journal of Latin American Studies* 15 (2): 491–503.

Clarke, Matthew, and Anna Halafoff. 2016. *Religion and Development in the Asia-Pacific: Sacred Places as Development Spaces.* London: Routledge Publishers.

Curry, Andrew. 2019. "The First Europeans Weren't Who You Might Think. Genetic Tests of Ancient Settlers' Remains Show That Europe Is a Melting Pot of Bloodlines from Africa, the Middle East, and Today's Russia." National Geographic, August. https://www.nationalgeographic.com/culture/2019/07/first-europeans-immigrants-genetic-testing-feature.

Deer, Sarah. 2015. *The Beginning and End of Rape: Confronting Sexual Violence in Native America.* Minneapolis: University of Minnesota Press.

Dentsu Inc. 2019. "Dentsu Diversity Lab Conducts 'LGBT Survey 2018.'" https://www.dentsu.co.jp/en/news/release/pdf-cms/%EF%BC%8B2019002-0110en.pdf.

Dugan, Kate. 2007. "Buddhist Women and Interfaith Work in the United States." *Buddhist-Christian Studies* 27: 31–50.

Ecklund, Elaine Howard. 2005. "Different Identity Accounts for Catholic Women." *Review of Religious Research* 47 (2): 135–149. https://doi.org/10.2307/3512046.

Fahs, Breanne. 2010. "Daddy's Little Girls: On the Perils of Chastity Clubs, Purity Balls, and Ritualized Abstinence." *Frontiers: A Journal of Women's Studies* 31 (3): 116–142.

Fershtey, Anastassiya, and Khamza Sharifzoda. 2019. "Life in the Closet: The LGBT Community in Central Asia." *The Diplomat*, January 29, 2019. https://thediplomat.com/2019/01/life-in-the-closet-the-lgbt-community-in-central-asia/.

Gebara, Ivone. 2008. "Feminist Theology in Latin America: A Theology without Recognition." *Feminist Theology* 16 (3): 324–331.

Gross, Rita M. 1993. *Buddhism after Patriarchy: A Feminist History, Analysis, and Reconstruction of Buddhism*. Albany: State University of New York Press.

Guang, Pan. n.d. "Shanghai: A Haven for Holocaust Victims." The Holocaust and the United Nations Outreach Programme. Accessed January 15, 2020. https://www.un.org/en/holocaustremembrance/docs/pdf/chapter6.pdf.

Hallum, Anne Motley. 2003. "Taking Stock and Building Bridges: Women's Movements and Pentecostalism in Latin America." *Latin American Research Review* 38 (1): 169–186.

Harris, Elizabeth J. 1999. "The Female in Buddhism." In *Buddhist Women across Cultures*, edited by Karma Lekshe Tsomo, 49–65. Albany: State University of New York Press.

Hong, Christine J. 2015. *Identity, Youth, and Gender in the Korean American Church*. 1st ed. New York: Palgrave Pivot.

Hong, Jeesoon. 2019. "Christian Education and the Construction of Female Gentility in Modern East Asia." *Religions* 10 (467): 1–14.

Human Rights Watch. 2010. "Q&A on Female Genital Mutilation." June 16, 2010. https://www.hrw.org/news/2010/06/16/qa-female-genital-mutilation.

Kaplan, Dana. 2009. *Contemporary American Judaism: Transformation and Renewal*. 1st ed. New York: Columbia University Press.

Kim, Grace Ji-Sun, and Susan M. Shaw. 2018. *Intersectional Theology: An Introductory Guide*. Minneapolis, MN: Fortress Press.

Kóczé, Angéla, and Julija Sardelic. 2016. "Contesting Myths and Struggling Realities." Dangerous Women Project, June 5, 2016. http://dangerouswomenproject.org/2016/06/05/romani-women/.

Kugle, Scott Siraj al-Haqq. 2013. *Living Out Islam: Voices of Gay, Lesbian, and Transgender Muslims*. New York: NYU Press.

Leung, Beatrice, and Patricia Wittburg. 2004. "Catholic Religious Orders of Women in China." *Journal for the Scientific Study of Religion* 43 (1): 67–82.

Lipka, Michael, and David Masci. 2019. "Where Europe Stands on Gay Marriage and Civil Unions." Pew Research Center, Fact Tank: News in the Numbers, May 30, 2019. https://www.pewresearch.org/fact-tank/2019/10/28/where-europe-stands-on-gay-marriage-and-civil-unions/.

MacDonald, Mary N. 2005. "Gender and Religion: Gender and Oceanic Religions." Encyclopedia.com. https://www.encyclopedia.com/environment/encyclopedias-almanacs-transcripts-and-maps/gender-and-religion-gender-and-oceanic-religions.

Madigan, Patricia. 2011. *Women and Fundamentalism in Islam and Catholicism Negotiating Modernity in a Globalized World*. Religions and Discourse, vol. 53. New York: Peter Lang. http://0-site.ebrary.com.fama.us.es/lib/unisev/Doc?id=10600526.

Marcotte, Roxanne D. 2010. "Muslim Women in Canada: Autonomy and Empowerment." *Journal of Muslim Minority Affairs* 30(3): 357–373. https://doi.org/10.1080/13602004.2010.515816.

McDonald, Mary. 2015. "Religion of Oceania." In *Understanding the Religions of the World: An Introduction*, edited by Will Deming, 237–268. Chichester, UK: John Wiley & Sons, Ltd..

Meeks, Lori. 2014. "Nuns and Laywomen in East Asian Buddhism." In *The Wiley Blackwell Companion to East and Inner Asian Buddhism*, edited by Mario Poceski, 318–339. Malden, MA: John Wiley and Sons.

Michel, Claudine. 2001. "Women's Moral and Spiritual Leadership in Haitian Vodou: The Voice of Mama Lola and Karen McCarthy Brown." *Journal of Feminist Studies in Religion* 17 (2): 61–87.

Nachtigall, Patrick. 2018. "Why Evangelical Churches Struggle in Europe." Three Worlds, May 25, 2018. http://three-worlds.com/diary/2018/3/19/why-evangelical-churches-struggle-in-europe.

Nelson, Sarah Milledge. 2008. *Shamanism and the Origin of States: Spirit, Power, and Gender in East Asia*. New York: Routledge.

Neuenfeldt, Elaine, ed. 2013. "Gender Justice Policy." Lutheran World Federation, October. https://www.lutheranworld.org/content/resource-lwf-gender-justice-policy.

Pena, Milagros. 1995. "Feminist Christian Women in Latin America: Other Voices, Other Visions." *Journal of Feminist Studies in Religion* 11 (1): 81–94.

Pew Research Center. 2017. "Orthodox Christianity in the 21st Century." November 8, 2017. https://www.pewforum.org/2017/11/08/orthodox -christianity-in-the-21st-century/.

Pye, Michael. 2018. "New Religions in East Asia." In *The Oxford Handbook of New Religious Movements*, edited by James R. Lewis, 1–22. Oxford, UK: Oxford University Press.

Robinson, Ira. 2013. *Canada's Jews: In Time, Space and Spirit.* 1st ed. Jews in Space and Time. Brighton, MA: Academic Studies Press.

Rodriguez, Jeanette. 1994. *Our Lady of Guadalupe: Faith and Empowerment among Mexican-American Women.* 1st ed. Austin: University of Texas Press.

Ruether, Rosemary Radford. ed. 2007. *Feminist Theologies: Legacy and Prospect.* Minneapolis, MN: Fortress Press.

Sherwood, Harriet. 2018. "Christianity as Default Is Gone: The Rise of a Non-Christian Europe." *The Guardian*, March 21, 2018. https:// www.theguardian.com/world/2018/mar/21/christianity-non -christian-europe-young-people-survey-religion.

Smidt, Corwin E. 2007. "Evangelical and Mainline Protestant at the Turn of the Millennium: Taking Stock and Looking Forward." In *From Pews to Polling Places: Faith and Politics in the American Religious Mosaic*, edited by J. Matthew Wilson, 29–51. Religion and Politics. Washington, DC: Georgetown University Press.

Swain, Tony, and Garry Trompf. 1995. *The Religions of Oceania.* New York: Routledge Publishers.

Valenti, Jessica. 2009. *The Purity Myth: How America's Obsession with Virginity Is Hurting Young Women.* Berkeley, CA: Seal Press.

Wadud, Amina. 1999. *Qur'an and Woman: Rereading the Sacred Text from a Woman's Perspective.* New York: Oxford University Press. http://ebookcentral.proquest.com/lib/osu/detail.action?docID= 431353.

Whitebear, Luhui. 2019. "VAWA Reauthorization of 2013 and the Continued Legacy of Violence against Indigenous Women: A Critical Outsider Jurisprudence Perspective." *University of Miami Race & Social Justice Law Review* 9 (1): 75–89. https://repository.law .miami.edu/umrsjlr/vol9/iss1/5.

Winfield, Nicole, and Rodney Muhumuza. 2018. "After Decades of Silence, Nuns Talk about Abuse by Priests." AP News, July 27, 2018. https://www.apnews.com/f7ec3cec9a4b46868aa584fe1c94 fb28.

Zumbrun, Joshua. 2007. "The Sacrifices of Albania's 'Sworn Virgins': A Rockville Filmmaker Tells of an Old Custom That Both Liberates and Limits Women." *Washington Post*, August 11, 2007. https://www.washingtonpost.com/wp-dyn/content/article/2007/08/10/AR2007081002158.html.

About the Editor and Contributors

THE EDITOR

SUSAN M. SHAW is professor of women, gender, and sexuality studies at Oregon State University. She holds a BA in English from Berry College, an MA and PhD in religious education from Southern Seminary, and an MAIS in women studies and English from Oregon State University. She is the author of *Reflective Faith: A Theological Toolbox for Women* and *God Speaks to Us, Too: Southern Baptist Women on Church, Home, and Society* and is the coauthor with Grace Ji-Sun Kim of *Intersectional Theology: An Introductory Guide*. She is a regular contributor to Baptist News Global and *Ms. Magazine* Online, and she is the general editor for ABC-CLIO's four-volume *Women's Lives around the World: A Global Encyclopedia*.

THE CONTRIBUTORS

ANUNCIA ESCALA is instructor emerita of Spanish at Oregon State University. She holds a PhD in romance languages from the University of Oregon and an MA in Spanish language and literature from New Mexico Highlands University. Her areas of interest are colonial and postcolonial narratives, with an emphasis on social justice and human rights in Latin America and Spain. She has led several delegations of students and professors to Guatemala to learn from human rights defenders.

KALI FURMAN is a doctoral candidate in women, gender, and sexuality studies at Oregon State University. She earned her bachelor's degree in history with minors in English and gender studies at Boise State University and her master of arts in women, gender, and sexuality studies and graduate certificate in college and university teaching at Oregon State University. She is the managing editor for the *ADVANCE Journal*, a journal of institutional transformation.

SHANNON GARVIN studied leadership and spiritual formation at George Fox University, where she received her DMin. She has worked as a pastor and community organizer and cared for individuals with end-stage cancer. She is passionate about people's ability to learn and grow. She currently teaches graduate courses online, focusing on students who are immigrants or in "Two-Thirds World" countries. She lives in her native Oregon, where her children currently attend university.

HANAN HAMMAD is associate professor and director of Middle East Studies at Texas Christian University. She holds a PhD in history and an MA in Middle East studies from the University of Texas–Austin. She is author of *Industrial Sexuality: Gender, Urbanization, and Social Transformation in Egypt*.

REBECCA J. LAMBERT received her PhD from Oregon State University in women, gender, and sexuality studies with a concentration in feminisms and racial justice. While there, she served as the managing editor for the journal *Feminist Formations*. Her research examines the affective experiences of women engaged in feminist, anti-racist social justice movements. Rebecca received her master's in gender and women's studies from Minnesota State University Mankato and her bachelor's degree from Indiana University.

JANET LOCKHART, MS, MAIS, collaborated with Susan Shaw on *Making Connections: Your Education, the World Community, and You*; *Writing for Change: Raising Awareness of Difference, Power, and Discrimination*; and *The Power of Words: Examining the Language of Ethnic, Gender, and Sexual Orientation Bias*. She contributed to *Teaching for Change: The Difference, Power, and Discrimination Model*; *Gendered Voices, Feminist Visions: Classic and Contemporary Readings*, seventh edition; and *Women's Lives around the World: A Global Encyclopedia*.

LEIDA KARIBU (L.K.) MAE is an artist and PhD student at Oregon State University, whose work is focused on Indigenous digital/material rhetorics. Recent publications and presentations include Wikipedia editing as feminist pedagogy, crip communities and care work in the institution, and identity mapping as mixed-race survivance and Skillshare praxis. L.K. holds a BA in English from York University and a BEd and MEd (with a specialization in women's studies) from Lakehead University.

KAREN G. MASSEY is associate dean for the master's degree programs at the McAfee School of Theology in Atlanta, Georgia. She received the MA and PhD degrees in Christian education from the Southern Baptist Theological Seminary in Louisville, Kentucky. She completed further doctoral studies in theology at Boston College and Harvard University. Dr. Massey teaches in the area of practical theology, with her major areas of interest being faith development, worship, and women's studies.

SUZANNE E. SCHIER-HAPPELL is a third-year PhD student in the Higher Education and Student Affairs program at Ohio State University. She earned a BA in religion and culture with a minor in anthropology from Emory University and completed an MA in history and critical theories of religion at Vanderbilt University. She later completed additional graduate-level coursework in languages and cultures of Asia at the University of Wisconsin–Madison. She currently teaches in the Religion and Philosophy Department at Capital University in Columbus, Ohio.

KAREN J. SHAW is director of development for gift planning at the University of Denver in Denver, Colorado. She is a 1988 graduate of Berry College in Rome, Georgia, and a career university advancement professional. Her work involves ensuring equality in and access to higher education through philanthropic support and engaged advocacy.

MARY-ANTOINETTE SMITH is associate professor of eighteenth- and nineteenth-century British literature at Seattle University, with graduate degrees from Loyola Marymount University (MA) and University of Southern California (MA, PhD). Her scholarship promotes praxis-centered race, class, gender/sexuality theory, and her publications include *Thomas Clarkson and Ottobah Cugoano: Essays on the Slavery and Commerce of the Human Species* (Broadview Press) and entries on "Lesotho" and

"Namibia" in *Women's Lives around the World: A Global Encyclopedia* (ABC-CLIO).

JENNIFER A. VENABLE is a doctoral candidate in women, gender, and sexuality studies at Oregon State University. She earned her MA in multicultural women's and gender studies at Texas Woman's University and her BS in psychology at the University of Louisiana at Lafayette. Her dissertation explores the ways that race, gender, class, and religion shape the identities of Cajun women. Her work has recently appeared in *The Southern Quarterly*.

LUHUI WHITEBEAR (Coastal Band of the Chumash Nation) is assistant director of the Oregon State University Native American Longhouse Eena Haws. She completed her PhD in women, gender, and sexuality studies at OSU. Her research focuses on Indigenous rhetorics, reclaiming Indigenous identity/gender roles, murdered and missing Indigenous women, Indigenous resistance movements, and national laws and policies that impact Indigenous people. Luhui is a mother, poet, and Indigenous activist who is passionate about disrupting systems of oppression.

AMINA ZARRUGH is assistant professor of sociology at Texas Christian University. She holds an MA and PhD in sociology from the University of Texas at Austin. She also teaches in the Middle East Studies and Gender and Sexuality Studies programs.

Index